THE INSTITUTE OF SOUTHEAST ASIAN STUDIES

The Institute of Southeast Asian Studies (ISEAS) was established as an autonomous organization in 1968. It is a regional research centre for scholars and other specialists concerned with modern Southeast Asia, particularly the many-faceted problems of stability and security, economic development, and political and social change.

The Institute's research programmes are the Regional Economic Studies (RES), including ASEAN and APEC, Regional Strategic and Political Studies (RSPS), Regional Social and Cultural Studies (RSCS), and the ASEAN Transitional Economies Programme (ATEP).

The Institute is governed by a twenty-one-member Board of Trustees comprising nominees from the Singapore Government, the National University of Singapore, the various Chambers of Commerce, and professional and civic organizations. A ten-man Executive Committee oversees day-to-day operations; it is chaired by the Director, the Institute's chief academic and administrative officer.

The Welfare State, Public Investment, and Growth

Selected Papers from the 53rd Congress
of the International Institute of Public Finance

Hirofumi Shibata and Toshihiro Ihori (Eds.)

 Springer

HIROFUMI SHIBATA, Ph.D.
Dean and Professor
College of Policy Science, Ritsumeikan University
56 Tojiin-Kitamachi, Kita-ku, Kyoto 603, JAPAN

TOSHIHIRO IHORI, Ph.D.
Professor
Department of Economics, The University of Tokyo
7-3-1 Hongo, Bunkyo-ku, Tokyo 113, JAPAN

ISBN 4-431-70222-9 Springer-Verlag Tokyo Berlin Heidelberg New York
Hardcover edition published in 1998 in Southeast Asia by the Institute of Southeast Asian
Studies, 30 Heng Mui Keng Terrace, Pasir Panjang, Singapore 119614, for exclusive distribu-
tion in Asia (excluding Japan), Australia and New Zealand.

Cataloguing in Publication Data

The Welfare state, public investment, and growth/edited by Hirofumi Shibata and
Toshihiro Ihori.
        Selected papers from the 53rd World Congress of the International Institute of
Public Finance
        at Kyoto 1997.
Public investments--Congresses.
Investments, Foreign--Congresses.
Fiscal policy--Congresses.
Welfare state--Congresses.
Shibata, Hirofumi.
Ihori, Toshihiro, 1952-
International Institute of Public Finance. Congress (53rd : 1997 : Kyoto, Japan)
HC79 P83 W44   1998   sls98-52205

ISBN 981-230-038-4

Printed on acid-free paper

© Springer-Verlag Tokyo 1998
Printed in Hong Kong
Typesetting: Springer-Verlag Tokyo from the authors' electronic files
Printing & binding:Best-set Typesetter, Ltd., Hong Kong
SPIN:10666654

Preface

This book presents fifteen papers selected from the papers read at the 53rd Congress of the International Institute of Public Finance held at Kyoto, Japan, in August 1997. Although organized under the general title of Public Finance and Public Investment, the Congress covered a wide range of topics in Public Finance.

One of the highlights of the Congress was a historic and brilliant debate between two of the greatest living authorities in the area of public finance, Professors James M. Buchanan and Richard A. Musgrave, on the nature of the welfare state and its future. Part I of this book is concerned with this debate and its empirical counterpart.

James M. Buchanan (Chapter 1) warns that the welfare state will be unsustainable unless it preserves generality or at least quasi generality in welfare programs. The introduction of overt discrimination in welfare programs through means testing and targeting can only diminish public support. He argues that a political version of the "tragedy of commons" will emerge if and when identifiable interest groups recognize the prospects of particularized gains as promised by discriminatory tax or transfer payments. Faced with mounting pressure from entitlement-like claims of special interest groups against public revenues on one hand and equally strong pressure against further tax burdens on the other, political leaders are attracted to solutions that single out the most vulnerable targets. Distributional disagreement among classes will then become a major source of political discourse and an impetus for class conflict.

Richard A. Musgrave (Chapter 2) rebuts Buchanan's thesis. Musgrave contends that the essential role of a welfare state is to give specific individuals or groups support in particular situations of need. By nature, the welfare state is "selective," not general. The concept of a truly general and nonselective welfare state, when carried to its logical limit, becomes an empty box. He also doubts if the foibles of politics would permit so decisive a case for general and against selective programs. General programs have wider appeal than selective programs and can draw on broader support. Finding coalition partners for a selective program is often a daunting task, and therefore such programs are more difficult to implement. In their favor is the fact that selective programs require less revenues than general programs. In any case, issues of distribution have to be addressed in a democratic society. Oftentimes such issues do not lend themselves to unanimous choice.

Frederick Zu-Liu Hu (Chapter 3) turns to empirical investigation of relationships between the major provisions of a welfare state (social security and welfare payments) and the state of democracy, demographic trends, and per capita income on a cross-country basis. Investigating data of many countries throughout the world, he finds that all three variables—democracy, aging, and per capita GDP—have highly significant coefficients, with expected signs, that explain over 80 percent of the variation in welfare expenditures. He then examines the effect of the welfare state on economic growth and finds that social security payments may have an adverse effect. He finds among the developed nations the well-known tendency for a pattern of steady increase in welfare spending over the past quarter century. Hu shows that if such patterns are replicated in developing countries in the coming years, the growth in the number of people over 60 years of age could reduce the rate of growth in per capita real GDP in East Asian countries by 1.5 percentage points. However, he observes that in East Asian countries there appears to be an increasing awareness of the cost and inefficiency of the prevalent social security systems in industrialized countries.

Part II deals with topics on public investment and economic growth. Vito Tanzi and Hamid Davoodi (Chapter 4) argue that corrupt politicians and high officials in government favor investment in large capital projects because larger projects make it more convenient for them to collect bribes and to enhance their political visibility. Capital investments are favored excessively over current spending on such things as operations and maintenance of existing infrastructure or spending on human capital, despite the fact that such current spending can promote growth more effectively than capital spending. They show empirical evidence of corruption that favors public investment, disfavors operating and maintenance expenditures, and allows shoddiness in public investments, thereby reducing economic growth. They caution that economists should be more restrained in their praise of public sector capital investment in countries where high levels of corruption exist.

Jan-Egbert Sturm, Gerard H. Kuper, and Jakob de Haan (Chapter 5) investigate empirically the impact of governmental capital spending on economic growth. They suggest three different ways to model the relationship between public investment and economic growth and compare them using data from the Netherlands. The three methods are the Production Function approach, in which the public capital stock is added as an additional input factor in a production function; the Behavioral

Approach, a cost or profit function in which public capital stock is included; and the Vector Auto Regression Approach, which uses as few economic restrictions as possible in order to solve some of the problems raised by the above two approaches. Their findings do not support the hypothesis that investment in infrastructure enhances economic growth. Their skepticism concerning the enthusiasm of many politicians who favor increased public investment echoes the views expressed by other authors in this volume.

Thomas I. Renström (Chapter 6) argues the desirability of less strictly enforced tax evasion policing as a mechanism for reducing the time-inconsistency problem in fiscal policy. He argues that unless a government can assure its citizens what future tax rates will be, it should tolerate tax evasion. As proof, Renström uses an elaborate model of capital taxation with two periods and two different types of individuals. The first are those who work only in non-tax-evadable activities, and the second are those (the self-employed) who could allocate their labor between tax-evadable activities and non-tax-evadable activities. Their allocations would depend upon the tax system, the probability of being audited, and the time period. By setting detection probabilities and punishment severity relatively low, the government commits itself indirectly not to tax capital income too heavily in the future and encourages activities on which the tax could be evaded, and thereby increases capital tax revenues in the second period.

Part III covers intergovernmental relations: international trading of emission quotas to control the global climate and interaction among member countries' fiscal policies in the European Union and the World Trade Organization. After reviewing theoretically the efficiency and distributional aspects of climate change policies, Peter Bohm, (Chapter 7) examines some possible distributionally acceptable and efficient international emission rights trading agreements to reduce carbon emissions. He pays special attention to emission quotas that are tradable among governments based on international agreements. He reports the results of an experiment using a tradable-quota system carried out by pubic officials and experts in four Nordic countries. Bohm finds that emission quota trade would reduce the aggregate cost of reaching the targeted reduction in carbon emissions by about 59 percent. He calls for awareness of the need to invest time and effort to obtain more information from these pilot tests and to carefully analyze the results.

Paul Bernd Spahn (Chapter 8) reexamines the traditional wisdom of centralized stabilization policy. The coming of the European Union (EU) is of course the reason for this exercise. On the one hand, Europeans widely accept the notion that monetary policy should be centralized as long as the policy is controlled by an institution independent of any EU member country. On the other hand, the idea of centralized fiscal policy in the EU is generally rejected for political reasons, as manifested in the subsidiary principle of the Maastricht Treaty. He carefully reviews various arguments in favor of and against centralized fiscal policy. His conclusion is that to make the system of decentralized fiscal policy workable, member countries must agree that arguments based on the old institutional arrangement no longer function under the new regime, and that institutional reform is required. Appropriate incentives and effective mechanisms of intergovernmental cooperation are needed, and budget surveillance and information exchange may constitute a subtle complement for achieving stability in the EU economy under decentralized government.

Alan A. Tait (Chapter 9) reviews rules of the World Trade Organization (WTO) affecting foreign direct investment (FDI) and compares them with rules of the International Monetary Fund (IMF). He illustrates the existence of a large number of exceptions and reservations attached to WTO rules as compared with the relatively small number of such qualifications attached to IMF standards. He acknowledges that differences in the two systems stem from differences in the nature of WTO and IMF, the former being a low-consensus adversarial system and the latter being a high-consensus obligation system. Tait's chapter points out that rather high costs are involved in the operation of a low-consensus adversarial system.

Part IV deals with tax competition to attract foreign direct investment. Shinemay Chen, Jorge Martinez-Vazquez, and Sally Wallace (Chapter 10) investigate the responsiveness of foreign direct investment to the tax policies in home and host countries for each pair of home and potentially competing host countries. The FDI investigated are from five developed countries (the United States, the United Kingdom, Japan, Germany, and France) to four host, potentially rival, countries in southeast Asia (Hong Kong, Malaysia, Singapore, and Taiwan). The unique feature of their chapter is their investigation of how potential tax competition among a set of host countries affects the distribution of FDI. Carefully studying large amounts of data, they find that FDI levels tend to be inversely related to the rate of effective taxation in the supplying country, and that the amount of FDI in a host country is sensitive to the tax system of other potentially competitive host countries.

Deborah L. Swenson (Chapter 11) investigates empirically the effect of taxes on foreign direct investment in the United States during the period between 1984 and 1994. She finds that aggregate data which show that higher-tax states appear to attract a greater level of investment obscure some distinctive effects of taxes on foreign investment. When the data are disaggregated by transaction type, different tax responses emerge across the separate classes of investment. She finds that states with higher taxes attract fewer new plants or plant extensions, but are not adversely affected in attracting foreign acquisitions of existing plants.

Part V describes the current situation of foreign investments in transitional economies—Russia and China. Vladimir I. Tikhomirov (Chapter 12) provides an extensive narrative on recent historical events and describes a series of extraordinary post-Soviet Russian economic and financial crises. His chapter is a history of the collapse of enterprise management, industrial production, and financial markets. Liberalization of Russia's foreign trade in 1992 opened a channel for capital flight out of the economy, and removing foreign exchange controls led to massive flight of the population's savings. Foreign direct investment did not save industrial production but went into servicing export-import operations and purchases of state bonds. The state has almost totally withdrawn from economic strategy and planning. Tikhomirov thinks that the state should play the main role in efforts towards reversing negative trends in the national economy. Public investment policy should be the center of such a strategy. International and external channels offering capital flight should be, if not closed completely, at least state controlled.

Zhang Xiaoqiang (Chapter 13) provides usually hard to obtain information about the present state of the Chinese economy as well as data on foreign direct investment in China, and the law and operations covering FDI in China. Areas like Guangdong, Jiangsu, and Shanghai, where the economy is relatively developed, have attracted certain foreign investment, but in the hinterland such as Guizhou and Ningxia, where the economy is poor, few FDI agreements have been signed so far due to the low expected rate of return on investment. He argues that many infrastructure projects have been undertaken for social benefits and exhibit poor financial rates of return. To develop infrastructure, he thinks that China must rely on her own efforts and resources in addition to FDI. The contrast between China and Russia in their dealings with economic transition from the state controlled to the market oriented inferable from this and the preceding chapters seems remarkable.

Part VI explains equalization transfer systems working in Japan and in Australia. Nobuki Mochida (Chapter 14) describes the Japanese revenue reallocation system between central and local governments. The system is designed to equalize, in terms of a set of formulas, financial resources available to each local government.

About 80 percent of the disbursement of the central government's general account is simply transferred to other accounts in which local government comprises the largest share. Thus it seems that Japan's local governments take a major role in local public finance, but in reality they rather simply administer the final disbursement of funds under the strict set of rules specified by the central government. But, he explains, the current system faces considerable challenges due to changing public preferences for stronger local autonomy in expenditure, more flexibility in tax rate setting, and enhanced transparency of the equalization transfer scheme.

Robert J. Searle (Chapter 15) explains in detail the system of transferring funds within the Australian Federation, particularly the largest among inter-governmental transfers, the transfers from the Commonwealth to the state and municipal governments. He also explains the role of the Commonwealth Grants Commission and its methods of operation and reviews comments on and reactions to the Australian transfer system as expressed by foreign observers.

On the whole, the papers assembled in the volume reflect the present and perhaps the enduring interests of public finance scholars. They more or less represent the current state of research activities in the international public finance field. The editor hopes that this volume may offer stimulation to the creative mind, expansion of the state of knowledge, and development of research techniques in the field of public finance.

This volume is not intended to represent the proceedings of the 53rd Congress of the International Institute of Public Finance (IIPF), for the set of papers included is only a small portion of the 200-odd papers presented at the congress. It is also not meant to represent the overall theme of the congress. Nevertheless, the book undoubtedly owes its origin to the congress. Therefore, I, as one of the editors of this book and the chairman of the Organizing Committee of the 53rd Congress of IIPF, wish to take this opportunity to acknowledge various support rendered to the congress, particularly in connection with publication of this volume. I wish to thank the Science Council of Japan, the Japanese Public Finance Association, Ritsumeikan University, and individual members of the Japanese Public Finance Association for their institutional and generous financial support. Thanks are due also to the members of the Organizational Committee of the Congress and to the Committee's vice chairman, Professor Kenichi Miyamoto, and secretary general, Professor Mitsutoshi Sakano, for their efficient administrative and logistical services. Likewise, we owe our gratitude to the members of the IIPF's Scientific Committee and to the committee's co-chairpersons, Professors Tatsuo Hatta and Toshihiro Ihori for their skillful program production. Toshihiro Ihori lent invaluable assistance as the other editor of this book. Last, we cannot fail to thank the paper presenters, session chairpersons, discussants, and above all the 750 participants in the Congress for their stimulating intellectual contributions.

The secretarial assistance rendered in connection with production of this book by Mrs. Yuriko Shimano and Miss Emiko Inoue, and the patient editorial services of Mrs. Eiko Kitamura of Springer-Verlag, Tokyo, are highly appreciated. Without the help of these individuals and institutions, publication of this book would not have been possible. I am most grateful to all.

Hirofumi Shibata

Contents

PART I. THE WELFARE STATE

CHAPTER1 THE FISCAL CRISES IN WEL-
FARE DEMOCRACIES:
WITH SOME IMPLICATIONS FOR PUBLIC
INVESTMENT[**]

JAMES M. BUCHANAN[*]

INTRODUCTION

It is generally acknowledged that Western welfare democracies, in Europe and
America (Japan may also be included in the listing), face severe fiscal crises.
Constituency demands for entitlement-like welfare transfers based on public
expectations for continuance of existing programs, exceed the revenues that the same
constituents are willing to provide in taxes. There is a political mismatch between
the two sides of the budgetary account. Only in the 1980s and 1990s did the
vulnerabilities of the extended welfare states become increasingly apparent, along
with emerging recognition of long-run nonsustainability. The "Swedish model,"
with generous programs of general income support along with very high rates of tax,
has been totally transformed, from a pattern to be emulated in the 1960s to a pattern
to be avoided in the 1990s.

There is little need to discuss the issues here through detailed and particularized
institutional descriptions country by country. The crises in the United States, in

---

[*]Center for Study of Public Choice, George Mason University, Fairfax, Virginia, USA

[**]Portions of this paper are also contained in a lecture, "The Crises in Welfare Democracies,"
presented in Rome, June 1997, under the auspices of Banca di Roma, to be published.
Earlier variants of some of the argument are included in James M. Buchanan, "Can
Democracy Promote the General Welfare?" (1997c), and in "The Metamorphosis of Western
Democracies at the End of the Century" (1997b). The analytical framework is derivative
from James M. Buchanan and Roger D. Congleton, *Politics By Principle Not Interest:
Toward Nondiscriminatory Democracy* (forthcoming, 1998).

Spain, in Italy, in Germany, in Sweden, in Japan, and elsewhere are sufficiently similar to allow for a discussion that is generally applicable.

In earlier papers, and in my forthcoming book, I have advanced the argument to the effect that, to insure survival, democracy must attempt to preserve *generality* or at least *quasi-generality* in its welfare programs, and, conversely, that the introduction of overt discrimination through means testing and targeting can only undermine public support, perhaps to the extent of making the welfare state unsustainable. A political version of the "tragedy of the commons" must emerge as, when, and if identifiable interest groups recognize the prospects of particularized gains promised by increasingly discriminatory tax or transfer treatment.

Unfortunately, Western welfare democracies are changing in a direction opposed to that which I suggest to be desirable. Faced with mounting pressures from entitlement-like claims against public revenues and matched by equally strong pressures against further tax burdens, political leaders (of all ideological persuasions) are attracted to seek solutions by picking out what they consider to be the most vulnerable targets. Why should "the rich," who may have participated in financing the welfare programs along with others, be allowed to secure the benefits when, clearly, members of this group "can afford" to finance their retirement support and pay for their own medical services? There is no recognition of the categorical distinction between a *general* welfare program and one that provides welfare support only to those who are somehow politically defined to be "in need." In terms of prospective political implications, it is important to distinguish between the "general welfare state" and the "discriminatory welfare state." And what I see happening is that Western democracies are rapidly converting themselves into the latter from the former, with little or no recognition of what is indeed happening.

For basically the same reasons, we observe that modern political leaders neglect genuinely productive public investments, which yield generalized benefits, as they seek to maintain welfare transfers to politically dominant groups.

In what follows, I shall first examine the historical development of the democratic welfare state, followed by a diagnosis of the dilemma in which modern welfare states find themselves. This includes diagnosis of some elements in the late century that have created the growing disparities between claims against the state and the ability to meet these claims. Following this diagnosis, I shall discuss in more detail the distinction between general and discriminatory programs. Finally, I suggest that the technologically determined openness of the world economy must place constraints on the working out of the welfare state dilemma in all countries.

THE WELFARE STATE IN HISTORY

It may be useful to commence with a contrast between eighteenth- and twentieth-century public attitudes toward politics. I have often asked audiences or readers to put themselves in the mind-set of the late eighteenth century, particularly as represented by David Hume, Adam Smith, and by the American founding fathers, especially James Madison. These, and other, major figures of the Enlightenment did not think in terms of how the state —the organized collective— could promote the well-being of individuals; their primary interest was in preventing the state from tyrannizing over individuals. How could political authority, which they acknowledged to be necessary both to accomplish the leap from and to prevent relapse into Hobbesian anarchy, be kept in check? How could the state provide the framework within which persons might carry on their ordinary pursuits without exceeding these limits? How to limit political power; this was the dominant theme. These social philosophers did not consider the question: How can the state actively promote the well-being of the citizen?

The eighteenth-century skepticism about politics and politicians, indeed about the whole politics of governance, disappeared in the nineteenth century. We can identify several sources for the shift. German romanticism emerged to counter the classical liberalism, and this romanticism encompassed the Hegelian notion that man finally realizes himself fully only in the collective experience. A second source invokes what I have called "the electoral fallacy." In the historical epoch in question, governments were in the historical process of being transformed from autocratic monarchies, with a distinct separation between aristocratic classes and all lesser ranks, into electoral democracies. The French Revolution did take place, and popular sovereignty took on genuine meaning in public attitudes. This shift would have been expected to produce a lessening of skepticism about the efficacy of politics, as well as the behavior of politicians. If we, the people, can indeed throw the rascals out, why should we be so concerned about checking their powers in advance?

Finally, the genius of Karl Marx should never be undervalued. Marx brilliantly juxtaposed the logical implications of the still incomplete classical economics and the observed undesirable features of early industrial capitalism. He, and his followers, wisely refrained from careful definition of the socialist alternative; in this way they allowed romantic imaginations to run free and to construct nonfeasible utopias.

This potted history helps us to understand Prince Bismarck's motivation in introducing the welfare state late in the nineteenth century. He feared both populist democracy and Marxist revolution, and he predicted that industrial workers could be kept loyal to the collective —to the state— if they were bribed by promises of social security. In one respect, Bismarck was successful; the appeal of Marxist ideology was never strong enough to be a major force in developed countries. But Bismarck did not reckon on the appeal of his programs for state-financed welfare in a political setting with an open voting franchise, even to the extent that it included welfare recipients as well as taxpayers.

The twentieth century is described by the maturing of the Bismarckian general, but limited, welfare state into the massive transfer states at the century's end —a process that was allowed to take place uninhibited only after the disruptions of the two great wars and the Great Depression between them. The modern welfare state emerged full blown only in the second half of the twentieth century. The fact that it did so in temporal lockstep with the resource demands of the Cold War attests to the political popularity of fiscal transfer programs and also suggests the potential for disruption when and if the unsustainable commitments fully come to inform public consciousness.

WHY NOT THE WELFARE STATE?

A critic may be prompted to ask what the problem is all about. If persons, through their democratically elected legislative representatives and parties, choose to expend some, or even a considerable, share of valued resources to finance fiscal transfers to support those deemed worthy of welfare assistance, why should political or governmental insolvency be a consequence? Why is the extended welfare state incompatible with democracy?

There are two distinguishable features of modern democracies that combine to generate the incompatibility. First, as the institutions of majoritarian democracy are organized, political decisions are not made through agreement or consensus by all persons, or their representatives. Instead, decisions are reached through the organization of majority coalitions who then exercise the authority to make decisions binding over all members of the political community. The "natural logic" of majority rule implies differential or discriminatory treatment of those persons and groups that are in the minority. In itself this basic discriminatory feature of majoritarianism need not create major problems if majority coalitions rotate over sequential electoral cycles and if the exploitation of minorities is kept within bounds by operative constraints.

When, however, a second feature is recognized —one that is also widely descriptive of modern welfare states— seeds of fiscal insolvency and/or taxpayer revolt are necessarily planted. If majority coalitions are authorized to initiate fiscal actions that not only implement transfers among separate groups or classes of citizens within the temporally defined electoral cycle, but also embody guarantees that fiscal transfers will continue to be made in periods subsequent to those that define electoral dominance, a continual ratcheting upward of total commitments must take place. The rotation of political authority between alternating majority coalitions cannot, in this setting, be self-correcting.

Consider the following illustrative example. A majority coalition, call it A, exercises its constitutional authority and initiates an entitlement program that designates all members of some group, t, to be eligible for fiscal transfers. If these transfers are authorized for one period only, or period-by-period, no particular difficulty need arise. An alternative coalition, call it B, might, when it acquires authority, simply eliminate the transfers to members of t or choose some other eligible group. In the modern welfare state, however, an open-ended entitlement program is widely interpreted to imply that, once defined to be eligible for fiscal transfers, members of a designated group have legitimate claims against revenues for *all* future periods. Modern politics proceeds as if the approval of a welfare spending program involves two separate components: (1) fiscal transfers in the period of enactment and (2) promises or obligations to make similar transfers in all subsequent periods. It is as if a debt has been created that embodies an obligation on the part of the political unit to meet claims against it by all those initially defined to be eligible for transfers.

Consider the situation faced by the alternative majority coalition, B, in this scenario. To refuse to honor the claims of members of t, the designated eligible group, amounts, in public attitudes, to default on public debt. Rather than pursue this politically suicidal course of action, the coalition will simply meet the claims against it and, on its own initiative, will seek to satisfy its own constituents by establishing yet an additional entitlement program. Any ratcheting downward in the size of the welfare-transfer sector in modern democracy is made impossible by the combination of majoritarianism on the one hand and debt-like entitlements on the other. We should not, therefore, be surprised at the difficulties in maintaining budgetary shares devoted to the financing of public inputs that enhance general productivity of national economies.

WHY NOW?

It becomes relatively easy to identify elements in the developments, both in political institutions and in public attitudes toward these institutions, that have either brought the problems to crisis proportions only in the late years of the twentieth century and which make any satisfactory resolution of these problems more difficult. There is, first of all, the *fatal conceit* of socialism (Hayek, 1988) which embodies separation between production and consumption of economic value (Buchanan, 1993). This conceit carries over directly into welfare-state extension, which is often supported in arguments that proceed as if the claims against economic value reflected in fiscal transfers can be settled from an inexhaustible preexisting and continuously renewable stock. The ending of the great socialist experiments, through the 1989-91 revolutions, did much to modify this fatal conceit, but its residues remain in public and political attitudes.

Second, there is the *Keynesian delusion* which was especially important in the critical middle decades of the century during which the welfare state was formed. In a mind-set that involved a total separation between the analysis of the workings of the macroeconomy and the politics of implementation, arguments were advanced that seemed to offer putative justification for deficit financing over and beyond those emerging from the classical principles of sound finance (Buchanan and Wagner, 1977). The lessening of concern about the creation of explicitly measured budgetary deficits carries with it some spillover complement through a lessening of concern about the implicit debts represented by the open-ended entitlement programs. Further, even if the future-period claims against revenues are fully recognized, the Keynesian-inspired absence of concern over deficit creation promotes acquiescence rather than avoidance. If the structures in place fail to generate revenues sufficient to meet claims, why not simply finance these claims by additional issues of debt?

These first two sources involved errors in thinking —bad science— that had important influences on the shape of political action. Additional exacerbating elements stem from changes in the structural setting within which the welfare state grew in the second half of the century and within which any changes must take place in the next decades. The third source of fiscal stress is familiar, it arises from the changing *age profile* in all of the Western welfare states. In every country, a major share of transfer outlay is that which takes value from productive income earners and provides payments to those who have retired from productive work. These systems are pay as we go structures, and, as such, the rate of taxation required to finance any particular level of payment to pensioners depends critically on the ratio between the sizes of these two groups. If the population is growing, either from natural rates of increase or from immigration, pension payments can be sustained, and increased, without creating undue budgetary pressures. If, by contrast, population growth slows down and the population, overall, ages, the rates of taxation required even to sustain existing levels of pension payments may become intolerable. And, as everyone recognizes, this ratio is moving in the wrong direction in all Western welfare states, almost all of which have massive pay as we go pension structures.

A final element that warrants specific mention here applies directly to the second major outlay component in modern welfare states —the financing of medical services. Here the claims tend to be open-ended, but, in dramatic contrast with pension obligations, these claims are not objectively defined in monetary units. The claims are, instead, to services in kind (medical care) which must be provided by a supplying industry. Issues of moral hazard aside, the necessary translation between services and costs might be accomplished without major difficulty in a setting where the *technology* of delivery is static or changes slowly. But, if the technology changes rapidly, and if the changes involve cost increases, there is a built-in inflationary element in the program, almost independently of how the supply of services is actually organized. The difficulty is made more severe if members of the public, as potential recipients of services, as well as their political agents, remain at the mercy of "experts" in the supplying industry in defining what is and what is not adequate service. With developments in modern medicine at century's end, it seems unlikely that any reorganization of the medical entitlement programs could possibly insure that outlay would be sufficient to keep up with the technology (Buchanan, 1990a).

THE GENERAL WELFARE STATE AND POLITICAL EFFICIENCY

Let me summarize the preceding argument. I have suggested that the operation of majoritarian democracy in a constitutional setting that allows debt-like entitlements to be introduced must produce a racheting upward in transfer programs. I have then identified several sources for the intensifying of fiscal pressures at the end of the century. The false ideas summarized as the fatal conceit of socialism and the Keynesian delusion led to the failure to reckon properly on the long-run consequences of actions taken. These consequences are, in turn, more serious than they might otherwise have been predicted to be because of the changing age profiles of populations in Western democracies and because of the explosive developments in medical technology.

The argument that I have advanced provides an explanation for the crises that are faced at the end of the century. There are two ways that the states may respond, and I have already expressed the fear that the responses are in the wrong rather than the right direction. It is useful to clarify the distinction further.

The Bismarckian welfare state can be accurately described as *general* or *quasi-general* in its primary features. By these terms, I refer to the fact that the programs have been financed by *general* taxation for the most part, and that the benefits have been made available *generally*, rather than discriminatorily or differentially, to designated categories of eligibles. I consider the pay as we go structures of retirement income support to meet criteria of quasi-generality. These structures do, indeed, involve massive transfers of value from one group in the polity to another. But generality is preserved in the sense that all persons expect to qualify for income support because all persons (who survive at all) get old. Similar features describe programs for medical services; not all persons become ill, but all who do become ill tend to be deemed eligible for support in the state-financed programs.

Generality or quasi-generality is a critically important element in determining the political efficiency of the inclusive set of welfare state programs. Consider the situation faced by a member of a successful majority coalition, or her political agent, in choosing among rates of tax and rates of outlay on this or that program, including choosing how such programs might be rescued from threatened fiscal distress. A general tax rate increase will necessarily apply over all members of the polity, including those who are in the majority coalition. Approval of a tax increase will not be treated as a direct levy on members of the minority coalition out of power; and similarly, for a change in benefits. Under a general or quasi-general program, political choices cannot reflect differential or discriminatory treatment as among separate groups of constituents.

Generality or quasi-generality may be maintained in response to developing fiscal crises by modifying rates of tax and/or rates of transfer payments for all members of the polity. For example, the pay as we go structure of pension payments may be brought within fiscal solvency by increasing general taxes on all income earners, by cutting back rates of benefits on all persons who reach retirement age, by changing the retirement age itself, or any combination of these three changes. The political efficacy of the overall structure is enhanced because, in any such changes, all persons and groups share in the adjustments. There is little or no advantage, as such, in securing membership in the majority political coalition.

These reforms may be contrasted dramatically with those that violate the generality or quasi-generality principle and reflect response to fiscal crises through the introduction or extension of discrimination in treatment, on either the tax or the outlay side. Consider the introduction of means testing to determine eligibility for receipt of old-age payments. If persons who earn income or accumulate wealth beyond certain defined limits are declared to be ineligible for transfer payments upon reaching the standard age, despite having been subjected to the general taxes to finance payments during their own working years, these persons will necessarily consider the system exploitative. Comparable shifts in attitudes will take place if taxes are increased only on some participants in the program while leaving other participants with reduced rates. Distributional conflict among classes will be moved to center stage in political discourse, and the political game itself will become the source for the formation of class conflict.

Any attempt to reform modern welfare states by moving away from general and quasi-general programs of income support must create incentives for political agents to invest resources in organizing majority coalitions. If welfare state programs come to be considered as means through which some groups, those who are politically successful, can secure gains at the direct expense of those who are politically unsuccessful, the resource wastage involved in majoritarian rent seeking will increase substantially. And consider how proposals to make publicly-financed investments in infrastructure, aimed to be generally beneficial to all members of the polity, might fare in such a political environment. In this political setting, neither the general welfare state nor the productive public sector, as we know it, will survive. The "churning state," as described provocatively by Anthony de Jasay (1985), will emerge, in actuality if not in name.

DEMOCRATIC WELFARE STATES IN THE GLOBALIZED ECONOMY

To this point, the discussion has proceeded on the implicit presumption that the separate national units are fully autonomous, one from another. As noted earlier, the problem of the maturing welfare democracies are remarkably similar, such that general discussion maintains cross-country applicability. The point I now want to emphasize, however, is that the separate nation-states, as political units, are not autonomous, and that the competitive forces generated in an increasingly integrated world economic nexus impose constraints on the set of policy options as well as on the directions for change pursued by each and every state.

Any welfare program, embodying both taxes and transfer payments, is economically inefficient in the narrow and conventional sense. A larger (more highly valued) bundle of goods and services can be produced in the absence of the tax-transfer process than in its presence. Inefficiencies of this sort may, of course, be reckoned as a cost that is superseded by the benefits that a welfare program promises in furtherance of an alternative objective —social security of varying forms.

Over and beyond these economic inefficiencies, familiarly referred to as excess burdens, welfare systems may create political inefficiency and in varying degrees of significance. And, as previously noted, the structure of a welfare program itself may determine its indirect efficiency loss. To the extent that a program differentiates among classes or groups, on either the tax or transfer side of the account, supplementary incentives are provided for investment in efforts to secure favorable treatment and to protect against unfavorable treatment. Political inefficiency takes shape through majoritarian rent seeking (Buchanan, 1995) measured by the amount of resources devoted to attempt to organize and join dominating majority coalitions in positions of political authority.

Political inefficiency is not totally eliminated in a welfare state described by adherence to a generality or quasi-generality norm in its programs. But closing off the major sources for discriminatory gains and losses must surely forestall massive resource wastage that might otherwise be predicted to occur. But what is there that might arise to prevent the natural forces of internal politics in a country from proceeding down the path of nongenerality? Here, or so it seems to me, competition among national units, actual or potential, directly or virtually experienced, can emerge to protect even majoritarian politics against the logically-derived excesses of distributional churning.

Western democracies, along with other developed countries, are increasingly open to flows of commerce and the mobility of capital value in an electronic age. International league tables come continually off the presses, and CNN offers anyone anywhere the opportunity to see what is happening everywhere. A majority coalition that finds its policies producing losses in the international comparisons will be unlikely to remain in authority. Relative size, of course, matters here. Pressures upon, say, New Zealand to transform its overextended welfare state in the 1980s were naturally greater than pressures, say, on the United States in the 1990s. Nonetheless, it seems appropriate to conclude that no modern state can remain grossly inefficient due to the excesses of its internal distributional conflicts. The dilemma-like setting in which all groups lose in some opportunity-cost sense will become too obvious; constructive reform will take place that restores generality to some extent at least, although program reductions may be a necessary consequence.

The same argument may be extended in application to programs for public investment. As the demands for welfare transfers have multiplied in past decades, the infrastructure, embodying publicly-financed investment, has been allowed to deteriorate in many polities. Pressures placed on national governments by increasing integration into the globalized economic nexus will make a reversal of such deterioration almost necessary. The budgetary trade-off that has allowed welfare transfers to burgeon as public investments in infrastructure are drawn down —this trade-off will almost surely be reversed.

Forces for competition are naturally opposed by forces for cartelization, and these offsetting forces operate in the international as well as the domestic arena. Supporters of overextended and discriminatory welfare states will make efforts to secure international agreements that will insure comparable degrees of income support in differing countries, thereby aimed to eliminate competitive pressures.

Europe warrants particular notice in this connection, since here the danger of effective cartelization seems quite real. My own interpretation is that Europe, in the early 1990s, missed its once-in-history opportunity to organize itself into a genuinely competitive federalism (see Buchanan, 1990b, 1997a). The *dirigiste* vision, emanating from Brussels and reflected in the terms of the Maastricht treaty, seems to have carried the day. And the separate nation-states are forestalled from competing, one with another, in an integrated European network of exchange. There has been a general failure to understand the critical distinction between uniformity as emergent from an operative competitive process and uniformity imposed as a means to prevent this very process from serving its functional purpose.

A Europe in which the separate welfare states are cartelized can anticipate losing out in the international comparisons to those countries in Asia, Latin America, and even in North America that reform their welfare programs along lines that will reduce the resource wastage of competitive rent seeking. The "social model" that many Europeans hold up as superior to the somewhat more limited welfare states elsewhere is not economically viable for the twenty-first century.

CONCLUSION

I have concentrated almost exclusively on the elements of the fiscal economic crises that Western democracies now confront because of the nonsustainable claims of the several welfare-transfer programs. I have only very briefly traced out the obvious implications for public sector investments as politicians respond to pressures to sustain nonviable transfer claims. I have not examined at all the whole set of larger issues that may exacerbate rather than attenuate the narrower fiscal crises. I refer here to the continuing, and indeed mainly salutary, dissipation of loyalties to historically defined national political units —to nation-states— along with implications for centralized democratic governance. Federalism, decentralization, privatization, devolution, communitarianism, civil society —these terms are in the air, and, in their several and partially intersecting implications do little to suggest that the welfare states, as we have come to know them, can survive. Perhaps their survival is simply not on. My central point is only to suggest that survival becomes possible only if generality is preserved. As I have stated on several occasions, the general welfare state may survive if it imposes a limit upon itself and does so generally; the discriminatory welfare-transfer state will not survive. If modern political leaders go down this strictly redistributionist alley, they face taxpayer revulsion and to the detriment of those most in need of public sustenance. In democracy, the "poor" can only ride along with others in the carriage; they cannot expect to ride alone, at least in tolerable comfort.

REFERENCES

Buchanan, James M. *Technological Determinism Despite the Reality of Scarcity: A Neglected Element in the Theory of Spending for Medical and Health Care*, (Little Rock, Arkansas: University of Arkansas for Medical Sciences, 1990a): 3-17.

_____. "Europe's Constitutional Opportunity,"in *Europe's Constitutional Future* (London: Institute of Economic Affairs, 1990b), 1-20.

_____. *Consumption without Production: The Impossible Idyll of Socialism* (Freiburg, Germany: Haufe, 1993), 49-75.

_____. "Majoritarian Rent Seeking," Center for Study of Public Choice, George Mason University, Fairfax, Virginia, working paper, 1995.

_____. "National Politics and Competitive Federalism: Italy and the Constitution of Europe," in *Post-Socialist Political Economy: Selected Essays* (Hants, UK: Edward Elgar, 1997a), 243-53.

_____. "The Metamorphosis of Western Democracies at the End of the Century," *Seventh Sinclair House Debate: "Is Industrial Society Disintegrating?"* (Bad Homburg, Germany: Herbert Quandt-Stiftung, 1997b), 8-13.

_____. "Can Democracy Promote the General Welfare?," *Social Philosophy and Policy* 14 (No. 2, Summer 1997c): 165-79.

Buchanan, James M. and Roger D. Congleton. *Politics by Principle Not Interest: Toward Nondiscriminatory Democracy* (New York and Cambridge: Cambridge University Press, forthcoming, 1998.)

Buchanan, James M. and Richard E. Wagner. *Democracy in Deficit: The Political Legacy of Lord Keynes* (New York: Academic Press, 1977).

de Jasay, Anthony. *The State* (Oxford: Basil Blackwell, 1985).

Hayek, F. A. *The Fatal Conceit: The Errors of Socialism* (Chicago: University of Chicago Press, 1988).

CHAPTER 2 COMMENTS ON JAMES M. BUCHANAN "THE FISCAL CRISIS IN WELFARE DEMOCRACIES"

RICHARD A. MUSGRAVE[*]

Professor Buchanan's paper, as we have learned to expect from him, carries a strong message. The welfare state can survive only if it discards discriminatory practices and returns to its earlier reliance on general programs. Unless this is done, it will be swamped by the political pressures of particular interest groups. As one who believes in the historical contribution of the welfare state, I welcome his concern for its survival and will join hands to save it. However, the more general thrust of his paper leaves me uncertain as to how strong an ally I have found.

In fact, I wonder whether his insistence on general programs and rejection of discriminatory (I would rather say "selective", a less loaded term) ones does not contradict the very idea of what the welfare state or, better, welfare democracy is about. A distinction needs to be drawn between (1) the role of the state in contributing to the general welfare by, say, raising per capita income and (2) its role in giving support to individuals or groups in particular situations of need. Both roles are important, but the task of the state *qua* welfare state deals with the latter; and as such it is selective in nature, not general.

The concept of a truly general and non-selective welfare state (as distinct from a state concerned with the general welfare), when carried to its logical limit, becomes

[*]H. H. Burbank Professor of Political Economy Emeritus, Harvard University, and Adjunct Professor of Economics, University of California, Santa Cruz

an empty box. A welfare state which pays a benefit of $100 to each person and finances it with a lump-sum tax of $100 is wholly general on both sides of the ledger but it does not accomplish very much. The purpose of the welfare state is to protect individuals or groups in situations of particular need and for this selective techniques are called for in order to avoid unnecessary and harmful churning in the budget. An illustration is given in the table.

Programs to Provide a Minimum Income of $15

	L	M	H	Total
Selective Program				
Income	10.00	50.00	100.00	160.00
Tax base	-	50.00	100.00	150.00
Tax rate (%)	-	3.33	3.33	3.33
Tax	-	1.67	3.33	5.00
Benefit	5.00	-	-	5.00
Net change	+5.00	-1.67	-3.33	-
General Program				
Income	10.00	50.00	100.00	160.00
Tax base	10.00	50.00	100.00	160.00
Tax rate (%)	11.54	11.54	11.54	11.54
Tax	1.15	5.77	11.54	18.46
Benefit	6.15	6.15	6.15	18.46
Net change	+5.00	+0.38	-5.38	-

Let there be three people, L, M and H, earning $10, $50 and $100 respectively. Suppose further that the policy goal is to assure a minimum income of $15. Under a selective program, M and H will be taxed at 3.33 percent to raise the required revenue of $5 from a base of $150 with $5 then transferred to L. L gains $5, while M and H lose $1.67 and $3.33, respectively. Under a general program all three receive the same grant and pay at the same rate of tax. In order to leave L with a net income of $15, a revenue of $18.46 is required. With a tax base of $160, this calls for a tax rate of 11.54 percent. L pays $1.15 and after receiving $6.15 is left with $15 as the program desires; M pays $5.77, receives $6.15 and is left with a net gain of $0.38; H pays $11.54 and after receiving $6.15 suffers a net loss of $5.38. A net benefit is extended to M who was not meant to be assisted, and a tax rate of 11.54 percent is needed rather than one of only 3.33 percent.

Where the program goal is to assure a minimum level of income for families with children, it will cost less if payments are made to families with children only, rather than to all families. If the purpose is to protect the aged, it seems sensible not to include babies in the beneficiary group. Thereby the needed budget will be smaller and the required rate of tax will be lower, as will be the efficiency cost of taxation, a point which I made at length in the '70s when the negative income tax was discussed. Efficient policy, therefore, should limit benefits to the target group, an obvious point which Professor Buchanan, though not a friend of high taxation, seems to set aside.

He may respond that this concern, while valid in principle, is outweighed by the way in which the political system responds to the two approaches. Use of selective or discriminatory programs is said to generate excesses which are avoided by general programs. Perhaps so, but even then this basic efficiency case for selective programs should be allowed for as part of the picture.

I am also not sure that the foibles of politics make so decisive a case for general and against selective programs. Such programs will become excessive, so Professor Buchanan argues, because majority coalitions can impose them against the will of the minority. The tragedy of the commons grows more tragic, the larger is the number of deals that can be made. Such may be the case in some settings, but I can also imagine opposite situations. General programs have wider appeal and can draw on broader support, and the more selective programs are, the more difficult it becomes to find coalition partners. Dividing up programs may limit rather than expand the budget.

Moreover, terms have to be defined more clearly. General programs, I take it, are programs which combine many target or beneficiary groups while selective programs are those with a single target group. General, therefore, need not mean large, and selective need not mean small. In most countries, the growth of welfare policy has been largely in two selective programs aimed at the aged and the sick. But these programs have carried such weight not because they are selective and invite multiple coalitions, but because they have a large clientele and involve costly benefits.

As a longstanding supporter of a broadly defined income tax base and critic of selective tax preferences, should I not now be sympathetic to the generalist approach? Income, as an index of capacity or well-being, should be defined in broad accretion terms, and the (now so popular) expansion of tax preferences is disgraceful where I come from. The analogy to welfare programs, however, is mistaken. The case for generality in the definition of income does not tell us that everyone should be taxed at the same rate. It only tells us that capcity should be measured uniformly. Similarly, if a welfare program is to assure a set minimum income or the availability of certain goods to low-income people, a comprehensive definition of minimum income is needed, but it does not follow that benefits should be paid to all.

A good deal more could be said about how programs should be packaged, but economy of time forces me to move on. I must turn to the broader frame in which Professor Buchanan views welfare democracy. The picture which he paints is not pretty and leaves me puzzled why the welfare state depicted in these terms should be saved.

The condensed history which he sketches offers a litany of mishaps. Enlightenment's sound and sceptical view of the state gave way to the franchise and popular democracy, with majority rule and its "electoral fallacy". Led by Marx's genius, consumption came to be separated from production, "that fatal conceit of socialism" as von Hayek is quoted. To top it off, there came Keynes with his "bad economics", finalizing what now has become the crisis of the welfare state. This may condense the pot a bit too much, but it brings out the essential message.

My own potted history, time permitting, would tell a somewhat different story. The pitfalls of the market system -- with all respect for its great productive powers -- did not vanish with the early stages of the industrial revolution, nor did the later blooming of classical economics prove that the market cannot fail. Bismarck may have been wrong in thinking that social insurance was needed in the 1880s, but he was correct from the longer perspective. The rise of the welfare state, along with the rise of democracy, was a necessary development, a needed complement to the market so as to permit its benefits to be enjoyed while cushioning its faults.

Obviously, production has to precede consumption, and rewards are needed to induce production. It does not follow, however, that market outcomes should be accepted as the final arbiters of all matters, including distribution. Factor pricing is one thing, and distributive justice is another. Both must be allowed for and a balance must be struck. The failure of socialism did not prove infallibility of the invisible hand and it did not void the need for social policy in a democratic society.

As for Keynes, recall that his case for deficits was made at a time of severe unemployment and deficient aggregate demand. Given his brilliant and pragmatic mind, he would not have counseled deficits when market forces are strong. I vividly recall a Washington seminar in 1945 when he expressed precisely that view. However, there is public as well as private investment, and spreading the cost over time is equally appropriate in both cases. Public investment in human resources is now increasingly recognized as a major concern of welfare policy, a theme which Professor Buchanan notes in the title of his paper, but which he addresses only briefly in the text.

I am also a bit worried about how Professor Buchanan views the working of a democratic society. He cites the rise of "a political setting with an open franchise even to the extent that it included welfare recipients as well as taxpayers", points to the likely abuse of minorities under majority rule, and stresses the unfortunate ability of incumbents to legislate programs beyond their electoral cycle. I hardly find it shocking to permit potential beneficiaries to join in program votes. Issues of distribution have to be addressed in a democratic society and do not lend themselves to unanimous choice. Nor would I call for letting programs be limited to legislative cycles. The goal of the welfare state is not only to provide security from one day to the next, but to offer continuity in thresholds. Changing circumstances will arise and call for program changes, but this does not void the case for continuity where possible. Nor does the more recent experience in the United States and now the United Kingdom suggest that such adjustments cannot be made. Political moods have their cycles, lessons are learned from experience, and the democratic process, though hardly smooth, has its way of surviving.

The crisis of the welfare state and its imminent collapse as portrayed by Professor Buchanan's paper is much overdrawn. The reforms accomplished since the Beveridge Report first appeared 56 years ago have been most successful, so much so that their essential message has come to be taken for granted, across political parties of varying persuasions.

Nevertheless, Professor Buchanan is correct when pointing to three serious problems that the welfare state must now face. They include demographic change, rising costs of medical services, and globalization. None of these difficulties can be traced to the evil geniuses of Marx or Keynes, or even to the bad habits of majority rule. They are exogenous to the nature of the beast, yet they will have to be met.

Aging of the population complicates old-age insurance but the difficulty can be resolved. Whatever the particular technique, per capita income of retirees has to be adjusted from time to time to keep it in a reasonable relation to that of the working population, net of what they pay into the system.

Health insurance poses a tougher problem. Aging of the population creates increased need, and advances of medical science offer increased possibilities of new if expensive remedies. Society may wish to dedicate a larger share of its income to health care, but the traditional premise that the cost of insurance be shared equally between the sickly and the healthy, calling for protection against adverse selection, may become increasingly costly for the latter.

Nevertheless, these are manageable problems, problems which should not wreck welfare democracy. The same may not hold for globalization. As I have argued for many years in the context of federalist design, distribution policy has to be an essentially central function. If pursued by subjurisdictions, mobile factors and capital in particular will flee high-tax areas and indigents will seek high-benefit havens. With globalization, national governments become local, and a downward spiral tends to result, a consequence which is well under way. This aspect of globalization may be tamed by international cooperation and tax harmonization, and I hope that this will be done. Intergovernmental competition is fine where directed at more efficient performance, but not where tax and welfare policies are reduced to their lowest common denominator. Professor Buchanan in turn rejects cooperation as "cartelization" and applauds unfettered intergovernmental competition. Once more I am left with the impression that Professor Buchanan, while throwing out a life preserver to the drowning welfare state, really would not greatly mourn if it were to drown.

CHAPTER3 SOCIAL SECURITY AND ECO-NOMIC GROWTH
—IMPLICATIONS FOR EAST ASIA

FREDERICK ZU-LIU HU[*]

INTRODUCTION

A remarkable fact about the development experience in East Asia is that the size of government stays small throughout the region despite rapid industrialisation and phenomenal increases in living standards. Government expenditures in East Asia averaged 22% of GDP in 1995, compared to 46% of GDP in OECD countries . A key factor behind the generally low levels of public spending in East Asia is that governments there have not played an active role in social protection activities such as old age provision and unemployment insurance. However, this situation may change soon as pressures are being built up for increasing the state's involvement in income redistribution and income maintenance. With fast declining fertility rates and rising life expectancy, East Asia will above all have to confront the challenge to meet old age pensions. While the percentage of the elderly (defined as people over 60 years old) in population is slightly under 10% in mid-1990s in the four newly industrialised economies - Hong Kong, Korea, Singapore and Taiwan - hence referred to as East Asian NIEs, for example, this ratio within a generation will rise to 22%, exceeding the 1995 level for OECD countries. How East Asian NIEs will respond to this challenge will have important implications for long-run growth and welfare.

In this paper, we first explore the determinants of social security and welfare

[*]Goldman, Sachs & Co, 37th Floor, Asia Pacific Finance Tower, Citibank Plaza, Hong Kong

The author is grateful to participants of the 53rd IIPF World Congress in Kyoto, especially to Ke-young Chu and Vito Tanzi, for invaluable suggestions and comments.

expenditures in a cross-country context to gain perspectives into how social security and welfare payments historically reacted to demographic trends and per capita income levels. We then explore what effects the expansion of the welfare state has had, if any, on economic growth. The final section examines implications of social security and welfare spending requirements for future economic performance in East Asia NIEs.

INTERNATIONAL PATTERN IN THE PROVISION OF SOCIAL SECURITY

Because of concerns on market failures and income redistribution, government is typically expected to play an important role in old age pensions, unemployment insurance, and various social transfer programs. However, there exist wide differences across country in the degree of government involvement in social security and welfare. Table 1 offers an international comparison in the level of central government outlays in social security and welfare as a share of GDP, based on data compiled from IMF Government Finance Statistics. While the public expenditure data fails to reveal the

Table 1. International comparison of social security and welfare provision ,1970-95 [a] (% of GDP, central government expenditures)

	1970-79	1980-89	1990-95
Anglo-Saxon [b]	6.8	9.6	10.3
EU [c]	13.0	16.3	16.8
Transitional economies		8.0	9.1
Latin America	3.1	3.5	4.2
Middle East [d]	1.9	2.4	3.0
Africa	0.6	0.7	0.4
South Asia	2.5	1.3	2.2
East Asia [e]	0.7	0.9	1.4
Japan	5.6	9.4	9.7
NIEs	0.9	1.3	2.2
China	0.5	0.4	0.2
Asean 4 [f]	0.5	0.6	0.7

Source: IMF, Government Financial Statistics 1996; and author's estimate

[a] Simple averages.
[b] Australia, Canada, Ireland, New Zealand, United Kingdom, and United States.
[c] Excluding Ireland and United Kingdom which are grouped in Anglo-Saxon.
[d] Excluding Israel.
[e] Excluding China and Japan.
[f] Indonesia, Malaysia, Philippines, and Thailand.

diversity in institutional structures and legislative differences in social security, it provides crucial information on the financing role of government in the provision of social security and welfare.

It is clear from the table that governments in industrialised countries typically spend a substantial amount of resources in social security and welfare. European Union stands out as having the largest welfare state. Member governments of the European Union on average have spent more than 16% of GDP on social security and welfare since 1980s. As part of their socialist legacies, transitional economies have also had fairly high levels of social security and welfare spending. The intermediate cases are Latin America and Middle East where governments on average have spent 2 to 4% of GDP on social security and welfare. The ratio for South Asia is around 2%, mainly owning to the relatively high level in Sri Lanka. At the other end of the spectrum lies East Asia, with an extraordinarily low level of government spending on social security and welfare, only slightly higher than Africa. It is especially striking to note that the East Asian NIEs have devoted only a little over 2% of GDP to social security and welfare in 1990-95.

Table 1 also shows that social security and welfare spending as a share of GDP has increased over time in all regions except Africa. Government outlays in this category rose by 3 percent of GDP in both Anglo-Saxon and European Union between 1970s and 80s, for example. Transitional economies experienced one full percentage point increase in these social expenditures between the 1990-95 period and the preceding decade, owing to a combination of falling output and rising unemployment in those economies. By contrast, the increases in social security and welfare spending in East Asia have been modest.

DETERMINANTS OF SOCIAL SECURITY SPENDING

What explains the differences in the size of the welfare state across countries? One hypothesis immediately coming into one's mind is that the international pattern in social security provision is simply generated by differences in income level, as measured by per capita real GDP. If countries are divided by their 1995 levels of per capita GDP in US dollars into 4 groups ranging from low-income to high-income countries, as defined by the World Bank, one can observe a positive relation between income level and the share of government social security and welfare spending, as shown in Table 2.

Another important factor determining social security expenditures is demographics. Variables such as the age structure of the population, especially the old-age dependency ratio, the rate of growth in population, fertility rate, the share of labor force in agriculture, and so on, all likely influence the level of social security spending.

One could also point to political and social factors in explaining international differences in social security. In some societies - notably developing countries, public insurance is limited to civil services while the protection of the majority of population is left to traditional insurance arrangements (Burgess and Stern 1991). In East Asia, for example, the low level of government spending on social security and welfare could be attributed to the functioning of traditional informal insurance mechanisms such as family and community-based support for the elderly. Alternatively the small size of welfare state in East Asia could be due to the lack of political democracy that allowed government to ignore the need or the popular demand for social outlays, especially those with redistributional elements. If democratisation induces the growth in the welfare state, then the transition to democracy in Taiwan and Korea since late 80s could prompt those two economies to raise their spending on social security and welfare to a level more in line with the average ratio in other high-income economies.

To assess the relative importance of these various factors, we present an empirical model for the determination of social security expenditure. The model relates

Table 2. Income level and government spending on social security and welfare (% of GDP, central government)

	1970-79	1980-89	1990-95
Low-income [a]	0.9	0.9	1.3
Lower-middle-income	1.4	2.1	3.1
Upper-middle-income	5.2	6.6	6.9
High-income I	8.6	10.9	11.8
High-income II [b]	10.7	13.4	14.2

Source: IMF, Government Financial Statistics 1996; and author's estimate

[a] Countries are grouped according to the World Bank classification.
[b] Excluding East Asian NIEs, Kuwait, and United Arab Emigrates.

government spending on social security and welfare, denoted as SSW, to income, demographic and political variables.

A. DATA DESCRIPTION

GDP: per capita GDP in 1970, expressed in 1985 international dollars. We use its logs in the regression. The data is drawn from Summers and Heston (1996).

Aging. We use the share of the elderly over 65 years old in the total population to measure the degree of ageing in 1970, the starting year of the sample period. The source of data is from World Bank (1994, 1997).

Aglabor: the share of labour force in agriculture in 1970. Social security is insignificant in agrarian societies and farmers are usually left out the formal public security system in many countries. This variable is intended to capture both the stage of development and the extent of coverage of public social security system.

Worker: the share of working age population (between age 15 and 64) in total population in 1970. Source: World bank (1997)

Democracy: approximated by the Index of political rights, averaged over the 1972-89 period (from 0 to 1; 1 = most freedom.) Source: Gastil (1982-83, and other years).

SSW: The share of consolidated central government expenditures on social security and welfare in GDP, period average for 1970-1995, expressed in percentage points. Source: IMF (1996), Government Finance Statistics.

Summary statistics for both dependent and independent variables are shown in Table 3.

Table 3. Summary Statistics of Regression Variables

Variable	Number of observations	Mean	SD	Minimum	Maximum
SSW	117	4.275	5.335	0.000	20.717
GDP	104	3286	3260	287	13299
Aging	106	0.052	0.034	0.017	0.141
Aglabor	111	0.5326	0.2862	0.0200	0.9400
Worker	103	0.4009	0.0962	0.2499	0.9167

B. REGRESSION RESULTS

Table 4 reports three sets of regression results. All three regressions use the same dependent variable, SSW, which is the share of central government expenditures on social security and welfare in GDP, averaged over the 1970-95 period, as described above.

In the first regression, all three standard independent variables - log (GDP), ageing, and democracy- have highly significant coefficients with expected signs. These three variables jointly explain over 80 percent of the variation in social security expenditures. Note that both the initial income variable and the ageing variable take values at the start of the sample period. Thus their relations with social security expenditures are unlikely caused by simultaneity bias. With a higher starting level of per capita income, a country is likely to have higher ratio of social security expenditures relative to GDP. This relation between initial income and subsequent social security expenditures can be seen in Figure 1.

Similarly, population ageing is strongly related to government social security spending. As shown in Figure 2, the higher the ratio of the elderly (above age 65) to total population a country started with in 1970, the larger its government spending on social security as a share of GDP. This is not surprising because old age pension, sickness, and survival benefits usually constitute the bulk of any social security

Table 4. Determinants of social security and welfare expenditures

Independent variable [a]	(1)	(2)	(3) [b]
log(GDP)	0.81	0.33	0.22
	(2.09)	(2.85)	(2.52)
aging	126.2	140.3	148.1
	(11.5)	(12.8)	(13.1)
democracy	0.33	0.35	0.64
	(2.19)	(2.47)	(2.95)
worker		-9.45	-8.49
		(-3.73)	(-3.21)
aglabor			-1.43
			(-1.03)
R**2(adjusted)	0.81	0.85	0.87
no. of observations	100	99	76

[a] t statistics are shown in parentheses.
[b] Corrected for first-order serial correlation.

28

Figure 1. Initial Income and Social Security Spending

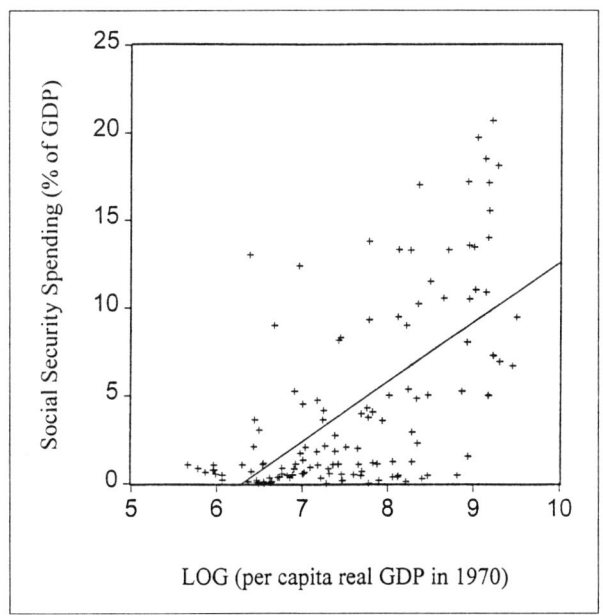

Figure 2. Social Security Spending and Population Aging

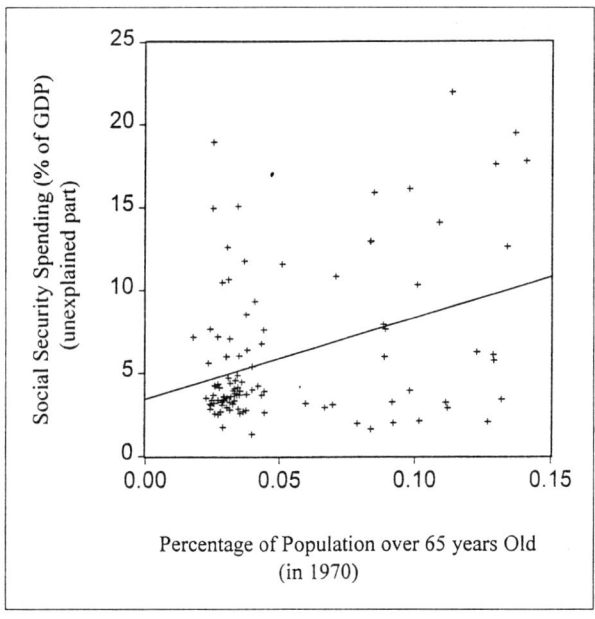

program in the world.

The democracy variable also turned out to be positive and significant. Thus government in a democratic society is more likely to expand the size of the welfare state, possibly to respond to popular demand for social outlays and especially to the political pressure from powerful interest groups such as retirees.

In the second and third regressions, we add additional variables such as the share of working age population and the share of labor force in agriculture. We find the share of working age population is significant with negative signs in both equations, while the share of labor force in agriculture does not add additional explanatory power for social security expenditures.

THE EFFECT OF SOCIAL SECURITY ON ECONOMIC GROWTH

Owing to the sheer scale of social security programs in many countries, there have been considerable academic and policy interests in the relationship between social security and economic performance. In particular, concerns have been voiced that the expansion in welfare state in Europe has adversely affected Europe's competitiveness and growth. Sachs and Warner (1996) argue that the poor scores for the European Union states in World Economic Forum's competitiveness rankings can be attributed to the European social welfare system. Atkinson (1996) provides

Table 5. Cross-Country Growth Regressions [a]

	(1)	(2)	(3)
Log(GDP), 1970	-0.0166 (-4.3423)	-0.0178 (-4.4744)	-0.0161(-4.6818)
SSW [b]	-0.0010 (-2.8788)	-0.0014 (-2.2978)	-0.0011 (-2.1921)
Fertility rate	-0.0033 (-1.6975)	-0.0040 (-2.0768)	-0.0051 (-2.0587)
Life expectancy	0.0019 (5.7364)	0.0017 (4.5195)	0.0016 (3.3064)
Government consumption		-0.0006 (-1.8739)	-0.0005 (-1.4219)
Schooling			0.0016 (1.4923)
Number of observations	95	92	64
Adjusted R**2	0.35	0.37	0.38

[a] Dependent variable is the average rate of growth in per capita real GDP in 1970-1995.
[b] SSW is the ratio of central government expenditures on social security and welfare to GDP averaged over over 1970-1995.

T statistics are in the parentheses.

an excellent review on the issues involved in policy debates as well as the available evidence from academic research.

As noted by Atkinson (1996), the evidence to date from aggregate empirics for the effect of social security on growth is quite mixed. While Weede (1986), Nordstrom (1992), Persson and Tabellini (1994) find some evidence for the negative impact of social security on growth, other studies such as Landau (1985), Korpi (1985), and Hansson and Henrekson (1994) find the effect of social security on growth either insignificant or in the positive direction.

Adding to the difficulty in weighing the collective evidence is that existing work suffers from the small sample problem. Without a single exception, for example, all the studies cited by Atkinson were confined to OECD countries.

In this paper we re-examine the relationship between social security and long-run growth in a much larger sample. The evident surge of interests in adopting or extending social security in developing and newly industrialised countries points to the need to examine the social security-growth connection applicable to a broader set of countries.

We have obtained a measure of social security expenditures, SSW, from IMF Government Finance Statistics for 117 countries, including low-income and newly industrialised economies as well as OECD countries. As shown above in Table 3, the variable SSW has a standard deviation of more than 5 percent of GDP, indicating substantial cross-country variation.

Apart from possible growth-reducing effects of social security and labor regulations, social security programs are financed by payroll taxes or general government revenues collected from various distortionary taxes. One channel for social security to affect growth is through the disincentive effect of taxation. To the extent income taxes reduce marginal returns to human capital and physical capital, they reduce long-run rate of growth. Moreover, social security benefits could affect individual's intertemporal consumption and saving behaviour though induced early retirement. Feldstein (1976) finds that the US pay-as-you-go social security program substantially depressed private savings.

To investigate the relationship between social security and growth, we include the SSW variable in a Barro-style cross-country growth model (Barro 1991). The dependent variable is the average rate of growth in per capita GDP, taken from Summers and Heston (1996). In addition to the presence of a measure of initial income to capture the convergence factor, the model also includes human capital indicators such as fertility rates, life expectancy, and adult schooling. The schooling

Table 6A. Sensitivity Analysis [a]

Independent variable [b]	(1)	(2)
log(GDP), 1980	-0.0149	-0.0138
	(-2.3259)	(-1.9054)
lagged SSW [c]	-0.0018	-0.0258
	(-2.6933)	(-2.4962)
Fertility rate (1980)	-0.0125	-0.0121
	(-4.3576)	(-4.0059)
life expectancy (1980)	0.0009	0.0008
	(1.7285)	(1.3149)
Government consumption		-0.0258
		(-0.5229)
Number of observations	69	68
Adjusted R**2	0.47	0.43

[a] Dependent variable is the average real per capita GDP rate of growth over 1980-95 period.
[b] t statistics are in parentheses.
[c] Lagged SSW is the average ratio of social security and welfare expenditures to GDP over 1970-79 period.

Table 6B. Estimation of the System of Equations: SUR Results

Dependent variable	Rate of growth in per capita real GDP [a]	Social security spending (% of GDP) [b]
Log (GDP) [c]	-0.013 (-2.141)	1.700 (3.191)
SSW [b]	-0.0019 (-2.438)	
Life expectancy [d]	0.0008 (1.295)	
Fertility rate [d]	-0.0122 (-4.522)	
Government consumption [e]	-0.0252 (-0.604)	
Aging [f]		119.579 (1.920)
Democracy		0.7566 (2.550)
R**2 (adjusted)	0.42	0.45
Number of observations	67	73

[a] Averaged over 1980-95.
[b] Averaged over 1970-79.
[c] Taking the 1980 value for the growth equation and the 1970 value for the SSW equation.
[d] Taking the 1980 value.
[e] Averaged over 1970-79.
[f] Taking the 1970 value.

t-values are in parentheses.

variable is the average years of schooling in the total population over age 25, taken from Barro and Lee (1993).

The cross-country regression results are reported in Table 5.

In the first equation, we regress per capita GDP growth on the log of per capita GDP (PPP dollars) in 1970, SSW, fertility rate and life expectancy at age zero in 1970. Note that the SSW variable has a negative coefficient with a t-value of 2.88, providing direct evidence that social security is negatively related to per capita GDP growth for a sample of 95 countries in 1970-1995. The inclusion of initial income in the regression is important since richer countries are expected to grow more slowly regardless of the level of social security spending. Failure to control for the catch-up effect would lead to drawing false causal connection between the lower rate of growth and higher level of social security spending as observed in OECD countries. Figure 3 shows the partial correlation between SSW and growth, after controlling for initial income and human capital indicators such as fertility rate and life expectancy at age zero.

Figure 3. Growth and Social Security Spending

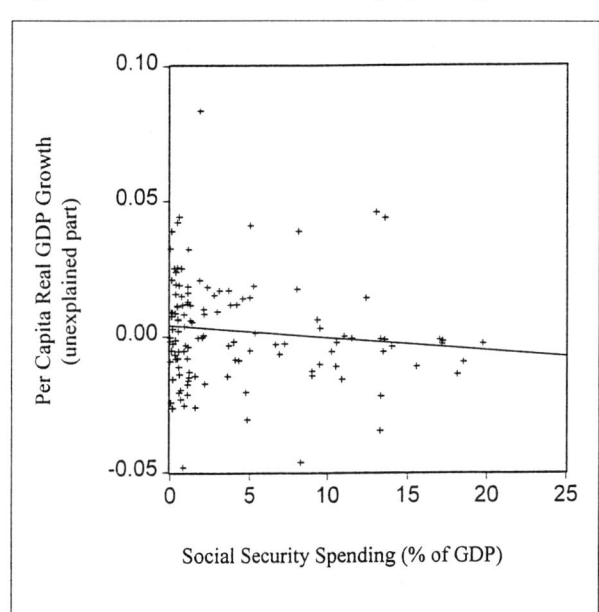

Transfers such as social security payments may be distinctively different from ordinary government consumption. Smith (1975) concluded that "it is less economically harmful for the state to raise taxes and make transfer payments than to consume resources directly," based on the finding that growth was negatively related to public spending excluding transfers but that the effect was smaller and less significant when public spending included transfers. Barro (1991) provided new evidence that government consumption is negatively associated with growth but he did not pursue the separate role of social security. It is possible that our SSW variable simply captures the effect of government consumption in the regressions presented here.

Table 7. Demographic Trends in East Asia: 1990-2020 [a]

Country	1990	2000	2010	2020
China	8.9	10.2	12.0	16.0
Hong Kong	13.0	15.6	18.8	27.3
Indonesia	6.4	7.3	8.3	10.9
Japan	17.3	22.7	29.0	31.4
Korea	7.7	10.7	13.9	19.5
Malaysia	5.7	6.5	8.0	11.0
Philippines	5.3	5.9	7.3	10.1
Singapore	8.5	10.9	15.6	23.9
Taiwan	9.7	12.0	14.1	20.6
Thailand	6.0	7.4	9.1	12.8

[a] Percentage of population over sixty years old.

Source: World Bank (1994).

Table 8. Social Security and Per Capita Real GDP Growth
— A Possible Scenario for East Asia

	Change in the Elderly/ Population [a]	Implied Increase in Social Security [b]	Impact on Growth [c]
Hong Kong	+14.3	+18.0	-1.8
Korea	+11.8	+14.9	-1.5
Singapore	+15.4	+19.4	-1.9
Taiwan	+10.9	+13.8	-1.4
Weighted average	+11.9 [d]		-1.5 [e]

[a] Change in the percentage of population over 60 years old between 1990 and 2020 (in percent).
[b] Government spending on social security and welfare (% of GDP), based on the point estimate in Eq.1, Table 4.
[c] Percentage points; based on the point estimate in Eq.1, Table 5.
[d] Using the 1995 population share as weights.
[e] Using the relative GDP size (measured in PPP) in 1995 as weights.

34

We thus include a separate measure of government consumption excluding education and defence in the growth regression (Eq.2). While government consumption has a significant and negative coefficient, consistent with the earlier findings by Smith (1975) and Barro (1991), the SSW variable has additional explanatory power for growth over and above that of government consumption.

In Regression 3, we also add a measure of human capital - the schooling variable. We find that the result that SSW is negatively related with growth is essentially unaffected.

To further evaluate the robustness of the negative relation between SSW and growth, we regress the average per capita GDP growth rate in 1980-95 on the average ratio of social security expenditures to GDP in the earlier period 1970-79. As can be seen in Table 6A, the lagged SSW variable again is highly significant and retains the negative sign. In the regression that includes government consumption as an independent variable, SSW is significant while government consumption is not. Since SSW is predetermined, the relation is unlikely affected by possible reverse causality or simultaneity bias.

We also treat the regression model for the determination of social security in section III and the growth model here as a system of equations and estimate them jointly using seemingly unrelated regression (SUR) technique. The results are presented in Table 6 B. Note that the estimated coefficients for the SSW variable and the "aging" variable are closely comparable to those obtained in Eq.1, Table 5 and Eq. 1, Table 4, respectively.

IMPLICATIONS FOR EAST ASIA

The above analysis illustrates how factors such as per capita income level, population aging, and the type of political systems could shape the pattern of social security spending. It also provides large sample cross-country evidence that social security may have adverse effects on economic growth.

In designing or reforming social security system, it is common to rely on projections about demographic trends and future growth rate of the aggregate economy while ignoring the feedback impact of social security system on growth itself. The evidence in this paper points to the need in social security reforms to take into consideration the effects of social security on long-run growth. East Asia has much to gain if it can achieve the optimal trade-off between social security and growth.

Table 7 shows demographic trends in East Asia. The share of the elderly (over sixty years old) in total population is expected to double between 1990 and 2020 in nearly all countries in the region. The rapid aging process takes place as East Asia has been successful in achieving rapid decline in fertility rates and raising life expectancy. By 2020, for instance, East Asian NIEs will be roughly as aged as today's Western Europe. Will East Asia follow Western Europe's example to support the elderly by drastically expanding the welfare state? Will East Asia adopt predominantly a pay-as-you-go public pension system or a fully-funded system? Can East Asia judiciously mix the respective role of government and the private sector in meeting the demand of social security?

If East Asia simply replicates the international pattern of social security spending over the past quarter of the century, the share of social security expenditures in GDP will rise substantially in the coming decades for the region. The projected share of the aged over 60 years old in total population implies that the ratio of social security expenditures to GDP will rise by about twelve percentage points by 2020 in the East Asian NIEs. Such an increase in social security spending could then reduce the rate of growth in per capita real GDP by 1.5 percentage points (weighted average) for the region. Such a scenario is illustrated in Table 8.

At the present time, there are two basic types of social security system in East Asia. One is the pay-as-you-go public pension system in Japan, Korea, and Taiwan. The other is the fully funded system – the Central Provident Fund in Singapore, Malaysia, and Thailand. The Special Administrative Region (SAR) government in Hong Kong is set to establish a central provident fund for its population.

The rest of the region is further behind in the development of social security, but there appears to be an increasing awareness of the cost and inefficiency of the prevalent social security system in industrialised countries. China, for example, has been very cautious about introducing a national social security plan to replace its current enterprise-based labor insurance and welfare programs, though the government has taken a keen interest in the central provident fund in Singapore (Hu, 1994, 1997).

Regardless of the institutional modalities adopted, so far East Asian countries have managed to keep the level of public spending on social security low by international standards. The key question is whether, as many East Asia joins the rank of high-income economies and goes through one of the rapidest population aging processes history has ever known, social security spending in the region will simply mimic the explosive growth Western Europe had experienced in the post WWII period . With luck and conscious efforts, East Asia could well move to a social security system that meets the objective of social protection but without the undesirable effects on savings and growth.

REFERENCES

Atkinson, A. B., (1996), "The Welfare State and Economic Performance," National Tax Journal, 171-198.
Barro, Robert, (1991), "Economic Growth in a Cross Section of Countries," Quarterly Journal of Economics, 106, 2 (May), 407-433.
——, and Jong-Wha Lee, (1993), International Comparisons of Educational Attainment," Journal of Monetary Economics, 32 9December), 363-394.
Burgess, Robin, and Nicholas Stern, (1991), "Social Security in Developing Countries: What, Why, Who, and How?" in Ahmad, Ehtisham, Jean Dreze, John Hills, and Amartya Sen, eds., Social Security in Developing Countries, Clarendon Press (Oxford).
Feldstein, Martin, (1976), "Social Security and Savings: The Extended Life Cycle Theory," American Economic Review 66, 76-86.
Gastil, Raymond, et al, (1982-83 and other years), Freedom in the World, Westport CT, Greenwood Press.
Hansson, Par and Magnus Henrekson, (1994)," New framework for Testing the Effect of Government Spending on growth and Productivity," Public Choice 81, 381-401.
Hu, F. Zuliu, (1994), " Social Protection, Labor Market Rigidity, and Enterprise Restructuring in China", IMF Paper on Policy Analysis and Assessment No. 22 (October), Washington DC.
—— , (1997), " Social Protection and Enterprise Reform: the Case of China," in Rein, Martin, Barry Friedman, and Andreas Worgotter, eds., Enterprise and Social Benefits after Communism, Cambridge University Press.
International Monetary Fund, (1996), Government Finance Statistics, Washington DC.
Korpi, Walter, (1985), "Economic Growth and the Welfare System: Leaky Bucket or Irrigation System?" European Sociological Review 1, 97-118.
Landau, Daniel L, (1985), " Government Expenditure and Economic Growth in the Developed Countries:1952-1976," Public Choice 47, 459-77.
Nordstrom, Hakan, (1992), "Studies in trade Policy and Economic Growth," Monograph No. 20, Stockholm, Institute for International Economic Studies.
Persson, Torsten, and Guido Tabellini, (1994), " Is Inequality Harmful for Growth? " American

Economic Review 84, 600-21.

Sachs, Jeffrey, and Andrew Warner, (1996), "The Social Welfare State and Competitiveness, " in Global Competitiveness Report 1996, World Economic Forum, Geneva.

Summers, Robert, and Alan Heston, (1996), "The Penn World table (Mark 5.5), Website Version."

Weede, Erich, (1986), "Sectoral Reallocation, Distributional Coalitions and the Welfare State as Determinants of Economic Growth Rates in Industrialised Democracies," European Journal of Political Research 14, 501-19.

World Bank, (1994), Averting Old Age Crisis, Washington DC.

——, (1997), World Development Indicators, Washington DC.

PART II. PUBLIC INVESTMENT AND ECONOMIC GROWTH

CHAPTER4 CORRUPTION, PUBLIC IN-VESTMENT, AND GROWTH

VITO TANZI[*] AND HAMID DAVOODI[**]

INTRODUCTION

Up to the time when a huge corruption scandal, popularly labeled "tangentopoli" (bribe city), brought down the political establishment that had ruled Italy for several decades, that country had reported one of the largest shares of capital spending in GDP among the OECD countries. After the scandal broke out and several prominent individuals were sent to jail, or even committed suicide, capital spending fell sharply. The fall seems to have been caused by a reduction in the number of capital projects being undertaken and, perhaps more importantly, by a sharp fall in the costs of the projects still undertaken. Information released by *Transparency International (TI)* [1] reports that, within the space of two or three years, in the city of Milan, the city where the scandal broke out in the first place, the cost of city rail links fell by 52 percent, the cost of one kilometer of subway fell by 57 percent, and the budget for the new airport terminal was reduced by 59 percent to reflect the lower construction costs. Although one must be aware of the logical fallacy of *post hoc, ergo propter hoc*, the connection between the two events is too strong to be attributed to a

---

[*] Director, Fiscal Affairs Department, International Monetary Fund

[**] Economist, Fiscal Affairs Department, International Montary Fund

[1] *TI* is a nongovernmental organization with headquarters in Berlin which traces corruption trends around the world and which has as its goal the elimination of corruption.

coincidence. In fact this paper takes the view that it could not have been a coincidence

The basic hypothesis of this paper is that corruption, and especially political or "grand" corruption,[2] is often tied to capital projects. Corruption is likely to increase the number of projects undertaken in a country, and to change the design of these projects by enlarging their sizes and their complexity. The net result is: (a) an increase in the share of public investment in GDP; (b) a fall in the average productivity of that investment; and, because of budgetary constraints and other considerations, (c) a possible reduction in some other categories of public spending, such as "operation and maintenance," education, and health. As a consequence of these and other effects of corruption on the economy, the rate of growth of a country where corruption is significant is negatively affected.

In the next section we discuss reasons why we assume that public investment is particularly sensitive to the existence of (political) corruption. We then present empirical evidence on the basic hypotheses. Finally, we draw conclusions.

CORRUPTION AND GOVERNMENT SPENDING

At least from the time, after World War II, when influential economists such as Harrod, Domar, Rostow, and others argued that countries need capital to grow and, more importantly, that there is an almost mechanical relation (the capital-output ratio) between increased capital spending and increased growth, there has been a strong intellectual bias in the economic profession in favor of capital spending. For example, when economists evaluate the allocation of public money between current and capital spending in government budgets, they tend to be critical of countries that allow the share of current spending to grow. On the other hand, they generally praise countries where the share of capital spending in total government expenditure goes up.

The above bias is enshrined in the "golden rule" that many economists advocate for countries. That rule essentially states that it is all right to borrow as long as the borrowing is for investment projects.[3] Thus, it is all right to borrow to finance the

---

[2] The literature distinguishes between petty or bureaucratic corruption and "grand" or political corruption.

building of new roads but not to finance the repairs of existing roads; or to borrow for the building of a new hospital, but not for the hiring of doctors or nurses or for buying medicines. This rule continues to be invoked as a good guide to policy even in the face of much evidence that some current spending--such as "operation and maintenance" that keeps the existing infrastructure in good condition or spending that contributes to the accumulation of human capital--can promote growth more than capital spending.

Politicians have internalized this bias and to some extent have exploited it. For example, ribbon-cutting ceremonies, when new investment projects related to roads, dams, irrigation canals, power plants, ports, airports, schools, and hospitals are completed and inaugurated, are very popular with politicians. They like to be pictured in newspaper articles in the act of cutting the ribbons and, thus, presumably, contributing to the future growth of the country. In a particular Latin American country, capital projects completed under the current administration have been painted orange to send a clear signal to the population that the present government is promoting growth. This pro-investment bias increases the investment budget. We will argue that another factor that also increases the size of the investment budget is corruption.

There is nothing routine about the investment budget and its composition. While much current government spending reflects, to a large extent, explicit or implicit entitlements or previous commitments,[4] thus allowing limited discretion, in the short run, to politicians and, especially, to specific politicians, capital spending is highly discretionary.[5] For the latter, high political figures--members of parliament, general secretaries, ministers, or even heads of state--must make some of the basic decisions. These decisions relate to: (a) the size of the total public investment budget; (b) the general composition of that budget, i.e., the broad allocation among different categories of capital spending; (c) the choice of the specific projects and their locations; and (d) even the size and the design of each project. In these decisions, and especially those in (c) and (d), some high-level individuals will have considerable control or influence. This will happen especially when some of the essential controlling or

---

[3] The rule simply states that only current expenditure needs to be balanced by ordinary revenue: a country can have a fiscal deficit equal to the net capital spending of the government.

[4] Pensions, interest payments on the debt, salaries, subsidies, and so on.

[5] Specific politicians generally do not have the power to change the pensions, salaries, or subsidies of specific individuals.

auditing institutions are not well developed and, therefore, institutional controls are weak.

Public investment projects tend to be large and in some cases they are very large. Their execution is often contracted out to domestic or foreign private enterprises. There is thus a need to choose the enterprise that will be responsible for undertaking the project. For a private enterprise, getting a contract to execute a project, and especially a large one, can be very profitable. Therefore, the managers of these enterprises may be willing to pay a "commission" to the government officials that help them win the contract.[6] In some countries, commissions paid by their enterprises to foreign politicians are both legal and tax deductible. Such "commissions" are often calculated as percentages of the total cost of the projects.

A commission of even a few percentage points on a project that costs millions or even hundreds of millions of dollars can be a large sum, one large enough to exceed the temptation price for many individuals.[7] When commissions are calculated as a percentage of projects" costs, the public officials who receive the payments for helping the enterprises win the bid will have a vested interest in increasing the scope or the size of the projects so that they can get larger commissions.[8]

The process of approval of an investment project involves several phases. For example, a civil construction project (roads, buildings, ports) requires decisions related to: (a) specification and design issues; (b) issue of tender (limited or open?); (c) tender scrutiny; (d) tender negotiations; and (e) tender approval and contracting process. The completion of the project will require verification that the work has been done according to the stipulated contract. It will also require some arbitration about points of disagreement. The writing of contracts for complex projects is very difficult and inevitably there will be many areas of uncertainty and eventual disagreement.

In some of these phases, it will be possible for a strategically-placed high-level official to influence the process in ways that lead to the selection of a particular enterprise.

---

[6] Commission is often a euphemism for what is essentially a bribe.

[7] Actually, in many cases the act of bribery may not start with the enterprises but with the officials who control the decisions. Foreign enterprises report that in some countries it is impossible to get a government contract without paying a bribe.

[8] For a useful discussion of corruption in public investment, see Patrick Meagher (1997).

44

For example, the specifications of the design can be tailor-made for a given enterprise. The issuance of tenders can be accompanied by the provision of insider information to favored enterprises, and so on.

The enterprise that pays the commission will not suffer from the payment of the bribe if it is able to recover that cost in several ways: (a) through up-front cost recovery if it can win the bidding competition with an offer that includes the cost of the commission; (b) it can have an understanding with the influential official that the initial low bid can be adjusted upward along the way, presumably, to reflect modifications to the basic design;[9] or (c) reduce its project costs by skimping on the quality of the work done and on the materials used, thus delivering, at completion, an inferior product.[10] In cases when the contract is stipulated in a cost-plus fashion, the enterprise can recover the cost of the commission by overpricing.

In all these alternatives which require the collaboration of the corrupt official, the country will end up with either a higher cost for the specified project than would have been the case in the absence of corruption; with a bigger or more complex project than would have been necessary; or with a project of inferior quality that will not perform up to the anticipated standards and will require costly upkeeping and repairs. The experience with public sector projects, especially in developing countries, is full of stories about roads that needed to be repaired a short time after completion, power plants that worked at much lower capacity than anticipated, and so on.

The above discussion has highlighted cases where corrupt high-level officials or political personalities steer the approval of investment projects towards particular domestic or foreign enterprises in exchange for bribes. This is an important part of the way in which corruption, defined in the broader sense of rent seeking, affects public investment. However, it is not the full story. Important cases of corruption exist also when political personalities steer public investments towards their home

---

[9] This second option may be less attractive to the enterprise if it fears that the official may require additional payments when the cost-increasing modifications are made or if it fears that the official may no longer have the power to influence the process. In countries where the same individuals remain in power for a long time, the strategy of the low initial bid followed by adjustments over the period when the project is executed is a common strategy.

[10] This has been a frequent occurrence in road building where the thickness of the base of the road may be much reduced. It has also been an occurrence in the building of bridges and buildings which, at times, have collapsed causing loss of lives and economic costs.

districts or their own land. In a recent case reported in the *Financial Times* of July 29, 1997, the President of a country was accused of having built an airport with public funds in his small home town even though there seemed to be little economic justification for it. This is far from an isolated case. At other times, projects are steered toward particular areas in order to increase the value of assets (such as lands owned by political personalities) in those areas.

In all of these cases, the productivity of the capital spending is reduced, thus reducing the growth rate of the country. Therefore, corruption can significantly distort the relationship between the capital input and the output generated by that capital, thus increasing the capital output ratio.

When the approval of investment projects comes to be much influenced by corrupt, high-level officials, the rate of return of projects as calculated by cost-benefit analysis ceases to be the criterion for project selection.[11] Capital spending becomes much less productive and much less of a contributor to growth than generally believed. Unfortunately, situations of this type are far from rare. In these situations, those who carry out the projects (the executing enterprises) come to care mostly about the profits that they make. And the political figures that authorize the projects and choose the enterprises care mostly about the bribes, or the other advantages that they get. Thus, corruption distorts the whole decision-making process connected with the investment budget. In the extreme case of a totally corrupt country, projects are chosen exclusively for their bribe-generating capacity and not for their productivity. The productivity of the projects becomes almost irrelevant.[12]

When corruption plays a large role in the selection of projects and contractors, the result of this process is a capital budget that is highly distorted. "White elephants" and "cathedrals in the desert" are produced. Some projects are completed but never used. Some are much larger and complex than necessary. Some are of such low quality that they will need continuous repairs and their output capacity will be much below initial expectations. In these circumstances, it is not surprising that capital spending does not generate the results in terms of growth that economists expect.

---

[11] In Italy, before tangentopoli, those hired to evaluate projects often found that they were totally ignored.

[12] This may be part of the reason why we observe extremely high capital-output ratios in some countries.

Widespread corruption in the investment budget will not only reduce the rate of return to *new* public investment, but will also affect the rate of return that a country gets from its existing infrastructure. The reasons are several.

First, to the extent that corruption is not a new phenomenon but one that has been around for some time, the existing infrastructure has also been contaminated because *past* investments were also misdirected or distorted by corruption.

Second, higher spending on capital projects will reduce the resources available for other spending. Of the other spending one that is not protected by the existence of entitlements or implicit commitments is "operation and maintenance," that is the kind of current public spending that is required to keep the existing physical infrastructure of a country in good working conditions. Therefore, a frequently observed phenomenon is the poor conditions of the existing infrastructure (roads with potholes, buildings badly in need of repairs, etc.). One often observes situations where new projects are undertaken while the existing structure is left to deteriorate.

Third, and more speculatively, in cases of extreme corruption, operation and maintenance on the physical infrastructure of a country may be intentionally reduced so that some infrastructures, such as roads, will deteriorate quickly to the point where they will need to be rebuilt, thus allowing some high-level officials the opportunity to extract another commission from the enterprise that will undertake the project. Some World Bank Reports have hinted that this may have happened in some countries.

A country can squeeze more output out of the existing infrastructure by keeping it in good working condition so that it can be used at close to 100 percent capacity.[13] It is easy to think of situations where the deterioration of this infrastructure retards growth more than the new capital projects add to growth. Additionally when generalized corruption in a country reduces resources because of the negative impact on tax revenue that is caused by corrupt tax administrators, operation and maintenance will be reduced far more than public investment because of the intellectual bias listed above that supports borrowing for capital projects but not for current expenditure.

---

[13] World Bank studies indicate that in many countries public infrastructure including roads, power plants, irrigation canals, often can be used only at a fraction of their full capacity.

EMPIRICAL ANALYSIS

A. DATA DESCRIPTION

In our empirical analysis we use indices of corruption data from two sources: *Business International* (*BI*) and *Political Risk Services, Inc.* The *BI* index has been used by Mauro (1995), among others, and is available for 68 countries over the 1980-83 period (one observation per country). The second source publishes a closely related index in the *International Country Risk Guide* (*ICRG*). Unlike the *BI* index, the *ICRG* index is annual; it covers the 1982-95 period and, depending on the year, is available for 42 to 128 countries. This index has been used by Knack and Keefer (1995) and many others.

Both indices are assessments of the degree of corruption in a country by informed observers, the *BI*'s network of correspondents, in the case of the *BI* index, and foreign investors, in the case of the *ICRG* index. The *BI* index has been discontinued, while the *ICRG* index is updated annually and is sold as part of a package to potential investors worldwide. Corruption in the *BI* indicates "The degree to which business transactions involve corruption or questionable payments". The index ranges from 0 (most corrupt) to 10 (least corrupt). In the *ICRG* index higher corruption indicates that "high government officials are likely to demand special payments" and "illegal payments are generally expected throughout lower levels of government" in the forms of "bribes connected with import and export licenses, exchange controls, tax assessment, police protection, or loans". The *ICRG* index ranges from 0 (most corrupt) to 6 (least corrupt).

We have re-scaled the *ICRG* index by multiplying it by 10/6 so that both indexes range from 0 to 10 and have spliced them to form a single corruption index from 1980 to 1995.[14] For ease of interpretation of the regression results, we have multiplied the resulting index by minus one so that higher values of the index imply higher corruption.

The discussion in the previous section underscored the interaction between corruption,

---

[14] The two indices are highly correlated with a correlation coefficient of 0.81. Other indices are also available including one issued by *Transparency International*. These indices are also highly correlated.

public investment, operations and maintenance (O&M) expenditures, and other aspects of the government's budgetary position. For public investment, capital expenditure data from the International Monetary Fund's *Government Finance Statistics* (*GFS*) are used. Unfortunately, cross-country data on O&M expenditures are not available. We have, thus, chosen two proxies called "expenditure on other goods and services" which includes O&M expenditures, and "wages and salaries as a fraction of current expenditures." The rationale behind these proxies will be explained below.

To investigate the impact of corruption on the *quality* of public investment, we use the following indicators of quality of infrastructure:

- Paved roads in good condition as a percentage of total paved roads
- Electric power system losses as a percentage of total power output
- Telecommunication faults per 100 mainlines per year
- Water losses as a percentage of total water provision
- Railway diesels in use as a percentage of total diesel inventory

The above data are often referred to as performance indicators of infrastructure and seem adequate for our purpose; they are measured from the perspective of both infrastructure providers and the users; they cover a large number of countries and most importantly, they have many characteristics that make them the responsibility of governments. These data are taken from International Telecommunications Union and the World Bank's World Development Indicators data base. Paved roads in good condition are roads substantially free of major problems and requiring only routine maintenance. Electric power system losses consist of technical losses such as resistance losses in transmission and distribution and non-technical losses such as illegal connection to the electricity and other sources of theft. System losses are then expressed as a fraction of total output. Telecommunication faults per 100 mainlines per year refer to the number of reported faults per 100 main lines for each year. Water losses include physical losses (pipe breaks and overflows) and commercial losses (meter under-registration, illegal use including fraudulent or unregistered connections, and legal, but not usually metered, uses such as firefighting). Railway diesels in use as a percentage of total diesel inventory measures technical and managerial performance.

Finally, government revenue data, taken from the *GFS*, are expressed as fractions of GDP. Data on GDP and real per capita GDP (the latter is a control variable in regression) come from the World Bankís *World Development Indicators* data base.

B. REGRESSION RESULTS

The previous discussions suggest testable hypotheses about the relationship between corruption on one hand and public investment, government revenue, O&M expenditures and quality of infrastructure on the other. We use regression analysis to test these hypotheses using cross-country data. It is of course difficult to draw causality statements from regression equations, and one must guard against spurious regression results. We do so by controlling for other variables, such as real per capita GDP, government revenue-GDP ratio, and public investment-GDP ratio.

(1) Corruption and public investment

Hypothesis 1: Other things being equal, high corruption is associated with high public investment.

To test this hypothesis, we regress the public investment-GDP ratio on a constant and the corruption index. We subsequently add real per capita GDP and government revenue-GDP ratio to see if the corruption-investment relationship is robust to the inclusion of these two variables. We add real per capita GDP since it is typically a proxy for the stage of economic development and different levels of development may require different needs for public investment. Government revenue-GDP ratio is added because the higher are these revenues the easier it is to finance public investment. The results are three regressions shown in Table 1. In all the regressions, we cannot reject hypothesis 1 at the 1 percent significance level.[15] Government revenue-GDP variable has a statistically significant positive coefficient indicating that such revenues are important sources of financing public investment. The results shown in Table 1 are for the world sample, but they also hold up for the sub-samples of developing countries and members of the Organization for Economic Cooperation and Development (OECD).

(2) Corruption and government revenues

---

[15] Note that corruption reduces aggregate investment (Mauro, 1995) which is the sum of public and private capital investment. Thus, corruption must reduce private capital investment by more than it increases public capital investment.

Table 1. The Effects of Corruption on Public Investment, 1980-95

(As a ratio of GDP; annual data)

Independent Variables	(1)	(2)	(3)
Constant	6.75	6.47	4.71
	(23.4)	(19.5)	(13.9)
Corruption index	0.38	0.27	0.48
	(8.97)	(4.15)	(7.48)
Real per capita GDP *		-0.71	-1.21
		(-2.94)	(-5.18)
Government revenue-GDP ratio			0.13
			(12.6)
Adjusted R^2	0.069	0.082	0.207
Number of observations	1,081	1,011	1,000

Sources: IMF, *Government Finance Statistics*; *World Tables*; *Business International*; and *Political Risk Services*. The corruption index is taken from Mauro (1995) and *International Country Risk Guide* compiled by Political Risk Services. A high value of the index means a country has high corruption; t-statistics are in parentheses. Estimation technique is OLS.
* Indicates that the coefficient is multiplied by 10,000.

Regressions in Table 1 show the direct impact of corruption on public investment and do not rule out the possibility of an indirect impact, say, through government revenues. Corruption can reduce government revenues if it contributes to tax evasion, improper tax exemptions or weak tax administration. This leads to the second hypothesis:

Hypothesis 2: Other things being equal, high corruption is associated with low government revenue.

To test this assertion we regress government revenue-GDP ratio on a constant and corruption. We then add real per capita GDP to control for stage-of-economic development effects. The results given in Table 2 for the world sample show that we cannot reject hypothesis 2 at the 1 percent significance level. Similar results also hold up for sub-samples of developing and OECD countries.

(3) Corruption and O&M expenditures

Table 2. The Effects of Corruption on Government Revenue, 1980-95

(As a ratio of GDP; annual data)

Independent Variables	(1)	(2)
Constant	9.99	12.9
	(12.1)	(13.7)
Corruption index	-2.51	-1.71
	(-20.4)	(-9.28)
Real per capita GDP *		3.73
		(5.34)
Adjusted R²	0.272	0.28
Number of observations	1,114	1,042

Sources: IMF, *Government Finance Statistics*; *World Tables*; *Business International*; and *Political Risk Services*. The corruption index is taken from Mauro (1995) and *International Country Risk Guide* compiled by Political Risk Services. A high value of the index means a country has high corruption; t-statistics are in parentheses. Estimation technique is OLS.

* Indicates that the coefficient is multiplied by 10,000.

An observation made previously, and one closely related to Hypotheses 1 and 2, is the underfunding of O&M expenditure. Since corruption and bribery are more effectively related to new investments, corruption may result in lower O&M expenditure. These observations lead to the third hypothesis:

Hypothesis 3: Other things being equal, high corruption is associated with low O&M expenditures.

As stated earlier, direct cross-country data on O&M expenditures are not available.[16] We therefore use two proxies: (1) "expenditures on other goods and services", a component of current expenditure, expressed as a fraction of wages and salaries; and (2) wages and salaries expressed as a fraction of current expenditure. These data are taken from the IMF's GFS data base. The rational behind the first proxy is obvious since, according to the GFS manual on Government Finance Statistics, expenditures on other goods and services include O&M expenditures. We have expressed this

---

[16] Ideally, we want shortfalls in O&M expenditures. This requires knowledge of the so-called "r" coefficients and actual O&M expenditures. The r coefficient is the ratio of net recurrent expenditure requirements to the total investment cost of a project; see Heller (1991).

Table 3. The Effects of Corruption on O&M Expenditure

a. Expenditures on Other Goods and Services, 1980-95
(As a ratio of wages and salaries, 1980-95)

Independent variable	World (1)	World (2)	OECD (1)	OECD (2)	Developing (1)	Developing (2)
Constant	72.9	97.2	-20.2	43.4	84.2	82.3
	(8.15)	(9.29)	(-0.558)	(1.19)	(7.08)	(6.65)
Corruption index	-3.54	4.44	-14	5.96	-1.24	1.43
	(-2.69)	(2.20)	(-3.53)	(1.23)	(-0.57)	(0.60)
Real per capita GDP *		0.42		0.81		0.63
		(5.55)		(6.99)		(3.93)
Adjusted R^2	0.006	0.038	0.037	0.182	-0.01	0.021
Number of observations	999	927	300	273	699	654

b. Wages and Salaries, 1980-95
(As a ratio of current expenditure; annual data)

Independent variable	World (1)	World (2)	OECD (1)	OECD (2)	Developing (1)	Developing (2)
Constant	47.3	42.2	34.2	30.8	39.7	39.7
	(41.7)	(33.2)	(12.2)	(11.3)	(26.1)	(25.2)
Corruption index	3.1	1.48	2.17	0.75	1.22	1.16
	(18.5)	(6.03)	(7.02)	(2.07)	(4.43)	(3.83)
Real per capita GDP **		-0.84		-0.65		-0.067
		(-9.13)		(-7.54)		(-0.327)
Adjusted R^2	0.255	0.319	0.139	0.31	0.026	0.023
Number of observations	1,000	925	300	273	700	652

Sources: IMF, *Government Finance Statistics*; *World Tables*; *Business International*; and *Political Risk Services*. The corruption index is taken from Mauro (1995) and *International Country Risk Guide* compiled by Political Risk Services. A high value of the index means a country has high corruption; t-statistics are in parentheses. Estimation technique is OLS.

* and ** Indicate that the coefficients are multiplied by 100 and 1,000, respectively.

expenditure relative to wages and salaries in order to highlight potential trade-offs between O&M expenditure and expenditure on wages and salaries. The ratio of wages and salaries to current expenditure is a reasonable proxy for O&M expenditures because governments often tend to award wage increases but cut O&M expenditures. Hence, increases in wages and salaries can be interpreted as cuts in O&M expenditures.

To test hypothesis 3, we regress each of the above proxies on a constant and a corruption index and, as usual for sensitivity analysis, we add real per capita GDP to each regression. The results are shown in Table 3. Unlike the previous regressions, we present the results for three samples (world, OECD and developing) as there are differences across these samples. With respect to the first proxy, results in Table 3 indicate that high corruption is indeed associated with low O&M expenditures. However, one can reject hypothesis 3 at the 1 percent significance level only for the developing country sample. Once we control for real per capita GDP, hypothesis 3 is rejected at the 1 percent significance level for all three samples. One interpretation of this finding is that the first proxy is a noisy indicator of O&M expenditure.

As regards the second proxy for O&M expenditures, we cannot reject hypothesis 3 for all three samples at the 1 percent significance level whether or not we control for real per capita GDP (Table 3, panel b). Countries with high corruption do tend to have high ratio of wages and salaries to current expenditure.[17] The evidence is much stronger statistically and economically for the developing country sample than the OECD sample.

(4) Corruption and quality of public investment

Infrastructure investments are often lumpy and require substantial up-front financial capital. It has been known for some time that corruption is most prevalent in the infrastructure sector (Wade, 1982; Rose-Ackerman, 1996). Regressions in Table 1 in this paper have provided evidence that high corruption is indeed associated with high public investment. See also Mauro (1997). However, this evidence links corruption to *quantity* of investment, and not the *quality*. We argued previously that countries take on new infrastructure investment without maintaining the existing infrastructure capital stock. Therefore, we expect the quality of the infrastructure to deteriorate and more so if corruption leads to O&M expenditure cutbacks. These observations lead to the fourth hypothesis:

Hypothesis 4: Other things being equal, high corruption is associated with poor quality of infrastructure.

To test this hypothesis we regress indicators of quality of infrastructure on a constant, the corruption index and real per capita GDP. The results are given in Table 4 for five indicators of quality of infrastructure. Hypothesis 4 cannot be rejected at the usual

---

[17] This does not mean that the level of salaries in corrupt countries is higher. In fact a recent study has found a negative relationship between salary levels in the public sector and corruption. See Van Rijckeghem and Weder (1997).

Table 4. Corruption and Quality of Infrastructure, 1980-95

(Annual data)

Dependent Variable	Constant	Corruption Index	Real Per Capita GDP ·	Adjusted R2	N
Paved roads in good condition	19.2 (4.97)	- 3.84 (-5.40)		0.052	513
Paved roads in good condition	15.5 (3.87)	-2.22 (-2.89)	5.4 (9.85)	0.268	373
Power outages	18.7 (27.7)	1.1 (8.69)		0.07	997
Power outages	18.8 (32.5)	0.95 (8.17)	-0.56 (-7.07)	0.162	922
Telecommunication faults	97.6 (6.93)	4.17 (1.63)		0.007	241
Telecommunication faults	94.5 (6.31)	-0.54 (-0.18)	-9.33 (-5.01)	0.127	201
Water losses #	43.8 (6.89)	2.25 (1.86)		0.089	26
Water losses #	43.6 (7.19)	1.52 (1.14)	-2.92 (-1.63)	0.186	25
Railway diesels in use ##	47.1 (7.45)	-3.66 (-3.80)		0.17	67
Railway diesels in use ##	59.4 (8.62)	-0.58 (-0.46)	1.37 (3.39)	0.285	67

Sources: IMF, *Government Finance Statistics*; *World Tables*; *Business International* ; and *Political Risk Services*. The corruption index is taken from Mauro (1995) and *International Country Risk Guide* compiled by Political Risk Services. A high value of the index means a country has high corruption; t-statistics are in parentheses. Estimation technique is OLS.

and ## denote averages of data over 1980-89 and 1990-95 periods, respectively.

· Indicates that the coefficient is multiplied by 10,000.

significance levels: Countries with high corruption do tend to have poor quality of infrastructure. In terms of statistical significance, the impact of corruption is strongest on the quality of roads (paved roads in good condition), power outages, and railway diesels in use. When we control for real per capita GDP, corruption changes its sign in only one regression (telecommunication faults) and looses its statistical significance at the usual levels in three regressions (telecommunication faults, water losses, and railway diesels in use). The fit of every regression improves, as judged by the adjusted

R-squared, when we add real per capita GDP. Moreover, real per capita GDP in every regression has the right sign: countries with higher real per capita GDP tend to have better quality of infrastructure. An important implication of the results in Table

55

4 is that the costs of corruption should also be measured in terms of the deterioration in the quality of the existing infrastructure. These costs can be very high in terms of their impact on growth.

Does corruption reduce the quality of infrastructure through public investment?

To answer the above question, we conduct a more rigorous test of hypothesis 4 for the quality of roads.[18] We regress paved roads in good conditions on a constant, real per capita GDP, the corruption index (i.e., the same regression as in Table 4) and two additional variables: public investment-GDP ratio and its interaction with the corruption index. Results are shown in Table 5. Columns (1) and (2) show that even when we control for public investment, we still cannot reject hypothesis 4 at the 1 percent significance level. The regression in column (3) shows that corruption is still significant in the presence of the interaction variable. If corruption reduces the quality of roads through public investment, we should find that corruption looses its significance when the interaction variable is added to the regression, given the presence of public investment-GDP ratio and real capita GDP. Comparison of columns (4) and (2)-- with and without the interaction term respectively-- shows this to be the case. In addition, the statistically significant interaction term in column (4) shows that the impact of corruption on the quality of roads depends on public investment. The negative sign on the interaction term suggests that the higher is the public investment, the higher is the negative impact of corruption on the quality of roads. This additional evidence is consistent with the finding in Table 1 that higher corruption is indeed associated with higher public investment.

Does higher corruption reduce the productivity of public investment?

Suppose that we measure productivity of public investment by improvements in the quality of roads per dollar of public investment. The regression in column (4) of Table 5 shows that the impact of investment on the quality of roads depends on the existence of corruption. Specifically, the negative sign on the interaction term shows that higher corruption can reduce the productivity of public investment.

---

[18] Results with other measures of quality of infrastructure are similar.

Table 5. The Effects of Corruption on Quality of Roads, 1980-95

Dependent variable: Paved roads in good condition as a percentage of total paved roads
(Annual data)

Independent Variables	(1)	(2)	(3)	(4)
Constant	-1.03	7.55	1.83	19.6
	(-0.150)	(1.01)	(0.193)	(1.82)
Corruption index	-7	-2.56	-6.51	-0.32
	(-8.68)	(-2.20)	(-4.74)	(-0.17)
Public investment-GDP ratio	2.03	3.09	1.15	-0.2
	(2.65)	(4.00)	(0.53)	(0.10)
Public investment-GDP ratio x corruption index			-0.16	-0.58
			(-0.44)	(-1.56)
Real per capita GDP *		0.24		0.25
		(6.38)		(6.57)
Adjusted R^2	0.186	0.326	0.184	0.329
Number of observations	322	269	322	269

Sources: IMF, *Government Finance Statistics*; *World Tables*; *Business International* ; and *Political Risk Services*. The corruption index is taken from Mauro (1995) and *International Country Risk Guide* compiled by Political Risk Services. A high value of the index means a country has high corruption; t-statistics are in parentheses. Estimation technique is OLS.
* Indicates that the coefficient is multiplied by 100.

CONCLUDING REMARKS

There are many channels through which higher corruption reduces economic growth. Mauro (1995, 1997) provides evidence and summarizes some of these arguments. The new evidence presented in this paper supports four additional arguments.

First, corruption can reduce growth by increasing public investment *while reducing its productivity*.[19] This finding is consistent with typical reduced-form cross-country growth regressions. For example, Devarajan, Swaroop and Zou (1996) have found that higher public investment is associated with lower growth, given other determinants of growth and Tanzi (1994) found that the relation between growth and investment is highly sensitive to the inclusion of a couple of countries.

Second, corruption can reduce growth by increasing public investment *that* is not accompanied by its recurrent current expenditure, i.e., adequate non-wage O&M expenditures. Our evidence shows that higher corruption is associated with higher total expenditure on wages and salaries. Wages and salaries are a large component of government consumption and higher government consumption has been shown to be unambiguously associated with lower growth (Commander et al, 1997; Barro, 1996; Barro and Sala-i-Martin, 1995).

Third, corruption can reduce growth by reducing the quality of the existing infrastructure. A deteriorating infrastructure increases the cost of doing business for both government and private sector (e.g., congestion, delays, break-downs of machineries, etc) and thus leads to lower output and growth. The importance of infrastructure in growth has been shown in many cross-country growth regressions (Canning and Fay, 1993; Easterly and Levine, 1996; Hulten, 1996).

Finally, corruption can reduce growth by lowering government revenue needed to finance productive spending.

The implication of this paper is that economists should be more restrained in their praise of high public sector investment spending and of rules such as the golden rule, especially in countries where corruption, and especially high level corruption, is a problem.

This paper has focused on the problem of corruption and not on solutions. As far as corruption relates to the activities of foreign enterprises, the OECD is currently attempting to induce industrial countries: (a) to make the payments of bribes to foreign officials not tax deductible; and (b) to criminalize the payment of bribes. So far the ministers representing the OECD countries have accepted these recommendations, but the legislative bodies of those countries must still act. The OECD proposal, however, would not affect public investment projects in non-OECD countries carried out by domestic contractors or by contractors from non-OECD countries.[20]

---

[19] Please note that because corruption reduces tax revenue, the relative increase in public investment (i.e., its share of the total government budget) is likely to be higher than the absolute increase in public investment.

[20] For a discussion of steps to reduce corruption, see Tanzi (1997).

REFERENCES

Barro, Robert J. (1996), "Determinants of Economic Growth: A Cross-Country Empirical Study," *NBER Working Paper,* No. 5698.

Barro, Robert J. and X. Sala-I-Martin (1995), *Economic Growth,* McGraw Hill, New York.

Canning, David and Marianne Fay (1993), "The Effect of Transportation Networks on Economic Growth," *mimeo,* Columbia University.

Commander, Simon, Hamid R. Davoodi, Une J. Lee (1997), "The Causes of Government and the Consequences for Growth and Well-Being," *World Bank Policy Research Paper* No. 1785.

Devarajan, Shantayanan, Vinaya Swaroop and Heng-fu Zou (1996), "The Composition of Public Expenditure and Economic Growth," *Journal of Monetary Economics*, 37, pp.313-344.

Easterly, William and R. Levine (1996), "Africa's Growth Tragedy," *mimeo,* The World Bank.

Heller, Peter S. (1991),. "Operations and Maintenance," *Public Expenditure Handbook*, edited by Ke-Young Chu and Richard Hemming, IMF

Hulten, Charles R. (1996), "Infrastructure and Economic Development: One More Unto the Beach," *mimeo,* World Bank and University of Maryland, College Park.

Knack, Stephen and Philip Keefer (1995), "Institutions and Economic Performance: Cross-Country Tests Using Alternative Institutional Measures," *Economics and Politics,* Vol. 7, No.3, pp 207-227

Klitgaard, Robert (1988), *Controlling Corruption*, Berkeley, University of California

Mauro, Paolo (1997), "The Effects of Corruption on Growth, Investment, and Government Expenditure: A Cross Country Analysis" in *Corruption and the Global Economy*, ed. By Kimberly Ann Elliott, Washington: Institute for International Economics

Mauro, Paolo (1995). "Corruption and Growth," *Quarterly Journal of Economics*, CX., No 3 (August), pp.681-712

Meagher, Patrick (1997), "Combating Corruption in Africa; Institutional Challenges and Response," paper presented at the IMF Seminar on Combating Corruption in Economic and Financial Management, Lisbon, May 19-21.

Olson, Mancur (1996), "Big Bills Left on the Sidewalk: Why Some Nations are rich and Others Poor," *Journal of Economic Perspectives*, 10,2, pp.3-24.

Pritchett, Lant (1996), "Mind Your P's and Q's: The Cost of Public Investment is not the Value of Public Capital Stock," Policy Research Working Paper, No 1660, The World Bank, Washington D.C.

Rose-Ackerman, Susan (1996), "When is Corruption Harmful?" Background paper for the *1997 World Development Report.*

Svensson, Jacob (1996), "Foreign Aid and Rent-Seeking," World Bank, Macroeconomics and Growth Division, *mimeo.*

Tanzi, Vito (1991*), Public Finance in Developing Countries*, Aldershot: Edward Elgar.

Tanzi, Vito (1994), "The IMF and Tax Reform," in *Tax Policy and Planning in Developing Countries*, edited by Amaresh Bagchi and Nicholas Stern, Delhi: Oxford University Press.

Tanzi, Vito (1995), "Corruption, Government Activities, and Markets" in *The Economics of Organized Crime*, edited by Gianluca Fiorentini and Sam Peltzman, Cambridge : Cambridge University Press.

Tanzi, Vito (1997), "Corruption, Governmental Activities and Policy Instruments: A Brief Review of the Main Issues," (*mimeo*: May 1997).

Van Rijckeghem, Caroline and Beatrice Weder (1997), "Corruption and the rate of Temptation:

Do Low Wages in the Civil Service Cause Corruption?" IMF *Working Paper.*

Wade, Robert (1982), "The System of Administrative and Political Corruption: Canal Irrigation in South India," *Journal Of Development Studies,* 18, pp.287-328.

Wei, Shang-Jin, "How Taxing is Corruption on International Investors," NBER Working Paper Series, *Working Paper* 6030.

CHAPTER 5 MODELLING GOVERNMENT INVESTMENT AND ECONOMIC GROWTH: A REVIEW AND SOME NEW EVIDENCE

·JAN-EGBERT STURM[*], JAKOB DE HAAN[*] AND
GERARD H. KUPER[*]

ABSTRACT

This paper reviews empirical research on the impact of government capital spending on economic growth. The pros and cons of three different ways to model the relationship between public investment and economic growth using time series (or panel data) are briefly reviewed, while some estimation results using a never employed dataset for the Netherlands are presented for illustrative purposes. We start with the production function approach in which the public capital stock is added as an additional input factor in a production function, which is then estimated at a national or regional level. Alternatively, a cost or profit function in which the public capital stock is included could be estimated by what we call the behavioural approach. A third way to examine the relationship between government investment and economic growth is the so-called VAR approach. By imposing as few economic restrictions as possible this approach tries to solve some of the problems raised by the production and behavioural approach. Our empirical results do not support the hypothesis that investment in infrastructure enhances economic growth.

[*] Department of Economics, University of Groningen, P.O.Box 800, 9700 AV Groningen, The Netherlands.

Keywords: goverment investment, public capital, economic growth
JEL-classification: D78, E22

1. INTRODUCTION

Governments can try to improve future living conditions in various ways: they can, e.g., stimulate private (foreign) investment, spend more on education and health programmes in order to enhance human capital, preserve the environment, or they can add to the stock of infrastructure. The past few years have witnessed growing awareness that the stock of public capital has been neglected by many OECD governments. As illustrated in figure 1, public capital spending as a share of Gross Domestic Product (GDP) declined in most OECD countries. During the 1970s and 1980s many countries have offset increases in debt interest payments and rising social security transfers by winding back public investment. Spain and Portugal are exceptions. In order to become more competitive within the European Union, these countries undertook extensive programmes of upgrading their stock of public capital. A small rise occurred also in Italy. Another conclusion that can be drawn from figure 1 is that the level of government investment spending varies considerably across countries, ranging between 1.3 per cent of GDP for the UK and 5.8 per cent for Switzerland in

Figure 1. Public investment as a share of GDP, 1970-75 versus 1987-92.

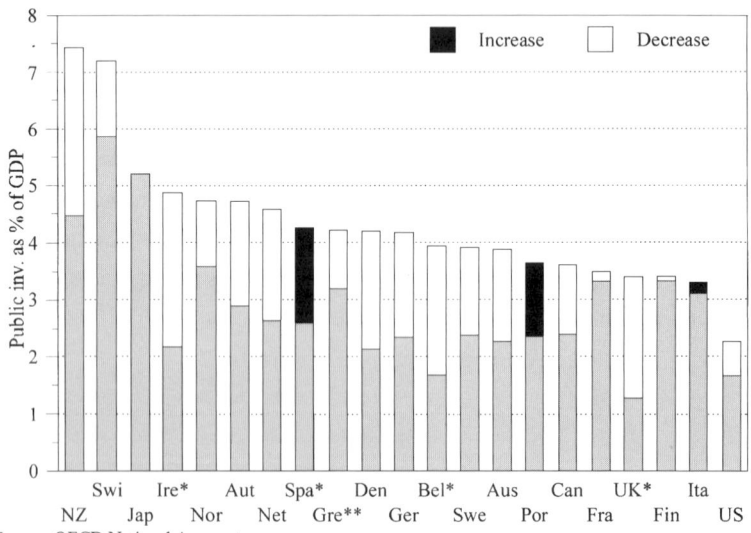

Source: OECD National Accounts.
* Only data available until 1991.
** Only data available until 1989.

1992.[1]

According to Oxley and Martin (1991, p. 161) the decline of government investment reflected "the political reality that it is easier to cut back or postpone investment spending than it is to cut current expenditures." De Haan et al. (1996) report evidence that during fiscal contractions government capital spending is indeed reduced more than other categories of government spending.

The simple fact that public investment has declined in most OECD countries in itself is no evidence that public capital is currently undersupplied. However, at approximately the same time that government investment spending declined, productivity growth plummeted almost everywhere. Aschauer (1989a) was the first to hypothesize that the decrease in productive government services in the US may be crucial in explaining the general decline in productivity growth in that country. Taking a production function approach and using annual data for the period 1949 to 1985, Aschauer found a strong positive relationship between productivity and the ratio of the public to the private capital stock. Based on his results, a 1 per cent increase in the public capital stock might raise total factor productivity by 0.39 per cent. The implications of these results for policymakers seem to be clear: public investment should go up to give a boost to the economy. Because of these well-received policy implications - higher infrastructure spending formed a major part of president Clinton's economic plans - the findings of Aschauer have sparked research into the impact of public sector capital spending on private sector output.

This paper will successively review three different ways to model the relationship between public investment and economic growth at a macroeconomic level (section 2).[2] We start with the production function approach in which public capital is added

---

[1] The data relate to consolidated general government and have been taken from the Standardised National Accounts compiled and published by the OECD.

[2] Sturm et al. (1996) also discuss two other modelling strategies. A fourth way to model the growth effects of public capital spending is to include government investment spending in cross-section growth regressions. Problems associated with these cross-section regressions include biases due to omitted variables and reverse causation. Conclusions based on cross-section regressions, especially in a cross-section of heterogeneous countries, are often not very robust and this is also true for the outcomes with respect to the growth-raising effects of public investment. A fifth way of modelling is to estimate the growth effects of public investment spending using structural econometric models. As pointed out by Sturm et al. (1996) the way this is generally done is not without problems.

to a (Cobb-Douglas) production function. Instead of adding the public capital stock as an additional input factor in a production function, a cost or profit function in which the public capital stock is included could also be estimated. By taking a cost or profit function dual to the production function and deriving factor-demand equations from it, a more behavioural approach can be followed. Thirdly, we review Vector AutoRegressions (VARs). This modelling technique tries to solve some of the problems related to the first two approaches. Section 3 presents some new estimation results for illustrative purposes using a new data set on the stock of infrastructure in the Netherlands in the previous century. The final section offers some general observations concerning all three approaches.

2. MODELLING THE IMPACT OF PUBLIC CAPITAL

2.1 THE PRODUCTION FUNCTION APPROACH

The stock of public capital (G) may enter the production function in two ways. First it may influence multifactor productivity (A). Second, it may enter the production function directly, as a third input:

(1) $Q_t = A(G_t) f(K_t, L_t, G_t)$

where Q is real aggregate output of the private sector, A is multifactor productivity, L is (aggregate hours worked by) the labour force of the private sector, K is the aggregate nonresidential stock of private capital, and G is the aggregate stock of nonmilitary public fixed capital. It depends on the functional form of the production function whether both effects can be identified. At the end of this section we will elaborate on this problem.

In this type of analysis generally an aggregated Cobb-Douglas production function in which the public capital stock is added as an additional input factor is used:

(2) $Q_t = A_t K_t^\alpha L_t^\beta G^\gamma$

Most authors have used his specification. Only a few studies have used a translog function, which is more general than the Cobb-Douglas function. Aschauer (1989a) introduces a constant and a trend variable as a proxy for A. The capacity utilization rate is added to control for the influence of the business cycle. Furthermore, he assumes constant returns to scale. As we will show in section 3, testing for the assumption of constant returns to scale may be crucial in terms of the results.

By adding the stock of public capital as an additional production factor to a Cobb-Douglas production function, initially high output elasticities of public capital were found. However, also taking into account more recent studies - which try to solve some of the shortcomings discussed below - the elasticity estimates vary widely. In their detailed review of empirical research to date - covering approximately 40 studies using this approach for OECD countries - Sturm et al. (1996) report estimates between -0.11 and 0.54. Especially in the more recent studies these estimates are found to be insignificant in many cases. Studies using aggregated national data for the US find higher production elasticities of public capital than those relying on more disaggregated data. Munnell (1992, pp. 193-194) ascribes this to possible spillover effects: "because of leakages, one cannot capture all of the payoff to an infrastructure investment by looking at a small geographic area." However, Holtz-Eakin (1992, 1994) and Holtz-Eakin and Schwartz (1995) find little evidence of spillovers in the US.

The three most serious objections to the production function approach, which often make normal interpretation of the elasticity estimates found impossible, relate to (1) specification issues, (2) reverse causation, and (3) time-series properties of the data. We will shortly elaborate on each of them.

Several *specification issues* should be mentioned. First of all, the Cobb-Douglas production function restricts - by definition - the substitution elasticities of the production factors to be equal to one. Another drawback of the estimated production functions is that labour and capital are exogenous; it is implicitly assumed that both factors are paid according to their marginal productivity.

Various authors have taken issue with other specification aspects of Aschauer's (1989a) model. For instance, Tatom (1991) argues that the reported large output elasticities are due to misspecification of the production function. He contends that the rising price of oil during the seventies made some private capital obsolete and therefore negatively affected productivity. Using another specification with energy prices included, Tatom (1991) finds little evidence that the public capital stock raises productivity. However, as relative prices do not belong directly in the production function, this approach can also be criticized. Instead, energy input itself should be included.

Another example of misspecification is the inclusion of the degree of capacity utilization. Aschauer (1989a) included this variable to account for business cycle fluctuations. Duggal et al. (1995) criticize studies in which this approach is followed since it is an additive factor in the estimated log equation, which implies that it is a multiplicative factor in the production function. A change in the capacity utilization causes an across the board change in the usage of all three factor inputs, such that the ratio of their marginal products remains the same. This is a very restrictive assumption. However, a specification in which the capacity utilization is not included at all is, of course, the other extreme.

A second issue is *causality*: does the levelling off of public capital reduce the growth of output, or does the reduced growth of output diminish the demand for public capital? To this criticism, Aschauer (1990, p. 35) has responded by stating that "this argument must confront the simple fact that public non-military investment expenditure ... reached a peak in the period between 1965 and 1968, while the usual dating of the onset of the productivity decline is around 1973."

A third reason to question the results of Aschauer (1989a) and others relates to the *time-series properties* of the data (Aaron, 1990; Tatom, 1991). Sturm and De Haan (1995) argue that if Aschauer's model is estimated in first differences - which is necessary as the variables used are neither stationary nor cointegrated - the model produces only ambiguous results. However, first differencing also has its problems. As pointed out by Munnell (1992) it is assumed that output growth in one year is only correlated with input growth in that same year; it eliminates the ability to estimate the underlying long-term relationship between production and factor inputs. Duggal et al. (1995, p. 6) argue: "The fact that first differenced equations generate a priori implausible labour and capital output elasticities is enough to question the capability of first differenced equations to capture the long run relationships." Indeed, researchers should examine not simply the extent to which variables are non-stationary, but also whether they grow together over time and converge to their long-run relationship, that is, whether they are cointegrated. Various authors have followed this approach, with rather mixed results. While Sturm and De Haan (1995) conclude, for instance, that public capital and private sector output in the US and the Netherlands are not cointegrated if data for the post Second World War period are used, Bajo-Rubio and Sosvilla-Rivero (1993) find for this period that both variables in Spain are cointegrated.[3]

A final problem according to Duggal et al. (1995) is that in all studies using the production function approach public capital is treated as a factor input, like private capital and labour. This violates standard marginal productivity theory in that it assumes a market determined per unit cost of infrastructure that is known to individual firms and can be used in calculating total costs. Aaron (1990) argues that absence of a market price, coupled with government pricing inefficiencies makes it impossible to assume that infrastructure as a factor input will be remunerated based upon its marginal product. The basic problem here is, however, that in a Cobb-Douglas function (estimated in log levels) it does not make any difference whether public capital is treated as a third production factor or as influencing output through the factor representing technology. Both ways of modelling the influence of public capital yield similar equations to be estimated. In other words, in these kinds of empirical models the direct and indirect impact of public capital cannot be disentangled.

2.2 THE BEHAVIOURAL APPROACH

A second approach is what we have dubbed the behavioural approach. Sturm et al. (1996) review in more detail 21 studies using this approach. By looking at a dual profit or cost function and deriving factor-demand or factor-share equations from it, this approach tries to model the economic behaviour of firms and to solve some specification problems related to the production function approach.

By taking flexible functional forms to specify the profit or cost function these studies assure that hardly any restrictions are placed on the underlying production function.

---

[3] In a recent paper Garcia-Milà et al. (1996) systematically test for various specification problems (including non-stationarity of the data) for the case of a state-level production function with public capital as an input. Although likely to be less of a problem with panel data sets, it is still possible that these kinds of estimates are contaminated by non-stationarity of the variables. Indeed, in the preferred specification, which is in first differences with fixed states effects, Garcia-Milà et al. (1996) report no significant effects of public capital, thereby refuting earlier evidence, including their own.

However, this appealing property of the behavioural approach also induces its biggest problem; the flexibility of the functional form implies that a lot of parameters need to be estimated and therefore requires a tremendous amount of information to be included in the database.

In general, these studies conclude that public capital reduces private sector costs or increases private sector profits. However, as shown by Sturm et al. (1996) the estimated effects are generally significantly smaller than those reported by Aschauer (1989a). Most studies roughly estimate less than half the impact reported by Aschauer (1989a), i.e. a public capital elasticity of output of approximately 0.2. In a variable cost function framework, the cost saving effects of public capital only arise if the substitution effect of some private inputs outweigh the complementary effects of other private inputs. Several studies find that intermediate inputs (and sometimes also labour) are substitutes for public capital.

Most authors clearly reject the hypothesis of constant returns to scale to all inputs. Exceptions are Conrad and Seitz (1992, 1994), Lynde (1992) and Lynde and Richmond (1992). Conrad and Seitz (1992, 1994) even reject the hypothesis of homogeneity of the cost function, which is assumed in most studies. However, imposing homogeneity results in accepting the hypothesis of constant returns to scale to all inputs. It can easily be seen that the behavioural approach boils down to allocating economic profits to increasing returns to scale, imperfect competition, and public capital. Therefore, imposing constant returns to scale and perfect competition on the model implies that all profits are automatically allotted to the public capital stock.

Two differences are conspicuous when comparing the behavioural approach with the production function approach. First, the use of a flexible functional form hardly enforces any restrictions on the production structure. For example, a priori restrictions placed upon substitutability of production factors - as encountered in the production function approach - do not apply. Apart from the direct effect that is focused upon when production functions are estimated, public capital might also have indirect effects. Firms might adjust their demand for private inputs, if public capital is a substitute or a complement to these other production factors. It seems very plausible that, for instance, a larger stock of infrastructure raises the quantity of private capital used and therefore indirectly increases production. By using a flexible functional form, the influence of public capital via private inputs can be determined. However, the flexible functional forms used do not guarantee global concavity of the cost function. Imposing this restriction on, e.g., a translog or generalized Leontief function may lead to biased estimates. Diewert and Wales (1987) have shown that the appropriate curvature conditions can be imposed on a symmetric generalized McFadden (SGM) functional form without destroying the flexibility property and without leading to biased estimates. Sturm (1998) is the only study using this functional form within this line of literature.

Second, as pointed out in the previous section, production function estimates may suffer from a simultaneous equations bias. Specifically, the right-hand variables in the various equations estimated by Aschauer (1989a) and Munnell (1990) include measures of labour input and utilization, and strong arguments have been made that such variables should be treated as endogenous. This problem does not arise in the behavioural approach, because costs or profits, and therefore input shares or demands, are directly represented. In the behavioural approach inputs are no longer exogenous to the level of output. However, input prices and - in case of the cost function approach, the level of output - are the exogenous variables. Therefore, the problem of possible endogeneity of variables remains, but does not concern the same variables as before.

Many authors adjust the stock of public capital by an index, such as the capacity utilization rate, to reflect their usage by the private sector. The impression exists that this is mainly done to artificially increase the variability of the data in order to cope with multicollinearity problems. On a theoretical basis two reasons have been advocated for adjusting the stock of public capital. First, public capital is a collective input which a firm must share with the rest of the economy. However, since most types of public capital are subject to congestion, the amount of public capital that one firm may employ will be less than the total amount supplied. However, the extent to which a capacity utilization index measures congestion is dubious. Second, firms might have some control on the usage of the public capital stock in existence. For instance, a firm may have no influence on the level of highways provided by the government, but it can vary its usage of existing highways by choosing routes. Therefore there are significant swings in the intensity with which public capital is used. Other authors explicitly "... refrain from all of these possible adjustment procedures because of their ad hoc character and because "proper" adjustment makes virtually all results possible" (Seitz, 1993, p. 230).

Despite the fact that time series properties are a main issue in the production function approach, they are hardly addressed in studies using the behavioural approach. Nevertheless, also in this line of research the results of many standard inference procedures are invalidated by non-stationary series. To make econometrically justifiable estimations one has to filter the time series to make them stationary or apply some kind of cointegration technique. The latter approach is followed by Lynde and Richmond (1993a, 1993b). They apply an error correction model (ECM) to capture the non-stationarity of the data.

Using an ECM approach also introduces dynamics in this framework. The standard behavioural approach assumes that all endogenous variables adjust to their equilibrium level within one period. Of course, it is hard to imagine that for instance the private capital stock fulfils this prerequisite. Not surprisingly, Sturm and Kuper (1996) report severe autocorrelation using the standard behavioural approach. Furthermore, they show that this can be overcome by adopting an ECM representation within a translog cost function. However, during the empirical implementation, they came up with other difficulties; several first-order conditions were no longer satisfied. Probably the increased flexibility was too much to be asked for given the available data.

Summarizing, the most appealing feature of the behavioural approach induces also the biggest problem; the flexibility of the functional form requires a tremendous amount of information to be included in the database. Furthermore, several problems raised in the production function approach still remain. In most of the studies using the behavioural approach energy is not included as an additional input, causality issues are not dealt with, and time series properties are not taken into account.

2.3 THE VAR APPROACH

A third way to analyse the impact of public investment on the economy, which we will label the Vector AutoRegression (VAR) approach, is primarily data-oriented. In a VAR model a limited number of variables is distinguished that are explained by their own lags and lags of the other variables, meaning that all variables are treated as jointly determined. By imposing as little economic theory as possible, this approach tries to solve some problems raised by the production and behavioural studies.

The production function studies derive single-equation models from first principles, which are then estimated while conclusions are based on the estimated elasticities. The multi-equation regressions in the behavioural approach are also deduced from first principles. In order to derive these first principles, some economic structure has to be assumed. Besides the potential specification problems, this also implies that the causal relationships are determined by theory. However, causality is often an issue when discussing the results of the production function approach as it is in the behavioural approach. An advantage of the VAR approach is that no a priori causality directions are imposed, or other identifying conditions derived from economic theory are needed. For instance, the causality might run from output to infrastructure, which is the opposite of what is usually assumed. It is standard procedure to carry out Granger-causality tests in a VAR framework.

An additional advantage - compared to the production function approach - is that public capital might indirectly influence output by its effect on a third variable, for instance private investment. Some authors, like Aschauer (1989b) and Erenburg (1993), report evidence for a complementary relationship between public capital and private capital, which suggests the existence of these indirect effects.

In case the time-series properties are taken into account properly, this approach therefore solves all three important objections raised with regard to the production function approach. However, as the VAR approach does not completely reveal the underlying production process, it is somewhat harder to get elasticity estimates. However, a VAR model can be analysed by observing the reactions over time of different shocks on the estimated system (innovation accounting). In this way one can get estimates of the long-run effects of different shocks.

Despite these advantages of the VAR approach, so far it has hardly been applied to the problem at hand. Sturm et al. (1996) have traced only four studies in which some variant of the VAR approach is conducted to test the effects of public capital spending on the private sector: Clarida (1993); McMillin and Smyth (1994); Sturm et al. (1995); and Otto and Voss (1996). To summarize these four papers: none of them finds clear evidence for the thesis that public capital spending influences output or productivity in the long run. However, not all four papers are on solid econometric ground or come up with unambiguous results. McMillin and Smyth (1994) and Otto and Voss (1996) do not take account of possible cointegrating relationships and present results that are possibly inconsistent or based on spurious regressions. Clarida (1993) reports that multifactor productivity and public capital influence each other mutually. Therefore, causation is unclear. The study of Sturm et al. (1995) is the only one which is conducted for the Netherlands. Using Granger-causality test and innovation accounting, they conclude that infrastructural investments have positively influenced output in the Netherlands in the second half of the nineteenth century. However, these positive effects eventually fade away in the long-run.

3. NEW EVIDENCE

This section present the results of new estimates for the case of the Netherlands. Using a new data set for the period 1853-1913 that has recently become available (sources of the data are mentioned in Sturm, 1998, Chapter 7.3), we start with the production function approach. Next we use a VAR analysis.

Dividing both sides of equation (1) by K_t, taking the natural logarithm, and assuming constant returns to scale across all inputs ($\alpha+\beta+\gamma=1$), gives:

(3) $\ln (Q/K_t) = \ln A_t + \beta \ln (L/K_t) + \gamma \ln(G/K_t)$

In contrast to other specifications in which K and G denote the private and public capital stock, respectively, in this section K and G denote the private and public capital stock of machines, equipment and buildings, and the public and private stock of infrastructure respectively. Following Aschauer (1989a) we use a constant and a trend as proxy for $\ln A_t$. Furthermore, we add the capacity utilization rate (CU) to control for the influence of the business cycle. Given the criticism concerning this specification as discussed in the previous section, we also have used a specification without the capacity utilization rate. We also explicitly test the assumption of constant returns to scale (i.e. $\alpha+\beta+\gamma=1$) by adding $(\alpha+\beta+\gamma-1)\ln K_t$; if the coefficient of $\ln K_t$ is zero the assumption of constant returns cannot be rejected.

Table 1 shows the Augmented Dickey Fuller tests on unit roots. It follows that (Q/K_t) is I(0), which implies that the stock of machines, equipment and buildings and GDP (Q) are cointegrated, since both variables are not stationary in levels. Except for the capacity utilization rate, all other variables are I(1), i.e. they become stationary only after differencing.

Table 2 presents the estimates of the production functions that we have estimated. The first column shows the Aschauer specification; as the Durbin-Watson statistic indicated the residuals were correlated, we have also estimated the model including an autoregressive term, but this does not affect our basic conclusions. In column (2) the capacity utilization rate is not included. It follows that this is not crucial for our main conclusion, which is that both estimates of β and γ are quite reasonable and indicate that both capital stocks affect productivity. In both cases the residuals are stationary so the Engle-Granger test indicates that all variables are cointegrated. However, as follows from columns (3) and (4) the restriction of constant returns to scale has to be rejected. Now the estimated coefficients do not make any sense. This finding confirms one of our main concerns raised in the previous section with respect to the production function approach.

As pointed out in the previous section, the VAR approach is more promising as many of the problems that plague the production function approach can be circumvented. In a VAR model a limited number of variables z_i, in our case $z_i = (Q_i, L_i, K_i, G_i)'$, is distinguished that are explained by their own lags and lags of the other variables, meaning that all variables are treated as jointly determined. If necessary, deterministic variables d_i, such as a constant, a trend and here also the capacity utilization rate, are included.

Table 1. Augmented Dickey-Fuller tests for non-stationarity

Series	Trend		Constant	
	Lags	t-value	Lags	t-value
$\ln(Q/K_i)$	0	-3.95 *	0	-3.91 **
$\ln(L/K_i)$	1	-1.98	1	1.48
$\ln(G/K_i)$	1	-2.92	1	-2.18
$\ln(K_i)$	1	-2.82	1	2.57
$\ln(CU_i)$	0	-4.30 **	0	-3.73 **
$\Delta\ln(Q/K_i)$	1	-8.87 **	1	-8.95 **
$\Delta\ln(L/K_i)$	0	-4.56 **	0	-4.22 **
$\Delta\ln(G/K_i)$	0	-3.34 +	0	-1.63
$\Delta\ln(K_i)$	0	-3.89 *	0	-2.56
$\Delta\ln(CU_i)$	0	-8.66 **	0	-8.74 **

Sample: the Netherlands, 1853-1913.
** Significant at a one per cent level, using the MacKinnon (1991) critical values.
* Significant at a five per cent level, using the MacKinnon (1991) critical values.
+ Significant at a ten per cent level, using the MacKinnon (1991) critical values.

Table 2. Estimation results using the production function approach [a]

$\ln(Q/K_t)$	(1)	(2)	(3)	(4)
constant	-1.78	-2.10	-29.67	-28.03
	(-2.50)	(-2.76)	(-4.81)	(-4.03)
trend	0.01	0.01	-0.05	-0.04
	(1.38)	(1.58)	(-3.39)	(-2.61)
$\ln(L_t/K_t)$	0.58	0.78	3.18	3.22
	(1.18)	(1.49)	(4.47)	(4.01)
$\ln(G_t/K_t)$	0.19	0.20	0.81	0.77
	(2.68)	(2.58)	(5.42)	(4.59)
$\ln(K_t)$			3.99	3.71
			(4.54)	(3.75)
$\ln(CU_t)$	0.80		0.88	
	(3.18)		(4.05)	
R^2 (adjusted)	0.37	0.27	0.54	0.41
Durbin-Watson	1.22	1.29	1.66	1.62
Engle-Granger [b]	-5.33	-5.46	-6.46	-6.20

Sample: the Netherlands, 1853-1913.
[a] The t-statistics are shown in parentheses.
[b] Tests whether the variables which were not stationary are cointegrated. At a five (one) per cent significance level the MacKinnon critical values are -5.01 (-5.71) in case of four variables, -4.68 (-5.36) in case of three variables, and -4.32 (-4.99) in case of two variables.

$$(4)\ z_t = \sum_{j=1}^{p} \Lambda_j Dz_{t-j} + \Omega d_t + \varepsilon_t$$

Matrices Λ_j and Ω are matrices of coefficients. In this approach usually Granger-causality tests are carried out. Some variable is said to 'Granger-cause' another variable, if the time series prediction of the latter from its own past improves when lags of the former are added to the equation. Therefore, Granger-causality is a statistical concept of antecedence, or predictability. Granger-causality tests address the question of whether one variable helps to explain the subsequent time path of another. This interpretation of causality is, of course, intuitively attractive. It has therefore become widely accepted, although some of its implications are still under debate (Granger, 1980).

Table 3 shows the outcomes of a VAR model, using Akaike's FPE-criterion (Akaike, 1969, 1970) to determine the number of lags.[4] We started with a maximum of 4 lags. The table shows the outcome of testing whether for each of the variables in $z_t=(Q_t$,

---

[4] A practical disadvantage of VAR is that the number of parameters to be estimated can easily become large. This reduces the degrees of freedom. Often a number of parameters hardly differs from zero. This property is exploited by Akaike's FPE-criterion (see Sturm, 1998).

Table 3. VAR-FPE model [a]

	ln(Q_t)-equation				ln(L_t)-equation				ln(K_t)-equation				ln(G_t)-equation			
	lags	χ^2	sum	χ^2	lags	χ^2	sum	χ^2	lags	χ^2	sum	χ^2	lags	χ^2	sum	χ^2
ln(Q_t)	3	11.24 *	0.43	8.64 **	0				1	6.68 **	0.02	6.68 **	4	10.75 *	0.01	0.14
ln(L_t)	0				2	551.69 **	0.87	512.66 **	0				1	10.06 **	-0.35	10.06 **
ln(K_t)	3	7.85 *	-0.35	2.17	1	7.75 **	-0.08	7.75 **	4	973.04 **	0.85	599.28 **	3	20.77 **	-0.24	12.39 **
ln(G_t)	0				3	27.57 **	-0.03	9.09 **	2	17.33 **	-0.03	10.71 **	3	766.35 **	0.86	764.68 **
R^2 (adj.)		0.99				1.00				1.00				1.00		

	Δln(Q_t)-equation				Δln(L_t)-equation				Δln(K_t)-equation				Δln(G_t)-equation			
	lags	χ^2	sum	χ^2	lags	χ^2	sum	χ^2	lags	χ^2	sum	χ^2	lags	χ^2	sum	χ^2
Δln(Q_t)	2	17.54 **	-0.77	17.53 **	0				0				2	5.35 +	-0.02	0.53
Δln(L_t)	0				1	15.50 **	0.44	15.50 **	1	3.19 +	0.21	3.19 +	0			
Δln(K_t)	0				0				3	51.81 **	0.76	42.65 **	1	2.38 **	-0.29	2.38
Δln(G_t)	0				2	12.21 **	-0.06	3.45 +	3	8.95 *	-0.03	0.37	2	118.28	0.84	117.15 **
R^2 (adj.)		0.32				0.30				0.63				0.76		

Sample: the Netherlands, 1853-1913.

[a] In the model in levels a constant, trend and the capacity utilization rate are included. In the model in first differences a constant and the first difference of the capacity utilization rate are included.

** Significant at a one per cent level.

* Significant at a five per cent level.

+ Significant at a ten per cent level.

L_t, K_t, G_t)' the individual coefficients of the corresponding lagged variabels are zero (first χ^2-statistic in table 3). The next column gives the sum of the lagged coefficients for each variable. The second χ^2-statistic tests for each variable whether this sum of the coefficients of all corresponding lagged variables is zero. The upper part of table presents the outcomes if the VAR model is estimated in levels, including the deterministic variables: constant, trend and the capacity utilization rate. It follows from the upper part of table 3 that the stock of infrastructure is not Granger-causing output; in fact, the variable is not even selected by the FPE-criterion (no lags). The only variable that Granger-causes output is the stock of machines, equipment and buildings, albeit that the sum of the coefficients does not differ significantly from zero. In other words, the effect of this capital stock fades out after some time. The lower part of table 3 shows the outcomes if the VAR model is estimated in first differences, using again the FPE-criterion to determine the number of lags. Again we do not find evidence that the stock of infrastructure affects output growth.

Besides conducting Granger causality tests, a VAR model can be analysed by observing the reactions over time of different shocks on the estimated system (impulse-response analysis). Rewriting the VAR into its Vector Moving Average (VMA) representation allows us to trace out the time path of various shocks on the variables contained in the VAR system. However, there are many equivalent VMA representations for one VAR model. Because of this identification problem some economic structure has to be imposed, which reduces an important advantage of the VAR analysis. Furthermore, the model needs to be stable in order to make the conversion. A sufficient condition that makes the model stable is that the variables used are stationary or cointegrated. As expected for both the models in levels and in first differences this is confirmed by impulse response analyses which are not shown here.

Problems concerning non-stationarity and cointegration of the data may be solved within the VAR framework by applying the Johansen (1988, 1991) cointegration technique (Gonzalo, 1994). This method consists of a VAR model in which an error correction mechanism is included, and is a statistical method in which all cointegrating relations in a system of variables can be found. A VAR model can be rewritten in vector error correction form:

$$(5)\ \Delta z_t = \sum_{j=1}^{p-1} \Gamma_j \Delta z_{t-j} + \Pi z_{t-1} + \Omega \Delta d_t + \varepsilon_t$$

Matrix Π contains information about long-run relationships between the variables in the data vector. The key feature is the rank of this matrix; the rank of Π is equal to the number of independent cointegrating vectors. Obviously, if rank(Π)=0, the matrix is null and the above equation is the usual VAR model in first differences. Instead, if the matrix is of full rank, the vector process is stationary, and the VAR model can be estimated in levels. In all other cases there are one or more cointegrating vectors, and the expression Πz_{t-1} is the error-correction factor. In the latter case the Π-matrix can be written as $\Pi = \alpha\beta'$, where β is the matrix of the cointegrating vectors, and α is the matrix of the weights with which each cointegrating vector enters the equations of the VAR model. In a sense, α can be viewed as a matrix of speed of adjustment parameters.

Using the software programme CATS in RATS and the same variables as before, we only found evidence for one cointegrating vector (see the upper part of table 4).[5] This cointegrating vector β reveals that there only exists a long-run relationship between GDP and the capital stock of machinery, equipment and buildings in the Netherlands in the 19th century.[6] The long-run relationship is

$$(6)\ \ln Q_t - 0.96 \ln K_t = 0$$

Table 4. The cointegration vector and its loadings

	$\ln(Q_t)$	$\ln(L_t)$	$\ln(K_t)$	$\ln(G_t)$
β-vector	1.00	0	-0.96	0
χ^2 [a]	20.02		21.24	
	α-vector	t-values		
$\Delta\ln(Q_t)$-eq.	-0.32	-2.24		
$\Delta\ln(L_t)$-eq.	0			
$\Delta\ln(K_t)$-eq.	0.03	3.60		
$\Delta\ln(G_t)$-eq.	-0.04	-2.70		

[a] The χ^2-statistics results from - besides restricting β_L=0, β_G=0, and α_L=0 - also restricting the specific coefficient to zero. At a five (one) percent level the $\chi^2(4)$ equals 9.49 (13.3).

---

[5] In our model we have three lags (p=3) as the fourth lag turned out to be insignificant.

[6] The imposed restrictions (β_L=0, β_G=0, α_L=0) cannot be rejected ($\chi^2(3)$=2.66, p-value=0.45).

As the augmented Dickey-Fuller test showed (table 1) that the ratio of GDP to the stock of machinery, equipment and buildings is stationary, this result is in line with our expectations. Note that infrastructure is not part of this long-run relationship! The deviation from the long-run relationship ($\ln Q_t - 0.96 \ln K_t$) plays a significant role in the equations for GDP, machinery, equipment and buildings, and infrastructure. The adjustment parameters α_Q and α_K have the expected signs (mean reversion). However, the negative sign of α_G in the equation explaining the change in infrastructure capital implies that if the deviation from the long-run relationship is positive, implying that GDP is too high, or the stock machinery, equipment and buildings is too low, the infrastructure capital stock tends to decrease.

4. CONCLUSIONS

We have reviewed the pros and cons of three different ways to model the relationship between public investment and economic growth. We started with the production function approach in which the public capital stock is added as an additional input factor in a production function, which is then estimated at a national or regional level. Initially, this approach yielded results "that were just too good to be true" (Aaron, 1990, p. 62). Indeed, the results of Aschauer (1989a) and Munnell (1990) have been criticized on various grounds. The most serious objections are related to the assumed causality between public capital and output, the specification and restrictiveness of the estimated model and the time-series characteristics of the data. With respect to this last issue, the proper way to proceed is to analyse whether the data are stationary or cointegrated. Applying this procedure for a new dataset for the Netherlands, it is concluded that the variables are cointegrated. However, the assumption of constant returns to scale has to be rejected and, consequently, the results are no longer plausible. This points to a serious shortcoming of much of the literature since most authors employ a Cobb-Douglas production function, thereby simply following the lead of Aschauer. This implies, however, that various restrictions are introduced.

An alternative for the production function approach is to estimate a cost or profit function in which the public capital stock is included. Some of the drawbacks of the production function approach can be eliminated by using this so-called behavioural approach. However, the flexibility of the functional form requires the database used to contain a tremendous amount of information. Furthermore, most problems raised in production function estimates still remain. In most of the studies using the behavioural approach energy is not included as an additional input, and time series properties are not taken into account. The issue of causality is also problematic. Most studies following the behavioural approach conclude that public capital reduces private sector costs or increases private sector profits. However, the estimated effects are generally significantly smaller than those reported by Aschauer (1989a).

A third way to examine the relationship between government investment and economic growth is the so-called VAR approach. By imposing as little economic restrictions as possible this way of modelling tries to solve some of the problems raised by the production and behavioural approach. An advantage of VAR models is, for instance, that no a priori causality directions are imposed or other identifying conditions derived from economic theory are needed. Indirect effects of public capital are also taken into account. As the VAR approach does not completely reveal the underlying production process, only impulse-response functions yield estimates of the long-run effects of different shocks. So far, there are only a few studies in which VARs have been used to analyse the problem at hand; therefore it is too early to reach definite conclusions. Using the new dataset for the Netherlands we find that the stock of infrastructure does not Granger-cause total output.

Summarizing, we come up with only very modest conclusions. First, public capital probably enhances economic growth (but not always). Second, we are less certain about the magnitude of the effect and this is a disappointing outcome, given the enormous amount of research in this field.

We end this paper with some general observations that apply to most of the research discussed in this paper. An issue that is not always dealt with carefully is that the concept of the stock of public capital includes rather diverging ingredients, like highways and streets, gas, water and electricity facilities, water supply, bridges, water transportation systems, etc. Most authors employ data in their analyses which are generally chosen on the ground of their availability, without analysing whether their conclusions are sensitive not only to the concept of the public capital stock (narrow versus broad definitions), but also to the way the capital stock has been constructed. For instance, most data on the capital stock are constructed using the perpetual inventory method, in which assumptions about the expected life of the assets are crucial. Few authors experiment with different definitions of the stock of public capital, which indeed, sometimes lead to diverging outcomes (Sturm and De Haan, 1995; Garcia-Milà et al., 1996). Although some authors, including Aschauer (1989a), differentiate between the total stock of non-military public capital and the stock of infrastructure, one may wonder whether this suffices. It is likely that regions and industries react differently to various types of public capital. Indeed, Pinnoi (1994) finds strong evidence in support of this view.

Another issue to which hardly any attention has been paid is the fact that what really matters from a theoretical perspective is the amount of services provided by the public capital stock. In all empirical research it is implicitly assumed that these can be proxied by the stock of public capital or the level of government investment spending, which may not be true. For instance, the amount of services provided is also determined by the efficiency with which services are provided from the stock of public capital. Indeed, according to Munnell (1993) there is substantial room for improving the efficiency.

A further general observation that we would like to make concerns the implicit assumptions about the time it takes for public capital to affect GDP growth. It may well be that there is a substantial lag before the existence of say a new road leads to new set ups of businesses. A simple Cobb-Douglas production function as often applied in the literature will probably not reflect this effect. Similarly, it does not allow for network effects, whereby the quality of the connections facilitated by infrastructure investments may be more important than the level of the public capital stock (Garcia-Milà et al., 1996). It may also make quite a difference whether the investment concerns infrastructure which previously did not exist at all, or simply more public capital (compare: a new two-lane road versus a two-lane road turned into a four-lane road). Indeed, the evidence of Sturm et al. (1995) suggests that the former may be more important than the latter.

The simple fact that public investment relative to GDP has declined in most OECD countries in itself is no evidence that public capital is currently undersupplied. A word of caution pertains to extrapolating the findings of some studies into the future. Even if infrastructure has been productive in the past, this does not imply that future investment will also be productive. The economic advantages associated with future infrastructure may be different from those of past infrastructure. For instance, it could be very beneficial to build a network of motorways while expanding this network may yield substantially less additional benefits. Simply looking at patterns in the past might tell us very little about future effects of public investment.

Nevertheless, infrastructure issues have moved to the forefront of the policy agenda in many OECD countries. Whether this will actually lead to higher spending levels remains to be seen. Indeed there is evidence that public capital spending is a relatively easy target during periods of fiscal contraction (De Haan et al., 1996). As many countries still have to redress their public finances, the lip-service of many politicians in favour of more public investment should not be taken for granted. The enthusiasm among policy-makers for increased infrastructure spending has been matched, if not surpassed by scepticism on the part of many economists (Munnell, 1993). Our paper only adds to this scepticism.

REFERENCES

Aaron, H.J. (1990), "Discussion", in: A.H. Munnell, editor, *Is There a Shortfall in Public Capital Investment?*, Federal Reserve Bank of Boston, Boston.

Akaike, H. (1969), "Fitting Autoregressive Models for Prediction", *Annals of the Institute of Statistical Mathematics*, **21**, 243-247.

Akaike, H. (1970), "Statistical Predictor Identification", *Annals of the Institute of Statistical Mathematics*, **22**, 203-217.

Aschauer, D.A. (1989a), "Is Public Expenditure Productive?", *Journal of Monetary Economics*, **23**, 177-200.

Aschauer, D.A. (1989b), "Does Public Capital Crowd Out Private Capital?", *Journal of Monetary Economics*, **24**, 171-188.

Aschauer, D.A. (1990), "Why is Infrastructure Important?", in: A.H. Munnell, editor, *Is There a Shortfall in Public Capital Investment?*, Federal Reserve Bank of Boston, Boston.

Bajo-Rubio, O. and S. Sosvilla-Rivero (1993), "Does Public Capital Affect Private Sector Performance? An Analysis of the Spanish Case, 1964-88", *Economic Modelling*, **10**, 179-184.

Clarida, R.H. (1993), "International Capital Mobility, Public Investment and Economic Growth", *NBER Working Paper No. 4506*.

Conrad, K. and H. Seitz (1992), "The 'Public Capital Hypothesis': The Case of Germany", *Recherches Economiques de Louvain*, **58**, 309-327.

Conrad, K. and H. Seitz (1994), "The Economic Benefits of Public Infrastructure", *Applied Economics*, **26**, 303-311.

Diewert, W.A. and T. Wales (1987), "Flexible Functional Forms and Global Curvature Conditions", *Econometrica*, **55**, 43-68.

Duggal, V.G., C. Saltzman and L.R. Klein (1995), "Infrastructure and Productivity: A Nonlinear Approach", paper presented at the 7th World Congress of the Econometric Society, Tokyo, Japan.

Erenburg, S.J. (1993), "The Real Effects of Public Investment on Private Investment", *Applied Economics*, **25**, 831-837.

Garcia-Milà, T., T.J. McGuire and R.H. Porter (1996), "The Effects of Public Capital in State-Level Production Functions Reconsidered", *Review of Economics and Statistics*, **78**, 177-180 .

Gonzalo, J. (1994), "Five Alternative Methods of Estimating Long Run Equilibrium Relationships", *Journal of Econometrics*, **60**, 203-233.

Granger, C.W.J. (1980), "Testing for Causality: A Personal Viewpoint", *Journal of Economic Dynamics and Control*, **2**, 1176-1196.

Haan, J. de, J.E. Sturm and B.J. Sikken (1996), "Government Capital Formation: Explaining the Decline", *Weltwirtschaftliches Archiv*, **132**, 55-74.

Holtz-Eakin, D. (1992), "Public-sector Capital and the Productivity Puzzle", *NBER Working Paper No. 4122*; published in *Review of Economics and Statistics*, **76**, 12-21 (1994).

Holtz-Eakin, D. (1994), "Public-sector Capital and the Productivity Puzzle", *Review of Economics and Statistics*, **76**, 12-21.

Holtz-Eakin, D. and A.E. Schwartz (1995), "Infrastructure in a Structural Model of Economic Growth", *Regional Science and Urban Economics*, **25**, 131-151.

Johansen, S. (1988), "Statistical Analysis of Cointegration Vectors", *Journal of Economic Dynamics and Control*, **12**, 231-254.

Johansen, S. (1991), "Estimation and Hypothesis Testing of Cointegration Vectors in Gaussian Vector Autoregressive Models", *Econometrica*, **59**(6), 1551-1580.

Lynde, C. (1992), "Private Profit and Public Capital", *Journal of Macroeconomics*, **14**, 125-142.

Lynde, C. and J. Richmond (1992), "The Role of Public Capital in Production", *Review of Economics and Statistics*, **74**, 37-45.

Lynde, C. and J. Richmond (1993a), "Public Capital and Total Factor Productivity", *International Economic Review*, **34**, 401-414.

Lynde, C. and J. Richmond (1993b), "Public Capital and Long-Run Costs in U.K. Manufacturing", *The Economic Journal*, **103**, 880-893.

MacKinnon, J.G. (1991), "Critical Values for Cointegration Tests", in: R.F. Engle and C.W.J. Granger, editors, *Long-Run Economic Relationships. Readings in Cointegration*, Oxford University Press, New York, Chapter 13, 267-276.

McMillin, W.D. and D.J. Smyth (1994), "A Multivariate Time Series Analysis of the United States Aggregate Production Function", *Empirical Economics*, **19**, 659-673.

Munnell, A.H. (1990), "Why has Productivity Growth Declined? Productivity and Public Investment", *New England Economic Review*, Jan/Feb, 2-22.

Munnell, A.H. (1992), "Infrastructure Investment and Economic Growth", *Journal of Economic Perspectives*, **6**, 189-198.

Munnell, A.H. (1993), "An Assessment of Trends in and Economic Impacts of Infrastructure Investment", in: *Infrastructure Policies for the 1990s*, OECD, Paris.

Otto, G. and G.M. Voss (1996), "Public Capital and Private Production in Australia", *Southern Economic Journal*, **62**, 723-738.

Oxley, H. and J.P. Martin (1991), "Controlling Government Spending and Deficits: Trends in the 1980s and Prospects for the 1990s", *OECD Economic Studies No. 17*, 145-189.

Pinnoi, N. (1994), "Public Infrastructure and Private Production. Measuring Relative Contributions", *Journal of Economic Behavior and Organization*, **23**, 127-148.

Seitz, H. (1993), "A Dual Economic Analysis of the Benefits of the Public Road Network", *The Annals of Regional Science*, **27**, 223-239.

Sturm, J.E. (1998), *Public Capital Expenditure in OECD Countries: The Causes and Impact of the Decline in Public Capital Spending*, Edward Elgar, Cheltenham.

Sturm, J.E. and J. de Haan (1995), "Is Public Expenditure Really Productive? New Evidence for the US and the Netherlands", *Economic Modelling*, **12**, 60-72.

Sturm, J.E., J.P.A.M. Jacobs and P. Groote (1995), "Productivity Impacts of Infrastructure Investment in the Netherlands 1853-1913", *SOM Research Report No. 95D30*, Groningen, forthcoming in: *Journal of Macroeconomics*.

Sturm, J.E. and G.H. Kuper (1996), "The Dual Approach to the Public Capital Hypothesis: The Case of The Netherlands", *CCSO Series No. 26*, Groningen.

Sturm, J.E., G.H. Kuper and J. de Haan (1996), "Modelling Government Investment and Economic Growth on a Macro Level: A Review", *CCSO Series No. 29*, Groningen, forthcoming in: S. Brakman, H. van Ees and S.K. Kuipers, editors, (1998), *Market Behaviour and Macroeconomic Modelling*, MacMillan, London.

Tatom, J.A. (1991), "Public Capital and Private Sector Performance", *Federal Reserve Bank of St.Louis Review*, **73**, 3-15.

CHAPTER6 TAX EVASION AS A DISCIPLI-NARY MECHANISM FOR FISCAL POLICY

THOMAS I. RENSTRÖM[*]

1. INTRODUCTION

This paper investigates the desirability of tax evasion as a mechanism for reducing the time-inconsistency problem in fiscal policy. It endogenises the auditing rates and punishment rates and shows that when the government cannot commit to future tax rates, tolerating tax evasion is optimal. The government can, by committing to low auditing and punishment rates, limit the effectiveness of income taxes in the future. Furthermore we seek to establish which types of economies that would rely on evasion as a "disciplinary mechanism."

The contribution of the paper, apart from endogenising the enforcement system, is to provide answers to several issues that have been raised in the evasion literature. We list the most important achievements of the paper below:

(1) Previous literature studying tax evasion and optimal auditing mechanisms generally concludes that maximum enforcement and consequently zero tax evasion are optimal (e.g. auditing everyone, or auditing very few and setting the punishment very high). However, despite the findings of the theory, actual governments seem to tolerate tax evasion. This paper provides an answer to the following question: Why

[*] Department of Economics, University of Birmingham, Edgbaston, Birmingham B15 2TT, UK. Email t.i.renstrom@bham.ac.uk.

I would like to thank Tim Besley, Torsten Persson, Peter Sinclair and Berthold Wigger for helpful discussions and comments. Thanks are also due to participants at the Public Economics Working Group at the Institute for Fiscal Studies, London, May 1996, and at the 53rd Congress of the International Institute of Public Finance, Kyoto, August 1997.

is tax evasion tolerated in equilibrium? We argue that an optimal outcome lies between the zero and the maximum enforcement. This is so because tax evasion may act as partial solution to the time inconsistency problem. The reason is that evasion makes the tax base more elastic and as a consequence the optimal tax rate lower. So by making the tax base more elastic the optimal tax rate without precommitment gets closer to the optimal tax rate with precommitment. Infact Boadway and Keen (1998) independently reached similar conclusions in a slightly different model than ours.[1]

(2) Standard models of tax evasion view the fiscal policy decision, at the time when it is taken, as distinct from the auditing-punishment decision. More precisely, when the tax system is decided upon the enforcement structure is taken as given. This reflects the idea that changing size of (or influencing) the inspection authority, or changing penalty structure, etc. can be done less frequently or less rapidly than changing fiscal policy. That is, the tax system is viewed as more *discretionary* than the enforcement system. However one could criticise this view by saying that a government *could* arrange differently, having a system with more discretion in enforcement. But if the tax system itself is discretionary (i.e. the tax rates cannot be precommitted to in advance) it may actually be *desirable* to operate the enforcement system under less discretion than the fiscal system. In this way the government strategically precommit to an enforcement system such that evasion occurs in equilibrium. This helps solving in part the precommitment problem in fiscal policy.

(3) As pointed out by some authors, theoretically an increase in the tax rate may reduce the evaded amount. This may happen when the income effect (from a tax increase) makes the evader less willing to take on risk, and therefore declares more income (i.e. distribute consumption possibilities more evenly across the risky states). However, this result depends entirely on the enforcement system. However, as we argue in this paper, such an enforcement system may not be desirable. That is, it may not be optimal to operate an auditing and punishment system such that when taxes are increased there is a reduction in tax evasion. Precisely because the evaded income has to increase as the tax rate increases, for tax evasion to act as a partial solution to a time-inconsistency problem. Therefore we would expect governments to arrange their enforcement systems accordingly.

---

[1] I was not aware that Boadway and Keen were working on this topic until Mick Keen sent me their paper just before the IIPF Kyoto conference.

(4) One point not properly dealt with in the literature is to explain why different countries experience different levels of tax evasion. Previous work says that different levels of the taxes or different institutional settings would cause this difference. This is not enough because these factors are endogenous. This paper goes behind in attempting to explaining primitives, for example the role of income distribution and the role of the level of aggregate income.

There are two papers, using two-period models,[2] that have reached the conclusion that some evasion may be desirable, Andreoni (1992) and Boadway and Keen (1998). The idea in Andreoni is that individuals may be credit constrained. If the government can set detection probabilities and fines relatively low, so that evasion occurs in equilibrium, individuals who evade effectively "borrow" from the government in the first period. If an individual is caught she pays the tax (i.e. the "loan") and the fine (i.e. "interest") in the second period. In this way some evasion in equilibrium may be efficient and welfare improving. Boadway and Keen (1998) analyse a two-period economy where a representative individual is taxed on her savings in the second period, when she also has the possibility of evading taxes. The tax receipts are used for provision of a public good. They reach the conclusion that when the government cannot commit to the future tax rate allowing some tax evasion may be optimal. The reason for this is that without evasion the capital tax base is inelastic and the government would choose the capital-tax rate too high if it cannot precommit to the tax . Tax evasion makes the tax base more elastic, and lowers the optimal tax rate under discretion making it closer to the optimal tax rate under precommitment. The idea underlying Boadway and Keen is closest to ours.

The paper is organised as follows. Section 2 develops the basic framework of tax evasion and focuses on the evasion-concealment decision in two-class framework: self-employed and "white-market" workers. Only the self-employed can evade taxes. Both classes are able to save. The self-employed have the possibility of supplying parts of their labour on the white market. The income earned on the white market is non-evadable.

Section 3 solves the two-period economic equilibrium. The self employed and the

---

[2] Weiss (1976) shows in a static economy that the randomisation induced by evasion may be desirable.

"white" workers decide in period one how much to consume and how much to save, knowing the level of enforcement and rationally expecting the government's fiscal policy decision in the second period.

In Section 4 we examine two types of governments: (*a*) the government is revenue maximising, and (*b*) the government is majority elected. We do not explicitly model the relative costliness of using auditing or punishment as enforcement. Therefore auditing and punishment become equivalent measures, and we refer to them simply as *enforcement*. We conclude the findings in section 5.

The major results of this paper are:

(1) Regardless the objective of the government, maximum enforcement is never optimal if the government cannot commit to future taxes. Thus, tax evasion acts as a disciplinary mechanism for fiscal policy.

(2) If the government is revenue maximising and if individuals are endowed with relatively low initial wealth the government tolerates more tax evasion in equilibrium. In these economies the tax rate and the revenue are lower.

(3) If the government is majority elected and future taxes cannot be committed to then the greater the initial wealth of the self employed, the greater is the politico-economic equilibrium enforcement rate, and the greater is the second-period politico-economic equilibrium tax rate.

2. THE BASIC FRAMEWORK OF TAX EVASION

In this section we develop a framework which is rich enough to capture the mechanisms we think are important in determining tax evasion and that allows us to pursue general equilibrium analysis.

(1) We distinguish between two classes of individuals: self employed and "white" workers, capturing the idea that self employed (in the "grey" sector) more easily can evade taxes as opposed to other groups in the economy. We will still allow individuals to differ within each class, since we would expect fiscal policy in general to depend on distributional characteristics. We will draw a sharp distinction by assuming that tax evasion and concealment can only be undertaken by the self employed, and that

no income earned by the "white" workers can be concealed or evaded. More precisely, the self employed have the opportunity to both hide income from the tax authorities at a cost (concealment or "laundry") and to under report the non-concealed income (evasion). Both of these choices are continuous.

(2) To allow for flows of labour from the grey sector into the white (and vice versa) the self employed choose the number of hours worked in their own businesses and on the white market.[3] This captures the idea that the tax system operating in the official market affects the employment in the grey sector. When making her labour allocation choice (as well as leisure) the self employed knows the tax rates, the auditing probability and the fines, and also takes into account her optimal choice of income evasion and concealment.

(3) We shall always have in mind a two-period economy, where investment has been made in the previous period, but we solve the equilibrium recursively, starting in the second period when all capital is fixed.[4] Indeed we then look at a tax-evasion economy very close to Allingham and Sandmo (1972). However, the economy we will use here will allow for a richer characterisation due to the following extensions: (i) simultaneous evasion and concealment decisions (ii) choice of hours worked on white market and in own business (iii) decreasing marginal product of labour in own business (iv) taxation of both labour and capital income.[5] These extended assumptions

---

[3] A self employed faces a concave production technology (in labour) in his own firm but an official after-tax market wage invariant to his labour supply.

[4] The self employed may save from period one to period two, but only in his own business. By this assumption we allow the groups "grey" and "white" to be separated. Thus the self employed have no other capital income in period two.

[5] We shall abstract from *income-source misreporting* (Yaniv (1990)). It will be assumed that of whatever income is declared the authorities can perfectly discriminate what is due to hours worked and what is due to investment, this automatically rules out the possibility of misreporting the *source* of income. If we were to study both simultaneously, the problem becomes very complex and less intuitive. We, for example, would need a differential punishment structure, presumably convex in each source of income misreported. Otherwise we would have corner solutions: the self employed would either report all income as due to capital or all due to labour, or possibly be entirely indifferent, why no interior solutions exist. Since our focus is on pure evasion and one-dimensional changes in the probability/ punishment structure it seems entirely reasonable to abstract from income source misreporting. Combining the two would indeed be an interesting research idea *on its own*, since sofar it has not been done. (Yaniv (1990) compares two cases, actually not combining them).

are not of crucial importance for establishing the *basic* argument of this paper, but they offer interesting implications for the government's optimal level of enforcement, and predictions of what *type* of economies would suffer (or benefit!) from higher degree of tax evasion.

2.1 THE SELF EMPLOYED

Entrepreneurs may choose how much to work in their own firm (the "grey" market) and how much to work on the "white" market. Hours in own firm are denoted ℓ^g and on the white market as ℓ^m, and total hours as $\ell = \ell^g + \ell^m$. The self employed has access to a constant returns-to-scale production technology $f(k^g, \ell^g)$, where k^g is the capital saved by the self employed. The self employed may conceal some income at a cost C. Denote the fraction of income that has not been concealed as s, so the cost of concealment is $C((1-s)f(k^g, \ell^g))$. Of the non-concealed income the self-employed declares a fraction, α, to the tax authorities (it is assumed that the tax authorities can determine from the reported income the proportions of labour and capital income). If the tax authorities detect tax evasion (this is with probability p) they detect all income evaded (but not the concealed one). The monetary punishment is a fraction, π, of non-reported income. The fiscal structure consists of a flat capital income tax (at rate θ), a flat labour income tax (at rate τ) and a lump sum benefit, b, equal for all individuals and all states (detected/non-detected). The consumption of the self employed if not detected is

$$Y = f(k^g, \ell^g) - \theta f_k \alpha s k^g - \tau f_i \alpha s \ell^g - C\big((1-s)f(k^g, \ell^g)\big) + k^g + b + \omega \ell^m \tag{1}$$

and if detected

$$Z = f(k^g, \ell^g) - \theta f_k s k^g - \tau f_i s \ell^g - C\big((1-s)f(k^g, \ell^g)\big) + k^g + b + \omega \ell^m$$
$$- \pi(1-\alpha)sf(k^g, \ell^g) \tag{2}$$

Given the savings made and given the hours worked, the individual chooses how much income to conceal and how much to report. The objective is to maximise expected utility

$$E[u] = (1-p)u(Y) + pu(Z) - v(\ell^g + \ell^m) \tag{3}$$

We shall make some simplifying definitions. Define a "composite" tax rate as

$$T \equiv \frac{\theta f_k k^g + \tau f_i \ell^g}{f(k^g, \ell^g)} \tag{4}$$

i.e. the effective marginal tax on income from self-employment (which of course depends on the individual's choice of labour supply and savings). Define the after-tax income, if all non-concealed income is declared, as

$$M \equiv (1 - sT)f(k^g, \ell^g) - C\big((1-s)f(k^g, \ell^g)\big) + b + \omega\ell^m \tag{5}$$

i.e. the after-tax income if the individual is not evading (only possibly concealing).

2.2 THE EVASION-CONCEALMENT DECISION

The decision to conceal and underreport is taken when all economic activity has been undertaken, i.e. after supply of labour in own business and on the white market. So taking ℓ^g and ℓ^m *as given* the individual chooses α and s so as to maximise (3). The first-order conditions imply

$$(1 - p)u'(Y)T = pu'(Z)\pi \tag{6}$$

$$C'\big((1-s)f(k^g, \ell^g)\big) = T \tag{7}$$

Equation (6) is the standard Allingham and Sandmo (1972) result, the marginal change in expected utility due to a marginal change in reported income shall be zero.[6] Equation (7) tells that the marginal cost of concealment shall equal the marginal benefit, i.e. the marginal tax rate on income from self-employment. Notice that the concealment decision does not directly depend on the evasion decision (possibly only indirectly via the labour supply decision).

2.3 THE LABOUR SUPPLY DECISION

Given the individual's optimal reporting strategy, the individual chooses his optimal occupation, i.e. the fraction of labour to devote to the white market and the fraction to the grey market. There are two necessary conditions for an interior optimum

$$\omega[(1-p)u'(Y) + pu'(Z)] = v'(\ell^g + \ell^m) \tag{8}$$

$$(1-p)u'(Y)\left[(1-T)f_\ell - \alpha sf\frac{\partial T}{\partial \ell^g}\right] + pu'(Z)\left[(1-T)f_\ell - sf\frac{\partial T}{\partial \ell^g}\right] = v'(\ell^g + \ell^m) \tag{9}$$

Equation (8) tells that the official market wage (after tax) times the marginal expected

---

[6] Or in other words, the marginal utility is orthogonal to the marginal return.

utility of consumption (evaluated at optimum evasion and concealment) equals the marginal utility from leisure. Equation (9) is the condition for self employment and states that the expected marginal benefit (in consumption units) from supplying labour in own business equals the marginal utility from leisure. We may further rewrite (9) by using (8) and (6) to obtain

$$\omega = (1-T)f_\ell - sf \frac{T+\alpha\pi}{T+\pi} \frac{\partial T}{\partial \ell^s} \tag{10}$$

This condition is more transparent than (9). It does not involve any marginal utility terms and thus is a condition for efficiency in self employment. The outside after tax wage rate should equal the after tax marginal product of self employment (as if all income was declared) minus a term reflecting the possibility of strategically affecting the mixture of capital and labour income. If this latter term is zero there are no such strategic possibility and we have a very simple efficiency condition. We see that the term is zero if the marginal (composite) tax rate on self-employment income is unaffected by the hours worked in own business. This happens in *either* of two cases:

(a) the capital income tax equals the labour income tax in self employment: $\tau = \theta$,
(b) the production function is Cobb-Douglas.

Thus, if either (a) or (b) is fulfilled the labour supply decision in own business is independent of the evasion-concealment decisions, and thereby also independent of the auditing-punishment structure.

2.4 TAX REVENUE FROM SELF EMPLOYED

By assuming that the auditing probability is the fraction of self employed actually audited (Kolm (1973)) the tax revenues collected from the self employed are[7]

$$R = (1-p)\alpha sTf + p[sTf + \pi(1-\alpha)sf] \tag{11}$$

or after some manipulation

$$R = [p(1+\pi/T) + \alpha[1 - p(1+\pi/T)]]sTf \tag{12}$$

We can verify that the tax revenues are increasing in p, the auditing rate.

---

[7] Provided that the self employed aggregate into a "representative individual", this will always be the case under certain conditions, see further Section 3.

3. THE TWO-PERIOD ECONOMY

3.1 ASSUMPTIONS

This section will make some simplifying assumptions in order to gain tractability.

A1 Individuals' Preferences
Individuals live for two periods. The utility function for each individual (regardless employed or self employed) is given by

$$U = \ln c_1 + \beta E_1 \left[\ln c_2 \right] + \beta \eta \ln(L - \ell) \tag{13}$$

A2 Individuals' Earnings
Self employed choose how much to invest in their own firm, and in period 2 how much to work in their firm and how much to conceal and declare of their income. They face the constraints

$$c_1^g + k^g = W \tag{14}$$

$$\tilde{c}_2^g = Pk^w + \omega \ell^w + b \tag{15}$$

where $\tilde{c} = \{Y$ if not detected, Z if detected$\}$.[8] The employed on the white market constitutes the majority of the population, their fraction of the population is denoted $n > 1/2$. They face the constraints

$$c_1 + k^w = W \tag{16}$$

$$c_2 = Pk^w + \omega \ell^w + b \tag{17}$$

where $P \equiv 1 + (1-\theta)r$ and $\omega \equiv (1-\tau)w$ are the after-tax returns from capital and labour respectively, and b is the lump-sum benefit. Individuals will be allowed to vary in their wage incomes (w and W).

A3 Production and Concealment Technologies in Grey Market
The production technology in the grey market is assumed to be of the Cobb-Douglas form[9] and the cost of concealing grey income, I^g, is assumed to be quadratic

---

[8] Where Y and Z are defined as in equations (1) and (2) respectively.
[9] We have established the role of Cobb-Douglas specification in the previous section. It will make labour supply in own business independent of the evasion and concealment decisions, even when differential taxation is allowed for.

$$f(k^g, \ell^g) = A(k^g)^{\varepsilon}(\ell^g)^{1-\varepsilon} \tag{18}$$

$$C(I^g) = \gamma(I^g)^2/2 \tag{19}$$

A4 Production Technology in the White Market

The production technology in the white market is assumed to be linear, i.e.

$$y = F(\bar{k}^w, \bar{\ell}^w + \bar{\ell}^m) = r\bar{k}^w + w\bar{\ell}^w + w\bar{\ell}^m \tag{20}$$

A5 Government

The government either

(*a*) maximises revenue

or

(*b*) implements the policy resulting from majority voting.

3.2 SECOND PERIOD ECONOMIC EQUILIBRIUM

Self Employed

For log-utility the condition for optimal evasion, equation (6) becomes[10]

$$\alpha^* = 1 - [(1-p)T/\pi - p]M/m \tag{21}$$

where

$$m \equiv sTf(k^g, \ell^g) \tag{22}$$

is defined as the tax payment if all non-concealed income is reported. It is interesting to notice that M/m is the ratio of after-tax income (if nothing is evaded) to tax payment (if nothing is evaded), and thus represents the inverse of "hypothetical" tax pressure. If the tax pressure is high, M/m is small and therefore α is large, i.e. a larger proportion of income is evaded. Then, consumption if not detected, consumption if detected, and indirect utility are

$$Y = (1-p)\frac{T+\pi}{\pi}M, \quad Z = p(1+\pi/T)M, \quad V = \Omega + \ln(M) \tag{23}$$

respectively, where $\Omega \equiv \ln(1+\pi/T) + (1-p)\ln[(1-p)T/\pi] + p\ln p$. M may be interpreted

---

[10] Recall that we may write $Y = M + (1-\alpha)Tsf$ and $Z = M - (1-\alpha)\pi sf$.

as the individual's income, to be allocated across two risky states. Because the utility function belongs to the HARA-family (Linear Risk Tolerance), the individual allocates *constant* fractions of her income across the states (the fractions are independent of M).[11] It should also be noted that the certainty equivalent is Me^{Ω}, therefore we may analyze the individual's concealment-, consumption-, labour supply-, and savings-decisions by looking at the certainty equivalent.

The quadratic cost function gives the optimal concealment decision, equation (7), as

$$1 - s^* = T/\left[\gamma f(k^g, \ell^g)\right] \tag{24}$$

so the concealed cost in optimum is $C^* = T^2/(2\gamma)$. Then

$$M = (1 - T) f(k^g, \ell^g) + T^2/(2\gamma) + b + \omega \ell^m \tag{25}$$

and

$$m = Tf(k^g, \ell^g) - T^2/\gamma \tag{26}$$

Finally the Cobb-Douglas specification gives the composite tax rate as

$$T = \theta\varepsilon + \tau(1 - \varepsilon) \tag{27}$$

and optimal labour supply in own business, equation (10), as

$$\ell^g = k^g \left[\frac{1 - T}{\omega}(1 - \varepsilon)A\right]^{\frac{1}{\varepsilon}} \tag{28}$$

Optimal labour supply on white market, equation (8), imply

$$\ell^m = \frac{L}{1 + \eta} - \frac{1 - \varepsilon + \eta}{1 + \eta} \frac{r^g k^g}{\varepsilon\omega} - \frac{\eta}{1 + \eta} \frac{T^2}{2\gamma} \frac{1}{\omega} - \frac{\eta(b + k^g)}{1 + \eta} \frac{1}{\omega} \tag{29}$$

where

$$r^g \equiv \varepsilon A^{\frac{1}{\varepsilon}} (1 - T)^{\frac{1}{\varepsilon}} \left[(1 - \varepsilon)/\omega\right]^{\frac{1-\varepsilon}{\varepsilon}} \tag{30}$$

turns out to be the after-tax return on self-employed capital.

Therefore

$$M^* = \frac{\omega L}{1 + \eta} + \frac{r^g k^g}{1 + \eta} + \frac{1}{1 + \eta} \frac{T^2}{2\gamma} + \frac{b + k^g}{1 + \eta} \tag{31}$$

---

[11] This is linear Engel curves in *state space*.

$$m^* = k^g TA^{\frac{1}{\varepsilon}} \left[(1-T)(1-\varepsilon)/\omega \right]^{\frac{1-\varepsilon}{\varepsilon}} - T^2/\gamma \tag{32}$$

$$V^* = \Omega + (1+\eta)\ln(M^*) - \eta \ln(\omega) \tag{33}$$

It should be noticed that none of the quantities (28)-(32) are directly affected by the auditing-punishment structure.

Employed on white market

In the second period labour supply is chosen as

$$\ell^{w*} = \operatorname*{argmax}_{\ell^w} \ln(Pk^w + \omega\ell^w + b) + \eta \ln(L - \ell^w) \tag{34}$$

with solution

$$\ell^{w*} = \frac{L}{1+\eta} - \frac{\eta}{1+\eta}\frac{Pk^w + b}{\omega} \tag{35}$$

We then obtain the "white" worker's indirect utility

$$V^{*w} = \Omega^w + (1+\eta)\ln(Pk^w + \omega L + b) - \eta \ln\omega \tag{36}$$

where $\Omega^w \equiv \eta\ln\eta - (1+\eta)\ln(1+\eta)$.

Tax Receipts

The tax receipts, G, will be the expected collection of taxes from the self employed plus the collected taxes from the "white" workers

$$G = (1-n)\left[m - \delta M + (w-\omega)\ell^m \right] + n\left[(w-\omega)\ell^m + \theta r k^w \right] \tag{37}$$

where

$$\delta \equiv \frac{T}{\pi}\left[1 - p - p\pi/T \right]^2 \tag{38}$$

We shall later on take δ as a measure of *tolerance* of tax evasion.

3.3 FIRST PERIOD ECONOMIC EQUILIBRIUM

Self Employed

Since

$$k^{g*} = \operatorname*{argmax}_{k^g} \ln(W - k^g) + \beta(1+\eta)\ln\left(M^*(k^g)\right) \tag{39}$$

we have

$$k^{g*} = \frac{\beta(1+\eta)}{1+\beta(1+\eta)} W - \frac{1}{1+\beta(1+\eta)} \frac{\omega L + T^2/(2\gamma)}{1+r^g} \qquad (40)$$

Employed on white market

The optimal savings is found as

$$k^{w*} = \underset{k^w}{\arg\max} \ln(W - k^w) + \beta(1+\eta)\ln(Pk^w + \omega L + b) \qquad (41)$$

with solution

$$k^{w*} = \frac{\beta(1+\eta)}{1+\beta(1+\eta)} W - \frac{\omega L + b}{[1+\beta(1+\eta)]P} \qquad (42)$$

4. FISCAL POLICY

4.1 THE REVENUE MAXIMISING GOVERNMENT: CAPITAL-INCOME TAXATION

In this section we shall assume that the government has only one tax instrument, the capital income tax, with the objective to maximise its tax revenues, i.e.

A5(a) Government

The government maximises revenue with respect to the capital-income tax, leaving no lump-sum transfer ($b=0$).

The tax receipts become

$$G = (1-n)(m - \delta M) + n\theta rk^w \qquad (43)$$

We shall focus on two regimes, one in which the government credibly can commit to future taxes, and one in which it cannot. We will examine the desirability of tax evasion, in particular what audit rates and punishment rates the government would choose. Since, within the framework outlined above, the audit rates and punishment rates are complementary instruments, and we have said nothing about the relative costliness of using them, we shall focus on a measure of how much evasion is tolerated. As a bench mark we take the case when the government does not tolerate tax evasion at all. This is the situation when either the probability of detection is one or when the punishment is infinite (and probability of detection goes to zero), the latter case is usually referred to as when we "hang tax evaders with probability zero," (Kolm (1973)). In these two cases δ is zero. The following definition seems natural

Definition 1 *Tax evasion is said to be **not tolerated** when $\delta=0$. The greater value of δ the more tax evasion is **tolerated**.*

Lemma 1 *The tax receipts from self-employed when all non-concealed income is declared, m, is a concave function of the capital income tax θ, for $0 \le \theta \le 2$.*

Proof: See the appendix.

The significance of Lemma 1 is that if all evasion is eliminated, we would expect that there exists an interior maximum to the revenue maximising problem. However, since "white" workers' capital income is inelastic we may have a situation where the maximising tax rate is large enough to completely discourage savings of both groups in the first period. In such a situation the commitment problem is severe and no capital exists in the second period and consequently government revenue is zero. This may happen when the "white" sector is large relative to the "grey" (when n is large), and when capital is highly productive (when r and ε are large). For example, for the self employed to save we clearly require $\varepsilon\theta < 1$.

Proposition 1 *In a one-period economy government revenue is maximised at $\delta=0$ (i.e. when evasion is not tolerated).*
(a) If there is no "white" sector, the maximising tax rate is less than 100%, except when concealment is infinitely costly, then the tax rate equals 100%
(b) If there is a "white" sector and concealment is infinitely costly the maximising tax rate is greater than 100%.
(c) If there is a "white" sector sufficient for maximised government revenue to be greater than zero is that $r < 1$, $\varepsilon < 1/2$, $\beta(1+\eta)W \ge wL/(1-r)$ and

$$\varepsilon[1-2\varepsilon]^{\frac{1-2\varepsilon}{\varepsilon}} A^{\frac{1-\varepsilon}{\varepsilon}} \left[(1-\varepsilon)/\omega\right]^{\frac{1-\varepsilon}{\varepsilon}} \ge \frac{n}{1-n} r \tag{44}$$

all hold.

Proof: Since M is positive $\forall \theta$ and independent of δ we have $\underset{\delta}{\max} (1-n)(m-\delta M)+nrk^w$

$= (1-n)m+nrk^w$. Next, maximising with respect to θ gives the first-order condition

$$G_\theta = m_\theta + nrk^w$$

$$= (1-n)\varepsilon(1-\theta)k^g[1-\varepsilon\theta]^{\frac{1-2\varepsilon}{\varepsilon}} A^{\frac{1}{\varepsilon}} \left[\frac{1-\varepsilon}{\omega}\right]^{\frac{1-\varepsilon}{\varepsilon}} -(1-n)2\varepsilon^2\frac{\theta}{\gamma}+nrk^w \tag{45}$$

If there is no "white" savings ($n=0$) we have $m_\theta\mid_{\theta=1} < 0$, (when $\gamma < \infty$) and by concavity of $m(t)$ (Lemma 1) the value of θ is too high. When $\gamma \to \infty$ we have $m_\theta\mid_{\theta=1} = 0$. When there is "white" savings and $\gamma \to \infty$, we must have $m_\theta < 0$ and consequently $\theta > 1$. To prove (c) we need to show that there is an interior solution where $\theta\varepsilon < 1$ and savings are positive. Suppose $\theta = 2$ and concealment is infinitely costly, then (45) becomes

$$(1-n)\frac{1-\theta}{1-\varepsilon\theta}r^g k^g +nrk^w = 0 \tag{46}$$

By using (40) and (42) we have that $k^w > k^g$ at $\theta=2$. Condition (44) is the same as saying $r^g/(1-2\varepsilon) \geq rn/(1-n)$. Then clearly (46) is negative at $\theta=2$, therefore $\theta\varepsilon < 1$. Since $\beta(1+\eta)W \geq wL/(1-r)$ white market savings are positive at $\theta=2$ and therefore k^g is also positive, and so government revenue.   QED

Part (c) gives the conditions for savings being positive at interior optimum for the capital tax. The conditions are only sufficient. If they were violated we could have a situation where the government is unable to raise any revenue at all (under discretionary fiscal policy).

Furthermore, we see that if capital is fixed the government cannot do better than eliminating tax evasion.

Lemma 2 *The following inequality holds*

$$M +\theta M_\theta > 0 \tag{47}$$

Proof: See the appendix.

We have, obviously, after-tax income (if nothing is evaded) M as a decreasing function of the capital tax θ: $M_\theta < 0$, but as Lemma 2 states its *elasticity* (in absolute value) is always smaller than one. This is so because the individual responds to changes in the tax by varying her labour supply.

Proposition 2 *In a one-period economy the tax rate is higher when δ=0 than when evasion is tolerated (i.e. when δ>0).*

Proof: Denote as θ' the tax rate that maximises government revenue when $\delta = 0$, then $(1-n)m_\theta(\theta')+nrk^w=0$. Denote as θ^* the maximising tax rate when $\delta > 0$, then

$$(1-n)\left[m_\theta(\theta^*)-\delta_\theta(\theta^*)M(\theta^*)-\delta_\theta(\theta^*)M_\theta(\theta^*)\right]+nrk^w = 0 \tag{48}$$

From the definition of δ [equation (38)] it follows that

$$\frac{\partial\delta}{\partial\theta} = \left(\frac{(1-p)\varepsilon\theta+p\pi}{(1-p)\varepsilon\theta-p\pi}\right)\frac{\delta}{\theta} > \frac{\delta}{\theta} \tag{49}$$

Using (49) in (48) we have

$$(1-n)m_\theta(\theta^*)+nrk^w > (1-n)\delta(\theta^*)\left[M(\theta^*)-\theta M_\theta(\theta^*)\right]/\theta^* \tag{50}$$

By Lemma 2 we see that the right-hand side is positive and therefore $((1-n)m_\theta(\theta^*)+nrk^w > 0 = (1-n)m_\theta(\theta')+nrk^w$, and by concavity of m we have $\theta^* < \theta'$.

QED

Proposition 2 shows how the possibility of tax evasion limits the effectiveness of the capital income tax. Tax evasion lowers the value of the Laffer optimal tax rate and therefore may act as a credibility mechanism in policy making in a dynamic economy. But let us examine the optimal punishment and auditing rates when the government is *able* to credibly commit to future the tax rate.

Proposition 3 *When the government **can** commit to future taxes, the government revenue is maximised at δ=0, with a tax rate lower than the one in Proposition 1.*

Proof: See the appendix.

Clearly, if the government can commit to future taxes it wishes to "hang evaders with probability zero." It should be noticed that the precommitted tax rate is *lower* than the one obtained in the static problem (this is due to the time-inconsistency of optimal policy).

Proposition 4 *When the government **cannot** commit to future taxes, the revenue is maximised at δ>0, i.e. evasion is tolerated.*

Proof: See the appendix.

In this case tax evasion is actually *desirable* since it acts as a credibility mechanism for fiscal policy in the future.

Proposition 5 *In economies where individuals are endowed with relatively low initial wealth, where the white-market return on capital is large, and where the number of white workers to the number of self-employed is large, the government tolerates more tax evasion in equilibrium.*

Proof: See the appendix.

This suggests that the time-inconsistency problem is more severe in low-income economies. When the number of individuals that cannot evade taxes is large, the greater the tolerance towards evasion has to be, i.e. the more the government has to rely on the relatively few evaders to make the tax base elastic.

4.2 THE REVENUE MAXIMISING GOVERNMENT: UNIFORM INCOME TAXATION

Here we shall assume that all income is taxed at a uniform rate. Still the objective is revenue maximisation, i.e.

A5(a') Government
The government maximises revenue with respect to a uniform income tax, leaving no lump-sum transfer ($b=0$).

The tax receipts are as in (37) where $\theta=\tau=T$.

Lemma 3 *The tax receipts when all non-concealed income is declared is a concave function of the income tax T.*

Proof: Follows by twice differentiating (37), when $\theta=\tau=T$, with respect to T using (29), (30), (32), and (35). The derivative is always negative.   QED

Here, because the tax is levied on labour income as well, the tax base becomes more elastic, and therefore the tax receipts is always a concave function of the income tax rate.

Similarly to section 4.1 we have

Proposition 6
(a) In a one-period economy government revenue is maximised at $\delta=0$ (i.e. when evasion is not tolerated).
(b) In a one-period economy the tax rate is higher when $\delta=0$ than when evasion is tolerated (i.e. when $\delta>0$).
*(c) When the government **can** commit to future taxes, the government revenue is maximised at $\delta=0$.*
*(c) When the government **cannot** commit to future taxes, the revenue is maximised at $\delta>0$, i.e. evasion is tolerated.*

Proof: See the appendix.

The above results (section 4.1 and 4.2) were derived for the *revenue maximising* government. We will now turn to a rather different (and perhaps more plausible) objective: the government objective determined in political equilibrium.[12]

4.3 ENDOGENOUS REDISTRIBUTIVE INCOME TAXATION

Here we shall assume that all tax receipts are redistributed lump sum to all "white" workers. We analyse the case of uniform income taxation.

A5(b) Government
The income tax is chosen through a majority vote in the last period, and all tax receipts are distributed lump sum to all individuals who are not self employed.

The political equilibrium we shall rely on, is the median-voter equilibrium.[13]

---

[12] Endogenous taxation.
[13] We do not address the question of how the equilibrium is reached.

Proposition 7 *In a one-period economy the tax rate that cannot loose under majority rule is less than the revenue maximising tax rate. The lower the wage and the lower the capital of the median voter the higher is the tax. If also evadability is voted upon the outcome is $\delta=0$ (i.e. when evasion is not tolerated in political equilibrium).*

Proof: See the appendix.

By assuming that self employed are in minority the median voter is a "white" worker. The median wishes to maximise the size of the redistribution towards herself. The size of the redistribution is maximised when no evasion is tolerated.

Proposition 8 *With precommitted enforcement, the tax rate that cannot loose under majority rule is higher when $\delta=0$ than when evasion is tolerated (i.e. when $\delta>0$). Furthermore,*
(a) the less capital the median voter owns in relation to the average for white workers, and
(b) the less the average capital for white workers is in relation to the capital of the self employed, and
(c) the smaller the wage of the median in relation to the mean,
the higher is the tax rate.

Proof: See the appendix.

The tax rate being higher when evasion is not tolerated confirms the possibility of evasion playing a role in limiting the effectiveness of fiscal policy. The role of redistribution is clear, the tax is greater the greater distance between the mean and the median among the group of white workers. Also there may be redistribution from the self employed to the white workers.

Proposition 9 *When the future tax rate **can** be committed to, full enforcement cannot loose under majority rule, δ is zero. The tax rate that cannot loose under majority rule is lower than the one in Proposition 7.*

Proof: See the appendix.

Proposition 10 *When the future tax **cannot** be committed to, δ is positive in politico-economic equilibrium and the second period tax rate is lower than the one in Proposition 7.*

Proof: See the appendix.

Thus, even though evaders are in minority tax evasion is tolerated in politico-economic equilibrium.

Proposition 11 *The smaller the initial wealth of the self employed, and the less the initial wealth of the median in relation to the mean for white workers, the lower is the politico-economic equilibrium enforcement rate.*

Proof: See the appendix.

5. SUMMARY AND CONCLUSIONS

This paper provided a theory where the size of the inspection authority and the size of the fines evolve endogenously. We found that if a society cannot commit to future taxes it may gain from committing to a small Inland Revenue Service and small punishments for tax evasion. The possibility of the public evading taxes limits the effectiveness of capital taxation. By setting detection probabilities and punishment relatively low, the government indirectly commits itself not to tax capital income too heavily in the future. The paper analysed the factors determining the level of tax evasion when taxes and enforcement are endogenous. In particular we found that societies with low level of initial wealth of the self employed, and more right-skewed distribution of wages, would experience a higher degree of tax evasion in politico-economic equilibrium.

The paper contrasts sharply *commitment* versus *discretion* in fiscal policy; either the government could commit to future policy (and maximum enforcement was desirable) or the government could not commit to future policy (and evasion was desirable). A natural extension of this model (which has not been undertaken yet) could be to allow for cases where the economy *partially* may commit to future taxes. We think that even in this case the tax evasion can still act as a disciplinary mechanism, but we would expect it to be used to a lesser extent. The intuition would be that societies with more commitment in fiscal policy rely less on tax evasion and would have higher enforcement rates ceteris paribus. However, we do not know if these countries would have higher taxes (because of their partial commitment).

The paper is closely linked to the *strategic-delegation* literature in the results. In the terminology of the strategic-delegation literature the government could benefit from delegating auditing and punishment decisions to a "soft" Inland Revenue Service and "soft" courts. Analogously to this literature this paper finds that a society may benefit from making the IRS and courts *independent* (or less subject to government intervention). A further extension of the paper could be to allow for a rather different way of limiting the auditing authority. This could be done by consciously appointing *corrupt* officials. Then we would find that this surely reduces the probability for a tax evader in getting fined and works in the same way as limiting the size of the inspection authority. Thus the government in this case would consciously allow corruption and find it desirable.

The paper studies *income taxes*, ignoring *expenditure taxes*. For expenditure taxes the time-inconsistency problem is generally less severe, and there is less gain from committing to lower rates of enforcement. Thus, we would expect VAT evasion to be punished and monitored to a greater extent than income tax evasion.

We have analysed the case when the enforcement is a variable completely free of choice to the government. However, in some societies the enforcement may not be a free choice variable, due to other sources of inefficiencies or technical problems (e.g. in developing countries) so the level of evasion may in these cases be in *excess* of what is desirable from a credibility point of view.[14]

We should not claim that tax evasion is the best way of solving time-inconsistency problems, other measures may be superior. However, in societies where these measures are not available, perhaps evasion is one of the only few "solutions."

---

[14] For example, to operate the enforcement, punishment needs to be exercised. In order to do this the auditor must be able to provide evidence of evasion, which may be difficult in societies where collection of data is difficult or where many transactions remain unrecorded.

APPENDIX

Proof of Lemma 1

The first derivative of m with respect to θ is

$$m_\theta = \varepsilon(1-\theta)k^g[1-\varepsilon\theta]^{\frac{1-2\varepsilon}{\varepsilon}} A^{\frac{1}{\varepsilon}}[(1-\varepsilon)/\omega]^{\frac{1-\varepsilon}{\varepsilon}} - 2\varepsilon^2\theta/\gamma \tag{51}$$

and the second derivative

$$m_{\theta\theta} = (1-\varepsilon)\varepsilon(2-\theta)k^g[1-\varepsilon\theta]^{\frac{1-3\varepsilon}{\varepsilon}} A^{\frac{1}{\varepsilon}}[(1-\varepsilon)/\omega]^{\frac{1-\varepsilon}{\varepsilon}} - 2\varepsilon^2/\gamma \tag{52}$$

which is negative as long as $\theta \leq 2$.   QED

Proof of Lemma 2

Differentiating M with respect to θ gives

$$M_\theta = -\frac{\varepsilon k^g}{1+\eta}[1-\varepsilon\theta]^{\frac{1-\varepsilon}{\varepsilon}} A^{\frac{1}{\varepsilon}}\left[\frac{1-\varepsilon}{\omega}\right]^{\frac{1-\varepsilon}{\varepsilon}} + \frac{\varepsilon^2}{1+\eta}\frac{\theta}{\gamma} \tag{53}$$

Premultiplying by θ (and rearranging somewhat) gives

$$\theta M_\theta = -\frac{\theta}{1-\varepsilon\theta}\left\{\frac{\varepsilon k}{1+\eta}[1-\varepsilon\theta]^{\frac{1}{\varepsilon}} A^{\frac{1}{\varepsilon}}\left[\frac{1-\varepsilon}{\omega}\right]^{\frac{1-\varepsilon}{\varepsilon}}\right\} + \frac{\varepsilon^2}{1+\eta}\frac{\theta}{\gamma} \tag{54}$$

but the term within curly brackets equals $M - [\omega L + (\varepsilon\theta)^2/(2\gamma)](1 + \eta)^{-1}$, then

$$\theta M_\theta = -\frac{\theta M}{1-\varepsilon\theta} + \frac{\theta}{1-\varepsilon\theta}\frac{\omega L}{1+\eta} + \frac{\theta}{1-\varepsilon\theta}\frac{1}{1+\eta}\frac{(\varepsilon\theta)^2}{2\gamma} \tag{55}$$

or by adding M on both sides

$$M + \theta M_\theta = \frac{1-(1+\varepsilon)\theta}{1-\varepsilon\theta}M + \frac{\theta}{1-\varepsilon\theta}\frac{\omega L}{1+\eta} + \frac{\theta}{1-\varepsilon\theta}\frac{1}{1+\eta}\frac{(\varepsilon\theta)^2}{2\gamma} \tag{56}$$

So equivalent of proving $M+\theta M_\theta > 0$ is to prove

$$(1+\eta)[(1-\varepsilon\theta)-\theta]M + \theta\omega L + (\varepsilon^2\theta^3)/(2\gamma) > 0 \tag{57}$$

The equation above is convex in θ. By evaluating at the minimum with respect to θ it can be verified that the minimum value is positive.   QED

Proof of Proposition 3

Government revenue is

$$G = (1-n)\left[m(\theta, k^g(\theta)) - \delta M(\theta, k^g(\theta))\right] + n\theta r k^w(\theta) \tag{58}$$

106

Since $M>0$ $\forall$ θ,k^g, G is maximised at $\delta=0$. The first-order condition for θ^{**} to be maximising is

$$(1-n)\left[m_\theta^* + m_k^* k_\theta^g(\theta^*)\right] + nrk^w(\theta^*) + nrk_\theta^w(\theta^*) = 0 \tag{59}$$

where m_θ^* is short hand for m_θ $(\theta^*, k^g(\theta^*))$, etc. Then clearly

$$(1-n)m_\theta^* + nrk^w(\theta^*) = -m_k^* k_\theta^g(\theta^*) - n\theta rk_\theta^w(\theta^*) > 0 = (1-n)m_\theta' + nrk^w(\theta') \tag{60}$$

Then we must have $\theta^* < \theta'$. Suppose the opposite $\theta^* > \theta'$, then we must have $k^g(\theta^*) < k^g(\theta')$ and $k^w(\theta^*) < k^w(\theta')$. Then we have m_θ $(\theta^*, k(\theta^*)) < m_\theta$ $(\theta^*, k(\theta')) < m_\theta$ $(\theta', k(\theta'))$, (the first inequality follows from $m_{\theta k} > 0$ and the second by $m_{\theta\theta} < 0$), and $rk^w(\theta^*) < rk^w(\theta')$. This is a contradiction. $\qquad$ QED

Proof of Proposition 4

We solve recursively, i.e. the second period first

$$\max_\theta (1-n)\left[m(\theta) - \delta(\theta)M(\theta)\right] + n\theta rk^w \tag{61}$$

Necessary for optimum

$$(1-n)\left[m_\theta(\theta) - \delta(\theta)M(\theta) - \delta(\theta)M_\theta(\theta)\right] + nrk^w = 0 \tag{62}$$

or

$$(1-n)\left[m_\theta(\theta) - \rho(\theta)\frac{\delta(\theta)}{\theta}M(\theta) - \delta(\theta)M_\theta(\theta)\right] + nrk^w = 0 \tag{63}$$

where

$$\rho(\theta) \equiv \frac{(1-p)\varepsilon\theta + p\pi}{(1-p)\varepsilon\theta - p\pi} > 1 \tag{64}$$

Let ξ denote a parameter reflecting the desired compliance, satisfying[15]

$$(1-n)\left[m_\theta(\theta) - \rho(\xi,\theta)\frac{\delta(\xi,\theta)}{\theta}M(\theta) - \delta(\xi,\theta)M_\theta(\theta)\right] + nrk^w = 0 \tag{65}$$

and $\rho'(\xi) > 0$, $\delta'(\xi) < 0$. This enables us to write $\theta = \Theta(\xi, k)$. Viewed from the first period $k = k(\theta)$, therefore $k = k(\Theta(\xi, k))$, and we may write $k = k(\xi)$. The first-period problem is

$$\max_\xi (1-n)\left[m\left(\Theta, k^g(\xi)\right) - \delta(\Theta,\xi)M\left(\Theta, k^g(\xi)\right)\right] + n\Theta rk^w(\xi) \tag{66}$$

Note that $(1-n)[m_\theta - \delta_\theta M - \delta M_\theta] + nrk^w = 0$, then the necessary condition is

---

[15] An example is fixing π, to say unity, and letting $\xi = p$.

$$(1-n)\left[m_k k_\xi^g - \delta_\xi M - \delta M_k k_\xi^g\right] + n\Theta r k_\xi^w = 0 \tag{67}$$

where functional arguments are suppressed. Since $\delta_\xi(\Theta,\xi)=0$ at $\delta=0$ we have

$$G_\xi = (1-n)m_k k_\xi^g + n\Theta r k_\xi^w \tag{68}$$

which is negative, since $k_\xi^g < 0$ and $k_\xi^w < 0$. QED

Proof of Proposition 5
From the proof of Proposition 4 we have

$$m_k = \frac{\delta_\xi}{k_\xi^g} M + \delta M_k - \frac{n}{1-n}\Theta r \frac{k_\xi^w}{k_\xi^g} \tag{69}$$

Since m_k, M_k, k_ξ^g, k_ξ^w and δ_ξ are all independent of the level of W, and that m_k, M, M_k are positive, then if M is large then δ is small and vice versa. QED

Proof of Proposition 6
Proposition 6 is proven in exactly the same way as Propositions 1-5.

Proof of Proposition 7
Using (34) and optimising with respect to T gives[16]

$$\frac{1}{Pk^w + \omega\ell^w + b}\left(-rk^i - w^i\ell^i + \frac{\partial b}{\partial T}\right) = 0 \tag{70}$$

The first term is marginal utility of consumption and is positive. Thus, at individual i's most preferred tax rate the following holds

$$rk^i + w^i\ell^i = \frac{\partial b}{\partial T} \tag{71}$$

By concavity of $b(T)$ (Lemma 3) it follows from (71) that $\partial T/\partial\ell^i < 0$ and $\partial T/\partial k^i < 0$. Single peakedness of preferences follows by concavity of $b(T)$, then the Median Voter Theorem applies. At the revenue maximising tax rate $b'(T)=0$, but for any majority elected tax rate $b'(T)>0$, thus the majority elected tax is smaller. Finally, evasion will just redistribute from white workers to self employed, thus all white workers agree upon $\delta=0$. QED

---

[16] Since optimisation also takes place over ℓ^i we can, by the envelope condition, ignore the terms involving labour supply.

Proof of Proposition 8

Denote as

$$\lambda(T) \equiv (1-n)Tw\,\ell^m + nTw\ell^w \tag{72}$$

the tax receipts collected from labour income. It is easily verified that $\lambda(T)$ is concave in T. Denote as T' the tax rate that maximises the median voter's utility when $\delta{=}0$, then $(1-n)m_T(T') + nrk^w + \lambda_T(T') = rk^i + w^i\ell^i$. Denote as T^* the maximising tax rate when $\delta{>}0$, then

$$(1-n)\big[m_T(T^*) - \delta_T(T^*)M(T^*) - \delta(T^*)M_T(T^*)\big] + nrk^w + \lambda_T(T^*) = rk^i + w^i\ell^i \tag{73}$$

Suppose instead that $T^* > T'$ is true. Then by concavity $(1-n)m_T(T^*) + nrk^w + \lambda_T(T^*) < rk^i + w^i\ell^i$, which combined with (73) gives

$$0 < -(1-n)\big[\delta_T(T^*)M(T^*) + \delta(T^*)M_T(T^*)\big] \tag{74}$$

but this is a contradiction since the bracketed term can be verified to be positive. Finally, because of concavity of $b(T)$ also when $\delta{>}0$, T^* is greater the smaller rk^i and $w^i\ell^i$. Next, notice that

$$\lambda_T(T^*) = (1-n)w\ell^g + nw\ell^w + (1-n)Tw\frac{\partial\ell^g}{\partial T} + nTw\frac{\partial\ell^w}{\partial T} \tag{75}$$

and rewrite (73)

$$(1-n)\big[\big(m_T(T^*) - rk^w\big) + w(\ell^g - \ell^w)\big] + r(k^w - k^i) + (w\ell^w - w^i\ell^i) = Z(T^*) \tag{76}$$

where

$$Z(T^*) \equiv (1-n)[\delta_T M + \delta M_T] - (1-n)Tw\frac{\partial\ell^g}{\partial T} - nTw\frac{\partial\ell^w}{\partial T} \tag{77}$$

Since $Z_T(T) > 0$ the right-hand side of (76) is large when T^* is large. Examining the left-hand side of (76) proves (a)-(c). QED

Proof of Proposition 9

(Sketch of proof) An individual specifying her preferred tax policy in period 1 to be implemented in period 2 will find it optimal to set[17]

$$rk^i + w^i\ell^i = \frac{db}{dT} \tag{78}$$

---

[17] Because of the envelope conditions.

For any level of T $b(T | \delta = 0) > b(T | \delta > 0)$, since T is precommitted to. Then white workers would be better off at $\delta = 0$, since regardless the decisive individual there would be greater redistribution from the self employed. $\qquad$ QED

Proof of Proposition 10

Solving recursively, i.e. the second period first, we have the first-order condition for the decisive individual as in (73). As in the proof of Proposition 4 let ξ denote a parameter reflecting the desired compliance. Then (73) gives the optimal tax as a function of ξ, and of the capital stocks k^i, k^w, k^g, i.e. $T = \Phi(\xi, k^i, k^w, k^g)$. Viewed from the fist period we may write $k^i = k^i(\xi)$, $k^w = k^w(\xi)$, $k^g = k^g(\xi)$. Then (after using all envelope conditions) optimising with respect to ξ in the first period gives the first-order condition (which is very similar to (67))

$$(1-n)\left[m_k k_\xi^g - \delta_\xi M - \delta M_k k_\xi^g + Tw\,\ell_k^m k_\xi^g\right] + nTrk_\xi^w + Tw\,\ell_k^w k_\xi^w = 0 \qquad (79)$$

Notice that by (29) and (35) $\partial \ell^m / \partial k^g < 0$ and $\partial \ell^w / \partial k^w < 0$. Since $\delta_\xi(T,\xi)=0$ at $\delta=0$, it can be verified (by using (26) and (35)) that (79) is negative at $\delta=0$, implying that compliance is too high. $\qquad$ QED

Proof of Proposition 11

(Sketch of proof) Using (79) in the same way as using (69) to prove Proposition 5 establishes the result. The part concerning the distribution follows from Proposition 9, since the second period tax is greater. A greater T in (79) establishes the result.

$\qquad$ QED

REFERENCES

Allingham, Michael G., and Agnar Sandmo (1972), "Income Tax Evasion: A Theoretical Analysis," *Journal of Public Economics*, 1: 323-338.

Andreoni, James (1992), "IRS as a Loan Shark: Tax Compliance with Borrowing Constraints," *Journal of Public Economics*, 49: 35-46.

Boadway, Robin, and Michael Keen (1998), "Evasion and Time Consistency in the Taxation of Capital Income," *International Economic Review*, (forthcoming).

Cowell, Frank A. (1990), *Cheating the Government: The Economics of Tax Evasion* (Cambridge, Massachusetts: MIT Press).

Kolm, Serge-Christophe (1973), "A Note on Optimum Tax Evasion," *Journal of Public Economics*, 2: 265-270.

Weiss, L. (1976), "Desirability of Cheating Incentives and Randomness in the Optimal Income Tax," *Journal of Political Economy*, 84(6):

Yaniv, Gideon (1990), "Tax Evasion under Differential Taxation," *Journal of Public Economics*, 43(3): 327-337.

Yitzhaki, Shlomo (1974), "A Note on Income Tax Evasion: A Theoretical Analysis," *Journal of Public Economics*, 3: 201-202.

PART III. INTER-GOVERNMENTAL RELATIONS

CHAPTER 7 PUBLIC INVESTMENT ISSUES AND EFFICIENT CLIMATE CHANGE POLICY

PETER BOHM[*]

Assuming an international policy target aimed at reducing the risks of climate change, I discuss here a special kind of immaterial public investment, namely investments in knowledge about a new policy option which appears to be a promising candidate for an efficient <u>international</u> climate change policy, but which was not yet been investigated thoroughly enough for practical application. What I refer to is a so-called international tradeable-quota (TQ) system, a version of which was proposed by the US for the meeting of the Rio Convention Conference-of-the Parties in Kyoto in December, 1997. The required investments in policy knowhow concern not only further theoretical analysis, but also extensive empirical cost studies as well as pilot testing of TQ systems. The discussion here relates primarily to the last step, how to go about testing the operation and the political acceptability of TQ systems.

First, however, I'd like to address a quite different issue, the implications of efficient <u>domestic</u> climate change policies for the marginal cost of public funds(MCPF), that is, funds to be used for public expenditure including public investments.

PART 1.
IMPLICATIONS OF EFFICIENT DOMESTIC CLIMATE CHANGE POLICIES FOR THE MARGINAL COST OF PUBLIC FUNDS

Assume an agreement has been reached among a set of countries, each bound by emission quotas, tradeable or non-tradeable. The emissions I will refer to are emissions of carbon, i.e., CO_2, the dominating greenhouse gas (GHG). Then, the individual

---

[*] Department of Economics, Stockholm University, Stockholm

signatory country can use whatever domestic policy it prefers in order to meet its carbon emissions quota. The following three major options can be identified:

(1) a carbon tax, that is, a tax on the carbon content of domestic fossil-fuel (FF) use --production *plus* imports *minus* exports of FF -- levied, say, on FF producers and importers; carbon emissions equal the carbon content of FF use as long as carbon removal is not an economically attractive option; or

(2) a domestic tradeable-permit (TP) system where those FF producers and importers who, under the first option, would have been tax liable are now permit liable, passing on permit prices to consumers just as they would pass on the taxes in the tax case, or

(3) some set of regulations of FF use, say, domestic non-tradeable permits.

If the international agreement is non-global, which seems likely at least initially, there is a significant risk of so-called carbon leakage -- that is, reductions in FF use in signatory countries may be partly offset by increases in FF use in non-signatory countries. The implications of the three domestic policy instruments may differ in this regard. But I will leave the carbon leakage problem aside here.

For a given national quota of carbon emissions, the required tax rate is essentially equal to the endogenous permit price in a comparable perfectly competitive TP system, giving the same allocation of emission abatement. Furthermore, these two market-based instruments can be made distributionally equivalent. If the permits were auctioned off, this would give the same revenue to the government as the tax alternative would, call this government revenue option A. At the other extreme, option B, permits are grandfathered, that is, given away to the permit-liable parties according to some distributional pattern, or the tax revenue, in the alternative tax case, is used for lump-sum redistribution to the tax-liable parties with the same distributional pattern. Here, distribution inside the non-government sector is again the same for the two alternative policy instruments.

The choice between the two market-based policy alternatives as now defined is of no concern when, as I will assume here, cost-effectiveness and distributional considerations are the only policy criteria. Hence, for the purposes of the present discussion these two instruments can be considered as one and the same. Furthermore, concerning the two options for distribution of the tax revenue/permit wealth between government and industry, there is the much discussed efficiency argument in favor of option A when there is a pre-existing distortionary tax system -- say, optimally distortionary with equalized marginal excess burdens. The revenue from the carbon tax or from auctioned permits could then be used to reduce pre-existing distortionary taxes. This presumes -- as I will continue to do here -- that no distribution considerations are violated by efficient revenue recycling.

Now, there has been a rather confusing double-dividend debate in the literature concerning the effect of introducing a revenue-neutral environmental tax, e.g. a carbon tax, relevant, of course, also for auctioned permits. Here, some economists have argued that the fact that other tax bases may be affected by the environmental tax would diminish the potential reduction in distortionary taxes (see e.g. Bovenberg and de Mooij, 1994, and Goulder, 1994). This argument has had a significant effect on the debate over carbon taxes, in particular.

The analytical basis for this conclusion has been that the environmental tax is compared with not introducing this tax, other things equal. My interpretation of this type of exercise is that it seeks to provide an answer to the question, what happens if an environmental target were to be introduced. But if an environmental tax in fact is introduced, there must exist an environmental policy target. Given such a target, which can be reached by the tax (auctioned permits) or some non-revenue-generating policy option, other things would not be equal if the tax (auctioned permits) were not introduced, because then another -- now non-revenue-generating -- policy instrument would have to be introduced.

Here, the given environmental target is analytically simple: a cap on carbon emissions. The baseline to the tax/TP option can then be either grandfathered permits or direct regulation. A baseline regulatory design could take a number of alternative forms, each with a potentially different set of implications as compared to the revenue-generating tax/TP option.

The important implications, in principle, of using the relevant counterfactual case for comparison, can be indicated for the standard regulatory case, where non-tradeable permits (NTPs) are distributed for free in the amount of the given domestic emission volume. We may even realistically assume that this distribution would be the same as the initial distribution in the TP system just discussed. Then, it can be shown that the indirect effects on other tax bases in the baseline case would be at least the same as in the revenue-raising tax/TP case. The increase in FF buyer prices in the baseline case would increase the consumer price index, reducing real wages and, by the conventional assumption made, also reducing employment and thus the revenue from labor taxes, all to at least the same extent as in the tax/TP case. This means that, as government revenue should be kept intact, distortionary taxes would have to be increased in the baseline case, since other tax revenues are reduced and there is no revenue from environmental policy.

To elaborate a little bit on the policy baseline case: If NTPs in Figure 1 happened to be efficiently allocated, which would be the case if the alternative had been a system of grandfathered tradeable permits, increases in FF buyer prices would be the same. But if the NTPs are inefficiently allocated, prices would increase even more, as indicated by point P, reflecting the differing marginal benefits of the NTPs. Hence, the indirect effects on labor tax revenue in the baseline case would at least outweigh the indirect effects in the tax/TP case, leaving at least the whole of the revenue of the tax/TP option for a reduction of distortionary taxes from the level of distortionary taxes in the policy baseline case. This is the relevant comparison, of course, even if the reduction in revenue from other taxes in the environmental tax/TP case exceeded the revenue from environmental policy.

The argument now made may be illustrated by taking a parallel case, where there is another policy target, a government revenue target, that can be reached by introducing

Figure 1. Reducing carbon emissions to target level: Aggregate marginal abatement costs (MAC) with a cost-effective vs. a non-cost-effective allocation of non-tradeable permits (NTPs)

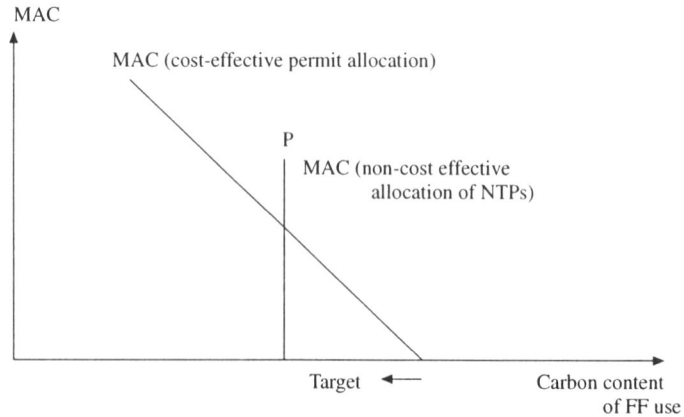

a certain financial tax T. To investigate the effect of this tax, given the target, the tax T has to be compared, not with not introducing the tax, period!, but with a relevant substitute instrument for reaching the target. The crucial point now is this. If both the tax T and its substitute or baseline have indirect effects on other tax bases, attention must be paid to both sets of indirect effects, not only the indirect effect of the tax T.

The importance of these arguments in the present policy context stems from the fact that climate change policy might eventually call for significant carbon emission reductions, hence high tax rates or permit prices and -- given an elasticity below one -- significant government revenue from the revenue-generating version of this policy. If so, the result could be a potentially significant reduction of marginal excess burdens in the economy, hence a reduction of the marginal cost of public funds (MCPF) and a consequent increase in the efficient level of demand for public expenditure, again in comparison to the relevant policy baseline.

Summarizing by taking a quick rear-view look at the past discussion of revenue-raising environmental policy, my interpretation of the history of the last 15 years or so is this:

1. During the 80's, conventional wisdom among environmental economists was that any given environmental policy goal, which politicians typically preferred to attain by regulatory instruments, would be attained more efficiently by using economic instruments, whenever feasible, one reason being that the revenue recycling then made feasible would reduce the excess burden of the tax system as a whole.

2. David Pearce applied this to the climate change policy case in an article in 1991. This also seems to be where the term double dividend was coined for the effects of revenue recycling of an environmental tax as compared to regulation. But up to that point, a partial equilibrium framework was used, implying that environmental tax revenue would constitute a net addition to government revenue prior to tax recycling.

3. In the early 90's a group of economists set out on a new track when now discussing the double dividend in a general equilibrium setting, where an environmental tax was compared with a baseline of no other environmental policy alternative. An important result of the general equilibrium analysis was the observation or highlighting of indirect effects on other tax bases, part of which was already implicit in a non-double-dividend-related paper by Sandmo in 1975. A less

fortunate implication of the new policy baseline was that at least two double-dividend concepts came to exist, making the short-hand use of this term troublesome.

4. The general equilibrium analyses investigated the effect of introducing an environmental target, then using a tax, and not the effect of introducing a tax given an environmental target. Given the latter issue and comparing revenue-raising policy with non-revenue-raising regulatory policy to reach a given environmental policy goal -- here, a given level of carbon emissions -- the importance of observing the indirect effects is reduced. If anything, replacing partial equilibrium analysis with general equilibrium analysis tends to make the difference in government revenue and hence in MCPF between the regulation case and the case with revenue raising instruments even larger.

PART 2.
ON EFFICIENT AND DISTRIBUTIONALLY AC-CEPTABLE INTERNATIONAL AGREEMENTS TO REDUCE CARBON EMISSIONS

We now move from implications of climate change policy at the domestic level to the problem of climate change policy at the international level -- more specifically, the design of an efficient and distributionally acceptable international agreement to reduce carbon emissions. Three potentially efficient policy options have been in focus here: An international carbon tax, harmonized domestic carbon taxes and a tradeable carbon emission quota system. While the general idea of the two tax options is pretty straightforward, the TQ system needs a word or two of explanation.

A TQ system is modeled after the principles of the TP system, of course. But, specifically, carbon emission quotas, referring to the carbon content of FF use of individual countries,

- can be regarded as being allocated to countries for moving, say, five-year periods
- are traded -- at least formally -- by governments, the contract parties
- can be traded e.g. on an international exchange, where a quota price is established
- are supported domestically *ex post* quota trade by instruments chosen by the individual country; in case a TP system is chosen, the national quota is allocated among domestic parties, to whom the government may wish to delegate also its international quota trade; this is an approach that the US might prefer.

In the Contribution by Working Group III to the Second Assessment Report of the Intergovernmental Panel on Climate Change (1996), a large group of economists summarized the conclusions of the Economics literature on Climate Change, peer reviewed by other economists as well as governments around the world. In the chapter on policy instruments, the TQ system emerged as the most promising instrument for efficient policy at the international level. However, the principles of this system do not seem to be generally well understood by many climate change policy negotiating parties. Partly for that reason, it seems, the system has met with opposition from a number of countries. This may be seen as a natural reaction, given that the principles behind its next-of-kin, TP systems, have been in use essentially in the US only and, in addition, that there is no real precedent for applying it at the international level.

Significant political opposition to a TQ treaty at this stage can have two undesirable implications: First, the negative first reactions can make also otherwise undecided countries negatively inclined -- I think my own country, Sweden, has been a good example of this kind of reaction. If such snowball effects occur, they obviously risk reducing the efforts to test and further analyze the properties of this solution. I would like to give you the results of an experimental test which tries to investigate the international political attitudes towards a specific TQ treaty proposal a little bit further, to check to what extent these attitudes in fact can be expected to be negative. If they are not, such a study, if at all enlightening, could contribute to setting the investigations of the details of a TQ system back on track.

Second, negative first reactions are, of course, also likely to make the number of participating countries in any pioneering TQ system quite small. Then, would a TQ system involving only a few, and probably only developed, countries be discouragingly ineffective as has been surmised, and hence contribute to stopping a development towards a larger and more effective such system? I'll report on another study, which investigates the efficiency of a TQ system with four small developed countries.

In both tests, the goal was to have countries represented in a way that would provide some relevant insight into the two issues, of course. This required identification of experimental subjects who could be expected to have some minimum knowledge important for the issue at hand. In addition, the experimental design had to provide incentives for such subjects to use this knowledge when responding.

THE EFFICIENCY OF A TRADEABLE-QUOTA SYSTEM WITH FOUR SMALL DEVELOPED COUNTRIES: AN EXPERIMENT

To begin with the second test just mentioned: In 1996, The Energy Ministries of Denmark, Finland, Norway and Sweden agreed to test the efficiency implications of hypothetical emissions trade among the four countries. They also agreed to

- appoint negotiating teams of relevant public officials and experts, quite close to the type of people that could be expected to be engaged in real emissions quota trade,
- have these negotiators take as given national commitments to stay at the 1990 carbon emission level by the year 2000; this is a target suggested in the 1992 Rio convention, and
- trade emission reductions, making an individual country able to exceed its national emissions target level by an amount that another of the four countries would sell, thus committing the latter country to undershoot its emissions target by that amount.

Incentives were provided to the negotiating teams in an attempt to mimic the likely incentives in a real trade situation, where each party would try to maximize its trade gains. Crucial for the test was that the teams also had agreed to give, prior to the trade negotiations, their negotiation-relevant social marginal abatement cost curves to an evaluation team of three non-Nordic experts (Scott Barrett, Jean-Charles Hourcade and Robert Stavins). After trade had taken place, this team would investigate not only to what extent actual trade had realized the potential -- as if perfectly

Figure 2. Marginal Social Abatement Costs before trade (centered around the year 2000 emission target levels)

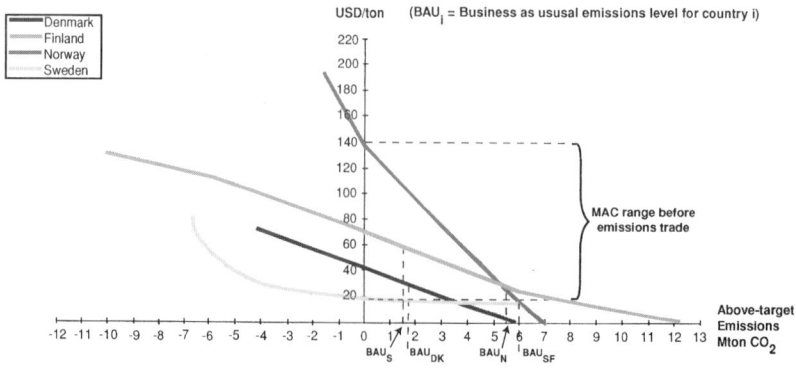

competitive -- aggregate trade gains, but also how successful each negotiating team had been in getting close to its particular potential trade gains maximum. This evaluation of their performance would then be published (see Bohm, 1997a).

The negotiations amounted to four days of bilateral trading by fax. Figure 2 shows the estimated negotiation-relevant MAC cost curves for the year 2000, centered at their respective emissions targets for that year. This reveals a considerable difference

Figure 3. Bids, Asks and Contracts
All countries

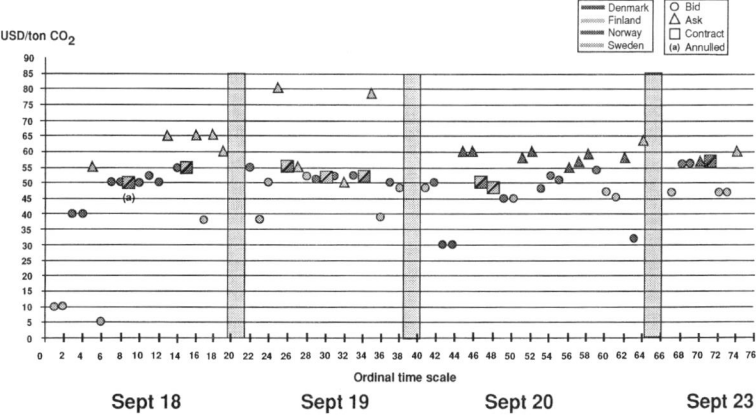

Figure 4. Marginal Social Abatement Costs after trade
(centered around the year 2000 emission target levels)

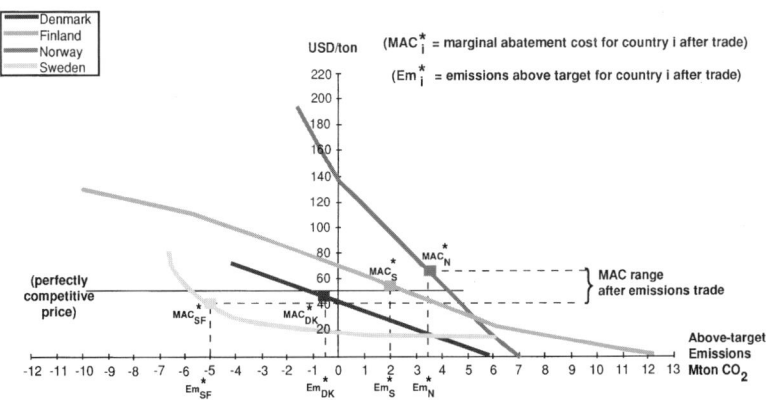

123

in MACs at the target level, actually much larger than has been presumed for so similar developed countries as these four. The BAU points in the Figure show where the countries expected their business-as-usual emissions level to be in the year 2000. Thus, the distance between BAU and the origin for each country indicates the predicted unilateral, or *ex ante* trade, emission reduction required to reach their emission targets.

Figure 3 is shown just to give a bird's eye view of the trade offers in terms of asks and bids that occurred during the four days and the squares show the six trade deals reached. Figure 4 shows where these deals took the four countries, two selling and two buying, where Finland -- the dominating seller -- and Denmark committed themselves to further reduce their emissions by Em^*_{SF} and Em^*_{DK} , and Norway and Sweden could exceed their target levels by Em^*_N and Em^*_S, respectively. This resulted in a sharp reduction of the MAC range, as can be seen from the Figure.

Recall the question posed for this study. Would a TQ treaty among a few developed countries be capable of achieving any significant reductions of the aggregate costs of commitments to binding emission targets? Specifically, how much of the aggregate perfectly competitive trade gains, relevant for a market with a large number of traders, could be attained? As can be approximately verified from Figure 4, the results were that

- the trade gains amounted to as much as 97% of the aggregate trade gains maximum, attainable if the market had performed as under perfect competition, and that
- emissions trade reduced the aggregate costs for reaching the targets by about 50%.

A TRADEABLE-QUOTA EXPERIMENT WITH DIPLO-MATS AS COUNTRY REPRESENTATIVES

We now move to the first test which is presented briefly only. Here, the purpose was to get an idea of how many countries -- in spring 1996, when the test took place -- could be willing to accept a specific TQ proposal, according to which

- all non-OECD countries were to receive carbon quotas large enough to keep them economically unharmed, and
- all OECD countries would share the costs of the reductions in global carbon emissions as implied by the treaty in the same proportion to GDP, around 1%, a figure often suggested in this context.

124

Remember that conventional wisdom at this time was -- and perhaps still is -- that a TQ agreement is a dead end. More specifically, the issue to be tested was how many in a world of 29 countries,
- including all the major players and
- with a reasonable coverage of the different regions of the world,
- all together covering some 90% of the world's carbon emissions,
would be willing to accept a take-it-or-leave-it proposal of the TQ treaty just indicated, at a future date that would be realistic for such a global proposal; the date suggested was 2005.

What approachable experimental subjects representing the 29 countries could say something interesting about this? For various reasons, it was deemed infeasible to get such responses from
- actual representatives of the countries
- country experts in an international organization like the World Bank, or
- academic country experts.
A more attractive alternative seemed to be to use, if possible, experienced generalist-diplomats in the service of one country's Ministry of Foreign Affairs -- persons who had recently been stationed in the country whose government they would be asked to represent and who had now left this country. To avoid revealing their identities to the governments in question or to any outside person, their names would be known only inside the Ministry.

These subjects would then be asked to carefully consider a necessarily rather comprehensive document describing the information issue, its background, the TQ proposal and its implications. They would also be told why they, as generalist diplomats, would be best suitable for evaluating 'their' government's likely reaction to the proposal against the background of their present -- 1996 -- knowledge of the government. This would mean that we would collapse the time between now and the assumed more realistic date for the proposal. Finally, they would have to be given a reason to respond. That reason, and hence the incentives for responding, would be given by a person at the top of the Ministry of Foreign Affairs who would ask the participants to cooperate in providing the solicited information. This information would also indicate that this person as well as others could read their responses inside the Ministry.

After a considerable period of discussion, the Swedish Ministry of Foreign Affairs allowed to let such a study be carried out. Number three in command at the Ministry agreed to write a cover letter, emphasizing that the reason for the Ministry's acceptance of the proposed study was that the study could provide relevant information for Sweden. The 29 participants were appointed, 24 of whom were ambassadors. In July of 1996, all 29 had responded by fax or mail to the Ministry.

Two rounds of questions were put to the participants. Here follows a summary of the responses in the first round only, where the question was: *Based on your knowledge of the government of the country you have been asked to represent, would this government be likely to say yes or no to the proposed treaty?*

- 17 of the 29 respondents said that "their" countries' governments would likely accept the proposal, which was
- true for 8 of 12 OECD countries, with all major countries (except Japan) saying yes, and
- true for 9 of 17 non-OECD countries, with the major countries -- China, India and Russia -- saying no.

A list of the 29 responses is presented in Table 1.

Taken at face value, the test indicates -- contrary to the views so far heard from several climate-change policy negotiators in the global community -- that a

Table 1. Responses to the TQ proposal

OECD countries (8 Yes, 4 No)			(Old) Non-OECD countries (9 Yes, 8 No)		
Australia	Yes		Brazil	Yes	
EU: Denmark		No	Chile	Yes	
Belgium	Yes		Mexico		No
Finland		No	China		No
France	Yes		India		No
Germany	Yes		Indonesia	Yes	
Spain		No	Israel	Yes	
Italy	Yes		Republic of Korea	Yes	
United Kingdom	Yes		Malaysia		No
Japan		No	Pakistan		No
Norway	Yes		Czech Republic		No
United States	Yes		Poland		No
			Russia		No
			Ukraine	Yes	
			Egypt	Yes	
			Kenya	Yes	
			Zambia	Yes	

considerable number of countries appear not to rule out joining a TQ treaty with implications of the type specified in the instructions. (For further information about this test, see Bohm, 1997b)

In summary, the two experimental studies indicate that TQ systems may attract a wider interest than from the US alone and that even a pioneering TQ treaty among a few developed countries can yield significant efficiency benefits. To some, these results might be taken to call for investments in more careful analyses and pilot testing of the TQ policy option than so far have taken place.

REFERENCES

Bohm, Peter. *Joint Implementation as Emissions Quota Trade: An Experiment Among Four Nordic Countries*, Nord 1997:4, Nordic Council of Ministers, Copenhagen, 1997a

Bohm, Peter. *Are Tradable Carbon Emissions Quotas Internationally Acceptable? An Inquiry with Diplomats as Country Representatives*, Nord 1997:8, Nordic Council of Ministers, Copenhagen, 1997b

Bovenberg, Lans and R. de Mooij, Environmental Levies and Distortionary Taxation, *American Economic Review*, vol. 84, no.4, September, 1085-1089, 1994

Goulder, Lawrence. *Environmental Taxation and the "Double Dividend": A Reader's Guide.* Paper presented at the International Institute of Public Finance 50th Congress, Cambridge, MA, August 22-25, 1994, also NBER Working Paper, no. 4896, 1994

Intergovernmental Panel on Climate Change (IPCC). *Climate Change 1995: Economic and Social Dimensions of Climate Change*, Contribution of Working Group III to the Second Assessment Report of the IPCC, Cambridge University Press, 1996

Pearce, David. D. The Role of Carbon Taxes in Adjusting to Global Warming, *Economic Journal*, vol. 101, 938-948, 1991

Sandmo, Agnar. Optimal Taxation in the Presence of Externalities, *Swedish Journal of Economics*, vol. 77, no. 1, 86-98, 1975

CHAPTER8 DECENTRALIZED GOVERN- MENT AND MACROECONOMIC CONTROL

PAUL BERND SPAHN[*]

INTRODUCTION

Recently, the option of channeling national resources through the budgets of lower tiers of government and of exploiting local tax potentials to a greater extent has found increasing attention. This is partly explained by successful development strategies based on regional rather than national initiatives (China); it is also nurtured by the forming of regional economic groupings (Mercosur, APEC) whereby the relationship between sovereign nation-states and centralized competencies has to be clarified.

As far as the allocation of resources is concerned, the benefits of decentralized government are usually unquestioned (see, however, Tanzi 1995). But, the multiplicity of government functions raises substantial problems for macroeconomic control at the national level. This is because local accountability calls not only for decentralized decision-making; it typically involves financial competencies as well—together with the right to borrow. Uncontrolled access to capital markets and mismanagement of budgets by local government may thus jeopardize efforts to stabilize the economy at the national level. Thus decentralization of government is not without risk for the stability of the economy.

---

[*] Fachbereich Wirtschaftswissenschaften, Johann Wolfgang Goethe-Universität, Frankfurt am Main, Germany.

THE CASE FOR CENTRALIZING THE STABILIZA-TION FUNCTION

The idea that decentralization of government jeopardizes macroeconomic stability goes back to Oates (1972) who presents a number of arguments in favor of centralizing monetary and fiscal policies. These arguments have recently been restated (Tanzi 1995, Prud'homme 1995) and they appear indeed intriguing. Generally, the case for centralizing macroeconomic stabilization policy is based on the following reasoning:

- The use of a national currency implies centralized monetary policy. Since monetary and fiscal policies are intertwined, centralized monetary policy seems to entail the case for centralizing fiscal policy.

- The monetization of public debt at local levels is likely to interfere with monetary policy. This may diminish the central bank's ability to pursue its national policy objectives.

- Any debt created through Keynesian demand management is internal for the nation, but external for regions. This entails inefficiency of decentralized stabilization policy through higher costs of borrowing.

- The impact of regional stabilization initiatives is usually negligible at the national level—because of its relative small size compared to the national budget. Furthermore, the openness of regional economies limits the effectiveness of local fiscal policy because any fiscal stimulus is exported to a high degree.

- Given regional spillovers of fiscal stimuli, local authorities will never provide enough stabilization because the costs are too high compared to the internal benefits of the policy.

- In order for centralized fiscal policies to be effective, further requirements have to be met however. The share of national taxes and government spending must be large relative to GDP; otherwise, the impact of national stabilization policies will be small. This means either a large government sector, a high degree of centralization, or both. Since local government can counteract central policies, a high degree of centralization is preferable.

EXAMINING THE CASE FOR CENTRALIZED STA-BILIZATION POLICY

More recently, the traditional wisdom of a centralized stabilization policy has been seriously questioned, mainly by European authors. On the one hand, Europeans widely accept the notion that monetary policy be centralized as long as sovereignty for this type of policy is vested in an institution which is independent from government.[1] On the other hand, the idea to centralize fiscal policy in the European Union (EU) is generally rejected. The political reasons for this are self-evident: In the EU, the thesis would lead to a strengthening of the supranational tiers, in particular through the widening of the European Commission's budget at the expense of nation states.[2] This would heavily inflict upon national sovereignty and contradict the 'subsidiarity principle'—formally adopted as a quasi-constitutional rule through Article 3b of the Maastricht-Treaty—which stipulates that the powers of EU institutions be limited to those functions that cannot be adequately performed by member states. This is an a-priori conjecture in favor of national sovereignty. Centralization is then the exception rather than the rule, and this must also apply to the stabilization function of government.

Although the rejection of centralized fiscal policy was mainly politically motivated, it calls for a thorough theoretical examination of the centralization hypothesis outlined above. Such examination was indeed successful in detecting a number of flaws in the conventional wisdom. The case for Keynesian demand management has most likely overemphasized the need for centralized macroeconomic policies, because

- *it assumes regionally symmetrical shocks.* One may well ask what the center government should do in the presence of regionally asymmetrical shocks that add to zero for the nation. There is no clear rule for fiscal policy in this case (Gramlich 1986);

- *it assumes a closed economy.* As Mundell (1963) has shown, any national fiscal

---

[1] Europeans have indeed been coordinating monetary policy through the EMS since 1979, and they now intend to create a Monetary Union (EMU) with a single currency by 1999. Monetary policy will be exerted by a European Central Bank which is independent from the Commission and from national and provincial government.

[2] Some authors have argued, however, that stabilization policy at the supranational level is possible with only very limited additional resources at the central level (see, for instance, Italiander and Pisani-Ferry 1992).

stimulus would be offset by an exchange-rate change in an open economy. The fiscal stimulus thus evaporates where the exchange rate is flexible. If there were an appropriate state fiscal response to regionally varying, but zero-sum shocks, this could eventually be neutral as to the exchange rate and still exhibit significant employment effects (Gramlich 1986);

- *it assumes segmented capital markets.* The idea that decentralized fiscal policy is more costly, because of higher borrowing costs for regional governments, is baseless for an economy where capital markets are free and access to international financing is unrestricted. Open, competitive capital markets will set a single interest rate for whatever debt is held by bondholders—abstracting of course from specific risk premia. Thus the debt of both tiers of government will, in principle, bear identical financing costs as expressed by the fixed rate of interest. Although specific risk premia may indeed exist for regional tiers of government, the assumption of centralized fiscal policy being less costly under these circumstances is unsound. It is not impossible that such costs will simply have to be borne by the central government—through explicit or implicit bail-out guarantees, or some type of 'national insurance'. This assumption is reasonable as long as capital markets are informed and rational. But worse: stabilization policy as national insurance against regional shocks may entail additional costs that could eventually exceed the cost of specific regional risk factors (see below);

- *it neglects supply-side effects of fiscal policy.* Fiscal policy is not simply 'demand management'. It will usually have an impact on the supply of goods and services through the way public resources are employed. This is particularly true for local public investment programs where the regional incidence of the supply effects is more evident. Here local governments are commonly better equipped to cope with local unemployment as they have easier access to pertinent information, can respond more speedily to local needs, and often control appropriate policy instruments for immediate implementation;

- *it neglects built-in stabilizers.* Fiscal stabilization is in great part automatic through built-in elements of the tax-transfer system. This is true in particular for highly elastic revenue (like the income tax) and selected expenditure components (e.g., unemployment benefits). But built-in stabilizers are not confined to the central government alone. They can work at all levels of government. This depends ultimately on the assignment of revenue and outlay functions. Moreover, trade among regions tends to cushion asymmetrical shocks and is therefore also automatically stabilizing without necessarily implying discretionary policy intervention.

- *it assumes non-cooperative behavior of lower tiers of government.* The case for centralized fiscal policy makes strong assumptions on non-cooperative behavior of local governments. This is often based on the assertion that local tiers have generally an inclination towards cash-flow oriented budget performance which would be pro-cyclical and hence destabilizing. Even if this thesis is accepted, any poise to run budgets on current revenue can be controlled through appropriate fiscal arrangements, a suitable assignment of revenue and outlay responsibilities and a well-conceived system of intergovernmental transfers. In practice, effective coordination mechanisms exist for decentralized fiscal policy. The problem is to avoid perverse incentives in the coordination machinery.

it assumes local borrowing to impinge strongly on monetary policy. In practice, centralized fiscal constitutions tend to consider money creation to constitute an alternative mean of financing the budget, and national governments then have to keep a firm grip on their central bank. It can be shown that central bank independence is usually greater under decentralized government (Huther/Shah 1996) which implies the chance for stronger monetary discipline and macroeconomic stability when fiscal policy is decentralized. Centralization of fiscal policy is then likely to put monetary stability more at risk than under decentralized government.

NATIONAL STABILIZATION POLICY AS AN IN-SURANCE DEVICE

As stressed before, central fiscal policy is tantamount to an insurance contract where the higher level government promises to even out income variations across regions that result from regionally asymmetrical shocks. Alternatively, regional governments could borrow 'abroad' (meaning 'outside the region', not necessarily on international capital markets) in order to stabilize its regional economy through appropriate local investment. However, the case for insurance compared to borrowing is relatively weak. This is in view of the following facts (CEPR 1993):

- In the case of supra-regional insurance of local economies there is always the risk of 'moral hazard' behavior of the latter. Local authorities could then be encouraged to inflict economic shocks upon their economies (e.g. through their budgets by bending to unrealistic wage claims) because they can hope to be eventually 'bailed out' by the insurer—the central government. Equally, national insurance tends to honor excessive consumption on the part of regional economies and governments whereby budget constraints are softened through the implicit or explicit guarantees of the insurance 'contract'.[3] The risk of moral hazard was widely perceived within the EU where the Maastricht-Treaty has defined quantitative budget limits for potential adherence to the Monetary Union, and a Stability Pact has introduced the possibility of financial sanctions against members in order to contain careless budget behavior after the creation of a monetary union. "The argument is that monetary union requires restrictions on member states to prevent the latter from overborrowing, because excessive debt may lead to a bail-out by the Union and threaten the stability of the single currency." (Eichengreen/von Hagen 1996, p. 2).

- Even where regional shocks are truly exogenous, insurance may be counterproductive where shocks are permanent rather than transitory. It is often difficult to decide whether unemployment is simply a response to a cyclical downturn or whether structural adjustment is needed in order to restore full-employment. Insurance may then deepen a recession by 'easing' hard budget constraints and by postponing the necessary structural adjustment (as unemployment insurance discourages labor mobility at the individual level). Conversely, borrowing by regional governments is likely to encourage more rapid adjustment policies because of the need to convince capital markets (and parliaments), and because the costs of non-adjustment are unfettered and more poignant.

- Equally important is the possibility that an insurance scheme could collapse under a long-lasting shock that was misinterpreted as temporary. This is particularly true if structural adjustment had not been initiated. It could then lead to tensions among local jurisdictions where some regions begin to perceive themselves as 'eternal paymasters' for other, poorer regions that lack the initiative for structural reforms (e.g. in Italy). Renegotiation of existing arrangements (or opting-out clauses) would however reduce the ex ante value of insurance because of a time-inconsistent behavior—which, again, entails additional costs. Time-inconsistency can also occur in the case of borrowing, but private capital markets should normally be able to limit such behavior more easily by smoothly accommodating their lending conditions to newly available information.

- And finally, macroeconomic shocks are not independently distributed among regions but highly correlated, which reduces the need for mutual insurance. Trade among open, but independent regions works as an implicit insurance device in this case.

- In the specific case of the EU, where autonomous budgeting of sovereign nations

---

[3] There are a number of examples which demonstrate that this eventuality is not simply theoretical, but relevant in practice. The German intergovernmental equalization rules are overly generous to regions with persistent and recurring budget deficits (e.g., Bremen or Saarland) which has so far had little effect on fiscal discipline and adjustment in these regions. (Compare the Saarland with Luxembourg in a similar, even slightly disadvantaged, geographical position where no bail-out guarantee exists, and the importance of fiscal discipline as an engine for structural adjustment will be understood.) In Argentina, the fiscal system provides overly generous transfers to the poorer and more sparsely-populated provinces in per-capita terms, again with little incentives to structural reform.

has to be respected, a further problem exists: adverse selection. Countries normally wish to link up with countries that are better risks than themselves, and they want to exclude those which appear less reliable.[4] In the aggregate, this is simply impossible, which precludes any collective insurance arrangement a priori. Federations can make insurance compulsory, but in the European Union there is a risk of a persisting political dead-lock among member states, or of a 'two-speed' process of monetary and fiscal integration and intergovernmental cooperation.

REVENUE AND EXPENDITURE ASSIGNMENT

There are essentially two distinct approaches to achieve stabilization under decentralized government. These hinge on the philosophy that guides the assignment of revenues and expenditures within the nation.

Either 'steadily flowing' revenue sources and cyclically invariant outlay functions are assigned to lower tiers which facilitates their budget planning and avoids the procyclical conduct of budgetary policies. The steady behavior of local governments will then act as an embedded, cyclically neutral, and hence stabilizing force, and demand management (if any) can be left entirely to the central government.

Or the Constitution assigns elastic output functions and volatile taxes to local tiers, then local budget flexibility is needed and special management tools have to be employed. Budget flexibility includes, of course, the right to borrow. From this follows that regional governments must have sufficient 'own sources' of revenue in order to minimize pressures for national bail-outs (von Hagen/Eichengreen 1996).

Since there is a clear case in favor of decentralizing the allocation function of government—and the provision of public goods at the local level is by its very nature steadfast and persistent (like services in basic education and health)—the first model of decentralization is often adapted which avoids the conflict with the objectives of macroeconomic stabilization. The financing of local budgets must then be based on stable local revenue sources (like a property tax or local fees for services) and on intergovernmental transfers that are ideally invariant to the whims of the business

---

[4] This is visible in the case of Germany where a majority of voters is said to object the forming of a Monetary Union in Europe. Germany has benefited from monetary stability more than other European countries in the past.

cycle. Grants have an advantage here over revenue-sharing means because the latter typically include cycle-sensitive taxes. Local borrowing can be confined to financing revenue-generating public investment at the subnational level that lie within the realm of their outlay responsibilities. This requires a set of institutional rules and central government surveillance, but little budget flexibility is needed for lower tiers of government.

If, however, local governments are to provide services that are sensitive to the business cycle—as for instance social assistance in the case of German municipalities or the states in the United States—flexibility is needed on both the revenue and expenditure sides of local budgets. These provisions should not encourage local governments to pursue an activist macroeconomic stabilization policy. On the contrary! But they should secure the full working of built-in stabilizers at lower levels of government under these conditions.

Budget flexibility is reduced

- when the budgeting process is rigid, i.e. when volume and structure of the budget are hampered to react to a changing business environment;

- when outlays and revenues are 'captured' in funds, or if a transfer of means across chapters of a budget is impossible;

- when revenue is earmarked to certain functions, in particular if the revenue is volatile (e.g., oil revenue tied to a road fund);

- when local borrowing is restricted or disallowed.

Only the last point is somewhat controversial and needs further discussion here although a full account of the problems of local borrowing cannot be given.[5]

In spite of the fact that institutional restrictions on local borrowing will reduce budget flexibility and hence jeopardize the full working of built-in stabilizers of the fiscal system, many countries limit such ability in some way or another. As mentioned already, the EU attempts to restrain even the borrowing of national governments through standard budget criteria and the onus of financial sanctions in the case of

---

[5] See, for instance, Ter-Minassian (1996) and Gandenberger (1996).

leniency. This is motivated essentially by concerns that local governments could—either through moral hazard or a misinterpretation of cyclical developments—incur debt that proves to be unsustainable in the long run, and the national government would then have to bail them out. It is for this reason that Eichengreen and von Hagen insist on a sufficiently high level of own resources for lower levels of government because this is indeed a necessary prerequisite for a credible pledge of the central government to let regional governments go bust eventually. The smaller is the relative importance of own resources at lower levels of government, the less trustworthy is a 'no bail-out' commitment of the central government. But the 'no bail-out' predicament is essential for private capital markets to assess specific lending risks correctly—which could then discipline regional governments implicitly through higher risk premia on interests. This is why the Maastricht budget criteria are neither needed to contain moral hazard, nor are they imperative for limiting debt exposure of European national governments as long as these control sufficiently large public resources of their own jurisdictions, and capital markets are allowed to adapt freely. It can even be argued that the Maastricht criteria could eventually jeopardize macroeconomic stability and hence become a source of inflationary pressures instead.[6]

INTERGOVERNMENTAL TRANSFERS

Own local revenue is the cornerstone of fiscal decentralization because it installs an efficiency-enhancing tax-benefit link and it fosters local accountability.[7] But whatever local tax system is established in a country, there will be need for grants or revenue sharing because local expenditure needs typically tend to outstrip local resources.

---

[6] The argument, made by Eichengreen and von Hagen (1996), is that states with a taste for tax-smoothing services—but hindered to supply them through the budget criteria—would exert pressure onto European institutions to supply them. This may lead to a larger accumulation of debt than if member states were free to borrow. This arguments is partly invalidated by the independence of the European central bank, partly by the balanced-budget requirement for the Commission (the European Investment Bank is unlikely to play a major role in this process). It must be noted, however, that the Maastricht budget criteria have exerted strong pressure onto governments to face the need for political, institutional and structural adjustment of their welfare systems, the provision of public services, and of budgetary processes—including the sourcing out and the privatization of government function. This in itself is a positive contribution of the Maastricht Treaty and its budget criteria.

[7] On the criteria for local taxation, see Spahn (1995).

This is particularly true for countries where social infrastructure is considered to be a public or merit good—for instance primary education or basic health—and responsibilities for such functions are decentralized—which they commonly are. Where such functions can be privatized (and outsourcing is socially accepted) the scope for mobilizing resources is, of course, much higher.

The design of any grants system is of prime importance. Whatever solution is adopted, intergovernmental fiscal relations should be based on stable, transparent, non-arbitrary, universal, and non-negotiable rules. These rules should avoid destabilizing incentives and must not interfere with the principle of accountability. The following may serve as a guidance:

If there is a vertical fiscal imbalance between local fiscal capacity on one hand, and outlay responsibilities assigned to lower tiers of government on the other, the gap is typically bridged through financial transfers in the form of unconditional revenue grants or through revenue sharing with the central authority. No strings are attached to these funds, but the transfers should be based on standard criteria of fiscal capacity or expenditure needs that cannot be influenced through strategic behavior of recipient governments. This together with the lower tiers' ability to pursue an independent tax policy guarantees that the latter can freely respond to variations in demand for local public services without penalty in the form of reduced transfers to the jurisdiction. It allows tax financing at least at the margin, which is a precondition for public sector efficiency. Pure 'gap filling' would be tantamount to a full bail-out, and it would encourage inefficient spending and waste.

Whether the emphasis is on the local provision of standard public services—with 'steady' behavior of lower level governments—or a more flexible budget approach, intergovernmental transfers should ideally avoid volatility. This is to allow local activities to evolve steadfastly within the stable-policy framework, and, in the flexible approach, it focuses their attention on those budget elements that are under their control: local taxation, expenditures and borrowing. Grants can be stabilized more easily than revenue sharing through 'closed funding'. Revenue sharing is usually based on rigid formulae and is therefore difficult to untie from the buoyancy of the national tax system. Therefore, the sharing of highly volatile taxes, in particular the sharing of natural resource taxes (e.g. on mineral oil), should be limited.

In order to render revenue sharing more steadfast, a 'stabilization scheme' is needed eventually. Under such a scheme, the lower tiers of government would not lose their entitlements to a shared tax, but the actual transfers are based on rules that 'sterilize' part of their revenue in periods of boom, and release it in periods of shortage.[8]

Narrowing the scope of revenue sharing onto the less volatile taxes does not solve the foregoing problem, because all buoyant taxes are typically revenue elastic. Moreover, this practice would focus the federal government's tax policy on taxes that are excluded from sharing and thus introduce a distortion into the national tax system.

However, the federal government should preserve the right to levy and vary non-shared taxes in order to have an instrument for macroeconomic stabilization at the margin.

A general-revenue grants system based on standard fiscal capacity and need criteria can establish vertical fiscal balance, it is neutral as to fiscal (dis)incentives, it can be made consistent with the idea of fairness among regions (equalization), and it can be conceived to be cyclically neutral and to foster macroeconomic stability. Australia has established such a system for the Commonwealth's general-revenue grants to the states (Spahn/Shah 1995, Rye/Searl 1996). But the Australian system is overly ambitious and very onerous in terms of information requirements. Simpler criteria will achieve similar results and still be efficient, equitable and stabilizing.

---

[8] The Colombian Oil Revenue Stabilization Fund is inspired by this philosophy. There are various possibilities to stabilize intergovernmental transfers: The tax base can be shared (instead of revenue) as revenue is typically more volatile for progressive taxes; tax sharing and grants formulae can be based on moving averages; revenue sharing can be indexed on macro indicators (like nominal GDP); the tax base can be 'capped' to exclude cyclical parts (e.g. only confined to the proportional 'floor' of a progressive personal income tax); and the yearly increments of transfers can be limited.

COORDINATION OF BUDGETS IN DECENTRAL-IZED GOVERNMENT

BENEFITS AND COSTS OF COORDINATION

As mentioned earlier, the case for centralizing the stabilization functions neglects the potentials of coordination among governments and budget surveillance and control. The benefits of budget coordination can be summarized as follows:

- Coordination can improve the allocation of public resources through a better exchange of information.

- Coordination among local jurisdictions and among the lower tier and the central government can 'internalize' spillovers conferred to other regions and to the nation.

- Concerted action can reduce the total burden of public debt by avoiding the overexpansion of uncoordinated fiscal policies.

But coordination is not obtained without costs.

- There are political costs of establishing clear and uniform criteria for joint action.

- There are costs of institutionalizing information exchange and operational procedures for coordination policy actions.

- There are costs relating to strategic behavior of all tiers of government because there may be a divergence between individual and collective rationality, and there is a 'free-rider' problem for governments at all levels.

Despite the importance of some costs of coordination, these will eventually have to be borne either because the benefits of a decentralized provision of local services may by far outweigh such costs, and/or because a centralized government sector is politically unfeasible (like, in the extreme, in Bosnia or West Bank-Gaza).

BUDGET AUTONOMY AND BUDGET SURVEILLANCE

Budget coordination in multilayer government has found increasing attention in recent years as a consequence of the Maastricht project for a Monetary Union in Europe. Stability-oriented European governments are concerned that a Central European Bank would have to finance large public deficits of non-cooperating member states—

directly or indirectly—which would jeopardize its ability to control the money supply, and hence inflation. For this reason, the European Central Bank will be independent from European institutions and from national governments. For the same reasons, formal budget criteria for public deficits and debt relative to GDP were defined for prospective entrants to the Monetary Union in order to coordinate their fiscal policies and to install budgetary discipline. Countries that do not fulfill these criteria do not qualify for entry—an effective sanction—, and, even after entry, the Maastricht criteria will continue to be surveyed with certain financial sanctions in the case of non-compliance. The Commission has to monitor the budgets of member states and to report regularly to the Council in the context of its medium-term economic and budgetary outlook. The Council continually forms judgments on 'excessive' deficits and debt, which will provide valuable information to capital markets. Markets are then assured to respond by adjusting corresponding risk premia which would create incentives to restoring budgetary discipline. Eventually, 'fines' of up to 0.5 per cent of national GDP could be imposed by the Council.

However, it is doubtful whether the EU will use the arsenal of financial sanctions in the case of non-compliance. After all, national governments remain sovereign in formulating their budget policies, and effective sanctions of a supranational body will be hard to implement without political tensions. Also, the market's ability to impose risk premia on certain government bonds is doubtful where it will speculate on the likelihood of an effective bail-out, by the Union, of defaulting member countries.[9] Some countries may lose interest in complying with the criteria, and 'moral hazard' could eventually become a problem.

This view has however one important shortcoming: it is essentially static and does not count on institutional evolution. Institutional arrangements tend to be modified in the light of economic and political transaction costs. This is also true for budgetary procedures and policies. The very objective of entering into the Monetary Union may change political conditions and constitutional arrangements rendering a more responsible fiscal policy possible in the longer run. Also, new arrangements and institutions will be formed that allow to effectively coordinate fiscal policies at the

---

[9] The Mexican crisis of 1994 and the Asian crisis of 1998 illustrate that countries such as the United States, and even the World Community and its international financial institutions would bail-out countries in financial difficulties even without formal commitments as may exist in a Monetary Union.

European level while preserving subsidiarity. Ultimately, new instruments to control and coordinate the behavior of national governments might be developed. In the meantime, the most effective instruments of policy coordination is information.

Coordination of budgets is a particularly sensitive issue in view of budget autonomy of lower tiers of government. This is why it should mainly be based on information exchange and guidance by formal principles or criteria. These are subtle, but powerful policy instruments. Formal budget coordination seems to be the only possibility to reconcile political autonomy with the need to achieve some degree of harmonization of budgets in federal states and unitary states with an autonomous local sector. Formal coordination may be extremely successful in material terms because it affects political behavior—as can be observed in post-Maastricht Europe. The very existence of the budget criteria has encouraged institutional reform and focused fiscal policies on the key issue: budget discipline.

As an example, Germany exercises formal budget coordination of federal and subnational governments through its Law on Budgetary Principles. Such principles may have a common significance for budget coordination for other decentralized government systems which warrants to discuss them briefly here.

FORMAL BUDGET COORDINATION PRINCIPLES

The Law on Budgetary Principles of 1969[10] attempts to coordinate the budget process and its implementation by guidance through uniform principles to be observed by all public authorities. Such principles extend from very general provisions (like the budget principles of gross estimates, comprehensiveness, unity, clarity, periodicity and antecedence, efficiency and cost effectiveness, authorization to spend and to commit resources) to more specific rules regarding the preparation of the budget, to accounting and the rendering of accounts (including the classification of the budget), to auditing and discharge, and to rules applying for special funds set up under federal or state legislation. Also, the budget process was made more transparent in order to assess the budget's effects on the general course of the economy. The second part of this legislation contains regulations that are generally and directly applicable to the

---

[10] This Law was published in English, together with other relevant material under the title 'Federal German Budget Legislation', by the Federal Ministry of Finance, Bonn, November 1988.

Federation and the states—like multi-year financial planning and the exchange of budget-related information.

The Law start from the premise that uniform national policy goals can only be realized if public budgets of central and subcentral governments can be monitored effectively and in a standardized fashion. Otherwise the coordination of budgets is bound to fail. This has led to a uniform framework of budget classification and outline whereby the need to form economic categories and to relate budget items to categories of the National Accounts has played a prominent role. Nevertheless, the accounting principles of the budget remain cash-oriented while the National Accounts attempt to realize an accrual concept. A cash-based budget concepts is, however, closely related to financial statements which record sources of funding the deficit and the net financial position of governments *vis-à-vis* private sectors. Obviously, given a harmonized framework of budget classification this must facilitate the consolidation of budgets across different authorities at various layers of government.

Although the annual budget is cash-oriented, *i. e.* only income and expenditure items are accounted for that are expected to lead to financial operations during the budget year, all authorities are obliged to assess—on separate accounts—the expected need for spending authorizations for future budget years.

The Law has reemphasized the classical principles of comprehensiveness of budgets and of accounting in gross (rather than net) terms. *All* public expenditure and revenue should appear on public budgets and be subject to national consolidation, and, ideally, no special funds should be tolerated that, once established, easily escape democratic control and create 'turf'.[11] 'Off-budget' funding is indeed a prominent instrument for circumventing budget constraints and to protect special interests. Moreover, expenditure items should appear in full cost terms and the consolidation of such expenditure with specific revenue items is ruled out. There are exceptions to this precept, however. Financing of public budgets through capital markets and the

---

[11] The only typical exception to this rule are social security funds. Moreover, temporary funds (like the *Treuhandgesellschaft,* an institution which was to privatize Eastern Germany's state firms and property, or the Germany Unity Fund which managed East German public debt) were established in the context of German unification, but later integrated in government budgets. In Latin America, there is often an excessive reliance on special funds and the earmarking of taxes and transfers for specific purposes, based on purely sectoral considerations (e.g. Colombia). This implies inefficiencies as discussed before.

redemption of public debt are shown in net (rather than gross) terms. This was seen to be more relevant for evaluating the impact of budgetary policy on capital markets and, eventually, on monetary policy.

Other rules for budget coordination are of a procedural nature, for instance those relating to the preparation, the establishment and execution of the budget as well as formal budget control and auditing.[12] Also, the annual budgets (calendar year) have to be embedded in a medium-term financial plan which is established jointly by a Financial Planning Council representing all three tiers of government. Its objective is to reach agreement on the coordination of general budgetary policy and to support the federal government in its statutory task to achieve a harmonized stability-oriented budgetary and fiscal policy. The Financial Planning Council is, however, bound by the Constitution to respect the autonomous and independent fiscal administration of states and the right of self-governance of municipalities. It therefore acts through recommendations which are non-binding yet have a strong impact on budget estimates and budget execution (including the level of borrowing). This requires, however, a cooperative environment in which independent budgetary authorities are willing to implement such recommendations within the realm of their responsibilities.

Medium-term financial planning is of prime importance in a situation where budgets are more and more determined by financially open-ended welfare programs. Such programs tend to establish eligibility criteria for certain transfers and services and legislation is often passed without regard to its long-term impact on budgets, because eligibility is difficult to anticipate (e.g. the need for old-age care). It also hinges on administrative criteria and value judgments (for instance, what kind of health treatment is society expected to support). Even where the financial impact of legislation is easier to evaluate (e.g. for public pensions through demographic projections), politicians—who tend to be myopic and loath to glance beyond the term of their mandate—often do not consider such consequences. Moreover, a cash-oriented

---

[12] Before the budgetary reform of 1969, not a single federal budget law was established before the beginning of the relevant fiscal year, yet, even after the reform, the implementation procedure did not function satisfactorily since the legislature tended to delay adopting the budget. A decision of the Constitutional Court of 1977 obliging parliament to approve the budget within the prescribed time limits was successful, however, and the federal budget was regularly established before the beginning of the fiscal year. Detailed instructions on financial and budgetary administration are entrenched in administrative regulations pertaining to the Budget Law.

budgeting system tends to underrate such consequences even though a medium-term financial plan may put short-run legislation into a longer perspective. This is true, at least, for the *immediate* consequences of investment projects, for instance. Whether this is sufficient, is doubtful, and suggestions to reform the budgetary process and its accounting framework emphasize the need to supplement the cash concept with an accruals concept for the public budget.

REFORMING THE FRAMEWORK OF PUBLIC BUDGETING AND CONTROL

In recent years, public budgeting has been criticized in view of the need to control fiscal policy and to coordinate budgets on the basis of a harmonized system of accounting and performance measurement (Buschor/Schedler 1994). It is acknowledged that traditional budgeting has its strengths in allowing a systematic presentation and control of policy implementation as to its financial resources imputed and used. It also facilitates to bridge the gap between policy implementation and financing the public purse. However, there are a number of drawbacks that need to be tackled in order to monitor public sector performance and to allow effective formal budget coordination in a multi-government setting.

- Public sector accounting should reflect the use of resources as costs like any private sector business institution.

- Public sector accounting should indicate the level of present commitments for future budgets and future generations.

- Public sector accounting should ideally allow some monitoring of performance-based or service-cost indicators.

- Public sector accounting should reflect the net asset position of governments at all levels.

New Zealand and the ACT in Australia have recently pioneered public sector accounting on the basis of Generally Agreed Accounting Principles (GAAP). The reporting system is accruals-based[13], but it also reports on cash flows. Moreover, it attempts to monitor net public debt as well as the impact of the budget's operating

---

[13] An example of the implications of shifting from a cash to an accrual basis is that if the Crown planned to dispose of an asset below fair market price (necessitating a write-off of part of the value) this would be recognized explicitly in the budget projections.

balance and revaluation changes on net worth. The purpose of such reporting is to add to the integrity and credibility of the government's statements. Such comprehensive and standardized reporting and financial planning could also be used to foster intergovernmental coordination and cooperation in a multilayer government setting and it may be used to corroborate a no-bail-out commitment of the central government. There are also attempts to measure governments' net wealth position, and interjurisdictional comparisons may serve to establish service/cost indicators in order to monitor public sector performance[14]. If the aim is to practice a 'golden rule' of public sector borrowing—i.e. access to capital markets is restrained to financing real public assets the benefits of which extend over several periods—it would be useful to split the budget into a current and a capital budget (as in some European countries, e.g. Luxembourg). New Zealand has extended this approach to monitor the development of net government value with the aim of controlling intertemporal budget restrictions.

Generational accounting is another tool that has come to some prominence in recent years (Auerbach/Gokhale/Kotlikoff 1994, Sturrock 1995). It attempts to evaluate the net redistribution of public resources across generations and the sustainability of fiscal policies in the longer run. A key concept is the net fiscal residuum. The present value of expected lifetime transfer receipts for each age cohort is subtracted from the percent value of expected life-time taxes for each group. This serves to measure the degree of fiscal redistribution among generations, and it allows to assess the explicit and implicit liabilities of welfare systems that will impinge on future budget positions—in particular those related with aging populations (Kuné 1993 and Chand/Jaeger 1996, International Monetary Fund 1996).

The implementation of such concepts requires highly controversial assumptions (e.g., on a single discount rate, the incidence of taxes, etc.) and it imposes a heavy demand on data. In addition, projections based on generational accounting methods are subject to uncertainties such as the rate of growth, demographic change (e.g., migration),

---

[14] Interestingly, the scheme for distributing unconditional grants to the states as developed by the Australian Grants Commission has generated a valuable set of information allowing such interjurisdictional comparisons of performance. It does not only provide useful information; it also combines with an incentive mechanism that tends to improve on sector performance since grants are accorded only at a 'standard level' of services. The opposite would result from 'gap filling' which would work as a disincentive to controlling costs.

and life expectancy. It is obvious that such concepts provide useful insights on the long-term sustainability of budgets, but they cannot substitute budgeting itself. Fiscal consolidation must always be carried out on the basis of 'hard' financial data and customary budgeting. Accrual accounts, generational accounts and additional information can only be subsidiary.

DECENTRALIZATION AND INFORMATION

Information policies are of key importance for decentralized government. Information is needed to render coordination effective, to inform lower-level governments and their electorates on national priorities, to foster interregional cooperation, to establish transparent rules for the distribution of financial resources among jurisdictions, to measure tax bases and potentials and to monitor the efficiency and cost-effectiveness of providing public services at the regional level. It is also important to spur competition among jurisdictions and to foster innovation.

The availability of data is therefore crucial for the success of decentralizing government. It is not sufficient to based policies on existing data and prevailing perceptions since these tend to support the status quo rather than decentralization as a means to improve social welfare. "New information would probably force a debate and induce a change in policies" (Inter-American Bank 1994, p. 192), which may alter the balance of interests. This largely explains the resistance against comprehensive information policies and new reporting schemes of certain influential groups which benefit under the present arrangements.

Information is also likely to affect existing institutions whose functioning (and even existence) may be questioned under the auspices of decentralization. This applies in particular to the vertical functional funds which thrive on earmarked taxes or grants. This may explain the resistance against information policies of bureaucrats and their 'clients' who benefit from the scheme. Despite such political frictions, decentralization must proceed through wider and better information in order to allow effective control and to built reliable new institutions for intergovernmental cooperation.

CONCLUSIONS

Decentralization can, but it must not jeopardize macroeconomic stability. Casual empiricism to the contrary neglects the fact that local tiers often have to operate in an unstable macro framework and their behavior thus reflects adaptive, but not necessarily unstable budget performance. The fact, for instance, that Argentina and Brazil have had severe problems in controlling lower tiers of government after their stabilization programs of the early 1990s is no proof that decentralization of government is *per se* jeopardizing macroeconomic stability. It simply reflects the fact that the 'old' institutional arrangements do no longer function under the new regime and that institutional reform is required.

Destabilizing behavior of local governments can be avoided through appropriate incentive structures and effective mechanisms of intergovernmental cooperation. Incentives can be economic and financial. They can also result from the workings of the political system, election rules, and the mechanisms that allow interest groups to inject their voice into the functioning of government. Economic incentives are directly related to the assignment of revenue and outlay responsibilities among the tiers of government. Ideally, a close link between taxes and expenditures is needed to enhance public welfare under decentralized government. Also intergovernmental transfers may convey wrong signals. But there is a set of criteria that can be used to design a transfer system that avoids disincentives and is prone to achieve fiscal balance, efficiency, equity and macroeconomic stability at the same time. Specific forms of intergovernmental cooperation, budget surveillance and information exchange may constitute a subtle complement for achieving stability under decentralized government.

REFERENCES

Auerbach, Alan J., Jagadeesh Gokhale and Laurence J. Kotlikoff (1994), 'Generational Accounting: A Meaningful Way to Evaluate Fiscal Policy', *Journal of Economic Perspectives*, Vol. 8, No. 1, 73-94.

Buschor, Ernst, and Schedler, Kuno (1994), eds., *Perspectives on Performance Measurement and Public Sector Accounting*, Haupt: Berne - Stuttgart - Vienna.

CEPR (1993), *Making Sense of Subsidiarity: How Much Centralization for Europe?*, Monitoring European Integration 4, A CEPR Annual Report (November).

Chand, Sheetal K. and Albert Jaeger (1996), *Aging Populations and Public Pension Schemes*,

IMF Occasional Paper, No.147, International Monetary Fund, Washington D.C., (December).

Eichengreen, Barry, and Jürgen von Hagen (1996), *Fiscal Policy and Monetary Union: Is There A Tradeoff Between Federalism and Budgetary Restrictions?'*, Working Paper No. 5517, National Bureau of Economic Research, Cambridge, Mass. (March).

Gandenberger, Otto (1996), *Coordination of Macroeconomic Policy and Fiscal Decentralization - A European Perspective*, Unpublished paper prepared for CEPAL/GTZ, University of Munich.

Gramlich, Edward E. (1987), 'Federalism and Federal Deficit Reduction', *National Tax Journal*, Vol. 40, 299-313.

Huther, Jeff and Anwar Shah (1996), *A Simple Measure of Good Governance and its Application to the Debate on the Appropriate Level of Fiscal Decentralization*, Unpublished draft paper, The World Bank, Washington, D.C., (September).

Inter-American Development Bank (1994), *Economic and Social Progress in Latin America*, Washington D.C..

International Monetary Fund (1996), *World Economic Outlook*, Washington D.C..

Italianer, Alexander and Jean Pisani-Ferry (1992), 'Systèmes budgétaires et amortissement des chocs régionaux: implications pour l'Union économique et monétaire', *Economie Prospective Internationale*, No. 51, 49-69.

Kuné, Jan B., and others (1993), *The Hidden Liabilities of the Basic Pensions System in the Member States*, Centre for European Policy Studies Working Paper, Brussels (November).

Mundell, Robert A. (1963), 'Capital Mobility and Stabilization Policy under Fixed and Flexible Exchange Rates', *Canadian Journal of Economics and Political Science*, Vol 29 (November), 475-85.

Oates, Wallace E. (1972), *Fiscal Federalism*, Harcourt-Brace Jovanovich.

Prud'homme, Rémy (1995), 'The Dangers of Decentralization', *The World Bank Research Observer*, Vol. 10, No. 2, 201-26.

Rye, C. R., and R. J. Searl (1996), 'The Fiscal Transfer System in Australia', in Ehtisham Ahmad, ed., *Designing and Implementing Inter-governmental Transfers*, International Monetary Fund (forthcoming).

Spahn, Paul Bernd (1995), 'Local Taxation: Principles and Scope', in Jayanta Roy (ed.), *Macroeconomic Management and Fiscal Decentralization*, EDI Seminar Series, The World Bank, Washington D.C., 221-32.

Spahn, Paul Bernd and Anwar Shah (1995), 'Intergovernmental Fiscal Relations in Australia', in Jayanta Roy (ed.), *Macroeconomic Management and Fiscal Decentralization*, EDI Seminar Series, The World Bank, Washington D.C. 49-72.

Sturrock, Jon (1995), *Who Pays and When? An Assessment of Generational Accounting*, Congressional Budget Office, Washington D.C.

Tanzi, Vito (1996), *Fiscal Federalism and Decentralization: A Review of Some Efficiency and Macroeconomic Aspects*, Annual Bank Conference on Development Economics 1995, The World Bank, Washington D.C., 295-316.

Ter-Minassian, Teresa (1996), *Borrowing by Subnational Governments: Issues and Selected International Experiences*, Unpublished IMF Paper on Policy Analysis and Assessment, International Monetary Fund, Fiscal Affairs Department (April).

CHAPTER9 FOREIGN DIRECT INVEST-
MENT : RULES VERSUS DISCRETION

ALAN A. TAIT[*]

INTRODUCTION

What can we learn about making international rules governing foreign direct investment (FDI) from existing practices? The only truly global rules on investment at present are incorporated in the Articles setting up the World Trade Organization (WTO).[2] These seek to reduce distortions and impediments to international trade, and to increase investment security when setting up establishments to gain market access by establishing a framework of transparent and enforceable rules within the ambit of a rules-based institution. However, outside trade circles, these WTO rules are not widely known, appreciated or understood; they tend to be complex and selective, yet their potential relationship to the proposed OECD rules on investment is important for the future development of international investment. An informed debate on foreign direct investment should not take place without an appreciation of these issues and the difficulties and options they present. Some lessons may be drawn.

Like a Shakespearean play, we have to get our characters on stage to know their names and relationships. Let us turn to the actors. The Marrakesh Agreement establishing the WTO is not the easiest document to find your way around [WTO,

---

[*] Special Trade Representative and Director, Geneva Office of the International Monetary Fund, Geneva, Switzerland [1]

[1] The views expressed are those of the author and do not necessarily represent those of the Fund.

[2] There are some 1,310 bilateral investment treaties involving some 161 countries, but these are very far from possible global investment rules.

1994]. Incorporating the Uruguay Round (UR) and its Ministerial decisions, the General Agreement on Tariffs and Trade 1994 (GATT 1994), but not the extensive schedules of tariff concessions and services commitments, still runs to 558 pages of fairly arid prose. But for good or ill, this rather unlovable document is crucial for the conduct of world trade. Until the UR, the trade covered by GATT meant trade in goods. The burgeoning importance of trade in services in the 1980s, and the later explosion of FDI,[3] drew attention to the importance of market presence (requiring FDI) and the need for rules to deal with trade in services and related investment. This led to the General Agreement on Trade in Services (GATS) and the Agreement on Trade Related Aspects of Intellectual Property Rights (TRIPs), embodied in the WTO Agreements. It also led, somewhat less directly, to the OECD negotiations on the Multilateral Agreement on Investment (MAI). All these inelegant acronyms are our cast of characters.

This paper reviews some of the important elements of the WTO rules affecting FDI and tries to evaluate the degree of discretion involved. We will look first at those incorporated in the Agreement on Trade in Goods, that is, Trade Related Investment Measures (TRIMs) and the Agreement on Subsidies and Countervailing Measures (SCVM), and second, at GATS subsuming TRIPs. Finally, some remarks on the MAI are made briefly,[4] and some general conclusions offered about the sorts of rules preferred and the institutional arrangements to oversee them.

TRADE IN GOODS: TRIMS

The TRIMs Agreement [WTO 1994, pp.163-167], as an integral part of the Marrakesh Agreement to which all WTO members subscribe, is the first multilateral attempt to enforce national measures affecting investment and to do so by prohibiting new restrictions and phasing out existing ones. However, exceptions and flexible transition periods create uncertainties. The first important partial treatment is that "trade related investment measures" relate mainly to requirements placed on manufacturers to

---

[3] FDI to developing and transition economies grew from US$18.6 billion in 1990 to US$83billion in 1995 (Table 23, p.86, IMF 1996).

[4] Originally, the MAI negotiations were supposed to be completed by May 1997; it now seems that a date of mid-1998 is more likely. This means any remarks about the MAI are based on partial reporting and relate to a moving target.

incorporate minimum locally produced inputs (by value or volume) in products for domestic sale; or the requirement that imported inputs are limited to a specified proportion of the volume or value of imports; or that access to foreign exchange is limited to some proportion of foreign exchange earnings [WTO 1994, pp.166-167]. What TRIMs does not cover are all the so-called positive incentives, such as direct fiscal help to particular forms of investment, regional tax incentives, or discriminatory planning incentives. By targeting only the "negative incentives" clearly, opportunities are created for countries to meet the TRIMs obligations and shift investment incentives to, say, fiscal bases. For example, a domestic resource requirement for car production could be phased out while an accelerated investment depreciation allowance to domestic car component manufacturers might achieve similar ends. Such shifts induced by TRIMs could increase or reduce investment uncertainty; the effect on economic efficiency is unclear [Buchs 1996, pp.47-48].

Another uncertainty involves a provision that allows a member to apply an existing TRIM to a new investment or enterprise so that it will not be put at a disadvantage compared to the older enterprise. This application (which must be notified to the WTO) is limited to enterprises producing "like products" and can only be used during a transitional phase.

The transitional phase by which members shall eliminate TRIMs is within two years of the start of the WTO (i.e., by 1/1/97). However, this rule applies only to developed countries; developing countries are allowed five years to adapt, and least-developed countries seven years (and this may be further extended). While this may appear a clear amendment to a clear rule, oddly enough there is no definition in the WTO Agreement of what constitutes the distinction between least-developed, developing and developed countries, despite the requirements of their own Article 5.2. For "least-developed countries" the WTO has adopted the UN General Assembly's list of LDCs, but the distinction between "developing" and "developed" remains uncertain. Countries more or less nominate themselves, that is, it becomes a matter for some discretion. Moreover, it is unclear whether the transition periods apply to new members acceding to the WTO from a clock started 1/1/95, or whether the clock is started afresh for each entrant.

Table 1. Notifications received under Article 5.1 of TRIMs

	Less Developed	Developing	Developed
Not in conformity with TRIMs	0	31	2 [5]
Consistent with TRIMs	1	6	3 [5]

Source: derived from Report (1996) of the Committee on Trade Related Investment Measures.

Table 1 shows those members that have notified themselves as not being in conformity with TRIMs, and clearly this is dominated by those in the "developing" category. Whether there really are no LDCs that are not in conformity with TRIMs, it does seem surprising that none has notified. Countries are not obligated to notify consistency with TRIMs but ten have done so, again dominated by the "developing" category.

The final discretion is one generally accorded to WTO members to allow a developing country member (again not defined in the Agreement) to deviate temporarily from the TRIMs provisions if their restrictive trade measures are adopted for balance of payments purposes. Of course, "temporarily" can be subject to elastic interpretation; for example, some "temporary" restrictive balance of payments measures in the trade in goods have lingered on for many (up to thirty) years.

So the apparent "rule" appears a good deal more flexible and subject to discretion than at first sight. A good example of a "rule" that only works if it bends. The question left, of course, is how far should a rule be allowed to bend before it ceases to be useful?

Such is the discretion possible that the immediate effect on investment is unlikely to be great. Indeed, because positive investment incentives are not covered, investment could be even further skewed if countries move to use them more (See Vocke 1997, Table 3). Probably, the most important effect is "the publication effect", in that countries may be increasingly unwilling to use such TRIMs if they know they will be subject to scrutiny by the WTO and debate by their peers.

Table 2, column 1 summarizes some of the discretionary elements under TRIMs discussed above.

Table 2. Complications in Some Rules

	Rules			
	1. TRIMs	2. SCVM	3. GATS	4. TRIPs
Discretionary elements				
Selectivity	Positive incentives not covered	General Subsidies tolerated: inapplicable to agriculture or services	Market access commitment	
Investment equally treated	Existing TRIM applied to new investment	Non-discriminatory and non-contingent subsidies allowed. Special rules for privatization subsidies		Patent protection on old technology grace period of 5 years
Transition periods	Up to 7 years extendable	Indefinite for some	Up to 5 years	Up to 11 years
Balance of payments protection allowed	Yes	No	Yes	No

Source: derived from Report (1996) of the Committee on Trade Related Investment Measures.

THE AGREEMENT ON SUBSIDIES AND COUNTERVAILING MEASURES

One way in which FDI could be put at a disadvantage would be if domestic producers were favored, through subsidies, compared to those undertaking the FDI. Of course, this is a complex issue with huge potential ramifications; for instance, government capital restructuring on preferential terms of, say, banks or airlines (not unheard of) could put others with FDI at a disadvantage. Although the WTO Agreement deals with only a limited sub-set of subsidies, this text is one of the longest and most complex in the Marrakesh Agreement. The rule appears fairly straightforward. Subsidies contingent on export performance and on the use of domestic over imported

---

[5] The distinction between categories of countries is unclear despite the requirement of TRIMs Article 5.2: to define less developed countries, the WTO has adopted the UN General Assembly's list of LDCs; however, the distinction between "developed" and "developing" is less clear. For this table, the IMF categorization of "advanced" countries (see WEO 1997, Statistical Appendix Tables A, B) and Central European transition economies has been used for the "developed" category.

goods are prohibited (WTO 1994, p. 266) and other specific subsidies can be countervailed. Supporting this, special duties levied to offset any such subsidy (i.e., countervailing measures) may only be imposed after investigations within the ambit of this Agreement.

Discretion enters at once on the definition of "subsidy" (which was not defined under the old GATT Agreement). The WTO is only interested in discriminatory subsidies contingent on exports or use of domestic over imported inputs or other specific subsidies. A domestic subsidy to a particular industry (which might have only one or two producers, e.g., steel or coal) that, say, sold 80 percent of its output to an export industry would not be forbidden as the subsidy would not be contingent on the export, or contingent on the use of the domestic good over, say, imported steel. So non-specific subsidies are allowed, even though they could have economic effects on exports similar to specific subsidies. Criteria are elaborated to define specificity (no limited access, automaticity, disproportionality, regionality [see WTO 1994, pp. 265-266].

Further, there are differing transition periods. Countries with a GNP per capita under US$1,000 are not required to remove export subsidies and other "developing" countries were given an eight year period of grace. The subsidies contingent on the use of domestic over imported goods can be removed over an eight-year period for LDCs and over five years for developing countries. The text continues with language which suggests that, on the one hand, a developing country, when export subsidies are "inconsistent with its developing needs", should eliminate the subsidies; on the other hand, if it deemed them necessary beyond the eight-year period, it would have to negotiate an extension with the Committee overseeing the application of the Agreement. In fact, fifteen paragraphs (WTO 1994, pp. 299-301) relate to "Special and Differential Treatment of Developing Country members" and with complex alternatives. The complexity of these rules may make it difficult for some members to interpret the Agreement.

Special time periods (seven years) are allowed for countries in transition from centrally planned to market economies. Also, subsidies for privatization are only classified as "actionable" in transition economies. "Actionable" means subsidies that injure the domestic industry of another member and cause "serious prejudice"[6] to the interests of another member and which can be challenged through the disputes settlement procedure or by unilateral use of a countervailing duty by the injured party.

Discretionary elements are also introduced because this agreement does not apply to services (and there could be subsidies to services) nor to agriculture (which is subject to a separate agreement). Regional subsidies are allowed provided they are non-specific within the region and the disadvantages (low incomes, remoteness, etc.) defining a region for aid are fairly generously drawn (WTO 1994, pp. 275-276).

Overall, this is a brave attempt to bring discrimination against FDI, through the use of subsidies, within the rule of WTO law. But it exemplifies the difficulties of applying the apparatus of the law to such a subtle and contentious area. Immediately, the text is drawn into thickets of doctrinal definition. What is subsidy, specificity, an adverse effect, service, prejudice, an actionable countervailing measure, injury, special and differential treatment for developing countries? It stands as a classic case of "what is simple cannot be fair, and what is fair cannot be simple". Unless a limited group of countries can agree on common simple rules with few (or no) exceptions, the wider the group extends the greater will have to be the exceptions and the more complex the text.

GENERAL AGREEMENT ON TRADE IN SERVICES (GATS)

The GATS is an extremely ambitious attempt to extend the focus of multilateral, binding, international agreements from trade in goods to include trade in services, recognizing that services are playing, and are likely to play, an increasingly major role in international trade or global integration. At first glance it might seem that FDI plays a trivial role in the supply of services. However, FDI in the GATS is important as a way "to overcome the lack of tradability of services compared to traditional forms of cross-border trade. In this respect, the agreement already constitutes a multilateral investment regime. It enables service corporations to become transnational by creating the conditions for an international corporate network for the supply of their services".[7]

---

[6] Naturally, "serious prejudice" requires another entire section (WTO 1994, pp.269-71) to be defined.

[7] Vocke, 1997, p.14.

However, the GATS is not designed as an international investment agreement. "The GATS does not contain the kind of investment protection provisions commonly found in many of the bilateral and regional investment arrangements..." (WTO, 1996, p. 71). Nor does GATS involve a principle of general application. By agreement among themselves, governments can condition national treatment or market access or grant it partially. Finally, GATS is not transparent in adopting a negative list approach; rather it is a hybrid "containing a positive listing of sectors and a negative listing of limitations on market access and national treatment" (ibid).

The rules governing trade in services are quite clear, except for a somewhat complicated definition of what constitutes the supply of a service. Supply is categorized in four senses: a) from territory to territory; b) supply in one territory to service a consumer in another; c) by a service supplier of one member through "commercial presence" in the territory of another; and d) by a service supplier using its personnel in the territory of another. The intent is to ensure that service supply covers not only the service transferred territorially but also the commercial presence of a service supplier.

This raises difficulties of definition. Clearly much service supply (e.g., financial, marketing) may require subsidiaries to be set up abroad. If these affiliates supply a service related to *marketing* goods, they are covered by GATS; if their service is related to *distribution* of goods, they are not. Uncertainty is created.

In general, the potential coverage of GATS is broad, but the actual coverage of GATS to date has been modest and the information needed to help the access of members, especially developing countries, is complex and not necessarily easy to interpret. Countries initially have made very limited commitments. Negotiations in important sectors became bogged down e.g., basic telecommunications, financial services, maritime transport services, and the movement of natural persons.

Discretion emerges first, of course, in members' market access commitments. Not unexpectedly, most commitments have been made by developed, high income countries. What is interesting about the GATS text is the way in which the WTO becomes involved in a multilateral FDI regime almost as an afterthought (actually through a footnote). Under Article XVI on market access, members are required to treat service suppliers no less favorably than provided for in their own schedules. A footnote (WTO 1994, p. 341) expands on this commitment to say "...if the cross-border movement of capital is an essential part of the service itself, that Member is thereby committed to allow such movement of capital" even if no commercial presence is required in the service importing country. If a member undertakes a market access commitment in relation to the supply of a service through setting up an affiliate (commercial presence), then the service importing country is "committed to allow related transfers of capital into its territory" (ibid).

These are important footnotes. They create the potential for WTO commitments and rulings to have significant effects on FDI. Broadly speaking, these provisions should liberalize FDI, however, the WTO Agreement is limited because it refers only to services, and only to services where members have made market access commitments.

The current negotiations over such commitments indicate how slowly such provisions may expand. Negotiations on Maritime Transport Services should have been completed by end-June 1996, instead they were suspended. Financial Services negotiations were completed only in December 1997. On Basic Telecommunications, the WTO has succeeded in wide-ranging schedules to liberalize a broad range of international telecommunications services.

Not only is the impact on FDI limited by the selection of service sector commitments made, it is also circumscribed by the application of the GATS Articles and WTO rules. GATS allows MFN inconsistent measures to be maintained for five years and longer (subject to review) (WTO 1994, p. 352). "Frontier zones" services may be given special advantages. If there is a serious balance of payments difficulty, restrictions may be introduced (paralleling the balance of payments provision of the GATT 1994). Schedules may be modified (Article XXI) subject to negotiations to agree compensation. This compensation procedure is open to arbitration and the whole GATS can be brought under the Disputes Settlement Understanding (DSU).[8] Further, the GATS allows for special treatment for emergency safeguard measures, government procurement in services, and subsidies; however, discussions in all these

---

[8] GATS violations have been cited in four cases: in terms of significant disputes GATS violations have not been a major element. Four disputes in which GATS has been cited are: bananas (GATS wholesaling and distribution); Helms-Burton Cuba (transparency, access); US vs Belgium telephone directory services; US vs Japan distribution services (photo films) large scale retail store law.

areas are continuing and their resolution could well introduce further discretionary elements.

TRADE RELATED ASPECTS OF INTELLECTUAL PROPERTY RIGHTS (TRIPS)

TRIPs may affect FDI by safeguarding copyrights, trademarks, patents and designs, ensuring the owner a return on their intellectual property. Such protection could lead to an expansion of FDI to create manufacturing facilities across borders, or it could reduce FDI as demand could be satisfied from parent plants through international trade in the protected goods and services.[9]

The application of TRIPs is, first of all, complicated by the sheer bulk and complexity of the notifications (the U.S. laws and regulations to TRIPs amounted to some 425 pages, exceeded by the United Kingdom at 800 pages).

The examination of these national notifications, to ensure the general most-favored nation clause (WTO 1994, p. 369) is respected, is a major task. For a developing country, a truly daunting task. And for a least-developed country, virtually impossible (and if the notifications have to be translated into the three working languages, a formidable task for the secretariat). The challenge to bring a case to the DSB under TRIPs seems substantial.

Discretion is again allowed in applying the provisions of the Agreement: all countries were allowed one year of grace (from 1/1/95 to 1/1/96), transition economies and developing countries five years, and least-developed countries eleven years. Any effects on FDI are likely to be diffuse. The removal of uncertainty should enhance FDI. However, the actual administration of the rules looks to be complex and compliance difficult to monitor.

---

[9] For a full discussion of those possibilities, see Vocke, pp.5-12.

RULES VERSUS DISCRETION: LOW AND HIGH CONSENSUS

What can we learn from this brief survey of these limited WTO rules that affect FDI? First, they give a flavor of the complexities involved. Of course, some complexities are generated by the opening up of completely new fields of responsibilities (e.g., GATS) and the heavy burden of notifications (e.g., patent and copyright law). Nevertheless, it is clear that simple rules can soon be subverted to accommodate a wider membership. As the WTO works under consensus, the quality and strength of the rules must accommodate that required consensus, and this means that we have what we might call a fairly low-level consensus position. As a WTO member said "we have fairly few rules but a lot of exceptions", and the more exceptions there are, the more borderline decisions must be made.

Undoubtedly, rules should be as general as possible. The simplest rules are the MFN, but in the WTO, as far as FDI is concerned, they have been undermined through selectivity and through deviations allowed for differing transition periods and balance of payments purposes. It has also been weakened by the limited and sometimes almost as an afterthought (cf. footnotes introducing capital mobility into GATS) coverage of FDI.

From this survey, it is also clear that transition provisions must allow for the differing pace of countries adaptation to full capital account convertibility. Especially, the transition should take account of the fragility or robustness of the monetary and financial sectors. Moreover, many countries are concerned about the potential volatility of investment flows and demand that provision must be made to allow for the rapid re-imposition of controls in the light of pressure upon their balance of payments.

Clearly, what is needed is a truly general, multilateral treatment of investment incorporating all these provisions. This is what the MAI hopes to achieve. The message for the drafters of the MAI from this modest survey would be to strive to maintain true generality: exceptions complicate and weaken the operation of agreements—though it is recognized that without exceptions there might be no agreement.

The MAI aims, apparently, to encompass a fairly broad definition of investment. The message from the WTO treatment of FDI would seem to be that the more simple the rules and the fewer the "carve-outs" and "carve-ins" and discretionary elements, the better. A smaller membership of like-minded members, of course, will be likely to make it easier to administer, and the OECD, with 29 members, has a much smaller membership than the WTO (130) or the IMF (181). Even with this limited membership, as conclusions get closer, members require more time to tackle the demands for derogations, etc. If the MAI is to be downloaded to the WTO, this is likely to create an even greater low-consensus set of rules. However, the MAI is likely to involve something similar to the WTO's Dispute Settlement Board (DSB) to settle disputes between signatories of the MAI. Indeed, it is possible it could go further and allow enterprise-to-state disputes to be heard. In the WTO, it is only members (i.e., nations) that have standing in the Dispute Settlement Procedure (DSP); however, in NAFTA, in addition to state-to-state DSP, enterprise-to-state is recognized. It appears possible that MAI might do the same.[10] The danger is that the lengthy quasi-judicial setting of an investment disputes settlement mechanism could lead to heavy reliance on elaborate legal briefs and presentations. The costs of dispute resolution rise. The larger, richer countries (and larger and richer companies) are able to fight more complex cases. Poorer nations could well be reinforced in their belief that this was a rich man's club. In turn, this could encourage countries to look to more accommodating regional and bilateral agreements than to an elaborate, legalistic and adversarial "court" in a far-off center.

What we have described is a rules-based system designed principally by lawyers. Lawyers, of course, see life in adversarial terms, and trade negotiators see it as complex patterns of bargaining where nothing is given or yielded without an offsetting receipt. Yet, as economists, we know that in international trade, one of the most robust pieces of analysis in the history of economic thought teaches us that countries, by unilaterally opening their markets to free trade, improve their position, regardless of what others do. It is frustrating to have this panoply of rules, administered at considerable expense, based on a false premise of necessary trade-offs. However, this is the reality.

Given that this is what we have, to what should we move? It may be interesting to

---

[10] An interesting question arises about the sanctions possible under enterprise-to-state disputes (see Graham, pp.26-28).

glance at the IMF's experience with its members. Although the Fund has a weighted voting system, in fact it also acts broadly through consensus. But because of the limited number of Articles of Agreement and the fact that it is not an adversarial body,[11] it is a high-level consensus organization. That is, there is a broad level of consensus throughout the Board on the mandate and operation of the organization under relatively few and succinct Articles of Agreement. The Fund is not adversarial. The Fund has not evolved through members bringing cases against each other. There is no equivalent in the Fund of the WTO's DSP. Instead, members agree, for instance, to adopt Article VIII "that no member shall, without the approval of the Fund, impose restrictions on the making of payments and transfers for current international transactions" (IMF 1993, p.21) as they feel able to "graduate". The flow of members adopting Article VIII over the years has been as the result of peer pressure and an increasing perception of the economic gains to be reaped. This procedure has not involved an evidence-based arrangement of the intended or actual effects of a measure. Instead, it is the nature of the measure, for example, whether or not it involves a "direct governmental limitation on the availability of foreign exchange as such" that is important, rather than the purpose or effect of the measure. Because effects do not have to be evaluated and members do not take retaliatory actions, no complex assessments of costs, fines or recompenses are needed. The process is relatively straightforward. Further, because the Fund has essentially a universal membership, then there is, more or less by definition, no discrimination between countries. The Fund approach is essentially non-discriminatory. This cannot be the case for agreements that do not have universal membership since, by definition, countries that accede to such agreements can discriminate against non-members.

Now, if there were an equivalent to Article VIII that enjoined members to place no restrictions on the capital account this could provide a mechanism whereby members could gradually adopt an agreement on the free flow of capital, parallel to Article VIII dealing with the current account. Over time, if all members adopted such an Article in much the same way as, over time, they have adopted the obligations of Article VIII, would there still be a need for the complex rules-based system affecting FDI of the WTO or MAI?

Regrettably, the reality is that no polar solution is likely. Even with the existing 140

---

[11] And perhaps because it is largely composed of macroeconomists and not lawyers?

agreements to the Fund's Article VIII, there are still restrictions and reservations (derogations) on those country commitments. Further, even if there were a new article to cover the capital account, it is unlikely that it would cover all direct investment; governments may wish to retain controls on inward foreign investment concerned that the country's economic, political, military or cultural independence may be threatened to the extent that specific assets or enterprises within the country are owned by foreigners. They may be wrong in this assessment; for instance, it would almost certainly be better to allow foreign banks and insurance companies to operate in competition with domestic financial concerns, but nevertheless the reality is that countries frequently wish to limit foreign ownership of "sensitive" enterprises. So, even in a new Fund article covering capital flows, there would probably have to be some cut-off point (say at 10 percent, as recommended by the OECD), above which the obligation not to impose controls would not apply. Even this might be controversial, and other ways might be sought to further exempt inward direct investment from Fund articles. Moreover, the liberalization of inward direct investment is contained in other international agreements. The MAI would cover, presumably, direct foreign investment, including portfolio investment, intangible assets, and some real estate. So no neat clear-cut solution is probable. Nevertheless, I think it is worthwhile drawing attention to the costs of the low-consensus adversarial system. Surely, the more we can put into the high-consensus obligation Fund-type agreements the better?

REFERENCES

Buchs, T., 1996, "Selected WTO Rules and Some Implications for Fund Policy Advice", IMF Working Paper 96/23 (Washington, International Monetary Fund).

Graham, E.M., 1996, "Foreign Direct Investment in the New Multilateral Trade Agenda", PSIO Occasional Paper, WTO Series Number 4, Graduate Institute of International Studies (Geneva, Switzerland).

International Monetary Fund, 1997, *World Economic Outlook*, May 1997 (Washington, International Monetary Fund).

——, 1996, *International Capital Markets, Developments, Prospects, and Key Policy Issues* (Washington, International Monetary Fund).

United Nations Conference on Trade and Development, 1997, "Bit by Bit; Understanding Development Implications of Bilateral Investment Treaties", Note to Correspondents No. 2, May 28, 1997 (UNCTAD, Geneva, Switzerland).

Vocke, M., "Investment Implications of Selected WTO Agreements and the Proposed Multilateral Agreement on Investment", IMF Working Paper 97/60 (Washington, International Monetary Fund).

World Trade Organisation, 1994, "The Results of the Uruguay Round of Multilateral Trade Negotiations: The Legal Texts", (Geneva, the GATT Secretariat).

——1996, *Annual Report 1996*, Vol. 1., (Geneva, World Trade Organisation).

PART IV. TAX COMPETITION AND FOREIGN DIRECT INVESTMENT

CHAPTER10 FOREIGN DIRECT INVESTMENT AND TAX COMPETITION IN SOUTHEAST ASIA

SHINEMAY CHEN[*], JORGE MARTINEZ-VAZQUEZ[**], AND
SALLY WALLACE[**]

I. INTRODUCTION

Foreign direct investment (FDI) is a unique form of international capital movement because it finances the construction of plant and equipment and also transfers technology and management skills from one country to another. Most developing countries use a variety of tax policies in an attempt to encourage investment and to channel this investment into areas that are considered national priorities. The study of the impact of tax policy on FDI can have significant policy relevance. If FDI is not responsive to tax advantages offered by the host country, the foregone tax revenues represent a windfall loss that have to be made up by raising other, likely distortionary, taxes in the host country. If inward FDI is sensitive to the host country's tax policies then policy design should attempt to strike a balance between foregone revenues and the benefits derived from capital technology and know-how transfers and future increases in tax base and revenues. Whether or not FDI is responsive to host country tax inducements also depends on the tax policies of home countries and may also depend on the tax policies of competing host countries.[1] Therefore, the host country's

[*] Department of Public Finance, National Chengchi University, Taipei.
[**] Economics Department, School of Policy Studies, Georgia State University, Atlanta.
The authors are thankful to Paul Benson, Barbara Edwards, and Arthur Turner for their very able assistance, and Mary Beth Walker for helpful comments.

[1] See Slemrod (1990). The notion of international tax competition is discussed by Fan (1991) and Chia and Whalley (1995).

design of tax policy also has to take into account home country tax policies and may have to take into account the tax policies of competing host countries.

This paper investigates FDI from five developed home countries (the United States, the United Kingdom, Japan, Germany, and France) to four host, potentially rival, countries in Southeast Asia (Hong Kong, Malaysia, Singapore, and Taiwan), and the responsiveness of FDI to the tax policies of each pair of host and home countries and those of potentially competing host countries.

The majority of the empirical literature has focused primarily on the effect of host country tax policies on FDI flows and has done that from the perspective of developed countries, in particular the United States. The literature has paid much less attention to the impact of home country tax policies on the developing country experience. Exceptions to this treatment include Chang and Cheng (1993) and Leechor and Mintz (1991) who examine home country tax impacts in developing countries, and Slemrod (1990) and Shah and Slemrod (1990) who explicitly introduce the home country tax regimes into their analyses. The literature has practically ignored the role of potential tax competition among a set of host countries in the distribution of FDI.

There are reasons why *a priori* we should consider the impact of tax policies from potentially competing countries on FDI. Many countries act as if foreign direct investment can bring substantial benefit to their economies. These countries want to keep or improve their competitive position to increase their share of FDI inflows. One way they may improve their competitive position is by offering more generous tax advantages to foreign investors (Tanzi, 1996). Other measures commonly used include establishing investment promotion offices and overseas offices to make investors aware of opportunities in their countries and to expedite the investment process.[2]

The tax policies adopted by the four countries studied here vary from Hong Kong's "laissez-faire" policy to Singapore and Malaysia's complex system of investment to attract FDI. Main features of the tax systems for the four countries are summarized

---

[2] The four host countries studied in this paper have this type of office: Hong Kong's Investment Promotion Office, Singapore's Economic Development Board, the Malaysian Industrial Development Authority (MIDA), and Taiwan's Industrial Development and Investment Center (IDIC).

in Appendix C. There is some evidence that the tax incentives granted by some of these countries are driven in part by tax competition with neighboring countries offering similar tax advantages (Chia and Whalley, 1995). These policies have persisted over the years despite the fact that they are suboptimal or ineffective (Boadway and Shah, 1995) and quite costly (Sanchez-Ugarte, 1997). Thus far, the tax literature has paid little attention to the phenomenon of intercountry tax competition and much less to the impact of this competition on FDI.[3]

The basic hypothesis explored in this paper is whether host countries are interdependent in the sense that production costs, including taxes in other host countries, affect the inward FDI to a particular host country. If the hypothesis proves to be correct, the study of the role of tax policy on FDI will require taking into account the tax policies of other potentially competing countries.

The sources of FDI are highly concentrated. The United States, the United Kingdom, Japan and West Germany were the leading sources of outward investment in 1988, accounting for 65.6 percent of the total stock of outward direct investment in 1988. Developing countries, which account for a relatively insignificant share of FDI outflows, received some 21.3 percent of inward FDI (Dunning, 1992). Within developing countries, the distribution of FDI has been highly concentrated in a few economically large and/or upper-middle income countries of Asia and Latin America. Between 1980 and 1990, almost 70 percent of all FDI to developing countries flowed to the following 10 countries: Singapore, Mexico, Brazil, China, Hong Kong, Malaysia, Egypt, Argentina, Thailand, and Taiwan in the descending order of their share of total FDI to developing countries (OECD, 1993).

Table 1 summarizes the percentage share for 1991 of FDI by country origin among the four countries studied in this paper: Hong Kong, Malaysia, Singapore, and Taiwan. Compared to its competitors, Hong Kong obtained the most FDI from every investing

---

[3] There is substantial literature on the impact of tax advantages offered by competing subnational jurisdictions in developed countries (Ihlanfeldt, 1994; Bartik, 1991 and Wasylenko, 1996). Although there is conflicting evidence, the most recent studies reach the conclusion that the tax policies of local or state jurisdictions do have an impact on the location of investment once firms have made up their minds about the general area in which to locate (in response to more dominant location determinants) such as access to market or raw materials. On the other hand, there is little evidence that subnational jurisdictions enter in competition, or even "stay in line," with neighboring jurisdictions (Ladd, 1992).

Table 1. The Distribution of Foreign Direct Investment by the Origin of Country (1991)

Major Investing Countries	Hong Kong (a)	Malaysia (b)	Singapore (c)	Taiwan (d)	Total (in US $1000) (a)+(b)+(c)+(d)=100%
Japan	49%	18%	14%	18%	$2,883,462
USA	49%	6%	22%	23%	$2,554,357
United Kingdom	52%	16%	23%	9%	$470,333
Germany	35%	18%	30%	17%	$116,081
France	34%	6%	52%	7%	$83,596
Average	*43.8%*	*12.8%*	*28.2%*	*14.8%*	

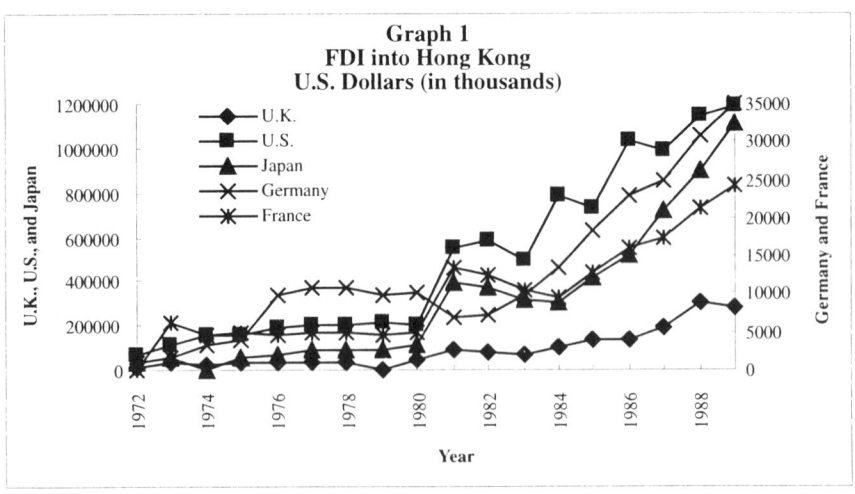

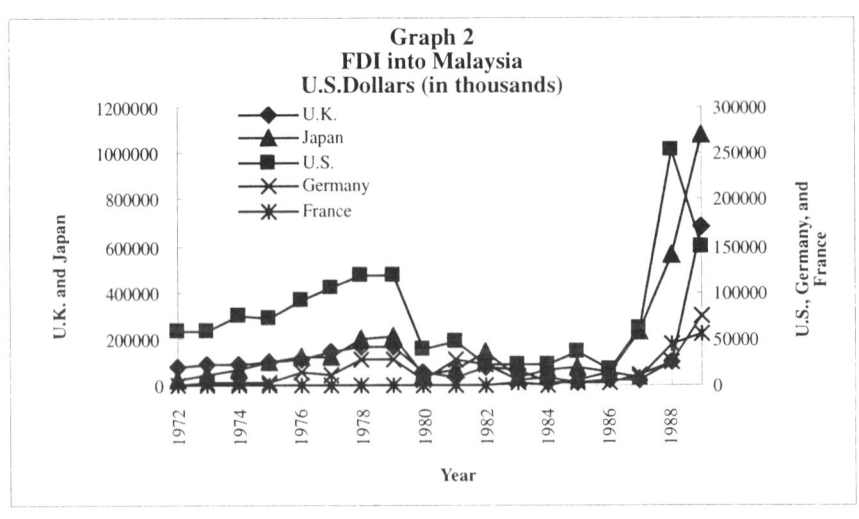

country except France. Singapore ranked second, followed by Taiwan and Malaysia. The time profile of FDI in each of the host countries is presented in Graphs 1 thorough 4. Note the different scales at each side of these graphs. While FDI into Hong Kong has grown steadily over the sample period, FDIs into Singapore and Malaysia have experienced more ups and downs. FDI into Taiwan is a more recent phenomenon and it has also been subject to significant fluctuations.

The remainder of the paper is organized as follows. The next section briefly reviews

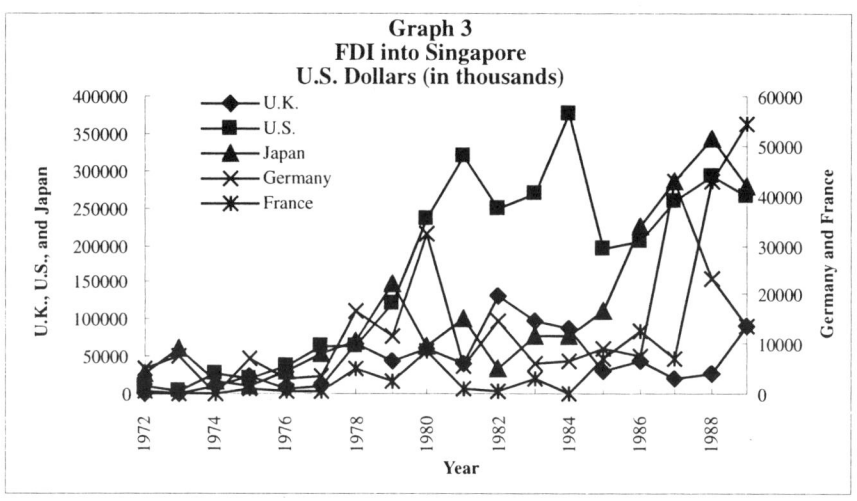

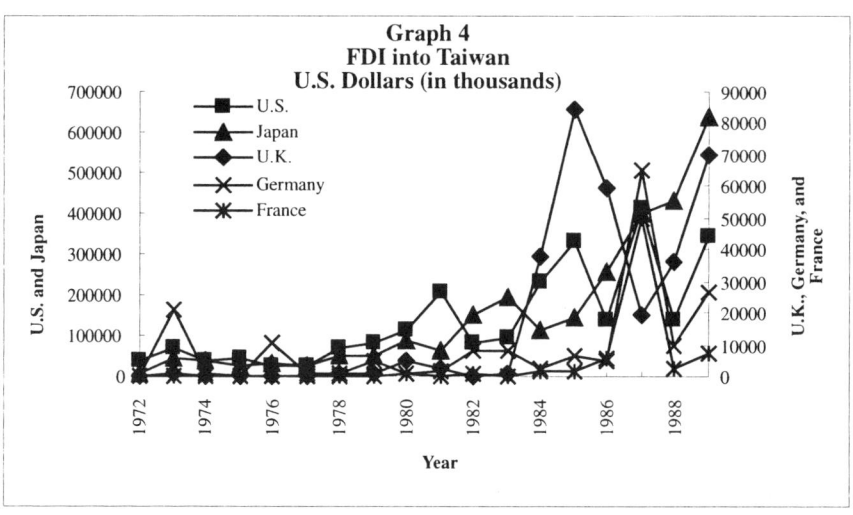

the literature on the determinants of FDI, focusing on the role played by taxes. In Section III, we posit an empirical model of FDI investment in which the tax policies of the host country, the home country, and competing host countries may all affect the level of FDI. In Section IV, we discuss data sources and variable definitions. In Section V, the empirical model is estimated using pooled cross-section and time-series annual data of 20 pairs of countries (home-host) over 18 years (1972-1989). The final section presents a summary and some concluding comments.

II. LITERATURE REVIEW

Foreign direct investment (FDI) is, in essence, the creation or expansion of firms' capital that operates across national boundaries. Several factors influence the level of FDI. Tsai (1991) dichotomizes these factors into demand-side and supply-side determinants. The supply-side determinants refer to firm-specific factors such as economies of scale or product life cycle. Much of the previous empirical literature has focused on the importance of the demand determinants such as a host country's market (Agodo, 1978; Green and Cunningham, 1975; Roo and Ahmed, 1979; Dunning, 1980; Schneider and Frey, 1985; Julius, 1990; and Ragizzi, 1993), relative labor costs (Riedel, 1975; Cushman, 1985; and Culem, 1988), and relative currency values (Frost and Stein, 1989; and McCulloch, 1993).

There is an expanding literature which analyzes the impact of taxes on FDI. Hartman (1984) pioneered the study of the effect of taxation on foreign direct investment into the United States. He estimated separate equations for foreign direct investment financed by retained earnings and FDI financed by transfers from abroad using annual data from 1965 and 1979. Hartman found that the inflow of FDI to the United States increased with the after-tax rates of return for foreign investors and for the U.S. economy as a whole, and that it decreased with the relative tax rate on foreign versus U.S. owned capital. The statistical results were stronger for FDI financed by subsidiaries' retained earnings than for FDI financed by parent companies' transfer of funds. Hartman did not control for home country taxes or rate of return outside the U.S. Subsequent studies by Boskin and Gale (1987), Newlon (1987) and Young (1988) find that Hartman's results are somewhat sensitive to specification and data periods, but nonetheless conclude that taxes do have an impact on FDI.

Slemrod (1990) extends the FDI-taxation debate by examining the effects of the United States' tax policies and seven investing countries on FDI in the United States. Slemrod tested two propositions on the effects of host country taxes on FDI; first, that FDI from exemption countries should be at least as sensitive to host country tax rates as FDI from foreign tax credit countries, and second, that this difference should be most apparent in the behavior of new transfers of funds. Using time series data and an estimate of the effective marginal tax rate on new investment, Slemrod estimated separate FDI equations for each of the seven major investing countries in the U.S. [4] His findings strongly support the hypothesis that a negative relationship exists between the U.S. tax rate (host country tax rate) and the FDI financed by transfers of funds. However, the estimated tax effect on retained earnings ranged from significantly positive to significantly negative, with no clear trend emerging and no obvious pattern by tax system. The four countries for which a significant tax effect on transfers and total FDI was found were evenly divided between exemption countries (the Netherlands and Germany) and foreign tax credit countries (Japan and the United Kingdom).

Shah and Slemrod (1990) studied the effects of Mexican (host country) and U.S. (home country) taxation on FDI in Mexico. Like Slemrod (1990) and Hartman (1984), Shah and Slemrod distinguished FDI financed by transfers and those financed by retained earnings. They also control for the credit status of multinationals, in particular the ability to defer the tax liability on subsidiaries' foreign-source income until the earnings are remitted, and for host country risk factors. They test a number of specifications of their model. In particular, they calculate and estimate a variety of tax measures using a marginal effective tax rate on investment in Mexico and the U.S. statutory corporate rate. They found that both the host and home country tax regimes are significant for FDI from the U.S. into Mexico. FDI financed by transfers were sensitive to the marginal effective tax rate on the new aggregate investment in Mexico and to Mexico's credit rating. Tax differentials between the U.S. statutory rates and Mexico's marginal effective tax rate did not play a significant role for FDI financed by transfers. However, FDI financed by reinvested earnings was quite sensitive to both Mexico's marginal effective tax rate as well as the tax differential.

---

[4] These countries are Canada, France, Netherlands, West Germany (exemption countries), Italy, Japan, and United Kingdom (foreign tax credit countries).

In a more recent paper Chang and Cheng (1993) also study the role of tax policy on FDI in a single developing country. Chang and Cheng used approvals data of FDI in Taiwan from 1972-1987.[5] They control only for the tax policy of the host country. For this purpose they use a measure of tax preferences in Taiwan, calculated as the difference between the highest marginal corporate income tax rate and the average effective tax rate.[6] Although Chang and Cheng found that FDI is responsive to GDP and labor costs, domestic tax policy, as proxied by tax preferences enjoyed by foreign investors, had no impact on FDI.

Finally, Cummins and Hubbard (1994) estimated a model of capital investment using 1981-1991 panel data on investment of U.S. subsidiaries in Canada, the United Kingdom, Germany, France, Australia, and Japan. Cummins and Hubbard found that subsidiaries' decisions on new capital investment are affected by tax factors through two channels. First, the cost of capital for investors is influenced by corporate income tax rates, investment incentives, and depreciation rules in the host country. Second, FDI from countries with residence-based tax (or foreign tax credit) systems is affected by the tax price on dividend repatriation and the foreign tax credit status of the parent company, and by the statutory tax rates of the home country.

In summary, the current empirical literature on the tax policy effects on FDI does lend support to the notion that tax policy plays a significant role for FDI. A limitation of previous work is that it does not consider the effects of *relative* tax policies of competing host countries. For reasons mentioned earlier, these relative policies may impact FDI flowing to potential host countries. We seek to fill this gap with the empirical approach detailed in the next section.

III. THEORETICAL FRAMEWORK AND EMPIRICAL MODEL

Two main sets of issues are raised in relation to the role of tax competition in FDI. The first is the nature of the tax competition among potential host countries and

---

[5] FDI data include the total amount of both the new investment and additional investment projects approved by the Investment Commission in the Ministry of Economic Affairs.

[6] Chang and Cheng also control for GDP level, wage costs, and export activity of foreign firms in Taiwan.

between home and host countries. The second is the extension of the conventional framework for studying the role of tax policy on FDI to the case where tax competition among host countries may exist.

This paper does not formalize nor test hypotheses on the nature of tax competition among host countries. Recently, there has been an increasing awareness of the extent and possible consequences of international tax competition (Tanzi, 1996). Some evidence exists that host countries have engaged in strategic tax competition to attract FDI. Chia and Whalley (1995) report tax competition among ASEAN countries in the form of a Stackelberg-type situation in which the concession of further tax incentives by Singapore is followed by other ASEAN countries, including Malaysia. The modelling of tax competition in the theoretical literature has primarily concentrated on the rivalry among home and host country tax authorities and much less on the rivalry among host countries.[7]

Our focus is on the extension of the FDI-tax empirical model to account for the possible existence of tax competition among FDI host countries. FDI by multinational firms may be driven by a multiplicity of objectives. There does appear to be a consensus in the large theoretical and empirical literature that multinationals' FDI is associated with the exploitation of multi-plant economies of scale arising from the ownership of knowledge-based assets and location-specific advantages.[8] But like any other profit maximizing firm, multinationals will seek, other things equal, to minimize their worldwide taxes. The impact of tax competition among possible host countries can be incorporated in a model of a multi-plant profit-maximizing multinational firm.[9] We can hypothesize that the level of FDI to any host country depends not only on the tax system of the host country and that of the home country (as is customarily in the literature) but also on the tax systems of other host countries that are potentially competitors. Note that this general statement of the hypotheses fits not only a world in which host countries undertake strategic tax policies to compete

---

[7] See Janeba (1995), Bond (1991), Mintz and Tulkeus (1990), Gordon (1990), and Hamada (1966).

[8] One reason multinational firms establish production in some host countries may be in order to bypass protective trade barriers. This may allow firms to sell in protected host markets at prices higher than international prices. This would appear to have been a key factor in FDI in European countries and in Latin America. FDI in Asia has been more generally oriented toward the export market (Markusen, 1991).

[9] See, for example, Caves (1982), Cushman (1985), Dunning (1981), and Lucas (1993).

for FDI, but also one in which multinational firms react to differential tax burdens in host countries even though the differences in tax systems are not the product of open tax competition among the host countries. In short, this paper tests the hypothesis that FDI is sensitive to competing tax systems. If host countries do engage in tax competition practices as the casual evidence indicates is the case in Asia, it has significant policy value to establish whether FDI is actually responsive to these practices.

The impact of the tax system of a host country and other rival host countries on incoming FDI depends on the complex interaction of statutory tax rates, deductions and other aspects of the definition of taxable profits, tax credits, and special provisions, such as tax holidays for new investments. The final impact of a host country's system on FDI may also depend on the ability of multinationals to shift net incomes across international boundaries through the use of transfer pricing, and on the tax system of the home country. [10]

Two separate methodologies have been used in the literature to measure the impact of the host country's tax system on foreign investors. [11] The first consists of the calculation of the marginal effective rate that an additional investment will be subject to in the particular host country and it is measured by the difference between the pre-tax and after-tax rates of return on the investment. [12] The computation of marginal effective tax rates requires detailed information on tax provisions and other economic variables that interact with the tax codes such as sources of finance, uses of profits, or the rate of inflation. Because we study FDI in four host countries from five different home countries over a period of 18 years, it is impractical to use a marginal effective tax rate approach.

The second approach used in the literature to measure the impact of the host country's tax system is the computation of an average effective tax rate. This is calculated by dividing actual taxes paid by an independent measure of income. In this paper we use a measure of the effective capital income tax rate following the approach of

---

[10] See Slemrod (1995) and Boadway and Shah (1995).

[11] These are discussed in Shah and Slemrod (1991).

[12] This approach is based on Hall and Jorgenson's (1967) derivation for the user cost of capital and applied, for example, in King and Fullerton (1984). Its application to developing countries is discussed by Auerbach (1995).

Mendoza, Razin, and Tesar (1994). The attraction of Mendoza et al.'s capital income effective rates is that they take into account all tax revenues from capital income, including capital income taxes paid by households, capital income taxes paid by corporations, all recurrent taxes on immovable property paid by households and others, and, where they exist, taxes on financial and capital transactions. As pointed out in Shah and Slemrod (1991), there may be an advantage in using data-based average effective tax rates over analytically-based marginal effective tax rates because the former may capture more aspects of the tax laws and better reflect other features incorporated in the marginal effective rate computations. The effective rate of taxation in the particular host country will be denoted by τ_h.

Besides the effective rates of taxation in the host and competing host countries, as pointed out, FDI in the host country can be affected by the ability of multinational firms to shift net profits across boundaries through the use of transfer pricing.[13] Because there is no available measure of how this ability may differ across countries, we will not be able to account for this factor.[14] The impact of the greater ability by multinational firms to use transfer pricing is to decrease or neutralize the importance of tax factors in the final location of FDI.

FDI in the host country may also be affected by the tax system in the home country in two different ways (Slemrod, 1990). First, increases or decreases in the effective rates of taxation in the home country can make FDI in any host country more or less attractive to multinational firms with a home base in the country. We will denote the effective rate of taxation in the home country τ_H, and it is computed in the same fashion as for the host countries. Second, the impact of the host country tax system may be affected by the home country tax system if the home country taxes the global income of its multinational firms. For the home countries in our sample that use a territorial principle (France and Germany), this effect does not exist because in these countries income earned by their multinationals abroad is exempt from taxes at home.

---

[13] Slemrod (1990) discusses this as a possible reason for a lack of significant difference in the tax response of FDI from exemption and credit countries.

[14] One would expect that multinational firms would have an easier time using transfer pricing techniques where the tax administration in the host country is less developed or sophisticated. The composition or nature of the FDI may also contribute to the use of transfer pricing. Unfortunately, we lacked information on either of these issues.

The impact of the home country tax system on FDI in those countries that use a global income approach (the United States, the United Kingdom, and Japan in our sample) is complicated by several factors.[15] Most countries with a global income approach (certainly the three home countries in our sample) give a credit to their multinationals against their home tax liability for the business taxes paid abroad, to avoid the double taxation of the same income. However, this credit is typically limited to the amount that the multinational would have paid on the same income according to home country tax rules. Thus the difference between the effective rate of tax in the host country, τ_h and the rate that would apply on the same income in the home country can be significant. However, it is not entirely clear how to measure this difference. Shah and Slemrod (1991) measure this difference as $(t_H - \tau_h)$ where t_H is the statutory rate or it should be defined as a rate closer to the home country statutory rate than to its effective rate, τ_H.[16] Now if $(t_H - \tau_h) < 0$, the home country tax regime has no effect on the role of host country taxes on FDI.[17] The level of τ_h is all that matters. If $(t_H - \tau_h) > 0$, the multinational firm will still owe tax in the home country. However, the home country typically will not impose a tax on the multinational firm until its profits are repatriated. Therefore, some benefits will accrue to the multinational firm until repatriation or no additional tax will be due if the profits are never repatriated. A further complication is that no additional tax or lower taxes will be due by the multinational firm if a tax sparing agreement exists between the home and host countries.[18] In our sample of home countries in the worldwide-income-plus-credit group, Japan and the United Kingdom have signed tax sparing agreements, but the United States has signed none.[19]

---

[15] See Slemrod (1995) for a lucid discussion of these issues.

[16] The reason Shah and Slemrod argue is that foreign-source income is not generally granted home-source tax benefits such as accelerated depreciation or investment tax credits.

[17] Note that the home country effective rate (τ_H) can still make it more or less attractive for the multinational to invest at home *vis-a-vis* foreign countries. With $(t_H - \tau_h) < 0$ the multinational firm is in an excess credit position. Home countries may allow the multinational firm to use these excess credits against the home tax liability owed on the repatriation of profits from other host countries where $t_H > \tau_h$.

[18] Under these agreements the home country allows the multinational firm to claim tax credits for taxes due in the host country at an agreed-upon rate even though in reality the multinational may have never paid the tax because of tax holidays or other incentives offered by the host country.

[19] A final factor to be considered is that the additional home tax may not exist depending on the source of funds of the FDI. According to Hartman (1984, 1985) if the FDI is financed with retained earnings of a foreign subsidiary rather than the transfer of funds, the host country tax burden is all that matters. This issue is not pursued any further in this paper because our data do not allow the identification of the source of funds.

To control for other factors affecting the flow of FDI, we include three other explanatory variables in the regression equations. First, FDI in any particular host country is expected to be negatively related to wage rate or hourly compensation cost in that host country and positively related to the hourly compensation costs in the other three host countries. Second, FDI in any host country is expected to be negatively related to the likelihood of currency depreciation in the host country and positively related to the likelihood of depreciation in the other competing host countries. The likelihood of currency depreciation is proxied by the number of months of imports covered by international reserves. Third, because much of FDI in the four host countries is export oriented, FDI in any host country is expected to be positively related to its export price index and negatively related to export price of the competing host countries.

The general form of the empirical model for FDI from home country i into host country j (F_{ij}) is represented by:

$$F_{ij} = f\left[v,\ \tau_i,\ \tau_j,\ (t_i - \tau_j),\ \bar{\tau}_{jo},\ w_j,\ \bar{w}_{jo},\ e_j,\ \bar{e}_{jo},\ p_j,\ \bar{p}_{jo} \right] \tag{1}$$

where v represents a time trend, τ_i the effective tax rate in home country i, τ_j the effective tax rate in host country j, t_i the statutory tax rate in home country i, $\bar{\tau}_{jo}$ the average effective tax rate in the other three hosts countries, w_j the hourly compensation cost in host country j, $\bar{w}_{jo}$ the average hourly compensation in the other three host countries, e_j the number of months of imports covered by international reserves in host country j, $\bar{e}_{jo}$ the average number of months of imports covered by international reserves in the other three host countries, p_j the export price index in host country j, $\bar{p}_{jo}$ and the average export price index in the other three host countries.

Due to the presence of serial correlation, the model is specified in a first difference form and is estimated as five sets of equations (one for each home country) with four equations in each set (one for each host country) over a period of 18 years, as follows:

$$\Delta F_{ij} = \delta_{ij} + \beta_{i,j1}\Delta\tau_i + \beta_{i,j2}\Delta\tau_j + \beta_{i,j3}\Delta(t_1 - \tau_j)$$
$$+ \beta_{i,j4}\Delta\tau_{jo} + \beta_{i,j5}\Delta w_j + \beta_{i,j6}\Delta\bar{w}_{jo}$$
$$+ \beta_{i,j7}\Delta e_j + \beta_{i,j8}\Delta\bar{e}_{jo} + \beta_{i,j9}\Delta p_j$$
$$+ \beta_{i,j10}\Delta\bar{p}_{jo} + \varepsilon_{ij.} \tag{2}$$

where ε_{ij} is the random disturbance term, and ΔF_{ij} is the annual change of FDI from home country i ($i = U$ [USA], K [UK], J [Japan], G [Germany], and F [France]) into host country j ($j = HK$ [Hong Kong], M [Malaysia], S [Singapore], and T [Taiwan]).

The disturbance terms cross-home country equations, that is, for home country i, ε_{i1}, ε_{i2}, ε_{i3}, ε_{i4} are likely to be correlated. Culem (1988) suggests that for a given year, FDIs from a specific home country toward different host countries may be positively correlated due to lower (or higher) growth rate of the home market compared to those observed in the rest of the world, or negatively correlated due to the fact that one of the host countries may become more attractive *vis-a-vis* the rest. To account for the possible correlation among the disturbance terms each set of four equations is estimated using a seemingly unrelated regression technique. Finally, and again because of the limited number of observations, we are forced to impose the restriction that the effect of the home country tax system is identical in each of the four host country equations.[20]

IV. DATA SOURCES AND VARIABLE DEFINI-TIONS

The model outlined above is estimated using cross-section and annual time-series data covering 20 pairs of countries over 18 years (1972-1989). Obtaining data for such multicountry estimation is difficult. The data for our estimation have come from a variety of sources. All of the variables and their computations are summarized in Appendix A. In this section, we highlight some issues involved in developing comparable data for a variety of countries.

---

[20] Relaxing this restriction did not lead to improvements in the estimation results but it produced a lack of statistical significance for some coefficients and the wrong signs for others.

The data for the dependent variable in each equation (the change in FDI flow from home country i to host j, ΔF_{ij}) are not entirely homogenous due to differences in reporting of FDI. For example, FDI data for Hong Kong refer to the total investment at the original cost which is the sum of the stock of fixed assets at the original cost and working capital. FDI data for Malaysia includes paid-up capital and loans, FDI data for Singapore refer to the value of gross fixed assets, and FDI data for Taiwan is composed of foreign currency, imports of machinery, equipment and materials, receipts of technical know-how or acquisition of patents, and reinvested earnings.

The effective capital income tax rates (τ_j and τ_i) are constructed using the approach of Mendoza et al. (1994). For the home countries, we use the Mendoza et al. series on τ_i and extend it through 1989. Because of the lack of complete data for all host countries we are forced in some cases to adapt the methodology of Mendoza et al. to fit the available data for these countries. These calculations are detailed in Appendix B.

The wage rate (w) is measured by the hourly compensation cost in U.S. dollars. The hourly compensation cost statistics for all countries except Malaysia are drawn from the *Handbook of Labor Statistics* by the Bureau of Labor Statistics, U.S. Department of Labor. The hourly compensation cost for Malaysia is derived from the annual real earnings (World Bank) per employee by assuming 44 hours worked a week. [21] Export price indexes (p) (unit value indexes) are all taken from the Asian Development Bank's *Key Indicators of Developing Asian and Pacific Countries*.

V. EMPIRICAL RESULTS

Table 2 summarizes the results for the tax variables, the main interest of this paper. For space reasons, the results for the control variables are only discussed, but the full set of results is available from the authors. While all tax variables in Equation 2 were included in the initial runs, the difference between the statutory rate in the home country and the effective rate in the host country was consistently not significant and this variable was dropped from the final set of regressions.

---

[21] The 44 hours is the average work week in Malaysia (Price Waterhouse, 1994).

Table 2. Tax Effects on Foreign Direct Investments

		Foreign Tax Credit Countries [3]			Foreign Tax Exemption Countries [3]	
		USA (ΔF_U)	UK (ΔF_K)	Japan (ΔF_J)	Germany (ΔF_G)	France (ΔF_F)
Home Tax [1]:		-4.8	1.6	10.4	0.04	1.18
(+)		(1.8)**	(2.87)*	(2.13)**	(0.06)	(2.87)*
Host Tax:	Hong Kong $\Delta\tau_{HK}$	-13.7	-2.4	-0.8	-0.02	0.3
(-)		(1.5)	(0.95)	(0.1)	(0.06)	(0.91)
	Malaysia $\Delta\tau_M$	-6.8	-21.8	-17.6	-4.26	0.8
		(1.77)**	(1.88)**	(2.54)*	(5.51)*	(0.16)
	Singapore $\Delta\tau_S$	-0.05	9.27	3.44	0.7	-4.9
		(0.05)	(1.35)	(0.27)	(0.3)	(6.52)*
	Taiwan $\Delta\tau_T$	6.6	-2.3	5.5	-2.13	-1.12
		(0.75)	(1.36)	(1.15)	(1.6)**	(1.56)**
Other	Other than HK	71.0	-4.6	18.9	-0.5	1.08
Host Tax [2]:	$(\Delta\bar{\tau}_{HKO})$	(3.26)*	(0.75)	(0.96)	(0.74)	(1.30)
(+)	Other than M	-5.2	73.7	79.6	13.6	-25.6
	$(\Delta\bar{\tau}_{MO})$	(0.40)	(1.985)**	(3.31)*	(5.6)*	(1.59)**
	Other than S	7.8	-11.7	18.3	-7.2	0.4
	$(\Delta\bar{\tau}_{SO})$	(0.76)	(1.7)**	(1.54)	(3.1)*	(0.56)
	Other than T	12.6	-2.8	14.8	-1.18	-0.09
	$(\Delta\bar{\tau}_{TO})$	(0.79)	(0.86)	(1.68)**	(0.49)	(0.07)

[1] Home country tax effects are restricted to be equal across each set of host countries to economize in degrees of freedom.
[2] The average of the other host country's effective tax rates is used to economize in degrees of freedom.
[3] The credit/exemption classification are based on the general treatment category from Price Waterhouse (1995). For many countries, the general treatment may be altered by treaties with specific countries.
* Significant at the 1-percent level; ** Significant at 5-percent level.

The coefficient for the home country effective tax rate (τ_H) is positive in four out of five countries and statistically significant for the United Kingdom, Japan, and France. As the domestic effective rate of taxation in these three countries increases, the level of FDI goes up in the four host countries. The positive and significant coefficient for France, an exemption or territorial system country, supports the hypothesis that the home country tax system is a determinant of FDI from both territorial and global income tax systems. [22] The coefficient for the domestic effective tax rate, τ_H, is negative and statistically significant for the United States. We do not have a good explanation for this result. It could be that for the United States τ_H captures, to a

---

[22] Slemrod (1990) also tested the hypothesis that FDI from exemption or territorial system countries should be positively related to the domestic effective tax rate, but found no empirical support for it.

larger extent than is the case for the United Kingdom and Japan, the negative effect on FDI of higher taxes on repatriated profits.[23] One institutional difference that may matter is that the United States has no tax sparing agreement with the four host countries, indeed with no country. On the other hand, the United Kingdom and Japan have had tax sparing agreements during the sample period (1972-89) with Singapore and Malaysia.[24] The presence of tax sparing agreements makes repatriation of profits less sensitive to changes in the effective rate of taxation in the home country.

The second set of empirical results in Table 2 corresponds with the coefficients for the effective rate of taxation in the host country, τ_h. Most of these coefficients, as expected, take a negative sign and they are statistically significant for Malaysia for FDI from all home countries with the exception of France, for Taiwan for FDI from Germany and France, and for Singapore for FDI from France.[25] Overall these results support those in the previous literature that have found sensitivity of inward FDI to the host country tax burden. The greater number of negative and statistically significant coefficients for τ_h for FDI from home countries with a territorial or exemption system also agrees with *a priori* expectations. FDI from territorial or exemption countries should be more sensitive to the host country tax system than FDI from global income or credit home countries. The lack of statistical significance for Hong Kong may reflect the fact that Hong Kong has had comparatively low tax rates, a simple tax structure and the lowest variation for the effective tax rate over the sample period with a standard deviation of 0.942. However, the lack of statistical significance for many of these coefficients for Singapore, Taiwan, and Hong Kong may reflect the observation error associated with the difficulty of measuring average effective rates of taxation.

The third set of coefficients in Table 2 measures the impact of the average effective rates of taxation in three other competing countries ($\bar{\tau}_o$). The results provide limited support for the hypotheses that FDI into any given host country is sensitive to changes

---

[23] We have no information on how much of the profits in the host countries is repatriated and how much is reinvested.

[24] The United Kingdom tax sparing agreement has been in force with Singapore from 1966 and with Malaysia since 1967. Japan's tax sparing agreement with Singapore has been in force since 1961 and with Malaysia since 1963. See Diamond and Diamond (1996).

[25] Chang and Cheng (1993) found FDI from the United States and Japan to be unresponsive to Taiwan taxes, the same result we obtained here. Chang and Cheng (1993) did not study FDI into Taiwan from any other home countries.

in the effective rate of taxation in competing host countries. This evidence is strongest in the case of Malaysia. FDI into this country from the United Kingdom, Japan, and Germany was quite sensitive to the average effective rates in the other three host countries. FDI from the United States into Hong Kong, and FDI from Japan into Taiwan also appear to have been responsive to average effective rates in the other three host countries. FDI from Japan appears to be most sensitive to tax burdens in alternative host countries. This was not expected, given that Japan is a global income or tax credit country. However, the tax sparing agreements between Japan and some of the host countries should enhance this sensitivity. The negative and statistically significant coefficients for Singapore for FDI from the United Kingdom and Germany, and for Malaysia for FDI from France were unexpected. The flows of FDI are relatively small in all these cases, which may mean that FDI is driven by a small number of multinational firms that have strong ties to the host countries for other reasons. The facts that Singapore appears to have often taken the lead and that its tax policy changes have been followed by other countries in the region (Chia and Whalley, 1995) may also complicate the actual impact of tax competition for Singapore. Nevertheless we have no straightforward interpretation for these results.

The rest of the estimation results (not shown in Table 2) for the control variables were mixed. These results are contained in 20 regressions and are difficult to summarize. From a home country perspective, the best overall performance, including statistical significance and expected signs for the coefficients, corresponded to the four regressions for the United States. From a host country perspective, the best performance corresponded to the five regressions for Hong Kong.

The coefficients for the host country for hourly compensation (w_j), exchange rate risk or months of imports covered by foreign exchange reserves (e_j), and the export price index (p_j) took the expected sign and were statistically significant in a number of equations. But some of these coefficients also were insignificant or took the wrong sign in several other equations. The same mixed pattern emerged for the coefficients of the variables measuring the average exchange rate risk, hourly wages, and export prices in the other host countries $\bar{w}_{jo}$, $\bar{e}_{jo}$, $\bar{p}_{jo}$.

VI. CONCLUSION

This paper studies the role of tax systems in the flow of FDI from a group of five industrialized countries into a group of four Asian countries. The analysis and estimation allows not only for the roles of the tax systems of each pair of home and host countries on FDI, as conventionally done in the literature, but also for the potential role played by the tax systems of competing host countries.

Our results support previous findings in the literature. With some exceptions, we find that FDI tends to be inversely related to the rate of effective taxation in the home country. This is so for both global income or tax credit home countries and territorial or exemption home countries. Also with some exceptions, FDI tends to be negatively related to the rate of effective taxation in the host country and this effect tends to be more pronounced for FDI coming from home countries with territorial or exemption systems.

In addition, our results lend some support to the hypothesis, not previously tested in the literature, that FDI into any host country is sensitive to the tax system of potentially competitive host countries. This sensitivity in more pronounced for Malaysia than for the other three host countries studied in this paper (Hong Kong, Singapore, and Taiwan). These results show that the tax policies of developing countries can put them in competition with each other for FDI.

Although suggestive, the results in the paper should be considered preliminary. Because of the limited number of observations, our empirical analysis imposes restrictions on the estimation of home country tax effects and it uses average figures for the effective tax rates of competing host countries. In the future, more complete data should allow unrestricted estimation and the differentiation by source of financing and by economic sector. Another avenue for future research is the formulation and estimation of behavioral models of tax competition among developing countries.

APPENDIX A

Data Definitions and Sources

Variables	Proxies	Data Sources	Note
ΔF_{itHK}: inward FDI data of Hong Kong	Total investment at original cost	*Survey of Overseas Investment in Hong Kong's Manufacturing Industries*, Hong Kong Government Industry Department	Sum of the stock of fixed assets at the original cost and working capital
ΔF_{iM}: inward FDI data of Malaysia	Foreign investment in applications received	Annual reports by the Malaysian Industrial Development Authority (MIDA)	Sum of paid-up capital and loans
ΔF_{iS}: inward FDI data of Singapore	Investment commitment in manufacturing	*Economic Development Board Yearbook*, Singapore's Economic Development Board	Value of gross fixed assets
ΔF_{iT}: inward FDI data of Taiwan	Approved foreign investment in all industries	*Statistics on Overseas Chinese & Foreign Investment, Technical Cooperation, Outward Investment, Outward Technical Cooperation*, Taiwan's Investment Commission	Sum of foreign currency, imports of machinery, equipment and materials, receipts of technical know-how or acquisition of patents, and reinvested earnings (Schive, 1990)
w: wage rate	Hourly compensation costs	For Hong Kong, Singapore and Taiwan, *Handbook of Labor Statistics* U.S. Department of Labor; For Malaysia, *World Tables*, World Bank.	w = weekly real earnings divided by 44 hours
p: export price	Export price index (unit value index)	*Key Indicators of Developing Asian and Pacific Countries*, Asian Development Bank	
e: currency depreciation risk	For countries except Hong Kong, the ratio of monthly international reserves to imports	For Malaysia and Singapore, *World Tables*, World Bank. For Taiwan, *Key Indicators of Developing Asian and Pacific Countries*, Asian Development Bank	
	For Hong Kong, nominal exchange rate	*Statistical Abstracts, U.S.*	International reserves for Hong Kong are not available
$\tau_{i,j}$: effective capital income tax rate.	See description in Appendix B.		

188

APPENDIX B

The Computation of Effective Capital Income Tax Rates

The effective capital income tax rate is constructed using the approach of Mendoza, Razin, and Tesar (1994). Basically, this effective rate is an income-weighted tax rate on capital income. To compute the tax rates on capital income, Mendoza et al. first estimated the households' average tax rate on total income, τ_d:

$$\tau_d = \left[\frac{taxes\ on\ income,\ profits,\ and\ capital\ gains\ of\ individuals}{household\ income} \right] * 100 \quad \text{(B.1)}$$

where household income is obtained from the sum of wages and salaries (W), property and entrepreneurial income (PEI) which includes dividend, interest, rent, royalties, and the operating surplus of private unincorporated enterprises ($OSPUE$). Then the effective capital income tax rate τ_k is constructed as:

$$\tau_k = \left[\frac{ICIT + CIT + PIT + CGT}{operating\ surplus\ of\ the\ economy} \right] * 100 \quad \text{(B.2)}$$

where $ICIT = \tau_d (OSPUE + PEI)$ are the capital income taxes paid by the households, assuming that all sources of the households' income are taxed uniformly, CIT are the corporate income taxes, PIT are all recurrent taxes on immovable property paid by households and others, and CGT are taxes on financial and capital transactions. The operating surplus of the economy, representing the before-tax capital income, is the gross product at the producers' values deducted by the sum and intermediate consumption, employee compensation, consumption of fixed capital and subsidies. Applying the same method and accessing the same data sources as Mendoza et al. (see Table B-1), we calculate 1972-1989 tax rates for the home countries (Japan, Germany, France, United Kingdom, and the United States).

The data used for the construction of the effective capital income tax for the host countries are summarized also in Table B-1. We adapted Mendoza et al.'s computations as follows. The Operating Surplus (OS) data for developing countries are obtained indirectly by applying the Mendoza et al.'s definition. In our setting, OS is calculated as:

189

OS = GDP at current market prices - indirect taxes less subsidies -
employee compensation - consumption of capital.

In the case of Hong Kong, the adjustments are minimal. The taxes levied under the Inland Revenue Ordinance are profits tax, salaries tax, property tax, and interest tax. There is no tax on the capital and financial transactions in Hong Kong, and, hence, CGT equals zero in this case. From the Departmental Report by the Commissioner of Inland Revenue and Ho (1994), tax revenue information on $ICIT$, CIT, PIT could be accessed and, hence, the total capital income tax revenue, the numerator of equation (B.2), is obtained.

In the case of Malaysia, there is a need to split the individual income tax, for which data are available, into wage income taxes and individual capital income taxes. First, an estimate for taxable income is calculated by taking the average annual earnings data per employee as annual before-tax income, and then deducting personal allowances. Second, the wage tax payment for a representative individual is obtained by applying the rate schedules. To get an estimate of the wage tax revenue for the economy as a whole, this amount is multiplied by the employed population. Subtracting total wages taxes from the individual income taxes gives a proxy for individual capital income tax. There is no tax on finance and capital transactions in Malaysia, and, hence, CGT equals zero in this case.

In the case of Singapore, only total tax revenues are available. We use the information in Asher (1990) to estimate the percentage shares of individual income tax revenue and corporate income tax revenue. The effective capital income tax rates for Singapore are then constructed applying the same techniques used for Malaysia.

In the case of Taiwan, τ_k can be derived easily. However, recurrent tax on immovable property (PIT) is proxied by the sum of the land value tax and land value increment tax.

Table B-1. Data Sources for the Computation of Effective Capital Income Tax Rates

Variables	Home Countries	Hong Kong	Malaysia	Singapore	Taiwan
Taxes on income, profits, and capital gain of individuals	*Revenue Statistics,* OECD	*Departmental Report,* Commissioner of Inland Revenue;	*Government Finance Statistics,* IMF;	*Government Finance Statistics,* IMF;	*Yearbook of Financial Statistics of the Republic of China,* Taiwan Department of Statistics, Ministry of Finance;
Household income:	*National Accounts: Volume II. Detailed Tables,* OECD	Ho (1994).	*National Accounts Statistics: Main Aggregates and Detailed Tables,* United Nations;	*National Accounts Statistics: Main Aggregates and Detailed Tables,* United Nations;	
Wages and salaries (*W*)					*Taiwan Statistical Data Book,* Council for Economic Planning and Development.
Property and entrepreneurial income (*PEI*)				*World Tables,* World Bank;	
Operating surplus of private unincorporated enterprises (*OSPUE*)			*Doing Business in Malaysia.*	*Doing Business in Singapore.*	
Corporate income taxes (*CIT*)	*Revenue Statistics,* OECD				
Recurrent taxes on immovable property paid by households and others (*PIT*)					
Taxes on financial and capital transactions (*CGT*)					
Operating surplus of the economy	*National Accounts: Volume II. Detailed Tables,* OECD				

APPENDIX C

Table C-1 contains a summary of the tax rates, depreciation methods and rates, tax holidays, and investment tax credits allowed in the four host countries for selected years covered by this study. This summary shows that taxing policies affecting foreign direct investment vary significantly among the four host countries. Hong Kong and Taiwan provide no tax holidays to attract foreign direct investment to their countries. Hong Kong's strategy for attracting foreign direct investment has been to provide low or no import and export duties, a low corporate tax rate, and no taxation of dividends. [*] Malaysia and Singapore target specific industries and types of activities (e.g., shipping, high technology industries, industries which employ a certain number of individuals, etc.) to receive tax relief and provide either reduced tax rates or tax holidays for as many as twelve years. In these two countries, most companies must receive permission to qualify for a tax holiday, adding more complexity to the tax system, but enabling the governments to tailor their policies more to the needs of their countries. Taiwan does not appear to target any specific activities to attract investment. Diamond and Diamond (1988) identifies Hong Kong, Malaysia, and Singapore as tax havens, but does not include Taiwan in its analysis.

---

[*] Hong Kong's corporate tax rates during the years 1972-1989 were the lowest of the four countries, ranging from 15-17 percent. Singapore and Malaysia had rates ranging from 32-45 percent; Taiwan used a graduated rate structure, with rates from 15-35 percent.

Table C-1. Selected Characteristics
Income Tax Systems of Hong Kong, Malaysia, Singapore, and Taiwan

County	Tax Rates	Depreciation Methods & Rates	Tax Holidays	Investment Tax Credit
Hong Kong	17 percent, except limited companies, which are 18.5 percent (Rates apply to tax years 1984-84; previous rates were 15 percent and 16.5 percent, respectively; in 1989, rate were 16.5 percent and 18 percent, respectively.	Straight-line method. System provides for initial allowances (first year) of service (e.g., in 1984, industrial buildings - 20 percent; machinery and equipment - 55 percent). Annual rates: generally, industrial buildings-4 percent; other assets - 10 percent to 30 percent.	Not granted--tax relief afforded in other ways such as the lack of import/export duties and tax on dividends.	Not applicable
Malaysia	40 percent + 5 percent development income tax for 1982-1988; 35 percent + 4 percent development income tax for 1989.	Straight-line method applies in most instances. For selected years, such as 1981-1985, accelerated depreciation allowance permitted for "qualifying expenditures." Initial allowances (first year): 10 percent to 60 percent for mid 1980s, but lowered to 10 percent-20 percent by the end of the 1980s. Annual rates: generally, industrial buildings - 2 percent; other assets - 6 percent to 20 percent.	From 1971-1989, rules changed numerous times. Generally, 2-12 year tax holidays available for pioneer companies, companies employing more than 50 employees, companies locating in certain sites, and companies in certain industries; other significant tax relief was also afforded certain industries and activities, such as hotels and shipping.	Allowed in some years (e.g., rates in 1984, 25 percent to 115 percent of the capital expenditures).
Singapore	40 percent in the early 1980s; lowered to 32 percent by 1989.	Straight-line method generally applies. Prior to 1981, could use declining balance method. 1981-1985 accelerated depreciation allowed for capital expenditures on construction. Initial allowances (first year): 20 percent to 25 percent, but cannot claim if elected accelerated depreciation. Annual rates: industrial buildings - 3 percent; other assets - 5 percent to 16 percent; higher rates afforded to high-tech equipment.	From 1972-1989, rules changed numerous times. In general, tax holidays of 5-10 years provided for pioneer enterprise, certain expansion by established enterprises, and export enterprises; longer tax holidays afforded to very large enterprises; other significant tax relief granted to enterprises engaged in specific activities or industries, such as trade and shipping.	Not applicable
Taiwan	Graduated rates of 15 percent to 35 percent in the early 1980s; by 1989, 2-rate system of 15 percent up to NT $100,000; 25 percent for income above that amount.	Straight-line, fixed percentage on declining balance or working hour methods can be used. No initial allow-ance (first year). Annual allowance: industrial buildings - 1 1/4 percent; other assets - 5 percent to 50 percent.	5 years for newly established productive enterprise. 4 years for plant expansion. 1-4 years for selected enterprises.	Rates varied significantly during 1980s, from 5 percent to 20 percent. Assets purchased in-country receive higher rate than imported capital assets.

SOURCES: Diamond and Diamond (1988); Deloitte, Haskins and Sells (1982a); Deloitte, Haskins and Sells (1982b); Deloitte, Haskins and Sells (1984); Deloitte, Haskins and Sells (1985); Coopers & Lybrand (1985); and Coopers & Lybrand (1990).

REFERENCES

Agodo, Oriye. 1978. "The Determinants of U.S. Private Manufacturing Investments in Africa." *Journal of International Business Studies* 9(3): 95-107.

Asher, Mukul. 1990. *Singapore's Fiscal System in International Perspective*. Paper presented at the Conference on the Fiscal System of Singapore.

Asian Development Bank. 1991. *Key Indicators of Developing Asia and Pacific Countries*.

Auerbach, Alan. 1995. "The Cost of Capital and Investment in Developing Countries." In *Fiscal Incentives for Investment and Innovation*, Anwar Shah, ed. Oxford: Oxford University Press.

Bartik, Timothy J. 1991. *Who Benefits from State and Local Economic Development Policies*. Kalamazoo, MI: Upjohn Institute for Employment Research.

Boadway, Robin and Anwar Shah. 1995. "Perspectives on the Role of Investment Incentives in Developing Countries." In *Fiscal Incentives for Investment and Innovation*, Anwar Shah, ed. Oxford: Oxford University Press.

Caves, Richard E. 1982. *Multinational Enterprise and Economic Analysis*. Cambridge: Cambridge University Press.

Chang, Ching-huei and Peter W. H. Cheng. 1993. "Tax Policy and Foreign Direct Investment in Taiwan." In *The Political Economy of Tax Reform*, Takotoshi Ito and Anne O. Kruger, eds., pp. 315-38. Chicago: University of Chicago Press.

Chia, Ngee Choon and John Whalley. 1995. "Patterns in Investment Tax Incentives Among Developing Countries." In *Fiscal Incentives for Investment and Innovation*, Anwar Shah, ed. Oxford: Oxford University Press.

Coopers & Lybrand. 1985. *International Tax Summaries - 1985: A Guide for Planning and Decisions*. New York: John Wiley & Sons.

____. 1990. *International Tax Summaries - 1990: A Guide for Planning and Decisions*. New York: John Wiley & Sons.

Culem, Claudy G. 1988. "The Locational Determinants of Direct Investment Among Industrialized Countries." *European Economic Review* 32: 885-904.

Cummins, Jason G. and R. Glenn Hubbard. 1994. "The Tax Sensitivity of Foreign Direct Investment: Evidence From Firm-Level Panel Data. Working Paper No. 4703. National Bureau of Economic Research.

Cushman, David O. 1985. "Real Exchange Rate Risk, Expectations and the Level of Direct Investment." *Review of Economics and Statistics* (May): 297-308.

Deloitte, Haskins and Sells. 1982a. *Taxation in Singapore*. New York: Haskins and Sells International Tax and Business Service.

____. 1982b. *Taxation in Taiwan*. New York: Haskins and Sells International Tax and Business Service.

____. 1984. *Taxation in Malaysia*. New York: Haskins and Sells International Tax and Business Service.

____. 1985. *Taxation in Hong Kong*. New York: Haskins and Sells International Tax and Business Service.

Diamond, Walter H. and Dorothy B. Diamond, eds. 1988. *Tax Havens of the World*. New York: Matthew Bender & Company, Inc.

____, eds. 1996. *International Tax Treaties of All Nations, Volume I-XV* and *Series B, Volume I-XXXVIII*. Dobbs Ferry, New York: Oceana Publications Inc. Release 96-3.

Dunning, John H. 1980. "Toward an Eclectic Theory of International Production: Some Empirical Tests." *Journal of International Business Studies* 11(1): 9-31.

____. 1981. *International Production and the Multinational Enterprise*. London: Allen and Unwin.

____. 1992. *Multinational Enterprises and the Global Economy*. Wokingham, England: Addison-Wesley.

Fan, Chuen-Mei. 1991. "An International Perspective on Tax Reform Strategies." *Australian Tax Forum* 8: 539-49.

Frost K.A. and Stein J.C. 1989. "Exchange Rates and Foreign Direct Investment: An Imperfect Capital Market Approach." Working Paper Series No. 2914. New York: National Bureau of Economic Research.

Gordon, R.H. 1990. "Can Capital Income Taxes Survive in Open Economics?" NBER Working Paper No. 3416.

Green R.T. and W.H. Cunningham. 1975. "The Determinants of U.S. Foreign Investment: An Empirical Examination." *Management International Review* 15: 113-20.

Hall, Robert E. and Dale W. Jorgenson. 1967. "Tax Policy and Investment Behavior." *American Economic Review* 57(3): 391-414.

Hamada, K. 1966. "Strategic Aspects of Taxation Foreign Investment Income." *Quarterly Journal of Economics* 80:361-75.

Hartman, David G. 1984. "Tax Policy and Foreign Direct Investment in the United States." *National Tax Journal* (December): 475-87.

____. 1985. "Tax Policy and Foreign Direct Investment." *Journal of Public Economics* 26: 107-21.

Ho, H.C.Y. 1994. "Effective Corporate Tax Rates on Capital Income in Hong Kong." In *Taxation and Economic Development Among Pacific Asian Countries*, Richard A. Musgrave, Ching-Huei Chang, and John Riew, eds, pp. 140-55. Oxford: Westview Press.

Hong Kong Government Industry Department. 1993. *Survey of Overseas Investment in Hong Kong's Manufacturing Industries*. Hong Kong: Hong Kong Government Industry Department.

Ihlanfeldt, Keith. 1994. "Tax Incentives for Economic Development in the State of Georgia." Staff Paper No. 2. of Joint Study Commission on Revenue Structure, State of Georgia. Atlanta, GA: Policy Research Center, Georgia State University.

Janeba, Eckhard. 1995. "Corporate Income Tax Competition, Double Taxation Treaties, and Foreign Direct Investment." *Journal of Public Economies* 56(2): 311-25.

Julius, DeAnne. 1990. *Global Companies & Public Policy: The Growing Challenge of Foreign Direct Investment*. New York: The Royal Institute of International Affairs.

King, Mervyn A. and Don Fullerton. 1984. *The Taxation of Income From Capital: A Comparative Study of the United States, the United Kingdom, Sweden, and West Germany*. Chicago: University of Chicago Press.

Ladd, Helen. 1992. "Mimicking of Local Tax Burdens Among Neighboring Countries." *Public Finance Quarterly* 20(4): 450-67.

Leechor, Chad and Jack Mintz. 1991. "Taxation of International Income by Capital-Exporting Countries: The Perspective of Thailand." In *Tax Policy in Developing Countries*, Javad Khalizadeh-Shirazi and Anwar Shah. Washington, D.C.: World Bank.

Lucas, Robert B. 1993. "On the Determinants of Direct Foreign Investment: Evidence from East and Southeast Asia." *World Development* 21(3): 391-406.

Malaysian Industrial Development Authority. Various Issues. *Statistics on the Manufacturing Sector of Malaysia*. Malaysia: Malaysia Industrial Development Authority.

Malaysian Industrial Development Authority. Various Issues. *Annual Report*. Malaysia: Malaysia Industrial Development Authority.

Markusen, James R. 1991. "The Theory of the Multinational Enterprise: A Common Analytical Framework." In *Direct Foreign Investment in Asia's Developing Economies and Structural Change in the Asia-Pacific Region*, Eric D. Ramstella, ed. Boulder and Oxford: Westview Press.

McCulloch, Rachel. 1993. *New Perspectives on Foreign Direct Investment*. In *Foreign Direct Investment*, Kenneth A. Froot, ed. Chicago: The University of Chicago Press.

McKenzie, K.J. and J.M. Mintz. 1992. "Tax Effects on the Cost of Capital: A Canada-U.S. Comparison." In *Canada-U.S. Tax Comparisons*, J. Shoven and J. Whalley, eds. Chicago: University of Chicago Press.

Mendoza, Enrique, Assaf Razin and Linda Tesar. 1994. "Effective Tax Rates in Macroeconomics: Cross-Country Estimates of Tax Rates on Factor Incomes and Consumption." Working Paper No. 4864. Cambridge, MA: National Bureau of Economic Research.

Mintz, Jack M. and Thomas Tsiopoulos. 1994. "The Effectiveness of Corporate Tax Incentives for Foreign Investment in the Presence of Tax Crediting." *Journal of Public Economics* 55: 233-55.

Mintz, J.M. and H. Tulkeus. 1990. "Strategic Use of Tax Rates and Credits in a Model of International Corporate Income Tax Competition." CORE Discussion Paper No. 9073.

Newlon, Timothy S. 1987. "Tax Policy and the Multinational Firm's Financial Policy and Investment Decisions." Ph.D. Dissertation, Princeton University.

OECD. 1992. *Revenue Statistics of OECD Member Countries*. Paris: OCED.

____. 1993. *Promoting Foreign Direct Investment in Developing Countries*. Paris: OCED.

____. 1994. *National Accounts: Detailed Tables, Volume II*. Paris: OECD.

Price Waterhouse. 1982a. *Doing Business in Singapore*. New York: Price Waterhouse.

____. 1982b. *Doing Business in Taiwan*. New York: Price Waterhouse.

____. 1994. *Doing Business in Malaysia*. New York: Price Waterhouse.

Price Waterhouse. 1985. *Doing Business in Hong Kong*. New York: Price Waterhouse.

____. 1995. *Corporate Taxes: A Worldwide Summary*. New York: Price Waterhouse.

Ragazzi, Giorgio. 1973. "Theories of the Determinants of Direct Foreign Investment." International Monetary Fund Staff Papers 20(2): 471-98.

Redel, James. 1975. "The Nature and Determinants of Export-Oriented Direct Foreign Investment in a Developing Country: A Case Study of Taiwan." *Weltwirtschaftliches Archiv* 3(3): 505-28.

Roo, F.R. and A.A. Ahmed. 1979. "Empirical Determinants of Manufacturing Direct Foreign Investment in Developing Countries." *Economic Development and Cultural Change* 27(4): 751-67.

Sanchez-Ugarte, Fernando. 1987. "Rationality of Income Tax Incentives." In *Supply-Side Tax Policy, Its Relevance to Developing Countries*, Ved P. Gandhi, ed. Washington, D.C.: International Monetary Fund.

Schive Chi. 1990. *The Foreign Factor: The Multinational Corporation's Contribution to the Economic Modernization of the Republic of China*. Stanford, CA: Hoover Institution Press.

Shah, Anwar and Joel Slemrod. 1990. "Tax Sensitivity of Foreign Direct Investment. Working Papers WPS 434. Washington, D.C.: The World Bank.

____. 1991. "Taxation and Foreign Direct Investment." In *Tax Policy in Developing Countries*, Javad Khalizadeh-Shirazi and Anwar Shah, eds. Washington D.C.: World Bank.

Singapore Economic Development Board. Various Issues. *Economic Development Board Yearbook*. Singapore: Singapore Economic Development Board.

Sinn, Hans-Werner. 1987. *Capital Income Taxation and Resource Allocation*. Amsterdam: North-Holland.

Slemrod, Joel. 1990. "Tax Effects on Foreign Direct Investment in the United States: Evidence from a Cross-Country Comparison. In *Taxation in the Global Economy*, Assaf Razin and Joel Slemrod, eds. Chicago: The University of Chicago Press.

___. 1995. "Tax Policy Toward Foreign Direct Investment in Developing Countries in Light of Recent International Tax Changes." In *Fiscal Incentives for Investment and Innovation*, Anwar Shah, ed. Oxford: Oxford University Press.

Taiwan Council for Economic Planning and Development. 1992. *Taiwan Statistical Data Book*. Taiwan, Republic of China: Council for Economic Planning and Development.

Taiwan Department of Statistics, Ministry of Finance. 1991. *Yearbook of Financial Statistics of the Republic of China* . Taiwan, Republic of China: Department of Statistics, Ministry of Finance.

Taiwan Investment Commission, Ministry of Economic Affairs. 1991. *Statistics on Overseas Chinese & Foreign Investment, Technical Cooperation, Outward Investment, and Outward Technical Cooperation*. Taiwan, Republic of China: Investment Commission, Ministry of Economic Affairs.

Tanzi, Vito. 1996. "Globalization, Tax Competition and the Future of Tax Systems." IMF Working Paper No. 96/141. Washington D.C.: International Monetary Fund.

Tsai, Pan-Long. 1991. "Determinants of Foreign Direct Investment in Taiwan: An Alternative Approach with Time-Series Data." *World Development* 19(2/3): 275-85.

United Nations. 1993. *National Accounts Statistics: Main Aggregates and Detailed Tables, 1991*.

United States Department of Labor, Bureau of Labor Statistics. 1989. *Handbook of Labor Statistics*.

World Bank. 1991. *World Tables*. Baltimore: John Hopkins University Press.

Wasylenko, Michael. 1996. "The Role of Fiscal Incentives in Economic Development. How Ohio Stands Relative to Its Neighbors." In *Taxation and Economic Development: A Blueprint for Tax Reform in Ohio*. Roy Bahl, ed. Columbus, OH: Battelle Press.

Young, Kan H. 1988. "The Effects of Taxes and Rates of Return on Foreign Direct Investment in the United States." *National Tax Journal* 41(1): 109-21.

CHAPTER11 INVESTMENT DISTINCTIONS: THE EFFECT OF TAXES ON FOREIGN DIRECT INVESTMENT IN THE U.S.

DEBORAH L. SWENSON[*]

I. INTRODUCTION

Most studies of taxation and foreign investment limit their investigation to the effects of tax changes on aggregate foreign investment flows. The reason is practical; little evidence is readily available that would allow researchers to consider the effects of taxes on individual firm investment decisions. However, it seems likely that this data limitation may in fact cause researchers to draw the wrong conclusions regarding the actual responsiveness of investment flows to tax differences. In part, there are reasons for firms to remain in a particular location once they have selected it once. This persistence of investment activity may cause most repeat investors to have little responsiveness to small tax differences, while newer investors will respond more vigorously.

The intensity of tax competition provides clear evidence that the empirical quantification of the magnitude of these tax effects is important. In fact, national and subnational governments often express public concern that they will need to compete aggressively if they are to attract foreign investment within their jurisdictional boundaries. At the national level, tax holidays, export processing zones and other investment inducements are the outcome of competition among countries, while

---

[*] University of California, Davis, Department of Economics and NBER.

I thank seminar participants at UC Davis Department of Economics, and the 53rd Congress of the IIPF for comments. Carissa Perez provided excellent research assistance. I thank the Institute of Governmental Affairs IGCC for research support. All remaining errors are my own.

subnational governments, such as U.S. states, compete to assemble fiscal packages in an effort to attract investors. Given the high level of concern over the escalation of fiscal inducements, it is puzzling to learn that many empirical investment studies find little or no role for tax policy in determination of foreign investment flows. In the case of outbound investment from the U.S. Brainard (1997) and Wheeler and Mody (1992) are representative of the failure to find that higher taxes consistently deter foreign investments.[1] As for inbound investment flows to the U.S., the results are mixed, although the studies that provide the most detailed measures of taxes more frequently identify a dampening effect of taxes on foreign investment.[2] This paper provides arguments and evidence regarding the distribution of foreign investment across U.S. states, to show that investment distinctions, especially those distinctions which are based on the transaction-type of investment, influence the tax elasticity one finds for the frequency of investments attracted.

There are many reasons for firms to remain in a particular location once they have selected it. This persistence in investment decisions can be driven by at least two factors. First, at an industry level, agglomeration externalities may cause firms to select sites that have been selected by their predecessors; the benefit of replicating these previous choices is that the firms will reap any externalities that are gained from operation within close proximity to other firms in the same industry. This effect has been shown in work on Japanese firm investments by Head, Ries and Swenson (1994, 1995). The second reason for persistence derives from the cost structure of multinational activity. In the context of exports Roberts and Tybout (1995) demonstrate how previous firm decisions can predispose firms towards continuation of prior activity. As described in Markusen (1995), Markusen and Venables (1996) and Brainard (1997), these are the benefits of concentration which arise when there are large fixed costs associated with the operation of multiple facilities. On the other hand, if a firm concentrates in a single location, it incurs transportation costs that are associated with the service of distant customers. This

---

[1] Hines (1996b) provides a summary of empirical studies of taxes and foreign investment decisions.

[2] Bartik (1991) and Wasylenko (1991) provide comprehensive reviews of the evidence. In general, more powerful tax effects are found for studies that look at smaller jurisdictions (such as metropolitan areas), as compared with interstate or international distributions of investment. Greater effects also tend to emerge in studies that tailor the tax terms to the particular investment industry, or investor characteristics.

places a countervailing incentive for dispersion of the firm - a "proximity" effect. It seems likely however that many of their arguments could be extended towards foreign investment as in Hallward-Driemeier(1996).

The practical implication of agglomeration economies, or lumpy costs of investment is that past decisions will affect current foreign investors' responsiveness to taxes. New investors may consider the benefits of locating near other investors in their own industry, but they will not be constrained by prior firm decisions. As a result, these investors should be more responsive to tax differentials than are firms who have established earlier operations in the U.S. The first part of the paper describes how the responsiveness of foreign investment to taxes is affected by the type of investment, and the nature of the firm's previous activities.

The second part of the paper tests these predictions in the context of U.S. data, to determine whether inter-state tax differentials within the U.S. affect the distribution of new U.S. investments. In the context of data on plant and property investments in the U.S., Hines (1996a) has used the residential versus territorial tax distinction to show that high state taxes appear exert a more inhibiting influence on the investments of those investors most affected by host country taxes - the territorial investors.[3] This paper will instead look at micro investment data that are available from the publication "Foreign Direct Investment in the United States: Transactions" which is published by the U.S. International Trade Administration.

The data contain information on a transaction basis, and include information on the name of the investor and their country of origin. These data also include the city and state location of the investment, the type of transaction (merger, greenfield, equity increase), 4-digit industry code and in many cases, transaction value. The presence of the industry classifications (in conjunction with data from the department of the Census), allow me to examine the potency of tax effects in the presence of agglomeration. In addition, the investment classifications that are provided with the data allow me to compare how different types of investment respond to tax

---

[3] Wolfson and Scholes (1992) describe how the residential versus territorial distinction would affect foreign investor's decisions. Auerbach and Hasset (1993) compute the tax rates for new investments versus acquisition. They question the Wolfson and Scholes hypothesis, since the relative intensity of acquisition activity after the U.S. Tax Reform Act of 1986 did not change systematically for worldwide as opposed to territorial investors.

differentials.

To test the importance of persistence, this paper examines the distribution of foreign investments across U.S. states between 1984 and 1994. Full controls for state characteristics, and industry-specific agglomeration economies are included in the regression specifications. When the data are aggregated, higher tax states appear to attract greater levels of investment. However, when the data are disaggregated by transaction type, different tax responses emerge across the separate classes of investment. The finding of a positive tax correlation in the full sample is driven primarily by merger and acquisition and equity increase activities. In contrast, new plant and plant expansion activities are strongly deterred by higher state taxes. These results demonstrate that aggregation of all investment types may lead to false inferences with respect to tax hypotheses.

The paper proceeds as follows. Section 2 develops a simple model of investment to motivate the importance of taxes and agglomeration measures, and to provide a background for the later econometric specification. Section 3 describes the construction of the data set, and provides some details regarding its construction. Econometric tests of the investment model are carried out in section 4, which is followed by a brief conclusion.

II. MODEL

I model the interaction of state tax differentials with investment type. At the basis of the model is the assumption that firms invest in the state that maximizes their overall profits. However, taxes will not affect all firms uniformly, as the firm's past activities, and the industrial composition of each prospective state affect the firm's current decisions regarding potential investment locations.

Suppose generally that the incremental profit a firm earns on a new investment placed in state s can be represented as:

$$\Pi s = \pi s(vs, \tau s, p)$$

The reduced form profit function represents the additional operating profit the firm

202

will generate if it chooses state s. The function includes arguments for input costs v, and taxes t, both of which are unique to the recipient states. The effect of state specific-factors or agglomeration economies are captured by the vector of input costs v. For example, a Japanese firm that produces electrical machinery may decide that it wishes to locate a new plant in the U.S. This firm will find it advantageous to choose one of the states that already has a high concentration of firms in this industry, as these states offer agglomeration externalities such as a well developed supplier network, or specialized labor. One distinct characteristic of agglomeration economies is that states become increasingly attractive to subsequent investors as the size of their industries grow.

In the long run, the specific-factors model exhibits different dynamic properties. Specific factors cause firms to be attracted to those states that are abundantly endowed with the relevant factors which they use intensively in their production processes. Since the relevant specific factors may not be available in every state, firms will be attracted to the subset of states that are able to supply the appropriate inputs. However, if state attractiveness is based the endowments of specific factors, the state's attractiveness will diminish over the time as the number of firms increases. This is because an increase in the relative concentration in one state will cause congestion, and this congestion will raise the price of the specific factors that are used as inputs. If one had a sufficiently long enough time series, and if it were possible to assume that the mix of industry factor demands did not change over time, it might be possible to disentangle investment incentives based on agglomeration economies from investment persistence driven by factor specific endowments. Throughout this paper, I will use the term "agglomeration" to describe any firm proclivities to cluster. Since my primary interest is in looking at tax effects, I will not speculate about the causes that result in this clustering, and whether the primary force is true agglomeration economies or specific-factor endowments.

Another element of the firm's profit function is the price of the firm's output p. However, I assume that the final sales price of outputs remains the same, regardless of the investment location; there are no compelling reasons to believe that the state location of production will influence the value of the product. As a result, although firm profits depend on the price of output, output prices will not exert any effect on the relative attractiveness of one state as compared with the others. For this reason, no measure of final product prices is included in the econometric specification.

Under this set of conditions, the firm places its investment in the state that yields the greatest profits, as long as the gain in operating profits justifies the fixed cost of investing in the new operations. While all investments involve a fixed cost, I assume that the fixed cost may vary with transaction type. For example, in comparing investment in new plants versus plant expansions it seems likely that the fixed cost of a new plant will exceed the fixed cost associated with a plant expansion.

There are many reasons why the fixed costs associated with a new plant are likely to exceed those of a plant expansion. To begin, differential fixed costs may represent the management complications that arise when a firm seeks to coordinate subsidiary operations of many geographically dispersed plants. The fixed cost differential may also represent the expense involved in developing new supplier networks. For example, if a firm that already has a plant in New York, it could expand its current New York facility. But it may also locate a new plant in another state. If it locates in another state, the firm is likely to forgo the ease of access to upstream and downstream suppliers that it has established through its prior operations in New York. Over time, suppliers may follow the firm if it locates outside of New York. But the initial transition will be less smooth than it would be if they were to repeat their choice of New York. In addition, the firm has already gained knowledge of the state in which it operates, and will have to incur costs of learning about a new state if it decides to locate elsewhere. All of these effects will cause the fixed costs associated with a new plant investment in a new state to exceed the fixed costs associated with a plant expansion. For this reason, I predict that state tax differentials will exert more influence on new plant decisions than on plant expansions.

Fixed costs that differ across investment type are only one reason that could cause the tax responsiveness of different investments to vary in magnitude. There are other reasons to motivate differential tax responses by transaction type. For example, in the case of joint ventures, it is often argued that the foreign partner seeks to pair itself with a U.S. firm which has developed an expertise that would be costly for the foreign partner to develop on its own. In this case, the foreign firm's U.S. activity will be dictated by the locations of potential partners. Unless the firm can identify many potential partners located in a multiplicity of U.S. states, these transactions will demonstrate little tax responsiveness. In contrast, if the foreign firm decides to erect a new manufacturing facility in the U.S., the firm presumably owns rights to the appropriate production technology. It will not be constrained in its choice of states, and for this reason, it should respond to taxes to the extent that state tax differentials alter the relative operating profits they will earn in each prospective state.

III. DATA

The econometric analysis relates the frequency of state investment transactions to the agglomeration and tax factors explained above. In this section I first describe the creation of the data sample, and then provide a sketch of the summary statistics.

The initial roster of foreign investments that are analyzed in this paper are collected from the publication, "Foreign Direct Investment in the United States".[4] The data define foreign direct investment as any transaction where a foreign firm has the direct or indirect ownership of 10 percent or more of the voting securities of an incorporated business enterprise, or an equivalent interest in an unincorporated business. The International Trade Administration collects data from a number of sources beginning with public sources, and transaction participants. The collection is supplemented by secondary sources, which include newspapers, magazines, and business and trade journals. Finally, the data comprise information collected from the public files of Federal regulatory agencies.[5] The primary federal agencies used in this collection effort are the Securities and Exchange Commission (SEC), the Federal Trade Commission (FTC), and the Federal Reserve Board (FRB).

Ondrich and Wasylenko (1993) study this data set in their analysis of state taxes. However, their work focuses solely on the new plant transactions completed between 1978 and 1987. They perform multinomial logit and nested multinomial logit

---

[4] The International Trade Administration of the U.S. Department of Commerce collects this data as stipulated by Executive Order No. 11858, dated May 7, 1975. The order places the responsibility "for the obtainment, consolidation, and analysis of information on foreign direct investment in the United States" with the Secretary of Commerce.

[5] This data differs from BEA foreign investment data in two significant ways. First, this data set includes transactions such as plant expansions, equity increases and real estate transactions that are not part of the BEA's collection effort. However, BEA aggregate data are based on reporting requirements that were established in 1979, and may be more comprehensive as a result. The Transactions Volume 1990 claims that there is a high correlation between the BEA series and the transactions data.

analyses, and use the estimated coefficients to determine the distribution of investment would have been different if states had chosen different tax and expenditure policies. Most of the specifications they estimated imply that corporate taxes reduce investment in new manufacturing plants. However, their analysis does not consider the responsiveness of other investment types.

I measure state taxes by corporate tax rates. These corporate tax rates were collected from publications of the *National Association of State Development Agencies*, and supplemented by tax charts from the *Advisory Council on Intergovernmental Relations*. The identification of tax effects is made possible by the changes in tax rates that occurred over the sample period.

The foreign investment data set characterizes the industry affiliation of the foreign transactions at the 4-digit SIC level. In order to measure agglomeration effects I use 4-digit SIC establishment counts that are collected from the Census Bureau publication, *Manufacturing USA*.

DATA DESCRIPTION

This paper examines transactions data for the eleven year span from 1984 to 1994. Although this data is based on individual foreign investment transactions, it is consistent with a number of trends that are noted in the aggregate data. For example, as panel A of Table 1 shows, the number of transactions is highest in the years 1987 and 1988 of the sample. After 1989, the number of transactions tapers markedly to a range of 300 per year in the early 1990's. This mirrors the peaking of aggregate investment into the U.S., which occurred at the end of the 1980's, and the decline in foreign investment was attributed to foreign economic downturns the early 1990's. The composition of the sample also reflects the international composition of aggregate foreign investment. As Panel C shows, the largest number of investments originated from Japan, followed by the United Kingdom. The origins of the investment have a bearing on the analysis of the data. As Japan and the United Kingdom tax their firms on a residential basis, any tax effects associated with these country's transactions are likely to be less powerful than those for investments that are completed by investors who reside in countries that tax on a territorial basis. Aside from the investments of Japan and the United Kingdom, Canada and Germany were responsible for over 400 transactions each. The remaining investments are spread among a large number of

**Table 1. Foreign Investment in Manufacturing Industries:
Sample Characteristics, 1984-1994.**

Panel A: Distribution of Investments by Year

Year	#OBS	#OBS w/ Value
1984	426	220
1985	440	190
1986	520	274
1987	699	350
1988	602	320
1989	568	312
1990	469	236
1991	347	167
1992	251	132
1993	234	124
1994	338	184
	4,894	2,509

Panel B: Distribution of Investments by Type

Type	Average Value	#OBS	#OBS w/ Value
Acquisition and Merger	$150.2	2229	1240
New Plant	36.9	896	505
Plant Expansion	47.1	534	314
Joint Venture	69.1	401	143
Equity Increase	191.2	313	188
Other	62.0	515	11

Panel C: Distribution of Investments by Country

Australia	120	Hong Kong	22	New Zealand	39
Belgium	46	Ireland	34	South Korea	45
Canada	423	Italy	95	Sweden	118
Finland	41	Japan	1862	Switzerland	162
France	266	Mexico	16	Taiwan	28
Germany	409	Netherlands	158	UK	763
		Norway	2		

countries.

Panel B of Table 1 considers the transaction value of the various investment types. The transaction value is not reported for many of the transactions, so I limit my discussion to the reported values. Acquisitions were the most prevalent transaction type, and at an average transaction value of $150.2 million, they were also the largest in average value. New plants and plant expansions were the next most common investment activities. Where known the transaction value of plant expansions actually exceeded that of new plants. New plants had an average value of $36.9 million while plant expansions had a value of $47.1 million. This is interesting for tax

207

Table 1. Foreign Investment in Manufacturing Industries: Sample Characteristics, 1984-1994 (continued).

Panel D: Distribution of Investments by Industry

Industry	All	AM	NP	PE	JV	EI
20 Food and Kindred Products	309	174	52	19	22	11
21 Tobacco Products	3	2	-	1	-	-
22 Textile Mill Products	8	30	30	8	6	1
23 Apparel and other Textile Products	46	28	9	1	4	3
24 Lumber and Wood Products	28	7	12	4	5	-
25 Furniture and Fixtures	35	7	14	1	8	2
26 Paper and Allied Products	94	42	19	14	7	4
27 Printing and Publishing	276	176	15	8	14	11
28 Chemicals and Allied Products	671	297	139	137	44	33
29 Petroleum and Coal Products	49	24	3	6	5	6
30 Rubber and Misc. Plastic Products	180	68	43	21	19	7
31 Leather and Leather Products	19	13	1	1	2	1
32 Stone, Clay, and Glass Products	178	92	38	9	15	18
33 Primary Metal Industries	250	82	45	43	48	22
34 Fabricated Metal Products	173	62	44	27	20	12
35 Machinery, Except Electrical	658	296	108	58	34	53
36 Electronic and Electric Equipment	664	288	120	68	48	38
37 Transportation Equipment	294	42	123	79	32	6
38 Instruments and Related Products	241	146	46	18	10	11
39 Misc Manufacturing Industries	83	41	23	8	3	2

Notes: The columns include, AM - Mergers and Acquisitions, NP - New Plant, PE - Plant Expansion, JV - Joint Venture, and EI - Equity Increase. The omitted category is Other.

policy, since it implies that a plant expansion may increase a state's productive capacity by a larger amount than a new plant would. If that is true, the fact that new plants may later expand, may increase the value to a state of attracting new plants. The last identified method of transactions was joint ventures, and these had an average value of $69.1 million during the sample period.

Finally, Panel D of Table 1 considers the industry distribution of the foreign investment sample, and the frequency of transaction types for each industry. Three industries attracted the bulk of the investment. These were Standard Industrial Code (SIC) industry 28, Chemicals and Allied Products, SIC industry 35, Non-electrical Machinery and SIC industry 36, Electronic and Electric Equipment. The type of transactions conducted in each of these industries mirrors the aggregate trends reported in Panel B. While acquisitions were the most common transaction method in these industries, both new plant and plant expansion activity were also common.

IV. REGRESSION SPECIFICATION AND RESULTS

The primary goal of my analysis is to gauge the responsiveness of different types of foreign investment to inter-state tax differentials in the U.S. I assume that the number of investments in state s, manufacturing industry i, and year t can be represented by I_{sit}. I begin with the simple estimating specification which describes the count of aggregate investments, and which is used as a baseline for evaluating the later results.

$$(1) \qquad I_{s,i,t} = \alpha + \beta Tax_{s,t} + \gamma Estab_{s,i,t} + \varepsilon_{s,i,t}$$

To capture the sensitivity of investment to taxes the independent variables include *Tax*$_{s,t}$, which is measured by the corporate tax rate. While the corporate tax rate does not vary across industries, it does vary over time. In contrast, since we know the industry classification of the investors, we can be more precise about the agglomeration properties of each state. The variable *Estab*$_{s,i,t}$ provides the count of firms in state s for industry i. The establishment counts are based on the data contained in the *Census of Manufacturing*. Unlike the foreign investment data, which are collected on an annual basis, the establishment counts are only available every 5 years. The most recent counts were conducted in 1982, 1987 and 1992. As a result, the independent variables that describe the frequency of establishment activity, were attached to recent year counts.[6] Foreign investments conducted between 1984 and 1986 were attached to 1982 counts of U.S. establishments, while foreign investments between 1987 and 1991 and between 1992 and 1994 were attached to the U.S. establishment counts of 1987 and 1992 respectively.

The initial results are presented in the first column of Table 2. Since taxes have a non-positive effect on income, I expect a negative coefficient on the tax variable. Contrary to expectation, however, I find that high tax states attracted significantly more foreign investment. The coefficient implies that a state whose taxes rose by 1 point, could be expected to receive 4 percent more investment relative to other states.

---

[6] It would be possible to create an interpolated series that would allow the variable *Estab* to evolve over time. However, the use of an arbitrary assignment scheme would induce measurement error. Another possibility would be to allow the variable *Estab* to grow in the intervening years according to some metric such as state income. However, this scheme is problematic too, since state income or other measures that could be used to apportion the changes, could independently influence investment.

The positive correlation between tax rates and investment frequency can be logically justified in some cases, especially if higher taxes fund business amenities that directly enhance firm profitability. However, since it is also possible that the tax results are driven by mismeasurement, or that the aggregation of the data affects the result for the full sample, further specification testing is warranted.

The second result that emerges in Table 2 is that state agglomeration characteristics, as measured by the variable *Estab*, are also associated with a higher probability of attracting subsequent investment in similar industries. The coefficients demonstrate that investors replicate the investment choices of their predecessors, and that combined influence of a state's specific-factors or agglomeration economies are a strong determinant of investment choice.

In the bottom half of the same column, the regression is augmented to include a full set of state dummy variables. The state dummy variables are added to capture cross-state variation that influences the attractiveness of states to prospective manufacturers. It is likely that amenities such as favorable climate, an effective transportation infrastructure, cultural opportunities, and other characteristics will enhance the attractiveness of some states in the eyes of all investors. The data support this presumption. I find that the joint value of the state fixed effects is highly significant, and that their inclusion in the regression specification increases the log-likelihood dramatically. The inclusion of these variables is important, since there may be unobserved state characteristics that are correlated with either state taxes or establishment agglomeration. If these correlations were present, we would incorrectly infer that taxes and agglomeration were affecting the investment flows, when underlying factors were instead responsible. Nonetheless, I find that the corporate tax variable remains positive in the new specification, and that its coefficient grows somewhat in magnitude, though it is less precisely estimated. At the same time, establishment agglomeration remains highly significant, though the magnitude of the coefficient falls. This is what we would expect if some states are uniformly more attractive to investors in most industries.

I next disaggregate the foreign investment by investment types k. Again, the six investment types I examine comprise new plant, plant expansion, merger &

Table 2. Poisson Regressions of Foreign Investment by State, 1984-1994.

	All	New Plant	Plant Expansion	Merger & Acquisition	Joint Venture	Equity Increase	Other
Corporate Tax	4.1111	-4.5981	-4.5406	13.6304	-4.5489	12.2753	6.9664
	(.6716)	(1.3095)	(1.6670)	(1.1554)	(2.1079)	(3.3329)	(2.1989)
Establishment Agglomeration	.1183	.1069	.0955	.1238	.1155	.0950	.1292
	(.0039)	(.0110)	(.0164)	(.0052)	(.0156)	(.0234)	(.0103)
Constant	-1.8326	-2.7531	-3.2352	-3.4296	-3.7105	-5.4606	-4.3540
	(.0512)	(.0926)	(.1180)	(.0939)	(.1492)	(.2685)	(.1711)
Log-Likelihood	-8112	-2763	-1899	-4306	-1303	-818	-1494
Corporate Tax	7.6888	-67.5803	-38.9709	81.5332	-37.7808	40.2319	1.7462
	(5.9744)	(10.6925)	(13.9683)	(8.8125)	(16.4870)	(28.1393)	(19.0946)
Establishment Agglomeration	.0553	.0529	.0261	.0609	.0556	-.0155	.0593
	(.0055)	(.0151)	(.0250)	(.0072)	(.0222)	(.0456)	(.0143)
State Dummies	Yes	Yes	Yes	Yes	Yes	Yes	Yes
Log-Likelihood	-6587	-2364	-1625	-3599	-1138	-697	-1231

Note: Standard Errors in ( ).

acquisition, joint venture, equity increase and other. The dependent variable is now partitioned so that the counts are performed according to investment type, as well as industry, time and state.

$$(2) \qquad I_{s,i,t,k} = \alpha + \beta \text{Tax}_{s,t} + \gamma \text{Estab}_{s,i,t} + \varepsilon_{s,i,t,k}$$

These results are displayed in the latter columns of Table 2. What is striking is that while establishment agglomeration is uniformly important across investment type, the effects of state corporate taxes are not. I find that there is a strong positive correlation between tax rates and the level of merger & acquisition activity as well as with equity increases and other. In contrast, new plant, plant expansion and Joint venture activity are strongly deterred by high state tax rates.

In economic terms, the results indicate that a state that increased its tax rate by one point, would only receive 95 percent of the new plants, plant expansions, or joint ventures relative to an otherwise similarly situated state. In contrast, the results suggest that this state will attract 14 percent more mergers and acquisitions. All else equal, we might expect that taxes should discourage the acquisition of targets that are located in high tax states. However, Scholes and Wolfson (1992) demonstrate that there may be a tax clientele effect for foreign investors from worldwide tax countries. Some evidence of this effect is also shown in Swenson (1994). In addition we would expect tax effects to be capitalized in the price of those firms which are acquired. As a result, when states enact unexpected tax increases, current capital owners will experience capital losses. New purchasers of the assets would pay a lower price for these assets, since they would now face higher future taxes on their subsequent earnings stream. Since the adjustment to higher state taxes would come through the change in asset prices, it would not be necessary, the frequency of acquisition to fall.

The bottom panel of Table 2 repeats the same set of individual transaction type regressions with the inclusion of state dummy variables. The findings confirm the results of the previous regressions, though the significance of the variables for equity increase no longer meet standard levels of statistical significance. In addition, the tax coefficient for the investment class "other" is no longer statistically significant.

To test my results for robustness, I augment the estimating equation to include

212

regressors that are argued to be important investment determinants, or which have been shown to be significant in other work. State characteristics X, such as population, state income and manufacturing wages, are common to all investors, and transform the estimating equation as follows.

$$(3) \qquad I_{s,i,t,k} = \alpha + \beta Tax_{s,t} + \gamma Estab_{s,i,t} + \delta X_{s,t} + \varepsilon_{s,i,t,k}$$

The new results are presented in Table 3. These results are consistent with the prior analysis, in that the tax coefficient is found to be positive in the aggregated sample, whereas the tax effects are shown to differ across investment types when the sample is disaggregated. Now plant expansions and new plants are negatively correlated with corporate tax rates, while all other investment types are positively correlated. The coefficients for plant expansion and merger are the only ones that are significant at conventional levels. The implied effects of these coefficients is that a state which increases its taxes by one point would receive only 61% of the plant expansion investment garnered by otherwise similar states, but that it would attract a larger portion of the merger & acquisition activity relative to comparable states. Once again, the reason for the strong positive correlation for mergers & acquisitions is unclear, though it may occur because a substantial number of acquisitions were completed by Japanese or British investors. Investors from these countries face a worldwide tax system on their foreign earnings, including those in the U.S. As a result, these investors would not necessarily be deterred by higher state taxes, and might actually represent a clientele for high-tax targets.[7]

One of my earlier predictions was that foreign investors building new plants would be more strongly deterred by high state taxes than foreign investors choosing to expand their plant capacity. Of the three sets of regressions, this is only borne out in the second panel, which includes individual state fixed effects, but no state covariates. The failure of the prediction may relate to one of the maintained assumptions in this analysis. I am assuming that the foreign investor wants to perform a particular type of transaction in the U.S. and that it is then determining the location for that transaction. In the case of new plants and plant expansions this is does not strictly hold. If the firm has no current U.S. facilities, it is constrained in its choice of transaction.

---

[7] See Wolfson and Scholes (1992), Swenson (1994) and Hines (1996a) for arguments about this point.

Table 3: Poisson Regressions of Foreign Investment by State, 1984-1994.

	All	New Plant	Plant Expansion	Merger & Acquisition	Joint Venture	Equity Increase	Other
Corporate Tax	12.5888	-32.1317	-48.6659	54.8073	38.4596	51.4033	46.6663
	(7.9086)	(18.8242)	(20.1485)	(12.3001)	(31.4202)	(40.3516)	(30.6152)
Establishment Agglomeration	.0559	.0710	.0566	.0572	.0513	-.0360	.0599
	(.0079)	(.0213)	(.0260)	(.0109)	(.0301)	(.0739)	(.0196)
Energy Prices	-.1608	.0893	-.3922	-.2095	.1959	.2060	-.1575
	(.0860)	(.2035)	(.2513)	(.1517)	(.3754)	(.7050)	(.2879)
Higher Education	-.0082	-.0061	.0092	-.0046	.0060	-.0519	-.0075
	(.0022)	(.0048)	(.0064)	(.0036)	(.0089)	(.0198)	(.0090)
Population	.0004	.0003	.0001	.0004	.0004	.0010	.0004
	(.0001)	(.0001)	(.0002)	(.0001)	(.0002)	(.0004)	(.0002)
Manufacturing Pay	.00001	.00004	-.0003	.0002	-.00005	.0001	.0003
	(.00005)	(.00009)	(.0001)	(.0001)	(.00014)	(.0003)	(.0002)
Percent Union	.1150	.893	.0210	.1221	.1857	.4230	.2078
	(.0143)	(.0379)	(.0475)	(.0204)	(.0549)	(.1804)	(.0568)
Percent Metropolitan	.1004	.1465	-.0974	.1316	.3586	.1139	.2145
	(.0318)	(.0379)	(.0863)	(.0533)	(.1203)	(.1667)	(.1232)
Per-Capita Income	-.00018	-.0004	.0004	-.0005	-.0001	-.0002	-.0007
	(.00009)	(.0002)	(.0002)	(.0001)	(.0002)	(.0006)	(.0003)
State Dummies	Yes	Yes	Yes	Yes	Yes	Yes	Yes
Log-Likelihood	-3794	-1269	-1014	-1869	-604	-405	-698

Note: Standard Errors in ( ).

214

However, if the firm already has a set of U.S. facilities, it can expand one of its current manufacturing plants, or it can locate elsewhere. In this sense, all expenditures directed towards plant expansions could have been deployed alternatively in the construction of a new plant. Since plant expansions have this character, I lose the direct comparability that I could otherwise exploit.[8]

Establishment agglomeration and states dummies remain significant in the comprehensive specification of Table 3. The added regressors meet conventional tests for statistical significance, which argue for the validity of their inclusion. What is notable is that many of these regressors, such as energy prices, have effects that differ substantially across investment type. Though the results are sensible. Plant expansions are shown to be adversely affected by high energy prices, while joint ventures and equity increases demonstrate no identifiable effects. This is further evidence that transaction type distinctions are not only important in thinking about taxes, but other underlying state economic factors.

V. CONCLUSIONS

This paper provides evidence on the effect of taxes on foreign investment into the U.S. between 1984 and 1994. The results suggest that analyses of aggregated data obscure some distinctive effects of taxes on foreign investment. In particular, I demonstrate that states with higher taxes attract fewer new plants or plant expansions. However, foreign acquisitions are not similarly deterred. If one analyses the full set of data, the results are driven by the merger & acquisitions sample, and a positive tax effect is found.

Further work with additional tax specifications is needed to analyze the importance of investment distinctions. Two directions in this area would include, analysis of more specific tax instruments, and an augmented regression specification that incorporates the expenditure side of government as well as the tax side.

---

[8] It is possible that firms make other choices such a new plant versus acquisition, or joint venture versus equity increase. However, work on the multinational as reviewed by Caves (1996), would suggest that there is little flexibility on these dimensions.

REFERENCES

Auerbach, Alan J. and Kevin Hassett, (1993), "Taxation and Foreign Direct Investment in the United States: A Reconsideration of the Evidence," in Alberto Giovannini, R. Glenn Hubbard, and Joel Slemrod eds. *Studies in International Taxation*, 119-144.

Bartik, Timothy J. (1991) *who Benefits from State and Local Economic Development Policies?* (W.E. Upjohn Institute: Kalamazoo, Michgan).

Brainard, Lael S. (1997) "An Empirical Assessment of the Proximity-Concentration Tradeoff between Multinational Sales and Trade," *American Economic Review*, 87(4):520-544.

Caves, Richard E. (1996). *Multinational Enterprise and Economic Analysis, second edition.* Cambridge: Cambridge University Press.

Coughlin, Cletus C., Joseph V. Terza, and Vachira Arromdee, (1991), "State Characteristics and the Location of Foreign Direct Investment within the United States," *Review of Economics and Statistics*, 68, 675-683.

Hallward-Driemeier, Mary. (1996) "Understanding Foreign Direct Investment by Firms: Market Pull, Cost Push and Knowledge Accumulation," Massachusetts Institute of Technology, manuscript.

Head, C. Keith, John C. Ries, and Deborah L. Swenson, (1994) "The Attraction of Foreign Manufacturing Investments: Investment Promotion and Agglomeration Economies," NBER Working Paper 4878.

Head, C. Keith, John C. Ries, and Deborah L. Swenson, (1995) "Agglomeration benefits and location choice: Evidence from Japanese Manufacturing Investment in the United States," *Journal of International Economics*, V38, no 3/4, p223-247.

Hines, James R. (1996a) "Altered States: Taxes and the Location of Foreign Direct Investment in America," *American Economic Review*, v86, no 5, p1076-1094.

Hines, James R. (1996b) "Tax Policy and the Activities of Multinational Corporations," NBER Working Paper, #5589, May.

Krugman, Paul R., (1991) "Increasing Returns and Economic Geography," *Journal of Political Economy*, 99:483-499.

Markusen, James R. (1995) "The Boundaries of Multinational Enterprises and the Theory of International Trade." *Journal of Economic Perspectives*, 9:(2) 169-189.

Markusen, James R. and Anthony J. Venables, (1996), "The Theory of Endowment, Intra-Industry, and Multinational Trade," National Bureau of Economic Research Working Paper # 5529.

Roberts, Mark and James Tybout. (1995) "An Empirical Model of Sunk costs and the Decision to Export." World Bank Policy Research Working Paper, No. 1436.

Ondrich, Jan and Michael Wasylenko, (1993) *Foreign Direct Investment in the United States: Issues, Magnitudes, and the Location Choice of New Manufacturing Plants*, MI: W.E. Upjohn Institute.

Scholes, Myron S. and Mark A. Wolfson. (1992) *Taxes and Business Strategy: A Planning Approach.* Englewood Cliffs, NJ: Prentice-Hall.

Sinn, Hans Werner, (1991). "The Vanishing Harberger Triangle," *Journal of Public Economics*, 45: 271-300.

Swenson, Deborah L. (1994) "The Impact of U.S. Tax Reform on Foreign Direct Investment in the United States." *Journal of Public Economics*, 54(2):243-66.

Wasylenko, Michael. "Empirical Evidence on Interregional Business Location Decisions and the Role of Fiscal Incentives in Economic Development," in Henry W. Herzon, Jr. and Alan M. Schlottmann, eds., *Industry Location and Public Policy*. Knoxville, TN: University of Tennesse Press, 1991, 13-30.

Wheeler and Mody (1992), "International Investment Location Decisions: The Case of U.S. Firms," *Journal of International Economics*, 33:57-76.

PART V. FOREIGN INVESTMENT IN TRANSITIONAL ECONOMIES

CHAPTER 12 INVESTMENT CRISIS IN POST-SOVIET RUSSIA

VLADIMIR I.TIKHOMIROV[*]

INTRODUCTION

Five years ago following the disintegration of the Soviet Union and the collapse of its political and economic management structures, the leadership of the Russian Federation announced its new policy of market reform. The main aim of the policy was decentralisation of the over-centralised state system of management of the national economy, privatisation of state-owned enterprises, and the formation of legal, financial and other structures facilitating the development of market economic mechanisms. In January 1992 the reform was started with the introduction of price, currency and trade liberalisation. At the end of the same year this was followed by the beginning of the privatisation campaign. Lifting of state control over prices almost immediately sparked off a huge inflation wave which very soon became one of the major obstacles to the continuation of the reform. Although the Russian government has been successful in controlling and lowering the inflation rate since 1995, this has not stopped the economy from sliding further and further into recession.

The dramatic falls in production indicators and standards of living experienced by Russia and the majority of ex-Soviet states in the post-1991 period could be attributed to a number of factors, the most important of which are: (a) the high level of mutual dependency, general backwardness and inflexibility of the socio-economic systems these newly independent states inherited from the over-centralised Soviet system which made independent management of their economies extremely difficult and greatly intensified the already existing socio-economic crisis in these states; (b) lack of experience in management and legal affairs in a market environment on the part

---

[*] Contemporary Europe Research Centre, The University of Melbourne, Melbourne, Australia.

of political and economic elites in these countries, which caused serious legal confusion and created too many legal loopholes, even a certain "power vacuum", resulting in an unprecedented growth in corruption as well as in economic and other crimes; (c) the economic difficulties and social costs caused by transition to the market economy in ex-Soviet states, which proved to be much higher than anticipated by reformists at the start of the reforms, forcing the majority of the leaders of these republics to make significant alterations to the initially proclaimed strategies which brought the whole reform process to a standstill and exacerbated the crises.

These factors affect developments in all of the former Soviet republics, although their strength and effects vary greatly. In some regions of the ex-USSR, like Transcaucasia and parts of Central Asia, post-Soviet political instability has led to a situation of on-going civil war which has had an even more devastating effect on economic and social transformations in these areas. At the end of 1994 political instability spread to the Russian Federation with the outbreak of the bloody Chechen War.

Despite the differences in terms of economic, social, political and ethnic background, not one of the former Soviet states has shown any signs indicating a genuine recovery. The key to successful change seems to lie in the ability of post-Soviet leaders to coordinate their transition policies, in such a way as to facilitate, rather than destroy, the existing benefits of their mutual cooperation. This raises the more general issue of the inter-relation between political independence (the nationalism factor) which frames the ideologies of the majority of ruling elites in these states, and the *de facto* economic dependency (moves towards integration) which these states was inherited from the Soviet Union. The clearest illustration of the struggle between these two tendencies is the history of the Commonwealth of Independent States (CIS). During the five years of its existence the CIS has failed to fulfil its proclaimed objectives of facilitating closer cooperation between its members, mainly because of strong internal pro-independence (ie. anti-integration) political pressures in most of its member-states.

The future of social and economic transformations in the former Soviet Union (FSU) is largely dependent on the success of the transition to democracy and a market economy in the biggest of its former republics, the Russian Federation. Russia accounts for 70-80% of the total industrial output of the FSU and, through energy supply chains, holds in its hands a very effective lever of control over developments in all of the other ex-Soviet states. Russia is also the indisputable military leader in the area and, in the event of a major crisis, still has the potential to bring all the other ex-Soviet states into its political and strategic domain. Since the collapse of the USSR Russia has also proved to be a clever and sometimes ruthless political manipulator in the area, on many occasions strongly and consistently safeguarding its own interests.

However, continuing attempts by the Russian leaders to reinstall Russia as the dominant force on the ex-Soviet territory are being blocked by the growing weakness of its economy (Table 1). Even Russian military might has become questionable following the humiliating defeat of Russian federal troops in the civil war in Chechnya. The economic difficulties of transformation are limiting the maneuverability of the Russian leadership drastically. Of all the economic matters requiring urgent attention of the current Russian leadership, the general financial crisis and the resulting collapse in investment seem to form the core of the problem. This study attempts to analyse the dynamics of both domestic and foreign investment in Russia during the post-Soviet period (1991-96).

Before discussing Russia's investment problems, a few words should be said on the issue of the reliability of official Russian statistical data which form the basis of the present analysis. Official Russian statistical materials are currently at the centre of a broad academic debate. The restructuring of the economy, changes in the ownership

Table 1. Annual Indices of Russian Economic Performance, 1990-96 (1990=100) [1]

	1990	1991	1992	1993	1994	1995	1996
GDP	100.0	95.0	81.2	74.2	64.7	62.0	58.3
Industrial Output	100.0	92.0	75.4	64.8	51.3	49.7	47.2
Agricultural Production	100.0	95.0	86.5	83.0	73.0	67.2	62.5
Capital Investment	100.0	85.0	51.0	44.9	34.1	29.7	24.3
Retail Trade Turnover	100.0	96.8	93.4	95.2	95.3	88.6	85.1
Average Real Salary	100.0	97.0	65.0	65.2	60.0	44.4	46.6

[1] Sources: Rossiiskii statisticheskii ezhegodnik. 1995, Moscow: Goskomstat, 1995, p.12; Sodruzhestvo Nezavisimykh Gosudarstv v 1995 godu, Moscow: Statkom SNG, January 1996, p.215-216; Sotsial'no-ekonomicheskoe polozhenie Rossii. 1995 g., Moscow: Goskomstat, 1996, p.254; Sotsial'no-ekonomicheskoe polozhenie Rossii.1996 g., No.12, Moscow: Goskomstat, 1997, p.7; Rossiya v tsifrakh. 1996, Moscow: Goskomstat, 1996, p.12.

of companies, the growth in market services that were non-existent in Soviet times, changes in accounting systems - all these factors have made the work of statisticians more difficult than ever. Since 1994 the Russian Statistical Committee (*Goskomstat*) and its regional branches have gradually been moving towards international statistical standards [2]. By mid-1996 the old Soviet system of formal accounting of production had been replaced by a system of national accounting. This brought the Russian statistical series in line with international standards, but did not help Russian statisticians to collect data from the so-called "unorganised" sectors of the economy and the shadow economy. Coefficients reflecting these developments had to be incorporated into the official statistical series. However, this sparked an on-going debate over whether these coefficients were truly representative of the real processes or whether they underestimated the real situation. In the most recent debates Russian statisticians are being accused, not of underestimating, but overestimating real production and GDP indicators [3].

The author of this paper supports the group of analysts who suggest that although Russian statistical series do have some faults, they are nevertheless in no way less reliable than statistics in many Western countries [4]. Moreover, the reliability of Russian statistical series that generally show a continuing decline in the economy is proved by numerous on-ground reports of a similar nature. Therefore, it is my view that, despite some inaccuracies, Russian statistics have generally managed to reflect the dynamics and trends of post-Soviet socio-economic developments correctly.

---

[2] See: "Rossiiskaya statistika ukhodit ot totalnogo utchyota", *Finansovye Izvestiya*. Cit. from *Biznes-TASS*, 31 August 1994.

[3] For instance, the official Russian inflation indicator in the consumer sector of 22% for 1996 was questioned by a leading Russian business newspaper which estimated that it should rather be at 60% (*Delovoy Mir*, 16 January 1997). In March 1997 *Goskomstat* was again accused of manipulating Russian GDP figures through increasing its allowance for the shadow economy from 20% to 23% (*The Financial Times*, London, March 25 1997, "Russia Shadow Economy Shown in Statistics", *Reuter*, 4 April 1997).

[4] See James H.Noren, "Statistical Reporting in the States of the Former USSR", *Post-Soviet Geography*, Vol.35, No.1, January 1994, pp.13-37; Stephen G.Wheatcroft, "Re-Visiting the Crisis Zones of Euro-Asia", *Russian and Euro-Asian Bulletin*, Melbourne, March 1997, Vol.6, No.3, p.6.

THE SCALE OF THE CURRENT FINANCIAL CRISIS IN RUSSIA

In the last two years the Russian economy has been almost totally paralysed by a serious financial crisis. The crisis began with the launching of the Russian reform in 1992 after the political disintegration of the USSR was followed by the break-up of economic ties between enterprises in the newly established states. This crisis was also greatly intensified by dramatic falls in the population's consumption, accompanied by rises in wholesale and retail prices. In event, many companies found it difficult to meet their payment obligations, first to suppliers and later to local and federal budgets.

Cuts in budget revenues meant that the state's capacity to assist the development of national industry and agriculture (through investment and subsidies) also started to shrink. In order to (even partially) meet its budgetary obligations the government raised taxes and introduced a complex system of control over cash and currency flows in and out of the country. This however failed to bring the necessary funds into the budget, forcing the Russian government to borrow more and more money, both domestically and abroad.

Increased borrowing helped the Russian government to balance the budget temporarily, but such a policy could not stop the spreading of the financial crisis. By 1993 delays in salary payments to state employees had become an everyday fact of life in Russia. Revenues from the privatisation of state property turned out to be much less than initially expected, but what was more important, the whole process of privatisation generally did not affect the way Russian companies were managed. Inefficient and loss-making enterprises inherited by Russia from the Soviet times, only became even more inefficient in the crisis situation. Bankruptcies were very rare for the sole reason that the government simply did not have funds to pay unemployment benefits to employees of bankrupt factories or to create new jobs for them.

The pace of the financial crisis in Russia was increasing since 1992, but it reached its culmination in 1996. In 1996 federal budget expenditures totalled 15.6% of GDP or $62 billion[5], which was less than the amount necessary to meet the government's

---

[5] This figure and the rest of data in the paper is in US dollars.

social policy obligations. 1996 budgetary revenues were 21% lower than expenditures and stood at $49 billion [6]. Budgetary payments to the economy were at a level of 1.84%, down from the 2.92% planned in the budget [7]. In mid-April 1997, the government's debt in back wages to public employees and delayed pension payments grew to an astronomical figure of approximately $9 billion [8].

While in 1992-94 the government was trying to solve the problem of falling tax collection by increasing tax levels and introducing new taxes, in 1995-96 the taxation burden almost reached its absolute limit [9]. This forced many Russian businesses to enter the "shadow economy" in order to evade tax payments. Emergency measures aimed at increasing tax flows were introduced at the end of 1996 and helped to raise some additional taxes. However, for the whole year of 1996 the Russian government managed to collect only 84% of planned taxes [10]. According to data released by the government, only 16.5% of Russian companies honoured their tax obligations in 1996. In November 1996, of 2.6 million registered firms in Russia, 436 thousand paid taxes regularly and in full, while at least 882 thousand companies (34%) published no accounts and made no tax payments whatsoever [11]. The majority of local governments also failed to pay their taxes on time. In 1996 only 6 out of 89 Russian administrative units met their obligations to the federal government fully [12].

By 1996 non-payments to suppliers had begun to hit the most successful Russian companies. Three of Russia's seven largest tax deadbeats were subsidiaries of

---

[6] This data corresponds to the officially released figure for the 1996 Russian budget deficit of 74.3 trillion rubles ($13 billion). However, it did not include the real yield paid on T-bills (state bonds) as part of the budget expenditure. That included, the budget deficit was 2.3 times larger at 174.3 trillion rubles ($30 billion). For a recent discussion on that issue see Stanislav Menshikov, "The Budget According to Chubais", *Johnson's Russia List*, 30 April 1997.

[7] "Russia: Budget Arrears", *Oxford Analytica East Europe Daily Brief (OAEEDB)*, 21 January 1997; *Open Media Research Institute Daily Digest (OMRI)*, No.38, Part 1, 24 February 1997.

[8] *Interfax*, 30 April 1997..

[9] In late 1996 out of every million rubles earned by business, up to 950,000 rubles went to taxes and other fees (Lidia Lukyanova, "Will Russia Get a 'Smarter' Tax Policy?", *Prism: A Monthly on the Post-Soviet States (Jamestown Foundation)*, Vol.II, November 1996, Part 3).

[10] *Izvestia*, Moscow, 14 January 1997.

[11] *Trud*, Moscow, 18 December 1996; *OMRI*, No.220, Part 1, 13 November 1996.

[12] *Rossiiskaya Gazeta*, Mosocw, 11 March 1997.

Gazprom, the natural gas monopoly. Their inability to pay taxes, however, is not an indication of their poor state; simply it indicates the inability of their customers to pay for gas supplies. In 1996 only 7% of retail natural gas purchases were settled in full in cash [13]. In late 1996 the total debt owed by large Russian companies to the federal budget was $1.3 billion [14].

In a situation when private banks were reluctant to credit indebted companies, the government was forced to step in by issuing state guarantees for commercial bank credits. It could be said that by the mid-1990s state-issued bank guarantees and tax exemptions had effectively replaced the old Soviet state subsidies to enterprises. In the first nine months of 1996 state-issued guarantees to the three largest credit providers alone exceeded $3 billion [15]. Another source of "hidden subsidies" are government-approved tax exemptions. In early 1997 it was reported that tax exemptions and offsets totalled $30 billion, two-thirds of which were exemptions granted by the federal government to local authorities [16].

In a cash-stripped economy such as the Russian economy had become by the mid-1990s, it is usual for various forms of surrogate money to appear as a replacement for the deficit cash. In the Russian case, many banks and local authorities started to issue bills of exchange (*vekselya*) order to facilitate payments between enterprises. In 1996 alone private banks issued $20 billion worth of bills of exchange with an additional $8 billion issued by local governments [17].

Rapidly falling tax collection and diminishing state foreign currency reserves [18] forced the Russian government to seek funding sources outside the country. Between 1991 and 1996 Russia's foreign debt increased by approximately 50% and reached $128 billion [19]. In 1996 the Russian government also started to issue state bonds (GKOs).

---

[13] *Monitor: A Daily Briefing on the Post-Soviet States*, Vol.III, No.50, 12 March 1997.

[14] Sergey Lukianov, Geoff Winestock, "Tax Collection Crisis: Is a Solution in Sight?", *St.Petersburg Times*, 18-24 November 1996.

[15] "Russia: Budget Arrears", *OAEEDB*, 21 January 1997.

[16] *Kommersant-Daily*, Moscow, 16 February 1997, p.1; *The Financial Times*, London, 25 February 1997.

[17] *OMRI*, No.50, Part 1, 12 March 1997.

[18] According to *Nezavisimaya Gazeta*, at the beginning of February 1997 the net gold and foreign currency reserves of Russia amounted to only $600 million (*Nezavisimaya Gazeta*, 25 March 1997).

[19] *Moskovskii Komsomolets*, Moscow, 19 February 1997.

During that year the sales of GKOs to foreigners were 3 times larger than the foreign direct investment and were at a level of $6.7 billion[20]. Foreign debt repayments became a heavy burden on the Russian economy. According to Russian Deputy Finance Minister Oleg Vyugin, the cost of servicing Russia's borrowing program was still "bearable" in late 1996, but he admitted that if the current borrowing rate continued financial resources "could run short by 1998"[21].

The financial crisis in Russia also had direct implications for savings and investment trends. A very good indicator of the population's faith in the government's ability to improve the economic situation are the dynamics of internal and external capital flight from Russia. Recent reports indicate that Russians were converting their savings in local currency into foreign currency on a massive scale, primarily into US dollars. In 1995 14% of the total population's income was spent on foreign-currency purchases; in 1996 this figure was already 18.5%[22]. According to the Russian Central Bank, in 1993-96 a total value of $84 billion was imported into Russia. Almost 3/4 of that sum were imported in two years - 1995 and 1996. Of the total amount of currency imports, $63.7 billion were net sales to individuals. About half of that money was later exported and in the beginning of 1997 it was estimated that $33 billion were in circulation among the Russian population[23]. This was more than half of the gross Russian money supply.

The scale of monthly internal capital flight in Russia in early 1997 was estimated at $5 billion[24]. Another $2 billion leave Russia each month in the form of external capital flight. In my recent article I estimated that the total amount of capital exported illegally from Russia during 1992-95 was $62 billion, with a further $20 billion leaving the country in 1996[25].

---

[20] *OMRI*, No.32, Part 1, 14 February 1997.

[21] "Russian Economist Warns of Crisis", *Associated Press (AP)*, 18 December 1996.

[22] *OMRI*, No.44, Part 1, 4 March 1997.

[23] *OMRI*, No.60, Part 1, 26 March 1997.

[24] *Rossiiskaya Gazeta*, 19 November 1996; *OMRI*, No.44, Part 1, 4 March 1997.

[25] Vladimir Tikhomirov, "Capital Flight from Post-Soviet Russia", *Europe-Asia Studies*, Glasgow, Vol.49, No.4, June 1997.

DYNAMICS OF DOMESTIC INVESTMENT IN RUSSIA

The decline in post-Soviet Russian industrial and agricultural production was greatly intensified by a dramatic fall in the volume of capital investment in Russia's economy. As early as by the end of the first year of reform, the need to renew capital stock of enterprises, industrial and agricultural alike, had become a major factor in their survival. Realisation of this fact had led many managers and directors of these enterprises to publicly demand a revaluation of the government's policies in the area of capital investment. The "directors' lobby" very soon became a powerful factor in post-Soviet Russian politics. By mid-1994 the demands of this lobby group received a new boost following the election of Mr Viktor Chernomyrdin (former head of the state gas monopoly *Gazprom*) as the new Russian prime minister. However, despite these growing pressures, the critical economic situation put drastic limits on the financial resources available to the government. While pursuing a policy of cutting all state expenses, including subsidies and investment in industry and agriculture, Russian reformers hoped that the growing gap in investment funding would be filled in by domestic private investors and through FDI. Numerous attempts made by the state in the last few years aimed at redirecting of population's savings and accumulated private bank funds into investment in production have not proved to be successful.

The long-term dynamics of capital investment in Russia show that in the decade between 1980 and 1990 the volume of investment was rising slowly. However, since 1990 it has been in decline, with the most dramatic fall occurring in 1992 (Table 2). There were also significant shifts in the structure of investment by branch of economy. In 1980-1985 investment in all areas with the exception of construction were growing steadily, with the most notable growth recorded in the fuel industry. Between 1986 and 1988 this tendency of growth continued. During that period the (industrial) construction sector experienced substantial growth which came mainly as the result of cuts in funding to agriculture.

When the Soviet leadership announced in 1989 that an increase in agricultural output would top its economic priority list, investment strategy was clearly re-oriented towards agriculture (with a more than two-fold increase in investment in one year!). In the same year investment in housing also increased substantially. The growth in public funding of agriculture and housing was accompanied by falls in the volumes

Table 2. Dynamics of Capital Investment in Russia, 1990-96 (1990=100) [26]

	1980	1986	1990	1991	1992	1993	1994	1995	1996
By Source									
Total	65.5	84.2	100.0	84.5	51.0	43.0	34.1	29.7	24.3
Public finance from all sources (federal &regional state funding)	159.4	200.6	100.0	66.3	40.9	43.5	29.2	25.3	12.3
Company funds (including bank loans and other borrowings)	0.0	4.5	100.0	89.4	68.9	48.1	42.7	36.2	31.5
All other sources (including FDI)	53.9	76.3	100.0	121.2	4.0	18.5	11.8	14.8	31.3
By Branch of Economy									
Industry	76.3	111.2	100.0	81.7	56.7	43.5	28.8	27.8	24.6
Agriculture	82.3	68.9	100.0	95.0	32.9	19.6	9.9	5.1	4.9
Construction	76.9	94.5	100.0	83.9	29.5	21.0	22.0	19.1	19.9
Transport and Communications	88.2	118.6	100.0	67.3	37.6	38.6	33.8	36.5	28.1
Housing	67.5	91.1	100.0	92.4	70.0	62.1	52.4	46.3	40.0
By Major Industries									
Industry total including:	76.3	111.2	100.0	81.7	56.7	43.5	28.8	27.8	24.6
Oil and Fuel	78.1 [a]	140.8 [a]	100.0	80.9	71.3	56.8	35.8	36.0	32.7
Machine-Building	85.7 [b]	125.8 [b]	100.0	70.8	29.1	23.0	14.1	10.8	8.8
Chemical and Forestry	107.4	113.6	100.0	87.9	55.9	32.3	23.8	24.8	18.9
Construction Materials	317.0	372.4	100.0	102.8	55.1	27.9	24.7	21.3	11.7
Electricity Production	-	-	100.0	103.6	110.1	94.8	67.4	68.5	77.3
Metallurgy	-	-	100.0	93.0	78.1	57.8	40.5	39.1	31.8
All other industries	51.8	66.8	100.0	76.4	37.5	30.3	19.6	18.4	14.1

[a] Including electricity production.
[b] Including metallurgy.

---

[26] Sourced and calculated from: Narodnoe khozyaistvo RSFSR v 1987 g., Moscow: Goskomstat, 1988, pp.326-328; Narodnoe khozyaistvo RSFSR v 1988 g., Moscow: Goskomstat, 1989, pp.612-614; Narodnoe khozyaistvo RSFSR v 1990 g., Moscow: Goskomstat, 1991, pp.522-527; Narodnoe khozyaistvo Rossiiskoi Federatsii. 1992, Moscow: Goskomstat, 1992, pp.537-542; Rossiiskaya Federatsiya v 1992 godu, Moscow: Goskomstat, 1993, pp.530-533; Rossiiskaya Federatsiya v tsifrakh v 1993 godu, Moscow: Goskomstat, 1994, pp.210-214; Rossiya-1994. Ekonomicheskaya konyuktura. Vypusk 1, Moscow 1994, pp.197-198; Narodnoe khozyaistvo RSFSR v 1988 g., Moscow: Goskomstat, 1989, pp.612-614; Narodnoe khozyaistvo RSFSR v 1987 g., Moscow: Goskomstat, 1988, p..326-328; Rossiiskii statisticheskii ezhegodnik. 1995, Moscow: Goskomstat, 1995, p.378; Sotsial'no-ekonomicheskoe polozhenie Rossii. 1995 g., Moscow: Goskomstat, 1996, p.56-59, 66; Rossiya v tsifrakh. 1996, Moscow: Goskomstat, 1996, pp.228-229; Sotsial'no-ekonomicheskoe polozhenie Rossii. 1996 g., Moscow: Goskomstat, 1997, pp.42-49,233-236; Sotsial'no-ekonomicheskoe polozhenie Rossii, yanvar' 1997 g., Moscow: Goskomstat, 1997, pp.42-49; Rossiiskii statisticheskii ezhegodnik. 1996, Moscow: Goskomstat, 1996, p.450; Sotsial'no-ekonomicheskoe polozhenie Rossii, yanvar'-fevral' 1997 g., Moscow: Goskomstat, 1997, pp.84-88.

of capital investment in all other major sectors of the economy, mainly in transport and communications, as well as machine-building.

In 1990 this tendency was again reversed when the share of agriculture in the total volume of public investment was significantly reduced. However, in the following year, when the general economic and financial crisis started to develop in Russia, a lack of investment funds pushed the Soviet and Russian governments to further investment cuts in all sectors of the national economy, although at that stage funds allocated to agriculture and public housing were reduced only marginally (by 5-8%).

The change of government at the end of 1991 resulted in a reassessment of Russia's public investment strategies. Investment emphasis was now placed on the revenue-generating sectors of the economy (the minerals and fuel industries). Capital-intensive and loss-making sectors were moved to the bottom of the new priority list. As a result, agriculture, (industrial) construction, machine-building (including the military-industrial complex), transport and communications, and social spending experienced much greater cuts in public funding than the minerals industry. The dynamics of investment in the housing sector also demonstrated a relatively smaller decline than in other sectors of economy, mainly because of an increase in private funding of housing. The 1993-94 deregulation of prices for transport and communications services made it possible to slow down investment falls in these sectors. Between the early and mid 1990s the largest falls in funding were experienced by agriculture, (industrial) construction and industry in general.

The investment dynamics shown in table 2 indicates that the volume of gross capital investment in Russia was constantly declining since the early 1990s. By the end of 1996 finances allocated to capital investment from all sources amounted to less than a quarter of the 1990 level. Investment in housing experienced the lowest fall - in 1996 they decreased by 40% of the 1990 level. On the other hand, the situation in Russian agriculture could be described as catastrophic: in 1996 the volume of capital invested in that sector in real terms amounted to less than 5% of the 1990 level. During the same period industrial construction also experienced a decline of more than 80%.

In 1990-96 the volume of capital investment in Russian industry as a whole fell by more than 75%. This figure, however, masks huge disparities between the various branches of industry: while in 1996 investment in electricity production in real terms constituted 3/4 of the amount invested in 1990, and in the fuel complex slightly less than a third of the 1990 level, funding in machine-building (engineering) fell by more than 10 times to 8.8% during the same period. Investment in production of construction (building) materials in 1996 was 11.7% of the 1990 level (Table 3).

Following attempts made by the former Soviet President Mikhail Gorbachev in late 1980s aimed at liberalisation and decentralisation of the Soviet economic system, the share of capital investment financed from company funds in the gross volume of capital investment was steadily increasing since 1986. This process was further boosted in 1991-92 after the collapse of central planning (and funding) in Russia. In the new environment all Russian companies (whether privatised and or still state-owned) were forced to rely more and more on their own financial resources and any external funding (domestic and foreign) that they were able to attract.

The privatisation of banks deprived the state of its former role as the main capital accumulator; deregulation and liberalisation of internal and foreign trade transferred the levers of control of financial flows from revenue-generating industries from state into private hands. As a result of the reforms undertaken in 1992-93, the Russian state effectively withdrew from its former role as the major (if not sole) redistributor of investment funds in the country. The share of public investment in gross capital investment in Russia fell from more than 90% in the mid-1980s to around 40% in the late 1980s and to less than 20% in the mid-1990s (see Table 3).

In the same period the share of company funding in gross capital investment increased dramatically: from less than 3% in 1986 to over 2/3 a decade later. In 1986-96 the share of non-state and non-company funding (see category "Other" in Table 3) more than doubled and reached 15%. The latter, however, was the result of a much less significant fall in expenditure on housing in 1990-96. By 1996 more than a third of all investment in housing came from the population's savings which was a three-fold increase since 1991[27]. Table 2 shows that in 1996 housing investment totalled 40% of the 1990 level. The decline in that sector was significantly lower than the falls of

[27] *Sotsialno-ekonomicheskoe polozhenie Rossii. 1996 g.*, Moscow: Goskomstat, 1997, p.47.
[28] After growing steadily in 1994-95 physical volumes of housing construction in Russia in 1996 declined by 10% (*Rossiiskaya Gazeta*, 25 January 1997).

up to 5 and 28% of the 1990 level experienced by other branches of the economy [28].

In the post-Soviet period there have also been important changes in the structure of gross capital investment in Russia. In 1990-96 the share of investment in industry in the total volume of investment remained relatively stable (30-36%). The share of investment in the spheres of transport and communications, after a fall in 1992-93, exceeded its 1990 level and stood at 13.6% in 1996. In the same period the share of investment in industrial construction declined from 4.5% to 3.7%. Once again,

Table 3. Structure of Capital Investment in Russia, 1990-96 (shares, %) [29]

	1980	1986	1990	1991	1992	1993	1994	1995	1996
By Source									
Total	*100.0*	*100.0*	*100.0*	*100.0*	*100.0*	*100.0*	*100.0*	*100.0*	*100.0*
including:									
Public finance from all sources (federal &regional state funding)	94.1	90.4	37.2	29.2	29.8	37.6	31.8	31.7	18.8
Company funds (including bank loans and other Borrowings)	0.0	2.7	51.3	54.2	69.3	57.4	64.2	62.5	66.3
All other sources (including FDI)	5.9	6.9	11.6	16.6	0.9	5.0	4.0	5.8	14.9
FDI only	n/a	n/a	n/a	n/a	n/a	2.4	1.7	2.8	4.0
By Branch of Economy									
Total	*100.0*	*100.0*	*100.0*	*100.0*	*100.0*	*100.0*	*100.0*	*100.0*	*100.0*
including:									
Industry	41.8	47.4	35.9	34.7	39.9	36.3	30.3	33.6	36.3
Agriculture	19.9	12.9	15.8	17.8	10.2	7.2	4.6	2.7	3.2
Construction	5.3	5.1	4.5	4.5	2.6	2.2	2.9	2.9	3.7
Transport and Communications	15.9	16.6	11.8	9.4	8.7	10.6	11.7	14.5	13.6
Housing	17.1	18.0	16.6	18.1	22.8	24.0	25.5	25.9	27.3
By Major Industries									
Industry total	*100.0*	*100.0*	*100.0*	*100.0*	*100.0*	*100.0*	*100.0*	*100.0*	*100.0*
including:									
Oil and Fuel	33.1 [a]	41.0 [a]	32.4	32.1	40.8	42.3	40.3	41.9	43.1
Machine-Building	25.9 [b]	26.1 [b]	23.1	20.0	11.9	12.2	11.3	8.9	8.3
Chemical and Forestry	13.1	9.5	9.3	10.0	9.2	6.9	7.7	8.3	7.2
Construction Materials	16.3	13.1	3.9	4.9	3.8	2.5	3.4	3.0	1.9
Electricity Production	-	-	6.2	7.8	12.0	13.4	14.4	15.2	19.4
Metallurgy	-	-	8.1	9.2	11.1	10.7	11.4	11.3	10.4
All other industries	11.6	10.3	17.1	16.0	11.3	11.9	11.7	11.4	9.8

[a] Including electricity production.
[b] Including metallurgy.

---

[29] For sources see Table 2.

agriculture was the main loser: the share of gross investment in that sector fell from almost 16% in 1990 to just 3.2% in 1996.

Table 4 shows the dynamics of capital investment in Russia during the first stage of privatisation ("voucher" privatisation which began in 1992 and ended on 1 July 1994). According to these data the growth of public and company funds anticipated by Russian reformers at the start of privatisation, failed to materialise. The volume of capital investment continued to decline rather rapidly after 1991 and by mid-1994 was just above 40% of its level three years ago. The structure of capital investment by source of investment remained relatively stable, with around 60% of the 1992-94 total investment volume still provided by companies and the rest mainly from various

Table 4. Quarterly Dynamics of Capital Investment, 1992-94 [30]

Total Capital Investment in Constant Prices (previous period 1991=100)

	I-92	II-92	III-92	1992	I-93	II-93	III-93	1993	I-94	II-94
Capital Investment	56	52	52	60.3	54.3	48.9	45.8	50.9	39.1	35.2

Structural Changes in Capital Investment by Source of Investment (%)

	1992	II-93	III-93	1993	I-94	II-94
All public investment, including:	31.3	31.0	31.0	32.5	28.0	27.0
from federal budget	15.8	16.9	14.6	17.5	16.0	15.0
from local budget	15.5	14.1	16.4	15.0	12.0	12.0
Preferential state credits	0.7	1.2	1.8	1.7	1.0	1.7
Centralised state investment funds	2.9	3.1	3.7	3.3	3.2	5.4
Company funds	61.6	55.0	60.0	59.0	64.0	58.0
All other sources (incl. FDI)	3.5	9.7	3.5	3.4	3.8	7.9
FDI	2.7	...	2.6	3.8	3.6	
Total	*100.0*	*100.0*	*100.0*	*100.0*	*100.0*	*100.0*

Structure of Investment by Ownership (%)

	III-92	1992	I-93	II-93	III-93	1993
State-owned companies	87.0	81.0	72.0	70.0	61.1	59.0
Leased enterprises	3.6	3.3	1.2	1.2	1.1	0.8
Joint-stock companies	2.7	6.7	14.3	19.0	26.4	28.9
Cooperatives	0.1	0.2	...	0.3	0.4	0.3
Partnerships, associations	3.8	1.3	...	3.0	3.5	3.3
Individuals	1.0	0.9	...	2.7	2.9	3.0
Other	1.8	6.6	12.5	3.8	4.6	4.7
Total	*100.0*	*100.0*	*100.0*	*100.0*	*100.0*	*100.0*

[30] Sourced and calculated from Statistical appendices to Goskomstat monthly statistical series (O razvitii ekonomicheskikh reform v Ross.Federatsii); Goskomstat monthly statistical series (Sotsialno-ekonomicheskoe polozheniye Rossii); Rossiya-1994. Ekonomicheskaya konyuktura. Vypusk 1, Moscow 1994, pp.197-198; Rossiya-1994. Ekonomicheskaya konyuktura. Vypusk 2, Moscow 1994, pp.155-157.

public sources (federal and local budgets, preferential credits, state-controlled investment funds).

During that period (1992-1994) important changes were introduced into the ownership structure of capital investment in Russia. The share of state-owned companies (enterprises) declined from 87% in the third quarter of 1992 to just 59% in mid-1994. The share of leased enterprises also dropped from 3.6% to 0.8%, while the share of investment coming from joint-stock companies increased ten-fold. These changes were a direct reflection of the 1992-94 privatisation process. The figure of 28.9% which represented the share of joint-stock companies in total capital investment at the end of 1993 was a significant indicator of the overall weight of these newly-privatised ventures in the national economy. It made clear it that, at least in its first stage, the Russian privatisation program had failed to produce any impressive results.

The above table also demonstrates that in the first two years of reform the Russian economy was still dominated by large and medium state-owned enterprises. It should be noted that in the period of 1992-94 all leased companied and the majority of joint-stock companies that were active in the Russian economy had been subjects of state property as recently as two-three years ago. During those years the combined share of state-run and newly-privatised (joint-stock) companies in the gross volume of capital investment remained at around 90%. At the same time the share of newly-established ventures (private companies, partnerships, associations, cooperatives, etc.) was still extremely low: it did not rise above 6-9% of the total capital investment. This meant that, at least in the initial phase of privatisation, the investment mechanism in the Russian economic system remained largely unchanged and was still dominated by (ex-)state companies, of which approximately one-third changed their titles to joint-stock companies between 1992 and 1994.

REGIONAL DISPARITIES IN INVESTMENT FLOWS

The gross volumes of capital investment in post-Soviet Russia mask the disparities in investment flows within the country. In order to compensate for this it is necessary to analyse, at least briefly, the structure and dynamics of capital investment in different economic regions[31] of the Russian Federation.

The regional structure of capital investment in Russia gives a more comprehensive picture of general investment flows and serves as an indicator of the economic priorities of the current Russian leadership. As can be seen from Table 5 below, predominantly mining-oriented regions, as well as the politically-important central areas, have always been on the top of the list of investment priorities of both the Soviet and post-Soviet Russian governments. These regions include Western Siberia (gas and oil), the Central region (which includes Moscow) and the Urals (the centre of the Russian metals industry). The combined share of these three regions in the total volume of capital investment in Russia was 47.6% in 1990. By 1996 this share had increased to 55.6%.

The three regional investment leaders also experienced the lowest falls in the volumes of real investment during the crisis years (1990-96). In 1996 the volume of investment in these regions amounted to 28-29% of the 1990 level. This differed significantly from falls of up to 14-24% of 1990 investment levels in all other Russian economic regions.

Russian investment priorities become even clearer if we single out those territories that have a clear economic profile from the economic regions and group them together. For instance, the territories of Kemerovo (coal production) and Tyumen' (oil and gas) in the Western Siberian economic region are among Russia's major mining areas along with the Republic of Sakha (coal, gold and diamond production) in the Russian Far East. All three areas also have manufacturing and agriculture, but mining is the dominant orientation. For the same purposes of comparison we have grouped together mainly manufacturing areas of St.Petersburg (North-West), Samara (Volga) and Khabarovsk (Far East) into the "manufacturing group", and Belgorod (Central ChernoZem), Krasnodar and Stavropol (both - North Caucasus) into the "agricultural group". It is worth mentioning that all 9 areas used for comparison are among Russia's leading economic territories and in 1996 had a combined share in the country's population of 17.6% .

---

[31] In statistical and economic terms Russia's 89 administrative regions (oblasts, territories and autonomous areas) are grouped into 11 economic regions and Kalinigrad (*Kalinigradskaya Oblast*). The 11 regions are: Northern, North-West (includes St.Petersburg), Central (includes Moscow), Volgo-Vyatka, Central ChernoZem, Volga, North Caucasus, Urals, Western Siberia, Eastern Siberia and the Russian Far East.

As illustrated by Table 5, the dynamics of change in investment flows to these groups of regions were different in the post-Soviet period. Predominantly mining areas experienced huge falls in investment (down to 32% of the 1990 level); but these

Table 5. Regional Structure of Capital Investment in Russia (%) [32]

	1985	1990	1991	1992	1993	1994	1995	1996
Shares of Economic Regions in Total Volume of Capital Investment (%)								
Northern	4.7	5.1	4.9	5.3	4.4	4.7	4.4	3.9
North-West	4.3	4.6	4.5	3.5	3.2	4.2	4.2	4.6
Central	17.5	17.6	15.8	15.6	18.0	22.4	22.5	20.3
Volgo-Vyatka	4.7	4.8	4.9	4.2	4.8	3.8	3.9	3.5
Central ChernoZem	4.8	4.6	4.4	4.6	3.8	3.4	4.2	3.8
Volga	10.8	10.3	10.8	10.7	10.6	9.5	9.7	9.3
North Caucasus	7.4	7.6	8.0	6.9	7.0	6.9	8.3	7.4
Urals	12.0	11.9	12.7	14.8	13.7	13.2	14.1	14.2
West Siberia	18.7	18.1	18.6	23.3	21.1	18.9	15.2	21.1
East Siberia	7.0	7.1	6.9	3.6	5.9	5.9	7.6	6.5
Far East	7.6	7.8	7.9	7.1	6.9	6.5	5.8	5.1
Kaliningrad	0.5	0.5	0.5	0.4	0.5	0.5	0.2	0.3
All RF	*100.0*	*100.0*	*100.0*	*100.0*	*100.0*	*100.0*	*100.0*	*100.0*
Dynamics of Capital Investment by Economic Region, 1990=100 (constant prices)								
Northern	70.3	100.0	80.3	53.2	36.9	31.4	25.2	18.3
North-West	72.5	100.0	82.1	38.4	29.7	31.3	26.7	24.0
Central	77.0	100.0	76.2	45.2	44.0	43.6	38.0	28.2
Volgo-Vyatka	75.6	100.0	86.3	44.1	42.9	26.9	24.0	17.6
Central ChernoZem	80.4	100.0	81.9	51.5	35.4	25.7	27.1	20.5
Volga	80.3	100.0	88.4	53.1	44.3	31.6	27.8	22.0
North Caucasus	75.3	100.0	89.2	46.3	39.7	31.1	32.7	23.8
Urals	77.9	100.0	90.5	63.4	49.6	37.8	35.2	29.1
West Siberia	79.5	100.0	86.7	65.7	50.1	35.6	25.0	28.4
East Siberia	76.5	100.0	82.9	25.6	36.0	28.6	31.7	22.3
Far East	74.8	100.0	85.6	46.2	38.0	28.1	22.0	15.7
Kaliningrad	73.1	100.0	83.6	39.7	45.9	33.8	13.1	14.4
All RF	*77.1*	*100.0*	*84.5*	*51.0*	*43.0*	*34.1*	*29.7*	*24.3*
Dynamics of Capital Investment by Groups of Regions, 1990=100								
Mining regions [a]	80.2	100.0	88.7	75.6	56.7	39.9	24.6	32.4
Manufacturing regions [b]	82.6	100.0	85.9	50.8	46.0	37.9	32.5	26.9
Agricultural regions [c]	70.2	100.0	90.9	51.5	44.5	33.8	28.3	24.4

[a] Kemerovo, Tyumen' and Sakha.

[b] St.Petersburg, Samara and Khabarovsk.

[c] Belgorod, Krasnodar and Stavropol.

---

[32] Sources: Kapitalnoe stroitelstvo v Rossiiskoi Federatsii, Moscow: Goskomstat, 1994, pp.11-12; Rossiiskii statisticheskii ezhegodnik. 1995, Moscow: Goskomstat, 1995, pp.842-844; Sotsial'no-ekonomicheskoe polozhenie Rossii. 1995 g., Moscow: Goskomstat, 1996, pp.339-341; Sotsial'no-ekonomicheskoe polozhenie Rossii. 1996 g., Moscow: Goskomstat, 1997, pp.233-234.

were still lower than the decline in manufacturing (27% of the 1990 level) and agricultural (24.4%) groups of regions. This trend confirms my earlier statement that since the fall of the Soviet Union mining industries have topped the Russian leadership's investment priority list, while agriculture and manufacturing have been moved to the bottom of the list.

Regional investment disparities in Russia are striking if we compare per capita volumes of investment by economic region to Russia's national average (Table 6). In 1985 per capita funding of investment projects in Russian regions varied between -35% and +88% of the national average. By 1996 the limits of variation had increased significantly: at a time when Kaliningrad was receiving per capita investment of less than half the Russian average, Western Siberian investment was twice the national average. Table 6 also demonstrates that the change in investment policies came in 1991-92, or precisely at the time when the Soviet government in Russia was replaced by Gaidar's reformist government. During 1994-95 a section of investment flows to Western Siberia was re-directed, mainly to the Central region (Moscow), but in 1996 this tendency was again reversed.

The ratios of per capita regional investment to national average were also high in the Urals and the Central region. Another leader was the Eastern Siberian economic region, where in the first year of Russian reform per capita investment fell to almost half of the national average, but subsequently grew to above average national levels. An explanation of these changes in investment flows should be sought in the fact that this region is the centre of Russian non-ferrous (particularly aluminium) industry and timber production. In the Soviet period this industry was a major supplier of metals and other materials to the military-industrial complex. After the collapse of central economic planning in 1991-92 and the huge falls in military production that followed, the Eastern Siberian metals industry found itself in an extremely difficult situation. This changed somewhat in 1993 when the industry was transferred into private hands. Eastern Siberia then became an important export revenue-generating region of Russia. This also had a visible positive impact on the flow of capital into the area.

Russian statistical series also allow us to analyse differences in investment flows between all the 89 administrative units that make up the Russian Federation. In order to make such an analysis easier and to produce clearer results, the table below lists

Table 6. Indices of Per Capita Capital Investment by Region (Russian average level = 100) [33]

	1985	1990	1991	1992	1993	1994	1995	1996
Northern	112.3	123.3	117.4	130.0	107.8	116.7	108.7	96.4
North-West	77.0	82.5	80.5	62.8	58.1	77.4	76.5	83.9
Central	84.7	85.5	77.4	76.3	88.5	110.7	111.4	101.1
Volgo-Vyatka	81.5	84.6	86.5	73.3	84.5	69.9	68.5	61.1
Central ChernoZem	89.4	87.4	84.9	88.3	71.4	65.1	78.3	72.0
Volga	96.3	92.5	96.6	95.8	94.2	84.0	84.5	81.5
North Caucasus	65.3	66.3	69.3	59.1	59.4	58.3	69.9	62.0
Urals	86.5	86.5	92.6	107.5	99.7	95.4	101.9	102.8
West Siberia	188.0	177.4	181.9	228.8	206.8	184.9	149.0	205.8
East Siberia	114.2	113.7	111.5	57.1	95.3	95.8	122.2	104.6
Far East	144.1	144.9	146.8	132.8	131.4	124.2	113.9	99.7
Kaliningrad	80.1	83.5	82.1	64.0	86.7	79.3	35.0	46.5
All RF	*100.0*	*100.0*	*100.0*	*100.0*	*100.0*	*100.0*	*100.0*	*100.0*

only 12 of these units (*oblasts* and republics) which fall respectively into categories of areas with the highest and lowest per capita investment in Russia. Among the six leading investment areas are Russia's capital (Moscow), four mining areas (Komi and Tyumen - oil and gas; Sakha and Magadan - gold and diamonds) and the Far Eastern area of Kamchatka which is one of the major centres of Russia's fishing industry. Although all of these six areas are leaders in attracting investment, on a per capita basis the disparities between them are striking. Oil and gas-rich Tyumen is an undisputable investment leader in Russia; per capita investment in Tyumen industry during last decade was between 3.6 and 7.4 times higher than the Russian per capita average. In 1996 Tyumen's share in the gross national volume of investment was the highest in Russia and stood at 14.6%. The second investment leader in Russia is Moscow, which attracted 12% of all 1996 investment in the Russian economy. Moscow was also a clear winner after the change in government in 1991-92: since 1992 its share in the total volume of investment in Russia has been increasing constantly. By 1996 per capita investment in Moscow was twice the Russian average; that was a remarkable change from the late 1980s level of 67-87% of the national

[33] Sources: Kapitalnoe stroitelstvo v Rossiiskoi Federatsii, Moscow: Goskomstat, 1994, pp.11-12; Rossiiskii statisticheskii ezhegodnik. 1995, Moscow: Goskomstat, 1995, pp.842-844; Sotsial'no-ekonomicheskoe polozhenie Rossii. 1995 g., Moscow: Goskomstat, 1996, pp.339-341; Sravnitelnye pokazateli ekonomicheskogo polozheniya regionov Rossiiskoi Federatsii, Moscow: Goskomstat, 1995, pp.119-121; Ekonomicheskoe polozhenie regionov Rossiiskoi Federatsii, Moscow: Goskomstat, 1994, pp.111-112; Sotsial'no-ekonomicheskoe polozhenie Rossii. 1996 g., Moscow: Goskomstat, 1997, pp.233-236.

average. In 1996 Tyumen and Moscow's combined population was less than 8% of Russian population but the two regions accounted for more than 26% of total investment in the Russian economy. In the post-Soviet period there was a significant decline in investment in real terms in both areas. However, these falls were much lower than for the rest of Russia. For instance, while the gross investment in Russia fell by more than 75% from 1990-96, investment in Tyumen fell by 66% and in Moscow by only 35%.

In 1996 the six leading investment areas attracted over 30% of all investment in Russia. In the same year the six areas with the lowest investment had a combined share of only 2.2% in the total investment in Russia. In 1985 the share of the six regional investment leaders was 10 times higher than that of the group with lowest regional investment; in 1996 it was already 15 times higher. With the exception of Ivanovo (the centre of Russia's textile industry) all of the latter group are predominantly agricultural areas. In the post-Soviet period only one of these areas experienced an increase in investment of any significance: this was Chechnya, where investment grew significantly during and after the Chechen War. However, the volume of these investment was heavily outweighed by the losses that the Chechen economy suffered during that destructive war.

The data in Tables 6 and 7 reveal another important development: due to the growing lack of investment funds, volumes of real investment were constantly falling in all Russian regions and areas since 1992. In the first one or two years of post-Soviet developments, investment in the majority of Russia's regions declined to the point where de-industrialisation became a reality and the political and social situation could easily begin to spiral out of control. Therefore, cuts in investment funds in the following years primarily affected the major investment-absorbing areas. Growing pressures from the latter coupled with existing financial constraints pushed the central authorities in Russia to balance these local demands by implementing a policy of "flexible" investment shares. This meant that additional public funds were allocated to those important economic areas where the need was most severe (or, alternatively, where political implications could be the most serious). These new allocations were made at the expense of other regions (areas) where new cuts in funding were made. However, these cuts immediately provoked resistance and growing pressures from other regions. Since 1992 the Russian government has been constantly balancing the demands for funding coming from different regions. In many cases the strength and

Table 7. Indices of Per Capita Investment by Selected Administrative Areas [36]

	1985	1990	1991	1992	1993	1994	1995	1996
Areas with Largest and Lowest Per Capita Indices of Capital Investment (Russian average=100)								
Komi Rep.	155.1	159.8	154.2	196.8	140.6	152.9	161.4	193.2
Moscow	87.7	77.5	67.0	78.9	115.2	189.0	196.9	204.5
Tyumensk.Obl.	630.2	487.5	503.6	739.7	647.2	523.0	360.3	676.9
Sakha Rep.	224.4	223.9	252.2	306.4	254.3	236.6	221.8	220.7
Kamchatsk.Obl.	140.9	134.4	129.1	109.9	210.8	165.2	116.5	92.2
Magadansk.Obl.	200.3	216.9	328.2	212.8	185.5	160.7	148.6	133.3
Ivanovsk.Obl.	60.9	65.4	71.4	53.2	38.5	38.6	35.3	28.1
Dagestan Rep.	44.8	44.6	46.3	41.8	46.6	41.6	30.0	41.7
Karachaevo-Cherkesia	63.8	76.7	75.7	67.6	54.2	44.6	40.6	54.2
North Osetia Rep.	60.8	50.7	56.9	40.1	41.5	41.5	39.5	40.6
Chechen & Ingush Rep.	48.1	46.3	47.4	14.0	...	...	230.5	107.9
Tyva Rep.	72.9	84.2	84.5	53.3	43.7	42.4	25.8	12.0
All RF	*100.0*	*100.0*	*100.0*	*100.0*	*100.0*	*100.0*	*100.0*	*100.0*
Dynamics of Per Capita Capital Investment in Areas with Largest and Lowest Levels, 1990=100								
Komi Rep.	76.2	100.0	81.3	62.6	37.9	34.8	30.0	29.5
Moscow	88.9	100.0	72.9	51.7	64.0	88.6	75.5	64.5
Tyumensk.Obl.	101.5	100.0	87.1	77.1	57.2	39.0	22.0	33.9
Sakha Rep.	78.7	100.0	94.9	69.5	48.9	38.4	29.4	24.1
Kamchatsk.Obl.	82.3	100.0	81.0	41.6	67.5	44.7	25.8	16.8
Magadansk.Obl.	72.5	100.0	127.6	49.9	36.8	26.9	20.4	15.0
Ivanovsk.Obl.	73.1	100.0	92.0	41.3	25.3	21.5	16.0	10.5
Dagestan Rep.	78.8	100.0	87.5	47.6	45.0	33.9	20.0	22.9
Karachaevo-Cherkesia	83.8	100.0	85.9	32.7	31.5	25.5	24.3	21.5
North Osetia Rep.	94.2	100.0	94.6	40.2	35.2	29.8	23.2	19.6
Chechen & Ingush Rep.	81.6	100.0	86.2	15.3	0.0	0.0	147.9	56.9
Tyva Rep.	67.9	100.0	84.6	32.2	22.4	18.3	9.1	3.5
All RF	*78.5*	*100.0*	*84.3*	*50.8*	*43.1*	*36.3*	*29.7*	*24.4*
Shares of Selected Areas in All-Russia Capital Investment (%)								
Komi Rep.	1.3	1.4	1.3	1.7	1.2	1.3	1.3	1.6
Moscow	6.6	6.0	4.0	4.7	6.8	11.8	11.5	11.9
Tyumensk.Obl.	11.3	10.4	10.7	15.6	13.7	11.9	7.7	14.6
Sakha Rep.	1.6	1.7	1.9	2.2	1.9	1.8	1.6	1.5
Kamchatsk.Obl.	0.4	0.4	0.4	0.3	0.6	0.5	0.3	0.3
Magadansk.Obl.	0.8	0.8	0.8	0.5	0.4	0.3	0.3	0.2
Subtotal largest	*22.0*	*20.6*	*19.1*	*25.0*	*24.6*	*27.6*	*22.7*	*30.1*
Ivanovsk.Obl.	0.6	0.6	0.6	0.5	0.3	0.4	0.3	0.2
Dagestan Rep.	0.5	0.6	0.6	0.5	0.6	0.6	0.4	0.6
Karachaevo-Cherkesia	0.2	0.2	0.2	0.2	0.2	0.1	0.1	0.3
North Osetia Rep.	0.3	0.2	0.3	0.2	0.2	0.2	0.2	0.2
Chechen & Ingush Rep.	0.4	0.4	0.4	0.1	...	...	1.8	0.8
Tyva Rep.	0.1	0.2	0.2	0.1	0.1	0.1	0.1	0.0
Subtotal lowest	*2.1*	*2.1*	*2.3*	*1.6*	*1.4*	*1.4*	*2.9*	*2.2*
All RF	*100.0*	*100.0*	*100.0*	*100.0*	*100.0*	*100.0*	*100.0*	*100.0*

---

[36] Calculated from sources to Table 6.

political importance of these demands, and not the national investment strategies, have been the main factors forming the national investment policy. In this event, by the mid-1990s the Russian economy had become even more resource-oriented, while development of agriculture, manufacturing and new industries was seriously hampered.

The data in Table 8 show the structure of capital investment in Russian regions by source of investment[34]. Between 1994 and 1996 the share of public funding (federal and local) in the total volume of investment in Russia declined from 40.5% to 18.8%. Some economic regions, however, continue to be highly dependent on state finance. The Central region, which includes Russia's capital city, is the most dependent on state funding: in 1996 more than 34% of all investment in the region came from federal and local state budgets. Other regions with a high proportion of public funding include the isolated Northern areas (in the Far Eastern and Northern economic regions) and Chechnya (North Caucasus). Regional shares in public investment in Russia reveal that the Central region (again, mainly Moscow) absorbed between 36 and 40% of all available state funds. The need for post-war reconstruction in Chechnya deprived both Moscow and Tyumen of a certain amount of funding in 1996. However, Table 8 shows clearly that, along with Eastern Siberia, these two areas are unrivalled leaders in the struggle for public funding in Russia. The structure of federal investment gives possibly the most accurate picture of the Russian government's investment strategy, with Moscow, Chechnya and mining industries taking the larger part of all available public investment funds.

In 1996 the mainly agricultural regions of Central ChernoZem and Volgo-Vyatka turned out to be the leaders in attracting private investment. However, the explanation of this development lies in the fact that, due to dramatic cuts in centralised investment to these areas in the post-Soviet period, the share of investment from other sources, primarily from private banks, had proportionally increased dramatically. In real terms, however, the volumes of all types of investment in these areas declined significantly.

---

[34] Unfortunately, for the period before 1994 no detailed data of this kind is currently available.

[35] In recent years funding from the banking sector to the Russian industry has become more scarce. For instance, in August 1996 one of the major Russian banks, *Promstroybank*, that is involved in funding industrial enterprises and that is "known for its readiness to invest money from partiotic motives" announced that credits to industry made up only 8% of its investment portfolio, a significant drop from 20% in 1994 (*Finansovye Izvestia*, 22 August 1996).

Russian private banks issue credits on a commercial (ie. profit-sensitive) basis which, in the Russian situation of high inflation, means that high interest rates are attached to these credits. Only a very small portion of these private banks are currently interested in development strategy [35]. Under these circumstances, when the financial situation of their debtors becomes critical, banks usually prefer to sell debtors' property, thus covering at least part of the loss. Another option successfully applied by many

Table 8. Regional Structure of Investment by Source (%) [37]

Structure of Capital Investment

| | 1994 | | | | | 1996 | | | | |
	State	Munic-ipal	Compa-ny funds	Other	*Total*	State	Munic-ipal	Compa-ny funds	Other	*Total*
Northern	37.2	6.1	44.3	12.4	*100.0*	10.8	9.5	68.3	11.4	*100.0*
North-West	41.9	21.5	26.4	10.2	*100.0*	7.7	9.8	62.5	20.0	*100.0*
Central	35.5	9.7	45.4	9.4	*100.0*	18.8	15.5	43.4	22.3	*100.0*
Volgo-Vyatka	44.1	13.0	27.8	15.1	*100.0*	5.8	12.9	70.4	10.9	*100.0*
Central ChernoZem	35.1	6.3	36.9	21.7	*100.0*	7.5	11.0	66.0	15.5	*100.0*
Volga	39.0	9.3	39.0	12.7	*100.0*	6.0	10.6	66.1	17.3	*100.0*
North Caucasus	35.2	10.0	29.7	25.1	*100.0*	22.3	4.5	49.1	24.1	*100.0*
Urals	35.4	9.4	42.5	12.7	*100.0*	4.9	11.0	69.9	14.2	*100.0*
West Siberia	27.0	5.7	62.2	5.1	*100.0*	4.4	10.5	70.8	14.3	*100.0*
East Siberia	45.2	10.3	36.8	7.7	*100.0*	10.9	9.2	74.3	5.6	*100.0*
Far East	43.8	7.7	41.9	6.6	*100.0*	15.2	7.9	49.6	27.3	*100.0*
Kaliningrad	51.1	7.8	30.0	11.1	*100.0*	22.7	4.5	55.4	17.4	*100.0*
All RF	32.4	8.1	39.4	20.1	*100.0*	9.2	9.6	66.3	14.9	*100.0*

Regional Shares in State-Funded Capital Investment

| | 1994 | | | 1996 | |
	Federal budget	Local budgets	Central investment fund	Federal budget	Local budgets
Northern	3.8	4.4	2.6	4.0	3.3
North-West	5.8	4.7	2.1	3.4	4.1
Central	40.4	25.5	9.3	36.5	28.8
Volgo-Vyatka	2.7	4.4	3.1	1.9	4.1
Central ChernoZem	2.7	2.5	3.2	2.8	3.9
Volga	4.9	10.9	10.9	5.4	9.0
North Caucasus	8.0	5.2	27.3	15.8	3.0
Urals	5.9	15.8	4.8	6.7	14.3
West Siberia	10.4	12.1	24.2	8.9	20.2
East Siberia	6.7	5.5	4.3	6.8	5.4
Far East	7.4	8.6	7.4	7.4	3.7
Kaliningrad	1.2	0.4	0.7	0.6	0.1
All RF	*100.0*	*100.0*	*100.0*	*100.0*	*100.0*

---

[37] Sourced and calculated from: Rossiiskii statisticheskii ezhegodnik. 1995, Moscow: Goskomstat, 1995, pp.845-850; Sotsial'no-ekonomicheskoe polozhenie Rossii. 1996 g., Moscow: Goskomstat, 1997, pp.233-236.

Russian companies and banks is that of using threats of selling property and/or going bankrupt. In the latter case such threats are directly aimed at blackmailing the Russian central and local authorities with the social and political consequences of such action. As on many occasions in Russia's recent past, the authorities prefer to issue new credits and bills of exchange to bankrupt industries rather than to face the social and political consequences of the mass closure of enterprises.

Table 8 also demonstrates that there is a direct relation between the volumes of public and private funding in all regions. Thus, cuts in state funding to North, Central, Urals, Western Siberia and the Far East were accompanied by increases in private funding. As it was already stated above, rises in private funding during 1994-96 in some agricultural regions can be explained by the fact that all of these regions generally suffer from gross under-investment, which consequently makes the volumes of private investment in them almost negligible. On the other hand, the majority of agricultural producers in these regions, particularly on the eve of and during the Russian harvest season (July-September), have no other choice but to try to fill the growing gap in public funding by increased dependence on private sources of finance.

FOREIGN INVESTMENT FLOWS

Between 1990 and 1996 the total volume of foreign investment in the non-financial sectors [38] of Russian economy amounted to $12 billion. This was six times less than the estimated need for investment in Russia during that period, and 25 times less than the investment that the People's Republic of China managed to attract in 1991-96 [39]. Despite of the size of its economy, in 1996 Russia received less investment than Hungary and Poland, Russia's former allies in the ex-Eastern bloc [40]. The share of foreign non-financial investment in Russia's gross volumes of investment from all sources in 1993-96 was between 2% and 4% (Table 3).

The dynamics of foreign investment in the non-financial sector of the Russian economy is shown in Table 9. According to these figures, $5.5 billion were invested in Russia between 1990-95. In 1996 a further $6.5 billion were brought into the

---

[38] All investment minus mainly purchases of state bonds (GKOs) and state debts.
[39] *Finansovye Izvestia*, 31 October 1996 and *Delovoy Mir*, November 10-14 1996.
[40] *Reuter*, 18 February 1997.

country. The latter indicates that last year there was a significant change in the attitudes of foreign investors to Russia. It is interesting that more than 2/3 of this money entered the country after the June 1996 presidential elections in Russia. This fact shows the extent to which trends in foreign investment flows are dependent on the course of Russian political developments. Among the largest investors in the Russian economy are the United States [42], the UK, Switzerland and the Netherlands. Together these four nations accounted for almost 70% of all foreign investment in 1990-96.

Table 9. Dynamics of Foreign Investment in Russia (excluding financial investment, million US dollars) [41]

	1990-1993	1994	1990-1994	1995	Jan-Mar 1996	Jan-Jun 1996	Jan-Sep 1996	1996	1990-1996	*1990-96 as % of all*
Net total [a]	1679.9	1053.4	2733.3	2796.7	884.0	2005.4	4496.8	6506.1	12036.1	100.0
USA	...	...	1226.9	812.9	359.7	510.8	882.1	1695.2	3735.0	31.0
UK	...	...	833.0	161.4	120.2	261.0	372.4	486.4	1480.8	12.3
Germany	...	...	470.4	293.5	60.7	132.3	194.4	288.9	1052.8	8.7
France	...	...	501.0	95.9	17.5	21.3	34.8	41.7	638.6	5.3
Switzerland	...	...	98.9	419.8	5.0	281.0	968.1	1323.4	1842.1	15.3
Italy	...	...	351.8	0.0	3.1	13.5	32.0	75.2	427.0	3.5
Netherlands	...	...	237.4	83.3	31.8	301.9	954.1	979.6	1300.3	10.8
Belgium	...	...	93.8	105.3	10.5	30.2	47.3	65.0	264.1	2.2
Subtotal	...	...	3813.2	1972.1	608.5	1552.0	3485.2	4955.4	10740.7	89.2
Other/ outflow(-) [a]	...	...	-1079.9	824.6	275.5	453.4	1011.6	1550.7	1295.4	10.8

[a] Russian statistics show only "accumulated foreign investment" to a certain date which is the net sum of gross investment and outflow of foreign capital.

---

[41] Sourced and calculated from: O razvitii ekonomicheskikh reform v Rossiiskoi Federatsii. Dopolnitelnye dannye za yanvar'-sentyabr' 1993 goda, Moscow: Goskomstat, 1993, p.172; Rossiiskii statisticheskii ezhegodnik. 1994, Moscow: Goskomstat, 1994, p.777; Rossiiskii statisticheskii ezhegodnik. 1995, Moscow: Goskomstat, 1995, pp.946-947; Sotsial'no-ekonomicheskoe polozhenie Rossii, yanvar'-sentyabr' 1994 g., Moscow: Goskomstat, 1994, pp.53-54; Sotsial'no-ekonomicheskoe polozhenie Rossii, yanvar'-oktyabr' 1995 g., Moscow: Goskomstat, 1995, p.95; Sotsial'no-ekonomicheskoe polozhenie Rossii, yanvar'-fevral' 1996 g., Moscow: Goskomstat, 1996, pp.67-70; Sotsial'no-ekonomicheskoe polozhenie Rossii, yanvar'-mai 1996 g., Moscow: Goskomstat, 1996, pp.68-70; Kapitalnoe stroitelstvo v Rossiiskoi Federatsii, Moscow: Goskomstat, 1994, p.35; "Russia: 1996 Investment Climate Statement from US Embassy, Moscow", BISNIS Briefs, 31 July 1996; Rossiya v tsifrakh. 1996, Moscow: Goskomstat, 1996, pp.244-245; Sotsial'no-ekonomicheskoe polozhenie Rossii, yanvar'-avgust 1996 g., Moscow: Goskomstat, 1996, pp.72-75; Ekonomika Rossii, yanvar'-noyabr' 1996 g., Moscow: Goskomstat, 1996, pp.53-56; Sotsial'no-ekonomicheskoe polozhenie Rossii, yanvar'-fevral' 1997 g., Moscow: Goskomstat, 1997, pp.84-88.

[42] The bulk of US direct investment in 1995 came from US tobacco and food companies: Phillip Morris, Master Foods, Pepsi Cola (*Nezavisimaya Gazeta*, 29 October 1996).

The rapid growth of investment from Switzerland and the Netherlands during 1996 could be largely attributed to the partial repatriation of the fugitive Russian capital through Swiss and Dutch banking systems [43].

Of an estimated gross volume of $13.2 billion invested by foreigners in all sectors of the Russian economy during 1996, foreign direct investment totalled just $2 billion which was slightly up from $1.8 billion in 1995 (Table 10). The bulk of money invested in Russia during that year went into purchases of Russian state bonds and other securities ($6.7 billion). The next biggest item after investment in the financial sector were trade credits and bank deposits ($3.3 billion) [44]. In 1996 portfolio investment in non-financial sectors of the Russian national economy had a very small share of all non-financial investment - less than 1%. In 1994-96 the share of FDI in foreign non-financial investment declined significantly: from 52% in 1994 to 32% in 1996. In the same period the share of foreign trade credits, bank deposits and other credits (see "Other" in Table 10) increased from less than a half to over 67%.

Since the beginning of reform in Russia significant changes have occurred in terms of the direction of foreign investment. At the start of the reform (1992-93) the major part of foreign investment was accumulated either as charter capital of various joint ventures with Russian enterprises (mainly in trade, oil exploration and processing, construction, metallurgy) or in the form of credits issued to Russian export-import companies [46]. These investment were generally aimed at facilitating export-import operations with Russian partners, at a time when most of the Russian economy was

Table 10. Foreign Non-Financial Investment in Russia by Type, 1994-96 [45]

| | million US dollars | | | % to total | | |
	1994	1995	1996	1994	1995	1996
FDI	548.9	1876.9	2090.0	52.1	67.1	32.1
Portfolio	0.5	30.0	45.4	0.1	1.1	0.7
Other	504.0	889.8	4370.7	47.8	31.8	67.2
Total	*1053.4*	*2796.7*	*6506.1*	*100.0*	*100.0*	*100.0*

---

[43] *Nezavisimaya Gazeta*, 29 October 1996.

[44] "Russia: Foreign Capital is $11 Billion", *AP*, 27 December 1996; *OMRI*, No.32, Part 1, 14 February 1997.

[45] Sources: Rossiiskii statisticheskii ezhegodnik. 1996, Moscow: Goskomstat, 1996, p.466; Sotsial'no-ekonomicheskoe polozhenie Rossii, yanvar'-fevral' 1997 g., Moscow: Goskomstat, 1997, p.85.

still owned by the state. The peak in these "joint-venture" investment came in the first half of 1994, before the end of the first stage of Russian privatisation. At that time more than 80% of all foreign investment in the Russian economy (excluding the financial sector) were directed towards industry. Half of the latter were invested in the fuel sector.

Privatisation of state-owned enterprises, many of which were turned into joint-stock companies in 1994-95, decreased the significance of "joint venture" investment. However, barriers on foreign ownership of Russian minerals companies that were imposed both by Russian legislation and by stockholders of the newly-formed private enterprises, greatly limited the direct flows of foreign capital into the national economy. While direct investment in the production sectors of the economy have been declining steadily since mid-1994, the major part of foreign investment has been redirected into stock market operations, banking and finance. Thus, the share of industry in the total volume of foreign investment in Russia fell from 80.4% in mid-1994 to 33.3 % at the end of 1996.

One of the major drawbacks in foreign investment in Russia is that a very small proportion of both direct and portfolio investment goes to productive sectors of the economy (industrial and/or agricultural enterprises). Some current estimates put the share of such investment during the whole reform period at below $800 million [47]. And this is happening at a time when, according to the president of the US Overseas Private Investment Corporation (OPIC), there is at least $30 billion in new US investment just waiting to go into Russia [48]. Another recent estimate indicated that around $50 billion could be invested into the Russian fuel and energy sector alone [49]. However, this foreign money will start to come into Russia only after the existing Russian environment for foreign investors changes.

Foreign investors are put off from investing by the under-developed nature of Russia's

---

[46] Moscow-based joint ventures that were trade intermediaries made up 82.6% of all JVs operating in Russia in early 1990s (*Nezavisimaya Gazeta*, 29 October 1996).

[47] Ibid.

[48] Robert Lyle, "Russia: Huge Foreign Investment Hinges On Reforms", *Radio Free Europe/ Radio Liberty News Service*, 13 January 1997.

[49] Bruce Clark, Chrystia Freeland, "Russia: $50bn Awaits Tax Reform", *The Financial Times*, London, 7 February 1997.

market structures; existing tax burdens and the general instability of the taxation system; problems associated with the methods and outcomes of privatisation; outdated accounting practices [50]; frequent legal confusion arising from contradictory legislative acts; and widespread corruption in the bureaucracy and law-enforcement agencies. Added to that are frequent attempts undertaken by Russian legislators and companies aimed at limiting or even banning foreign participation in some areas of the economy [51]. The combination of all these factors explains the extremely modest scale of long-term foreign (direct) investment in the productive sector of the Russian economy. At the same time, attempts made by the Russian government in the recent years to attract foreign capital and credits, have opened up new opportunities for short-term but highly profitable foreign investment in Russia's emerging securities and stock markets.

The year 1996 saw the Russian stock markets booming. Billions of dollars of foreign portfolio investment were directed into purchases of Russian loans, state bonds and company shares, making Russia the most lucrative equity market in the Emerging Markets' group of countries [52]. Between mid-1995 and the end of 1996 the share of investment in banking and finance in the total volume of non-financial foreign investment increased by 2.5 times from less than 20% to 54%. Since mid-1996 Russian statistics have also started to list volumes of foreign portfolio investment in "the financial sector" or stock market operations. In the first half of 1996 the total volume of investment in that sector was 3.5 times larger than gross foreign investment in all other sectors of the Russian economy (Table 11). After the results of the Russian

---

[50] Very often foreign investors reported as one of the major problems the so-called double accountuing often practised by Russian companies which did not allow investors to keep track of cash flows at an enterprise.

[51] For example, in February 1997 it was reported that the lower house of the Russian Parliament, *the Duma*, passed in the first reading amendments to the law on foreign investment banning foreign investment in many sectors of the economy, including telecommunications and electrical power distribution. Next month Russia's gas monopoly *Gazprom* blocked an attempt by foreign investors to buy its domestically traded shares ("Duma Urges Wide Ban on Foreign Investment", *Reuters*, 21 February 1997; "Defensive Gazprom", *OAEEDB*, 3 March 1997).

[52] For example, according to the data from the Emerging Markets Traders Association (EMTA) between end of 1995 and end of 1996 the average bid price on Russia's *Vneshekonombank*'s Yen loans changed by 141.67% making it the largest change on the EMTA's list (see V.Tikhomirov, "Russia: The Stock Market Boom", *Russian and Euro-Asian Bulletin*, Melbourne, January 1997, Vol.6, No.1, pp.10-14.

[53] Calculated from sources to Table 9.

presidential election became known, the flow of foreign capital into productive sectors of the economy increased, bringing the ratio between portfolio and all other types of investment down: in 1996 foreign investment in financial sector (purchases of state bonds and company shares) amounted to $6.7 billion, against $6.5 billion of investment in all other spheres of the national economy.

The shift in orientation of foreign investment flows in Russia from "joint-venture" to "finance" was also reflected in the regional structure of investment (Table 12). Resource-rich areas (Northern and Western Siberian regions) and key transport regions (Far East) were the main centres of foreign investment in the early "joint venture" period. However, in later years these areas largely lost their attractiveness to foreign investors: for example, between 1993 and September 1996 the share of the Western Siberian region in the gross volume of non-financial investment fell from 14.7% to 5.5% and that of the Far East from 12.3 to 5.8%. During the same period the share of Tyumen in the total volume of investment made by foreigners in the Russian economy declined from 11.6% to 3.3%.

While investment in Russia's industrial regions were steadily falling in 1993-96, the country's capital city developed into the major centre for foreign investment in Russia, with its share in the gross foreign investment rising from 15.9% in 1993 to 70.7% in

Table 11. Structure of Foreign Investment in Russia, 1993-96 (% to total, excluding stock market operations) [53]

	1993 Jan-Jun	1993 All	1994 Jan-Jun	1995 Jan-Jun	1995 Jan-Sep	1995 All	1996 Jan-Mar	1996 Jan-Jun	1996 Jan-Sep	1996 All
All industry, incl.:	53.9	...	80.4	58.9	...	43.0	35.6	33.4	11.1	33.3
Fuel	17.7	49.7	41.7	13.5	10.3	9.3	...	...	...	...
Chemical	2.1	...	2.3	15.2	8.1	5.9	...	...	...	...
Machine-building	2.5	...	6.8	...	...	5.9	...	...	...	...
Wood-processing	6.3	6.1	7.1	...	6.5	5.7	...	...	...	...
Food	7.5	...	...	12.3	...	10.1	...	...	...	...
Construction	13.8	8.3	3.2	...	...	7.1	...	...	...	...
Trade & catering	19.4	6.3	11.1	9.9	14.7	16.9	16.4	6.8	...	...
Credit, finance, insurance	3.1	...	...	...	19.6	19.2	30.2	47.0	23.6	53.8
Other	9.7	42.2	5.2	31.2	40.7	13.9	17.8	12.8	65.3	12.9
Total	*100.0*	*100.0*	*100.0*	*100.0*	*100.0*	*100.0*	*100.0*	*100.0*	*100.0*	*100.0*
Investment in stock market operations as % to all other	...	...	...	...	...	...	...	348.8	144.6	103.1

Table 12. Regional Structure of Foreign Investment in Russia (%) [56]

	1993	1995	Jan-Mar 1996	Jan-Jun 1996	Jan-Sep 1996	1996
Foreign Investment by Economic Regions						
Northern	33.3	2.8	...	...	...	...
North-West	5.4	6.7	9.3	5.8	5.3	5.1
Central	17.4	58.4	59.8	65.4	73.5	73.8
Volgo-Vyatka	0.2	2.3	...	...	...	...
Central ChernoZem	0.6	0.2	...	...	...	...
Volga	7.9	9.6	6.7	5.9	4.6	2.9
North Caucasus	5.5	1.7	...	...	...	...
Urals	0.9	1.8	...	...	...	...
West Siberia	14.7	8.5	6.1	7.1	5.5	6.2
East Siberia	1.4	0.8	...	...	...	...
Far East	12.3	6.8	8.8	6.2	5.8	5.6
Kaliningrad	0.5	0.4	...	...	...	...
Subtotal	*100.0*	*100.0*	*90.7*	*90.4*	*94.7*	*93.6*
All RF	100.0	100.0	100.0	100.0	100.0	100.0
Areas with Largest Shares in Foreign Investment						
Moscow	15.9	46.9	45.0	62.8	70.7	66.0
Tyumensk.Obl.	11.6	3.7	4.3	4.4	3.3	3.9
St.Petersburg	5.1	5.5	3.2	2.8	2.2	2.2
Moskovsk.Obl.	0.5	...	12.1	...	...	...
Tatarstan Rep.	2.4	5.7	5.1	3.1	1.5	1.4
Khabarovskii Krai	2.5	...	3.3	2.5	1.6	1.2
Primorskii Krai	2.5	1.7	2.7	1.6	0.8	0.8
Sakhalinsk.Obl.	4.2	1.8	...	...	...	1.1
Leningradsk.Obl.	0.1	...	5.1	2.3	2.5	2.2
Samarsk.Obl.	0.7	2.5	0.4	1.5	2.4	...
Nizhegorodsk.Obl.	0.1	2.1	...	...	...	...
Subtotal	*45.5*	*70.0*	*81.4*	*81.0*	*85.0*	*78.8*
All RF	100.0	100.0	100.0	100.0	100.0	100.0

---

[54] In January-September 1996 43% of registered joint ventures in Russia were operating in trade and catering (*Ekonomika Rossii, yanvar'-noyabr' 1996 g.*, Moscow: Goskomstat, 1996, p.79).

[55] *Nezavisimaya Gazeta*, 29 October 1996 and *Ekonomika Rossii, yanvar'-noyabr' 1996 g.*, Moscow: Goskomstat, 1996, pp.79-80.

[56] Sources: Kapitalnoe stroitelstvo v Rossiiskoi Federatsii, Moscow: Goskomstat, 1994, pp.36-37; Sotsial'no-ekonomicheskoe polozhenie Rossii, yanvar'-fevral' 1996 g., Moscow: Goskomstat, 1996, p.69; Sotsial'no-ekonomicheskoe polozhenie Rossii, yanvar'-mai 1996 g., Moscow: Goskomstat, 1996, p.69; Rossiya v tsifrakh. 1996, Moscow: Goskomstat, 1996, p.244; Sotsial'no-ekonomicheskoe polozhenie Rossii, yanvar'-avgust 1996 g., Moscow: Goskomstat, 1996, pp.72-75; Ekonomika Rossii, yanvar'-noyabr' 1996 g., Moscow: Goskomstat, 1996, pp.53-56; Rossiiskii statisticheskii ezhegodnik. 1996, Moscow: Goskomstat, 1996, pp.466-467, 1096-1098; Sotsial'no-ekonomicheskoe polozhenie Rossii, yanvar'-fevral' 1997 g., Moscow: Goskomstat, 1997, pp.86-87.

September 1996. This spectacular development was mainly due to the fact that Moscow is home to the absolute majority of Russian national stock exchanges, banks and other financial institutions. Therefore, the bulk of foreign portfolio investment in Russia were naturally coming to Moscow.

By 1996 Moscow had also become the absolute leader among Russian regions in attracting "joint venture" foreign capital. The larger part of this capital is now invested not in the production sectors, but in trade, services and financial structures [54]. In September 1996, of the total number of joint ventures in Russia 44.8% were based in Moscow; Moscow's JVs had a combined share of 43.4% in the gross exports made by joint ventures from Russia during the first nine months of 1996 [55].

CONCLUSION

The profound social and economic crisis that has been developing in Russia since 1991 has had an extremely negative effect on public finance and investment. In the post-Soviet period, an acute financial crisis that almost paralysed the Russian national economy forced the government to make even larger sacrifices to its investment strategy. Increasing pressures from unpaid public employees, mounting state debts to internal and foreign creditors, shrinking state currency and gold reserves, and huge tax collection arrears put the already weakened financial system under great strain. It could be argued that short-term needs of political survival have largely replaced long-term economic and investment strategies on the current priority list of Russian reformists. During the last few years funding demands coming from a variety of political, social and regional quarters have been the main factors forming the national investment policy. In today's Russia, state investment policies (both with respect to the various branches of the economy and to the regions) are more and more reminiscent of the old Russian story about Trishka's coat ("Trishkin kaftan"): the continual appearance of new holes in a poor man's old coat means that he is forced to keep ripping off sections of the same coat.

By mid-1990s the need to cover the growing state budget deficit became the dominant objective of the Russian government's economic policy. Almost all of the government's other economic concerns were in one way or another subjugated to the achievement of this major aim (tax policies, foreign borrowing, demonopolisation and privatisation, state social and investment expenditures). In the decade between 1986-96 the Russian state to all its intents and purposes withdrew almost completely from pursuing any viable investment policy: during that period the share of public finance (federal and local) in the gross volume of investment fell from 90.4% to 18.8%. In 1996, in real terms, the total volume of all state investment in the national economy amounted to just over 6% of the 1986 level.

Public investment cuts resulted in a rapid growth of the share of non-state investment in the gross volume of investment in the national economy from 2.7% in 1986 to over 66% ten years later. However, this growth cannot be attributed to increased interest on the part of private investors in funding of Russian economy. In real terms, volumes of company investment in Russia fell by more than two-thirds over the past six years.

In the Russian economy the real volume of investment from all sources has fallen by more than four times in the post-Soviet period. In the last two years these greatly reduced flows of investment capital were mainly directed to the major Russian exporting industries (oil and gas extraction, timber, non-ferrous metallurgy), the city of Moscow and the post-war reconstruction of Chechnya. This has been done at the expense of funding all the other Russian regions and sectors of the economy. This investment policy has serious strategic implications for Russia's future:

(a) it is leading to the de-industrialisation of the Russian economy (for instance, gross volumes of investment in engineering fell by over 90% in 1990-96);

(b) growing dependency on food and agricultural imports is becoming inevitable (during the last six years the share of agriculture in all investment declined from 16% to 3.2%, while in real terms money invested in that sector in 1996 was equal to less than 5% of agricultural investment in 1990);

(c) the deterioration in investment funding of social needs (education, research and development, culture) will, in the long run, greatly undermine Russia's chances for the successful modernisation of its economy.

The deep crisis in the Russian financial system and economy is also reflected in the dynamics of foreign investment. The share of foreign investment in the total volume of all investment in Russia has never exceeded 4%. Since mid-1994 foreign investors have been directing less and less money into the production sectors of the Russian economy. At the same time, budgetary needs have forced the Russian government to borrow growing amounts of money by issuing internal and, since late 1996, external bonds. The interest rate on these bonds was significantly higher than the inflation rate and this immediately attracted both local and foreign investors. In 1996 the Russian equity market became the most lucrative area of investment in the financial sector in the non-Western world. During that year the volume of foreign investment in the Russian non-financial sector grew by 2.3 times over the 1995 level and exceeded the total sum of money invested by foreigners in Russia in the five previous years. However, of $13.2 billion of 1996 foreign investment in all sectors of the economy, only $2 billion were invested in Russian industry. The reminder was invested in purchases of Russian state bonds and debts or issued as trade and other credits to Russian companies and state agencies.

The collapse of state investment and the continuing decline in real private funding of the national economy has led to dramatic falls in Russia's industrial and agricultural production. Unless this adverse tendency is changed, it is hard to expect any substantial economic growth in Russia. Fundamental changes need to be made to the current Russian investment strategy without delay. Despite the acute shortage in state funds, there are massive and grossly under-utilised non-public financial resources available in Russia that are not being invested into the national economy. These include the population's uninvested foreign currency savings (which are increasing by $5 billion each month) and the capital that is invested abroad (at a rate of $2 billion a month). Although there were signs in 1995-96 that some of this money was coming back into the national economy, only miserable amounts were invested in the production sector. The bulk of the money went into servicing export-import operations and purchases of state bonds.

It could also be argued that to a great extent it was the post-Soviet Russian government's actions that led to the situation where it is left with very inadequate financial resources and very limited means of controlling the development of investment in the country. Liberalisation of Russian foreign trade in 1992 opened up the main channel of capital flight out of the country and significantly reduced the funds available to the state, while the lifting of foreign currency controls led to a massive flight of the population's savings from quickly depreciating ruble into low-inflationary foreign currency. Privatisation of the state-owned economy resulted in the collapse of the system of state redistribution of funding between different branches of the economy. Thus, through losing control over revenue flows from export-oriented industries and foreign trade, the government cut itself from a major source of budgetary funding. At the same time the bulk of loss-making companies that in 1996 made up almost half of the Russian economy [57] remained dependent on state subsidies. But the state cannot declare most of these companies bankrupt, because this would effectively mean leaving millions of their employees without any source of income. The current financial crisis has left the Russian government without any resources that could be directed into paying unemployment benefits to these people. On the other hand, the deep investment crisis means that fewer new jobs are created each year.

It would be unrealistic to expect that this dilemma will solve itself without government intervention. At present all of the state's economic activities in Russia are directed towards increasing cash flows into the nation's shrinking budget. This, in my view, is a highly questionable policy because in the situation of major socio-economic crisis that exists in Russia the state has almost totally withdrawn from economic strategy and planning. Instead, the state's main efforts should be directed towards reversing negative trends in the national economy. Public investment policy should be the centre of such a strategy. Internal and external channels of capital flight should be, if not closed at all, at least state-controlled. If not, the government - if it continues to stand firm in implementing its current policies - will inevitably become even more isolated from the society and may resort to undemocratic (administrative and/or authoritarian) measures more frequently in pursuing its proclaimed strategic goals. And this would hardly bring the proclaimed objectives of democratisation and formation of the market economy in Russia any closer.

---

[57] According to *Goskomstat*, in 1996 43% of industrial, 75% of agricultural , 58% of transport and 35% of construction companies were making losses (*Sotsial'no-ekonomicheskoe polozhenie Rossii, yanvar' 1997 g.*, Moscow: Goskomstat, 1997, p.145).

CHAPTER 13 THE INFRASTRUCTURE DEVELOPMENT AND FOREIGN DIRECT INVESTMENT IN CHINA

ZHANG XIAOQIANG[*]

PART A: BASIC INFORMATION

1. With years efforts, China has achieved great improvement in the infrastructure. For example, its installed electric power generation capacity reached 215 million KW by the end of 1995, of which 16 million KW was newly increased within that year, recording the first all over the world. The switching telephone amounted to 85 million lines in the same year, of which 16 million lines was for 1995, which also was the number one in the world. From 1980 to 1995, China's annual urban water supply capacity increased to 49.7 billion tons from 8.8 billion tons. From 1990 to 1995, China's high-class expressways increased to 10,000 KM from 2,000 KM. Obvious progresses have been made in the ports, railways, civil aviation, urban road and environmental protection (Table-1).

2. Because of the poor economic foundation and the huge population in China, basic improvement of the out-of-date infrastructure has not been realized. For instance, the installed electric power generation capacity per capita account for

Table-1 China-The Infrastructure Development

	1980	1985	1990	1995
1. Power Generated (billion Kwh)	300.6	410.7	621.2	1007.7
2. Telephone Switch (million)	4.43	6.13	12.32	72.04
3. Highway (thousand KM)	880	940	1030	1160
4. Urban Water Supply (billion ton)	8.83	12.8	38.2	49.7
5. Urban Road (thousand KM)	29.5	38.3	94.8	130

[*] Director-General, Foreign Capital Utilization Department, State Planning Commission, People's Republic of China.

only one eleventh of that in U.S.A., the telephone number every 100 persons is only 6.33, which lags far behind the average standard of the developing countries. And the railways in operation are less than 60,000 KM, lower than those in India. Amongst the total 670 cities in China, more than 300 are severely running shortage of water supply.

3. The Chinese Government positively manages to mobilize more investment for infrastructure. In 1990, 36.14 billion RMB out of 291.8 billion RMB which was for the state-owned-entity's fixed asset investment went to power sector, accounting for 12.1% of the total, 27.9 billion RMB went to transportation, 9.4% of the total and 7 billion RMB went to telecommunication, 2.3% of the total investment. In 1995, total investment for the state-owned-entity reached 1,089.8 billion RMB, of which 15.7% or 171 billion RMB was used for power industry, 13.7% or 149.8 billion RMB for transportation and 7.1% or 77 billion RMB for telecommunication. In 1995, power, transportation and telecommunication industries received about 36.5% of the total state-owned-entity fixed asset investment, and accounted for 19.9% of total investment of China in same year (Table-2).

4. During the past years, the saving rate and the investment rate reached as high as more than 32% in China. In the eighth five-year-plan (1991-1995), the nation's fixed asset investment totaled 6,600 billion RMB, the investment rate was 35%. From 1980 to 1995, China's total fixed asset investment increased 22% annually. The economic system reform has changed China's investment picture greatly. The percentage of state-owned-entity investment within the total investment has been reduce from 81.9% in 1980 to 66.1% in 1985 and only 54.3% in 1995(Table-3). For the purpose of controlling inflation and raising the people living standard and enhancing efficiency, during the ninth five-year-plan (1996-2000), we are proposed to decrease the investment rate to 30%, the total investment of the five years is planned to 13,000 billion RMB. From 2001 to 2005, China's total investment of the five years may reach to 20,000 billion RMB according to my estimation. Put these two figures together, from 1996 to 2005, China's total investment will be 33,000 billion RMB (4,000 billion dollars).

5. In accordance with the ninth five-year-plan and the 2010 long term target program (which were approved by the National People's Congress in March 1996), for the

Table-2 The State-Owne d-Entity Investment in Certain Main Infrastructure Sectors

in billion RMB

	1985		1990		1995	
Total State-owned-entity Investment	168.05	100%	298.69	100%	1089.82	100%
Electric power	12	7.10%	36.14	12.10%	171.03	15.70%
Transportation (1)	18.8	11.20%	27.91	9.40%	149.84	13.70%
Telecommunication	3.85	2.30%	6.98	2.30%	76.99	7.10%
Water supply	0.87	0.50%	2.29	0.80%	12.3	1.10%
Subtotal	35.52	21.10%	73.32	24.60%	410.16	37.60%

(1) "Transportation" implies highway, railway, civil aviation, ports, etc..

(2) From 1994 till now, the exchange rate of local currency RMB to U.S. dollar is 8.3 RMB=1 USD

Table-3 China-Total Fixed Asset Investment

in billion RMB

	Total	State-Owned-Entity	Collective Entity	Private	Others(1)
1980	91.09	74.59	4.6	11.9	
	100%	81.90%	5%	13.10%	
1985	254.32	168.05	32.75	53.52	
	100%	66.10%	12.90%	21%	
1990	451.76	298.69	52.96	100.12	
	100%	66.10%	11.70%	22.20%	
1995	2001.93	1089	328.94	256.02	330.32
	100%	54.30%	16.40%	12.80%	16.50%

(1) "Others" includes FDI, share holding system economy, etc..
  Since there were seldom these kinds of investment before 1990, detailed
  statistic began available after 1993.

next 15 years, the China's GDP is to grow at the rate of around 8%. Accordingly sustainable development is needed for the infrastructure. For example, from 1996 to 2000, it's necessary to newly increase another 80 million KW of installed electric power generation capacity (for the year of 2001 to 2010, 200 million KW will be needed), switching telephone is planned to increase by 90 million lines, high class expressway 11,000 KM. Anticipated by the World Bank, as much as 800 billion U.S. dollars will be invested to the infrastructure in China for the next 10 years. Based on China's previous experience and estimated demand in next 10 years, my estimation is that power, transportation, telecommunication, water supply and other infrastructure industries will receive about 20% of the country's total investment. The investment amount in these sectors may be 6,600 billion RMB (800 billion dollars).

6. For better infrastructure construction, Chinese Government will continue widening

the channel of capital mobilizing, encouraging the state-owned-entity, collective corporations, private and foreign capital to invest in infrastructure field, and will gradually change the situation existed in the past years that investment in infrastructure relies too heavily on the state-owned-entity. According to primary statistic, up till now more than 95% of total investment in the following 4 sectors: electric power, transportation, telecommunications and urban water supply are from public entities. For the next 5-15 years, the above percentage is probably reduced to 80%, the remaining 20% will be met by introducing foreign and domestic private capital, in which foreign capital will be more than half.

7. China is continuing reforming its fixed assets investment management system. In the past 17 years reform, the following apparent progresses have been achieved: (1) the sources of investment are becoming diversified. As Table-3 indicates, within the total fixed asset investment, the part owned by state accounted for 81.9% in 1980, but the rate fell to 54.3% in 1995. Investment in forms of share holding, foreign direct investment (FDI) were less than 3% of total investment in 1985, but it rose to 16.5%. (2) Based on the principle of socialist market economy, investments are divided into 3 categories: public welfare, basic and competitive. The government appropriation is mainly used for the public welfare investment like hospitals and schools. The basic investment, that supports projects of irrigation, railways, rural roads and so on which mainly yield social benefits, is to be realized mainly through government budget funds and policy banks' financing. For those "Basic" projects with better financial benefits like expressways, thermo-power plants, public enterprises, private and FDI are allowed to invest with financing more and more through commercial channels instead of mainly relying on government budget funds. For those competitive projects like processing industry, commercial real estate development, the enterprises can mobilize funds through commercial channels according to market situation. (3) The right of investment decision making has been decentralized gradually. For example, the right of approving FDI projects at provincial level has been risen to 30 million dollars. The large-scale enterprise groups have been authorized the same right as a province has. The local government can approve those local infrastructure projects that are not supported by central budget funds like urban roads, medium- and small-sized water plants, etc.. (4)We develop capital market and try to make it perfect, and reform financial system. Great progresses have been achieved in the development of stock market and bonds market. And the

corresponding managing acts and regulations have been published or will be issued. Corporations listed in the stock market in China are near 800, and the investment agencies and private who opened accounts amounted 30 million. Since 1994, some policy banks such as State Development Bank, The Export-Import Bank of China have been set up successively. Meanwhile, the commercialization of other state owned banks like China Construction Bank, China Industry and Commerce Bank has been sped up.

8. In China, the rate of private saving is comparatively high. Most of the savings are from the deposit in banks where the public enterprises borrow for investing. The investment conducted directly by private accounts for around 13% of the total fixed asset investment (256 billion RMB in 1995). However almost two thirds of it are for residential buildings, the others for processing industry, small scale servicing sector and agricultural production and so on. For the next several years, the investment conducted by private will account for more proportion in total fixed asset investment, but is estimated to still mainly flow to residential buildings construction. At the same time, the Government also encourages the development of private economy. The experiments for introducing private economy and individuals to infrastructure construction through stock investment, bonds purchase as well as direct investment are getting enlarged. In recent years, certain private enterprises have already invested in roads, bridges, ports and small power plants, and have gained some primary experiences. Hopefully there will be further development in future.

9. The source of state-owned-entity investment in China changed greatly in the past more than 10 years. In 1981, among the whole state-owned-entity investment 63.8 billion RMB, 43.2% was from the state budget. But the proportion of budget capital decreased to 24% in 1985, 13.2% in 1990 and only 5% in 1995. On the other hand, the proportion of the funds mobilized through domestic and foreign loans, entity's funds rising (using company depreciation, bond issuing, etc.) investment to the total state-owned-entity investment gradually rose from 56.7% in 1981 to 95% in 1995(see Table-4). From the above figures, it's not difficult to find that in the past more than 10 years the investment system and finance system reforms induced profound influence. The burden of investment from government budget has been relieved to a great extent. Now it undertakes the expenditures of education, public health, public administrations, national defense and so on and

Table-4 China-The Source of State-Owned-Entity's Investment

In billion dollar

	1985		1990		1995	
Total	168.05	100%	298.69	100%	1089.82	100%
1. State Budget Funds	40.3	24%	39.44	13.20%	54.5	5%
2. Domestic Loans	38.71	23%	70.56	23.60%	258.7	23.70%
3. Utilized Foreign Capital	8.86	5.30%	27.22	9.10%	85.94	7.90%
4. Self-mobilized Funds (1)	67.94	40%	128.96	43.20%	530.72	48.70%
5. Others	12.25	7.30%	35.58	11.90%	173.18	15.90%

(1) "Self-mobilized Funds" includes share issuing, bonds issuing, enterprises' depreciation and profits.

so forth. The funds for the state-owned-entity investment mainly depend on enterprises' self-mobilization (bonds issuing, enterprises profits, depreciation and funds recruiting) and banks' loan. In this sense, the policies adopted by China that introduce foreign capital into infrastructure are mainly aimed at making up the insufficient of domestic saving and enhancing technology standards and managing levels and raising efficiency rather than directly releasing pressure of government budget.

PART B: THE FOREIGN DIRECT INVESTMENT (FDI) IN CHINA

1. To accelerate the modernization of China and to make up with the insufficient domestic capital, since late 1970s the Chinese Government has been carrying out the policy of opening to the outside and utilizing foreign capital resulting in significant achievement. From 1979 to 1996, its real utilized foreign capital has accumulated to 310 billion dollars, of which foreign investment 180 billion dollars, every kinds of overseas loans 130 billion dollars. In the year of 1996, the real utilized foreign capital approached to near 60 billion dollars, out of which foreign investment reached 42 billion dollars, positioning the first place in the developing countries. The ratio of foreign capital to the Chinese fixed asset investment increases gradually, 5.4% in 1985, of which 2.3% for FDI, 11% in 1990, of which 4% for FDI, 21% in 1995, of which 16% for FDI (see Table-5).

2. Based on the situation of the economic system reform, managing ability and legislating process, China adopts a step-by-step way for those industries that are proposed to open to foreign investment. In early 1980s, we mainly opened

Table-5 China-The Proportion Of Foreign Capital to Total Fixed Asset Investment (%)

	1985	1990	1995
Total Foreign Capital	5.4	11	21
	4.65 bln USD	10.3 bln USD	48.1 bln USD
Foreign Investment	2.3	4	16
Foreign Loans	3.1	7	5

processing industry and real estate. After the mid-1980s, banks, electric power, highways, ports were opened gradually. Since 1990s, the opened industries have covered insurance, retail commerce, railways, civil aviation, urban infrastructure (water supply and transport). But telecommunication is not open yet.

3. Up till now, the FDI in China still highly concentrate on the general processing industry and real estate. Till the end of 1995, about 50% of foreign investment in China focused on the processing industry such as light and textile industries, 32% for real estate, hotels and restaurants. Less than 10% flowed to energy, transportation and urban infrastructure, of which around 1.85% for transportation, 7% for energy (4% for the petroleum exploration and development both offshore and on land, 2.5% for electric power). Power industry is one of the industries that make use of foreign investment the most in China's infrastructure. With foreign investment, about 5 million KW electric power generation capacity has been installed, really utilized foreign capital 3.5 billion dollars, and 7 million KW electric power generation capacity are under construction, utilizing foreign capital around 4.5 billion dollars.

4. The Chinese Government will insist on widening the opening to the outside, positively utilizing foreign capital, and will focus on FDI. We will optimize the structure of foreign investment, encourage foreign capital to invest to agriculture and irrigation, the energy industry with center of electricity, the transportation with the center of highway, and to urban water supply, high value-added processing industries. In June 1995, the State Planning Commission (SPC) of the People's Republic of China and other related government ministries stipulated *The Temporary Regulation for Instructing Foreign Investment,* and *Category for the Guidance of Foreign Investment Industries.* In these documents the energy and transportation are categorized as *encouragement.* Many infrastructual industries for the first time are clearly listed into the *Category,* including urban metro, highways, civil-airports, local railways, different kinds of power stations.

5. The Chinese Government encourages mobilizing foreign capital to invest on infrastructure by multi-means. We not only permit establishment of joint-venture, cooperative and solely-foreigner-owned enterprises, but also explore new approaches. For example, some corporations listed in Chinese stock market issue B share which can be held by foreign investors, the Chinese electric corporations were listed in the Hongkong and New York stock markets, pilot BOT (Build-Operate-Transfer) scheme projects (Guangxi Laibin Power Station 2×350 MW)has already completed bidding procedure and negotiation under the instruction of the Chinese Government, and are ready to commence construction. The Government has agreed to start the BOT scheme bidding procedure for Chengdu Water Plant, Sichuan Province. The Government has also approved a group of Sino-foreign joint-venture power plants to use the approach of *project financing*. In order to improve legal system and to increase the policy transparency, SPC issued *The Temporary Regulation for Project Financing Overseas* in April 1997. The regulation regarding to BOT, drafted by SPC, has been presented to the State Council for review and approval.

6. It's anticipated that there will be 30 billion to 40 billion dollars foreign investment flowing into China annually for the next 5 to 10 years. The ratio of foreign investment to the fixed asset investment of China, around 10-12%, would be lower comparing with that of 1995 (16%). What we most concern is to optimize the structure of foreign investment. We hope that the ratio of foreign capital invested in infrastructure to the total could be raised from present less than 10% to 20%-25%. In next 10 years, if the FDI to China reaches to 350 billion dollars and 25% of it flows to infrastructure sectors, the size will be 87.5 billion dollars. This figure means that FDI would be around 10% of China's total investment for infrastructure sectors in next 10 years (see Table-6). Electric power and transportation will be the main sectors. Take the electric power sector for instance, the Chinese Government has successively approved nearly 20 large- or medium-sized electric power stations with foreign investment in last two years, and the whole power generation capacity amounted to 11 million KW, the contractual amount of foreign capital was about 6 billion dollars. In next 5-10 years, FDI power plants may reach to 15% of all new installed power generation capacity in China. Some provinces and cities are exploring to transfer part of the property rights of existing highways, bridges and ports to foreign investors in order to quicken the construction of transportation facilities.

Table-6 China-Domestic Investment and FDI in Infrastructure: 1996-2005

in billion dollar

	Total	Domestic (Public and Private)	FDI
1. Power	260	221	39
2. Transport	250	225	25
3. Telecommunication	150	141	9
4. Water Supply	40	36	4
5. Others	100	90	10
Subtotal	800	713(89.1%)	87(10.9%)

Note: This table is based on author's personal estimation.

7. Some policy issues.

(1) Energy (coal, oil, power), transportation (highways, railways, ports, bridges, civil aviation) and urban public facilities (water supply, sewerage, roads, metro) have been opened by the Government for foreign investment. But for the reasons of state security, economic stability and public interests, in the sectors like hydro-power stations with the capacity over 250,000 KW, nuclear power plant, oil pipeline, gas pipeline, air-transportation, airports, public wharves, metro and the artery railways, Chinese sides are normally required to be the majority share holding party. In local railways, water transport projects 100% foreign owned investment is not allowed. But in expressway, coal-power plant, water plant projects, there are no any limitation on foreign shares. In power grid and urban networks of water supply, FDI is still not allowed. In the telecommunication sector, only a few mobile telecommunication projects are invested by foreigners, but they are not allowed to involve directly in operation and administration. In the future, China will conditionally open this sector in accordant with the commitment reached between China and WTO.

(2) To prevent monopolization and to protect consumers' benefits, the Chinese Government implements a service charge (price) examination and approval system for the sectors like electric power, transportation, etc. no matter it's of foreign investment or domestic capital. But the investors' benefits and reasonable profitability are put into consideration in the system. According to China's experience of FDI, FDI infrastructure projects usually ask the government to allow them charging relatively high tariffs than the state-owned

one, for the purpose of profit. In power, expressway and water plant, this is very common and therefore some inflation pressures are formed. The government must handle this matter properly to reach a reasonable balance between pricing system reform, consumers' benefits, attracting FDI to develop infrastructure and inflation control.

(3) In principle, Chinese Government would not limit the "rate of return" of foreign investment. Since foreign investment is a commercial or a market conduct, Chinese Government is not able to ensure a fixed rate of return like borrowing externally or issuing bonds overseas. The real rate of return of foreign investment depends on factors as markets situation and the enterprises operation and management. It's permissible that investors attain higher real investment rate of return than predicted in their feasibility study reports by means of decreasing investment and operation costs, increasing output and so on.

(4) In order to encourage foreign merchants to invest in infrastructual fields, Chinese governmental agencies have made a series of incentive policies like exemption of income tax, preferential land price and so on for those infrastructure projects with large investment and long period of investment return. For example, import duty on large-scale power plant equipment (300-600 MW unit) is 6%, this is far below the national average import duty level (23%). FDI power plant, expressway, port facility can get two year tax holiday and additional three years 50% tax reduction. The FDI expressway projects may enlarge their scope of business to real estate, restaurants near the project site with the government approval. For Sino-foreign joint venture projects borrowing by share holders (company), it's permissible for domestic financial institutes to provide guarantees to foreign lenders who provide loans, but the amount and ratio is limited to the proportion Chinese side contributed to the registered capital. For those projects with the scheme of "project financing", according to international practice, the Government requires collateral security by the projects' property since these financings are non-recourse or limited recourse loans. The risk could be lowered and scattered through a set of contracts (for example, the price agreement, electricity selling contract and the fuel supply contract in electric power projects). The governmental

administrative organizations are due to ensuring the contracts to be carried out legally. Because the infrastructure projects usually can not earn foreign exchange directly, Chinese government provides the guarantee for availability of foreign exchange to insure the FDI receiving enough amount of foreign exchange to meet their reasonable demand for debt service, production and dividends. In December 1996, Chinese government realized its commitment for convertibility of RMB under current account. This development created a much more favorable environment for FDI in China's infrastructure sectors.

(5) As most developing countries, Chinese Government implements the system of examination and approval to FDI projects. The current system is that a provincial government has the authority to approve a project whose total investment is below 30 million dollars. The central government is responsible to approve the projects whose total investment is above 30 million dollars. By learning the foreign successful lessons, Chinese Government adopted the approach of international competitive bidding to select investor in the pilot BOT project, (Guangxi Laibin Power Plant). By the view of practice, the approach of bidding could shorten the time of project preparation, and make us to choose the investor who is the best. Foreign investors also think that the approach made the competition fair and transparent. In the future, open bidding procedure would be utilized more and more in the sectors like electric power and highways. The approval procedure for BOT project with the total investment above 30 million dollars is these: A. local authority submits the application to the State Planning Commission (SPC) for project development and BOT type operation. B. After the approval of SPC, local authority organizes the international competitive bidding for the project, negotiation with the best tenderer and prepares the BOT contract (draft). C. Local authority submits the BOT contract (draft) to SPC for final approval, then sign the BOT contract with winner.

(6) In recent 10 years, certain changes happened to the traditional situation that it's government and public agencies that are responsible for the whole infrastructure investment. Private capital, especially foreign private capital invested in infrastructure projects in the developing countries are getting more and more. Including China, many developing countries have adopted the

policies encouraging foreign capital to invest in infrastructure. However, the infrastructure is an important industry relating to social and economic development, and to people living. Many infrastructure projects as urban public transport, irrigation facilities are still concentrated on social benefits with poor financial rate of return. Even the projects like power plants and expressways are not all suitable to private investment. Take the China case for instance, in the areas like Guangdong, Jiangsu, Shanghai where economy is relatively developed, because of good industrial enterprises efficiency, high residents income and big market demands, foreign merchants can get relative high profits by investing power plants and expressways. In these years the provinces attract certain foreign investment. But in the hinder land, like Guizhou, Ningxia where economy is poor, though efforts have been made to introduce FDI to these fields for infrastructure development, few contracts are singed up till now due to low investment rate of return. Therefore I think that developing countries should take more positive policies to encourage FDI to infrastructure sectors. The inflow of foreign capital will speed up the infrastructure development and can also facility the reform of economic system, increasing the efficiency of infrastructure. But we still should mainly rely on our own effort and resource and carry out the policies adopting diversified capital mobilizing channels like public sectors, private sectors and FDI to develop infrastructure.

PART VI. INTERGOVERNMENTAL TRANSFER SYSTEMS

CHAPTER14 AN EQUALIZATION TRANS- FER SYSTEM IN JAPAN

NOBUKI MOCHIDA[*]

1. INTRODUCTION

According to OECD statistics, Japanese local public finance occupies an important position, accounting for 70 per cent of general public expenditure, excluding social welfare funds, which is comparable to federal system such as Canada and Germany. In recent years, however, decentralization has became to be the top of Japan's political agenda. In 1993 the government has enacted the Decentralization Promotion Law, which will be effective for five years. These development are all the more welcome nearly half a century after Prof. Carl Shoup delivered his recommendation in 1949. However, there is tendency today for people to jump on the decentralization bandwagon without asking either what tune the band is playing or where the wagon is headed. One reason for the slow progress may be lack of clear understanding of the strength and weakness of Japan's intergovernmental fiscal relations.

There exist a few valuable case study of Japan in fiscal federalism literature [1], while these efforts are focused on general overview. The purpose of this paper is to consider

[*] Faculty of Economics, University of Tokyo, Japan
E-mail:mochida@e.u-tokyo.ac.jp

The author wishes to thank in particular Jun Ma, Anwar Shah, Farrukh Iqbal, Dubravko Mihaljek for helpful suggestion and comments. The earlier draft was prepared for the World Bank's EDI workshop on "International Experience on Intergovernmental Fiscal Transfer" held in Hanoi, Vietnam (March 27-29,1996).

[1] See, for example, Yonehara, J.[1987]; Ishi, H [1993]; Mihaljek, D.[1997].

an equalization transfer system in Japan both historically and in comparison with other countries. It offers the key to understanding of Japan's fiscal system. Resources in the form of the ability to support public services through taxes are not evenly spread across the various subnational units of government in any country. On the other hand, resource disparities coexist with differences in need characteristics. To the extent that these disparities remain, low resource areas with high needs for public services must tax themselves at a higher rate in order to finance the same level of resources as higher resource area. Given regional gaps in the tax revenues and financial needs, some means of fiscal equalization is necessary to provide local public services in poor areas. The most important means devised to handle this problem is the unconditional tax-sharing grant. In Japan, the local allocation tax system (Chihokofu-zei) plays a key role as the equalization transfer system [2].

The second part of this paper stresses the importance of fiscal equalization in Japan. The third part explains the computation formula of Local Allocation Tax and analyzes practical effect of fiscal equalization. Discussions in the fourth part considers issues and policy direction for decentralization. The final part is concluding remarks.

2. IMPORTANCE OF FISCAL EQUALIZATION IN JAPAN

We begin by considering the importance of fiscal equalization in Japan in terms of 1) reallocation of tax revenue among national and local governments; 2) equalization effects on financial resources; and 3) an international perspective. Large scale reallocation of revenue takes place in Japan through earmarked and general subsidies. Table 1 shows the tax shares and fiscal transfers between the central and local governments from the historical perspective. In 1989, national and local tax revenues totaled 84,891 billion yen. Before fiscal transfers, local taxes account for only 35.7 per cent of total revenue . However a substantial portion of national taxes is transferred to the local governments in two main forms. Unconditional transfers are tax-sharing grants on a lump-sum basis financed by the local allocation tax. Conditional grants are matching-type categorical grants which are called specific-purpose grant. After reallocating the tax sources among different levels of the government,the final share

---

[2] As to literature written in English concerning with the local allocation tax, see Ito, H. [1967]; Yonehara, J. [1987]; Ishi, H.[1993].

Table 1. Reallocation of Tax Revenue in Japan (%)

	1890	1900	1910	1920	1930	1940	1950	1960	1970	1980	1985	1993
(1) Government Expenditure												
Net Total/GNP	11.5	17.2	21.5	14.2	21.5	22.1	23.6	18.8	20.3	29.4	27.6	30.0
Net National/GNP	7.5	7.5	14.2	8.2	9.5	13.7	10.4	5.9	5.9	9.9	10.2	10.3
Net Local/GNP	4.0	4.0	7.3	6.0	12.1	8.4	13.2	12.8	14.4	19.5	17.4	19.6
(2) Tax Allocation before Fiscal Transfer												
National Tax/Total Tax	69.4	63.2	70.5	62.1	64.3	78.5	75.2	70.8	67.5	64.1	62.6	63.0
Local Tax/Total Tax	30.6	36.8	29.5	37.9	35.7	21.5	24.8	29.2	32.5	35.9	37.4	37.0
Income Tax/Total Tax	0	0	5.9	5.9	10.0	26.9	38.6	21.7	31.2	38.1	39.4	36.9
(3) Fiscal Transfers												
Transfer as % of general account	3.7	2.7	1.8	4.0	10.6	13.8	35.1	47.2	48.7	44.0	38.5	36.0
Local allocation tax as % of general account	-	-	-	-	-	6.1	17.1	17.8	22.0	18.7	17.8	20.4
Transfer as % of local revenues	6.7	5.4	2.8	4.7	8.2	21.2	40.8	39.3	37.7	40.8	34.7	31.8
Local allocation tax as % of local revenues	-	-	-	-	-	9.2	19.9	14.8	17.0	17.3	15.5	18.0
(4) Final Share of tax after Fiscal Transfer												
of National government	68.4	62.2	70.1	61.3	60.8	74.9	65.2	57.0	51.1	46.0	45.3	47.5
of Local government	31.6	37.8	29.9	38.7	39.2	25.1	34.8	43.0	48.9	54.0	54.7	52.5

(Source) Mochida, N.[1993], p.57.
Note: transfer includes both local allocation tax and specific-purpose grant.

of total tax revenue accruing to local governments increases to 52.2 per cent. This ratio has been unchanged for a nearly three decades. This means that one fourth of central tax revenue is used at the local level. As shown in Table 1, the reallocation of revenues between national and local governments started in 1940. After being revised according to Shoup recommendation in 1949, the local share of revenues reached almost 30-37 per cent for the next four decades.

The second key aspect of the local allocation tax system is its equalization effects on financial resources. Intergovernmental transfer is needed not only to balance the budget at the subnational level but also to offset the regional inequality created by the lack of population mobility. Given regional gaps in the tax revenues and financial needs, some means of fiscal equalization is necessary to provide local public services in poor areas. The most important means devised to handle this problem is the unconditional tax-sharing grant. In Japan, the local allocation tax system plays a key role as the Equalization Transfer System.

Comparing per capita local tax revenue and per capita revenue from general fiscal sources (i.e. local taxes and local allocation tax) at prefecture level in 1993, the

Table 2. Fiscal Equalization by local allocation tax (47 prefecture, FY 1993)

prefectures		prefectural tax revenue (hundred million)	local allocation tax (hundred million)	general revenue (hundred million)	per capita (thousand of Yen)		
					prefectural tax	local allocation tax	general revenue
A	aichi	9,552	69	10,017	143	1	150
	osaka	11,369	272	12,232	130	3	140
	kanagawa	9,210	124	9,765	115	2	122
B	shizuoka	4,495	927	5,853	122	25	159
	saitama	6,286	1,563	8,145	98	24	127
	chiba	5,652	1,448	7,408	102	26	133
	hyogo	5,738	2,286	8,400	106	42	155
	kyoto	2,800	1,213	4,221	108	47	162
	tochigi	2,188	1,240	3,621	113	64	187
	ibaragi	3,122	1,742	5,049	110	61	177
	fukuoka	4,363	2,394	7,039	91	50	146
	gunma	2,121	1,203	3,513	108	61	179
	hiroshima	2,930	1,837	4,971	103	64	174
	gifu	2,201	1,546	3,927	107	75	190
	shiga	1,398	1,079	2,574	114	88	211
	mie	1,949	1,469	3,586	109	82	200
	miyagi	2,342	1,661	4,183	104	74	186
C	okayama	1,925	1,752	3,830	100	91	199
	ishikawa	1,290	1,217	2,688	111	105	231
	nagano	2,266	2,116	4,606	105	98	214
	kagawa	1,064	1,072	2,220	104	105	217
	toyama	1,261	1,388	2,750	113	124	246
	fukushima	2,120	2,222	4,549	101	106	216
	nara	1,150	1,348	2,580	84	98	288
	fukui	1,082	1,152	2,317	131	140	281
	yamaguchi	1,505	1,757	3,394	96	112	216
	niigata	2,539	2,828	5,607	103	114	227
	yamanashi	879	1,228	2,202	103	144	258
D	hokkaido	5,205	7,114	12,837	92	126	227
	ehime	1,253	1,854	3,224	83	122	213
	wakayama	941	1,560	2,600	88	145	242
	kumamoto	1,364	2,306	3,816	74	125	207
	oita	1,003	1,865	2,984	81	151	241
E	yamagata	1,007	1,938	3,068	80	154	244
	saga	740	1,476	2,288	84	168	261
	nagasaki	1,095	2,320	3,528	70	148	226
	iwate	1,093	2,489	2,714	77	176	262
	kagoshima	1,200	2,743	4,085	67	153	227
	tokushima	688	1,565	2,319	83	188	279
	miyazaki	815	1,958	2,862	70	167	245
	okinawa	735	1,800	2,605	60	147	213
	akita	919	2,198	3,218	75	179	262
	aomori	1,041	2,471	2,626	70	167	245
	tottori	486	1,356	1,914	79	220	311
	shimane	615	1,848	2,546	79	237	326
	kochi	590	1,863	2,531	71	226	307
F	tokyo	23,191	---	24,447	196	---	206
	average	138,779	80,878	229,456	112	65	186

(source) Ministry of Home Affairs.

272

disparity in the financial resources among rich and poor districts is considerably reduced by LAT. In Table 2, a marked difference is observed in per capita prefectural tax revenues among localities in FY 1993, the largest being Tokyo 196 thousand of Yen, the smallest Okinawa with 60 thousand of Yen. More local allocation tax is provided disproportionately to those areas with lower resource bases to achieve some degree of equalization. As a result, per capita revenues from general sources in the area with low tax bases increases considerably. A surprise can be found that coefficient of variation in prefectural tax revenue accounting for 0.2408 differs little with that in general revenue which accounts for 0.2293. However this phenomenon resulted in a reversal of the rank ordering of disparities among prefectures rather than deterioration of equalization effect.[3] After fiscal transfer the prefectures with lower tax capacity, as measured by prefectural tax revenue, had the higher total resources, as measured by general revenue. It may be assumed that Japanese equalization system reduces territorial fiscal inequalities quite extensively, though many questions relating its mechanism remain unsettled.

It is helpful to compare the extent to which local resource disparities are reduced through equalization system in different countries. As Wolman H. and E. Page [1987] pointed out clearly, a number of countries, such as United States, Italy and France through grant system place little emphasis on resource equalization. The intergovernmental system of Canada, Denmark and Germany largely realize such potential, while the performance of the English grant system is less equalizing in this respect. However, grant system in Japan as well as Australia have the potential of reversing the impact of income distribution on public services, as shown by the relative wealth of low income districts after equalization.[4] The extent of resource disparity among local units in each country was measured through calculation of the coefficient of variation in the Notional Tax Income(NTI). Wolman H. and E. Page produce statistical evidence for the correlation between per capita tax capacity and per capita grant. According to their findings, in Canada, Denmark, and Germany, the distribution of grant appears to follow the principle of equalization fairly closely. In England, the relationship is weaker,yet still conforms to expectations of resource equalization, while in the United States the distribution of the grant does not.

---

[3] The rank order correlation between per capita prefectural tax and per capita general revenue is - 0.5195.

[4] Wolman H. and E. Page [1987],pp.82-98.

Table 3. Reduction of Resource Disparities Through Grant Systems (1980s)

	Notional Tax Income	Notional Equalized Revenue	Difference	Percent Difference
Australia	0.04	0.12	+0.08	+200
Canada	0.22	0.06	-0.16	-73
Denmark	0.11	0.03	-0.08	-73
England	0.13	0.11	-0.02	-15
Germany	0.13	0.08	-0.05	-38
United States	0.13	0.12	-0.01	-8
Japan (caseA)	**0.14**	**0.27**	**+0.13**	**+92**
Japan (caseB)	**0.14**	**0.22**	**+0.08**	**+63**

(source) H. Wolman and E. Page [1987]. Data as to Japan is estimated and added to by the author.
Note:CaseA:unconditional and conditional grant. CaseB:unconditional grant only.

The actual degree of equalization could be measured as the difference between the coefficient of variation in Notional Tax Income(NTI) and Notional Equalized revenue(NER) . As is shown by Table3 , Canada and Denmark, grants serve to reduce resource disparities quite extensive, as might be expected-by 73 percent in each. In Germany the system of intergovernmental transfers has a moderate equalizing effect(38 percent), while in England and United States the relatively weaker equalizing distribution of grants means that intergovernmental transfers have only marginal impact on resource inequalities. It should be noted that the major surprise can be found in Australia and Japan,[5] where resource disparities actually increased after equalization. Grant system in Japan as well as Australia have the potential of reversing the impact of income distribution on public services, as shown by the relative wealth of low income regions after equalization.

3. FORMULA AND EFFECT OF EQUALIZATION

A. EVOLUTION OF FISCAL EQUALIZATION [6]

The first regular scheme for equalizing local finance was the Local Distribution Tax in 1940 which was carried out in connection with tax reform of central and local

---

[5] Data relating to Japan is calculated and added to the original table by the author.

[6] This section is based on Mochida, N.[1993],Chap. 5- 6.

governments corresponding to the quasi-war situation.[7] The local distribution tax was a kind of national tax the proceeds of which were shared with local units.[8] They were distributed among localities without restriction not by the tax source principle but by a formula designed to provide equalization. However, the local distribution tax had some defects from the viewpoint of local autonomy. First, the tax sharing ratio varied in practice from year to year according in part to the fluctuation in receipts caused by the sensitivity of income taxation, and part to the fiscal deficit in national finance. Second, in the distribution tax, the total amount to be given to individual local units was divided into two parts, which were apportioned separately: one according to the need for services, the other according to fiscal capacity, bearing no relation to each other.

A big change in the basic structure of fiscal equalization system was brought about by the US occupation after the Second World War. Great stress was placed on the importance of local autonomy in a democratic nation, and the prewar system was completely restructured in order to encourage decentralization. In accordance with the Shoup Recommendation, distribution tax was converted in 1950 to " the local finance equalization grant " (*chihozaisei heiko-kofukin*).

It is true that the equalization grant was more reasonable than the distribution tax so far as the idea of the scheme was concerned. Equalization grant was computed respectively by means of the formula which contained two parts, the first relating to the measure of the local need for basic services, and second relating to the measure of local financial ability. Then the total financial capacity was subtracted from total financial need, the difference being the basis for computing the grant of each particular locality. In the case of the equalization grant, the total amount was determined more closely in accordance with the difference between fiscal needs and resources of localities, irrespective of national tax revenue.

However four years' experience revealed that it had not worked as well as was hoped.

---

[7] A marked territorial inequalities in per capita prefectural tax revenue was occurred in the era of Great Depression. As device to counter depression, "provisional grant"(rinji-chihozaisei hokyukin) was introduced.

[8] The aggregate amount to be distributed among local units was the sum of (1) 17.38 percent of the yield from income tax and corporation tax, (2) 50 percent of that from admission tax and amusement, eating and drinking tax.

For the aggregate sum of the grant was not paid out of the general funds of national government as computed by the formula but was determined every year, taking into consideration among other things the degree of stringency in national finance. So, every year it gave rise to frictions between local and national officials in the determination of the total amount. In view of above considerations, the equalization grant was abolished in 1953 and in its place Local Allocation Tax (LAT) was introduced in 1954.

B. FORMULA OF LOCAL ALLOCATION TAX

LAT is governed by "Local Allocation Tax Law". This law stipulates that LAT should be based on uniform formula; the final authority to approve the distribution lies with the National Assembly. According to the LAT Law, the Ministry of Home Affairs is responsible for its operation (calculating the amount of LAT) of the transfer and determining modification coefficients. The fact that MOHA does not have the final authority to approve the formula and unit costs is an important mechanism to deter any attempt to manipulate distribution. On the other hand, a certain degree of flexibility is given to MOHA as it has the authority of determine modification coefficients, which marginally affect the distribution of LAT. [9]

In addition, MOHA also has the responsibility to collect data, which are used for calculation LAT. Each local government is duty-bound to present these data to the MOHA. What kind of role do local governments have on operating the LAT? As to the LAT for prefectural government, all prefectural governments' staffs are bound only to collect data and present them to the MOHA and Local Autonomy Information Center. These legal framework ensure that no single locality or senior official effectively influence the distribution of LAT in favor of a particular region without affecting many other regions. [10]

LAT has continued to the present with some minor alterations. The framework of the local allocation tax is founded in the main on that of the former distribution tax enforced between 1940 and 1949, retaining on the other hand the formula used in the equalization grant for the distribution of funds to localities. In the LAT system, the

---

[9] Fujiwara, T [1996],pp.10-12.
[10] Yamauchi, K [1996],p.5.

total amount to be distributed to local authorities is a fraction of yields from major national taxes. Present system is no other than the shared tax in which a share in the proceeds of national taxes is granted to poor localities without limitation as to use. The total amount of the local allocation tax is calculated as follows.

$$TT = 0.32*(NT_y + NT_c + NT_a) + 0.29*NT_v + 0.25*NT_t \qquad (1)$$

Where TT denotes total financial pool of transfer, NT_y is the total yield of personal income tax, NT_c is that of corporate income tax, NT_a is that of alcoholic tax, NT_v is consumption tax revenue, NT_t is total yield of tobacco tax. These prescribed percentage of five major taxes of national government, is apportioned among local bodies in proportion to the amount of the difference of need and revenue. This is expressed by following equation.

$$LAT_i = N_i - C_i \qquad (2)$$

Where LAT_i denotes local allocation tax to ith region, N_i is basic financial needs of ith region, C_i is basic financial capacity of ith region. It is annually paid to local governments whose basic financial needs exceed basic financial revenues. Those rich localities whose revenue exceeds need are neither eligible for the grants nor liable to contribute money for fiscal adjustment, as is the case in some countries.

Before calculating basic financial needs, public services for each prefecture and municipality are divided into some service items(*gyosei-komoku*). Regarding prefecture there are 24 service items such as police, road-bridge, primary school and as for municipality there are 24 service items such as city planning, park, garbage collection and so on. Basic financial needs of ith local authority is calculated according to following formula.

$$Ni = \Sigma k \, (I_{ik} * U_{ik} * M_{ik}) \qquad (3)$$

Where I_{ik} is measurement unit for service K of ith region, U_{ik} is unit cost for service K of ith region, M_{ik} is modification coefficient for service K of ith region. For each local body, according to the formula mentioned above basic financial needs for each service item is calculated as the number of measurement units by multiplying the unit cost, adjusted by modification coefficients. The total basic need in each locality is the sum of the amounts needed for all service items combined. First step is to select measurement units. A measurement unit reflects the size of the beneficiaries of a particular expenditure. For example, a measurement unit of education is number of school pupils, that of social welfare is number of population and that of road is length of roads.

Second step is to determine an unit cost. The unit cost is a kind of net standard cost per measurement unit for each service item. Assuming a certain local body with standard condition and scale, the unit cost for each service item is calculated based on following formula. In case of prefecture only one fictitious local body whose population is 1.7 million and land area is 6500 square kilometers is assumed as "standard local body"; in case of municipality population 0.1 million and land area 160 square kilometers.

$$U = (C_g - R_s)/S \tag{4}$$

Where U is unit cost, C_g is gross standard cost, R_s is special revenue and S is a figure of measurement unit. Third step is to determine modification coefficients. The unit cost, however, is uniform throughout the whole country, and due regard is paid neither to the peculiar type of services nor to the special circumstances of localities. So an exceedingly complex adjustment is made as to the unit cost applicable to such types of service and localities by means of detailed modifiers decided in accordance with their differences. Currently modification coefficients are classified according to eight categories.[11]

On the other side, the basic financial revenue of each locality, on the other side, is expressed as a combined total of two types of revenue: (1) 80% in the case of prefectures, 75% in the case of municipalities of the sum of the yields of all regular local taxes, assuming that each is levied at the uniform rate or standard rate prescribed in the Local Tax Law, (2) the sum of revenues from local transfer taxes. This is expressed following equation.

$$C_i = G\ (\Sigma_j B_{ij} * t_j) + LTT_i \tag{5}$$

---

[11] As to modification coefficient, see Ishi,H. [1993] p.273.

Where G is 0.75 (case of municipality) and 0.80(case of prefecture), B_{ij} is ith region's jth tax base, t_j is standard tax rate on the jth tax base, LTT_i is revenue from local transfer tax. There are two reason for adopting such prescribed percentages. First, it is impossible to measure completely the basic financial needs of all local governments by a uniform formula. Second, it is necessary to retain incentives for local governments to collect their own taxes. On the other hand, all revenue allotted from the local transfer tax are included, mainly because it is collected by the national government and has no relation to the tax collection effort at the local level.

The available pool of transfer calculated in advance, however, does not necessarily cover the sum of the entitlement, i.e.,aggregate amount of the deficiencies of local governments whose basic financial needs exceed their basic revenues. A currently used methods is to adjust the pool of transfer to the sum of the entitlemens. In this regard, attention should be paid on the role of Ministry of Home Affairs and Local Public Finance Program. A legal definition of the central-local fiscal relations is not sufficient to guarantee its strict implementation. In Japan, the conflict between the Ministry of Finance (MOF) and the Ministry of Home Affairs (MOHA) reflects one of the main points of Japan's central-local fiscal relations, the latter institution representing a vital counter power in the central bureaucracy against MOF incursions into local matter. [12]

One of the most important role of MOHA is to formulate Local Public Finance Program.In Japan, the chief executive officer and the member of assemblies of all local authorities are elected by direct popular vote today. Each local government has own budgeting accounts which compile the revenue and expenditure necessary for its activities. In addition to these micro-budgeting system, however,there is another central guidance on local public finance budget. The local public finance program serves as a tool to estimate annual aggregate local revenue sources to cover standardized total local spending. The MOHA assumes the role of formulating the local public finance program every year. The MOHA has primary responsibility to ensure that local governments have enough revenue to balance the program. On the

---

[12] MOHA began as the Ministry of Interior and was founded in 1873, in the early period of the Meiji Era. After the Second World War, the US General Headquarters of the occupation dismantled the MOI. It was thirteen years after the crush of the MOI that the current MOHA was founded.

expenditure side, the local public finance program covers the whole of local governments' standard activities except for local public enterprise special accounts which are basically run on an independent profit system and a few other special accounts. On the revenue side of the program, it covers all the standard local revenue sources such as local taxes, local allocation tax, national disbursement , local loans, fees and tuition.

The most important function of the Local Public Finance Program is to ensure fiscal responsibility, because if the estimated program does not balance for the year, the MOHA has to propose some measure such as local tax amendments, increase of Local Allocation Tax, increase of local loans. During the formulation of Local Public Finance Program, MOHA negotiates very hard with the Ministry of Finance in order to secure the sources of revenue of local governments. Some special measure has took place to increase the total amount of LAT. These special measure can be divided into following five types.[13] (1). borrowing from special account of Fund Management Board of the MOF. (2). carrying forward of local allocation tax. (3). cancellation of local allocation tax cut. (4). transfer of provisional local grant. (5). special addition/reduction of local allocation tax.

Beside above mentioned special measure, final adjustment is necessary to adjust the size of the entitlement proportionally according to the size of the fund by using an adjustment coefficient α. The actual amount of ordinary allocation tax granted to a local government is calculated according to following formula. Where LAT_i denotes local allocation tax to ith region, N_i is basic financial needs of ith region, C_i is basic financial capacity of ith region and α is adjustment coefficient.

$$LAT_i = (N_i - C_i) - \alpha \times N_i \qquad (6)$$

D. PRACTICAL EFFECTS OF FISCAL EQUALIZATION [14]

Now we proceed to analyze practical effects of Japanese system on the general revenue of local body. To determine the actual degree of equalization achieved I added the per capita local allocation tax to the per capita local tax in order to obtain a notional total reflecting the area's resources after the fiscal equalization; this is termed General

---

[13] For detail of these special measure, see Mochida, N [1996],p.9-10.

[14] This section is based on Mochida, N.[1993].Chap.6.

Financial Resources (GFR). I then determined the disparity, as measured by the Gini coefficient in the GFR and compared it with the initial disparity in local tax per capita. The extent of the improvement (or deterioration) could then be measured as the difference between the Gini coefficient of local tax and that of GFR divided by the former. This measure can be expressed as the following equation.

$$\phi = (G_2 - G_1) / G_2 \qquad (7)$$

Figure 1. Extent of fiscal equalization by LAT

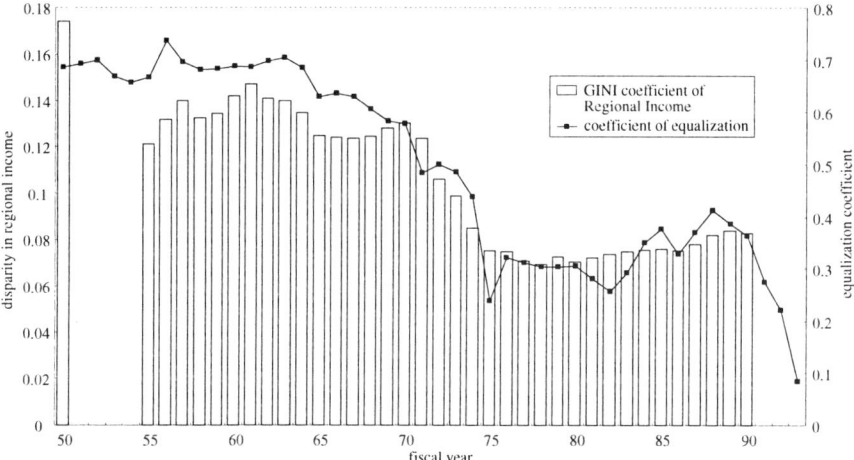

Figure 2. Regional distribution of financial sources

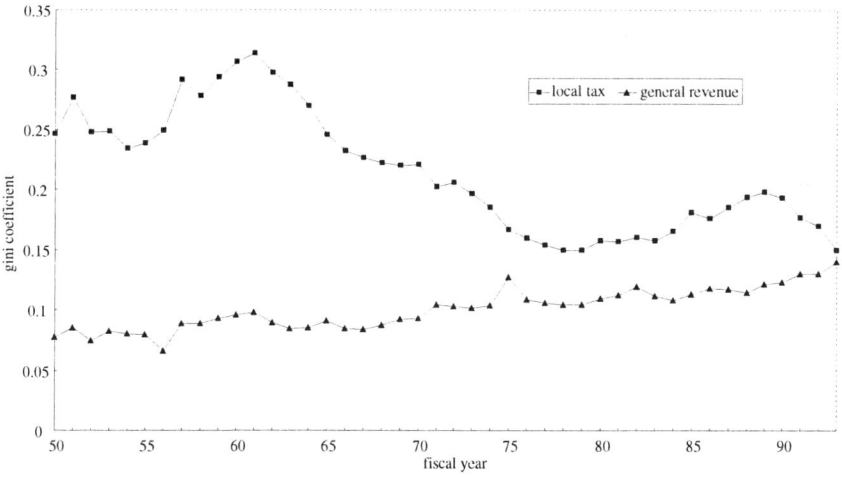

Where G_1 stands for the Gini coefficient of GFR, G_2 for the Gini coefficient in local tax. ϕ denotes the extent of the improvement; this I have termed the Equalization Coefficient in this paper. Figure 1 indicates the change in the extent of improvement measured by the Equalization Coefficient. As this figure demonstrates, the extent of improvement has changed drastically every ten years.

The first half of rapid growth era (1954 to 1964). Increase in pre-grant disparity is a peculiarity of this period. As figure 2 demonstrates, the disparity in financial resources among rich and poor local authorities became to be bigger and was maintained at high level. A large number of young people moved from rural area to the metropolitan area such as Tokyo, Osaka, Nagoya. To deal with this social problem, the political slogan of "Improvement of Regional Disparity" became to be one of main national policy goal and was embodied in the National Comprehensive Development Plan established in October 1962. In line with this national policy guideline, local allocation tax was distributed mainly to the backward districts in inverse proportion to their financial capacities. As a result, local allocation tax served to reduce resources disparities quite extensively by 70 percent in each year.

The latter half of the rapid growth era (1965 to 1974). The reduction of pre-grant disparities and reversal of the rank ordering is a distinctive characteristic of this period. There was sharp decrease in the disparities among rich and poor districts. As figure 1 indicates, the Gini coefficient of per capita regional income decreased from 0.1248 in FY 1965 to 0.0753 in FY 1975. This improvement of regional disparities was not caused by success of the National Comprehensive Development Plan but by the dispersion of factories around the country and increase in the number of people employed in the local public works. Nevertheless, the distribution of local allocation tax followed the principle of equalization all the more. As a result, resources disparities actually increased after the equalizing effect of local allocation tax is taken into account(figure 2). However, this increase actually resulted in a reversal of the rank ordering of disparities among prefectures. We should notice that the sharp "decline" in the Equalization Coefficients means enforcement of improvement rather than deterioration of equalizing effect.

Oil crises and thereafter(since the mid-1970 up to mid-1980). Gradual increase in pre-grant disparity is a characteristic of this period. During this period, the disparities in per capita local tax has began to increase again as a result of population concentration on the Tokyo metropolitan area caused by the internationalization of financial market. As the figure 2 demonstrates, the Gini coefficient of per capita local tax has increased gradually after oil crises. On the other hand, the negative correlation between per capita tax revenue and per capita local allocation tax became to be weaker than before, because of the shortage of total amount of local allocation tax. As a result of these trends, reversal of the rank ordering of disparities among prefectures was corrected somewhat.

So called "bubble economy" and thereafter (since 1985 up to the present). A sharp reduction of pre-grant disparities and reversal of the rank ordering is a characteristic of this period. There was marked decrease in the regional disparities as figure 2 indicates. GINI coefficient of local tax declined from 0.19 in FY 1988 to 0.15 in FY1993. As a result, the Equalization Coefficient has been dropped drastically from 0.4120 in FY 1988 to 0.085 in FY 1993. It is noteworthy that there is little difference between pre-grant disparities and area's resource disparities after the addition of local allocation tax. However, these trend does not mean deterioration of equalization effect, as mentioned above, but a reversal of the rank ordering of disparities among prefectures. These trends can be explained by both fundamental tax reform and collapse of "bubble economy".

4. ISSUES AND POLICY DIRECTION

Japan experienced large regional disparity in the early stage of post-war economic development. Japanese government simultaneously responded to the issue of regional disparity. As for this regard, an attention should be paid on the significant role of local allocation tax as mentioned above. However, current system faces considerable challenge in the medium term, given the changing preference of the public with respect to local autonomy.[15]

A. DEVOLUTION OF SPENDING RESPONSIBILITY

In Japan, the central government directly perform relatively few public functions such as national defense, pension-related public welfare expenditure and expenditure

---

[15] As to current issue and decentralization debate, see Jinno, N. [1995], Kaneko, M. [1995], Ito, K.[1996], Miyajima H. [1996], Mochida, N. [1997].

to repay a debt. About 80 per cent of disbursement of national government' general account are simply transferred to other accounts of which local government comprises largest share. In contrast, local governments are responsible for a major share of public spending, including on national land conservation and development expenditure, school education expenditure, social education, police and fire-defense, social welfare, sanitation and general administration. Although the ratio of national to local public expenditure in Japan is 30.8 to 69.2, on a final disbursement base, the ratio of the distribution of tax revenue is just reverse, namely, 63.5 to 36.5 in favor of national government. Intergovernmental fiscal relations are marked by a vertical fiscal imbalance in Japan. This means that Japan's local public finance system is administered locally rather than centrally and central government's role is to guide the local governments towards a common fiscal situation by means of subsidies, local allocation tax and control on local bonds.

Strength of Japan's system is the fact that considerably more public spending takes place at the local level than at the national level itself. The assignment of expenditure responsibilities is determined by national legislation (such as the Local Finance Law, the Local Autonomy Law) and cannot be altered at the discretion of the central government.[16] The central government has no legal right to issue unfunded mandates to local governments.

On the other hand, however, the national government remains heavily involved in almost every aspect of local public spending. Unlike American and Canadian system,[17] there is no clear separation of central and local function. As a result, major program(education, health, public works) are formulated by national ministries and financed by many specific grants. Therefore, the issue for Japan is not so much to change/enlarge the expenditure assignments themselves, but to redefine responsibilities for designing, implementing and financing these assignments.[18]

Recently, reexamination of agency-delegated function (*Kikan-Inin Jimu*) and reduction in number and volume of specific purpose grants became to be serious political agenda in decentralization debate. The agency delegated function (ADF) is

---

[16] In some transition economy, such as China and Vietnam, the central government sometimes changes the responsibilities of localities without approval of parliament.

[17] For Canada, United States, see Shah, A. [1994],pp.5-9.

[18] Mihaljek, D. [1997], p.304.

representative of Japanese central-local relations. Before Second World War, local leaders were appointed by the central government. The Occupational Reform dismantled the Ministry of Interior and introduced direct election for governor, mayor and member of local assembly. The central government was able to reestablish local influence trough the ADF, which required local leaders to act as agents of the central government in implementing assigned functions. Agency-delegated function has been supplemented by the mandamus proceedings in which the minister of national government could order prefectural governor to carry out certain action and if the governor did not obey such order, he could be removed from office by the national minister, subject to certain legal appeals. While there are 561 kinds of ADF prescribed in Local Autonomy Law, the Committee for Promotion of Decentralization in the national government released its interim report in the end of 1996 and recommended the complete abolition of agency delegated function in near future.[19]

Specific purpose grants has swollen to a vast sum as powerful means to guide local governments towards a common fiscal situation. However these grants are distributed on strict condition that the recipient follow the directives issued by the national government. For example, diversion of vacant classroom for primary and secondary school into social welfare program requires approval of the Minister of Education one by one. Strict conditionality tends to restrict local discretion over spending responsibility as follows. 1) too complicated and time consuming application procedure, 2) taking into account local preference not sufficiently, 3) many trifling grants and its inefficiency. If a local government fail to observe national directives, it is requested to refund the disbursement in whole or in part. Against this background, the Committee for Promotion of Decentralization 's second report released mid 1997 recommended the national government to reduce specific purpose grants substantially and to limit national treasury obligatory share to a minimum.[20]

B. ACCOUNTABILITY AND LOCAL TAX

Major sources of local government total annual revenues are local taxes (33 per cent), local allocation tax (16 per cent), central government disbursements (15per cent), loans (17 per cent), charge &fees (2.3 per cent) and local transfer tax (2 per

---

[19] Chihobunken Suisin Iinkai [1996], pp.28-34.
[20] Chihobunken Suisin Iinkai [1997], pp.8-10.

cent). There are 14 kinds of prefectural taxes and 9 kind of municipal taxes. Among prefectural tax, enterprise tax comprises the largest share, 35.2 per cent, prefectural inhabitants tax accounts for 28.9 per cent, automobile tax accounts for 11.8 per cent, light oil delivery tax accounts for 10.0 per cent. Among municipal taxes, fixed assets tax comprises largest share, 44.1 per cent, municipal inhabitants tax accounts for 43.2 per cent, city-planning tax occupy 6.8 per cent.[21]

Local governments in Japan have relatively large receipts from local taxes that makes a good score for revenue response to economic growth. On the other, local tax revenues fluctuate strongly during business cycle, large difference in tax base between localities exists, the flexibility in determining tax base and rate is strictly limited.

A good local tax system, in general, should satisfy several criteria. The first criteria is revenue response to economic growth.[22]   In the long run, it is desirable that local revenue increase/decrease in line with local expenditure needs. Although a buoyant tax base allow windfall revenue gains to local government, this problem can be overcome provided that the long run local elasticity of the tax base to economic growth is equal to one. It should be noted that unlike United States and United Kingdom where local governments rely/ relied predominantly on property tax, Japan's local tax system makes a good score for revenue response to economic growth. This is mainly due to the fact that major source of local own revenue is a kind of tax base sharing which are similar to surtax on national income tax base. Approximately 60 per cent of prefectural taxes revenue and 40 per cent of municipal taxes revenue are imposed on income of individual or corporation.[23]   There is good evidence to show that elasticities of local taxes are fairly higher than unity. The elasticity of tax revenue to economic growth is 1.26 and 1.35 respectively, for prefecture and municipality during 1971-90. Among local taxes, municipal individual inhabitants tax is highest, 1.74, prefectural individual inhabitants tax accounts for 1.43, municipal corporation inhabitants tax accounts for 1.42. Contrary to general belief, the responsiveness of

---

[21] On this subject,see Ishi, Hiromistu [1993] pp.254-263., Ministry of Home Affairs[1996a],pp.5-8.

[22] Bennett, Robert. J. and Gunter, Krebs[1987], p.251.

[23] The inhabitants tax has two forms;(1)per capita and (2)income. The former is a lump sum component, while the latter is levied on income of previous year in a manner similar to the collection of the national individual income tax.

property tax,which is called the fixed assets tax by MOHA, is not less than unity. This is mainly due to sharp rise in market value of land in the late 1980s and assessment made at regular interval. According to these elasticity, the share of local tax in total tax revenue is relatively high in comparison with other unitary states.

The second criteria is small revenue fluctuation over time.[24] Strong fluctuations in revenue during business cycle can be regarded positively for a national tax, but this is not true for local taxes. First, local expenditure needed is fairly continuous and revenue fluctuation make planning difficult. Second, local expenditure should not run contrary to national economic policy, although the scope for local authority to pursue a counter-cyclical budget policy is rather limited. Property tax produces fairly stable revenue in Japan. In contrast to this, corporation inhabitants tax and enterprise tax fluctuate strongly during business cycle, since these taxes are generally imposed on net income, not on sales or turnover. Individual inhabitants tax fluctuates smaller than corporation inhabitants tax and enterprise tax. Apparently instability of enterprise tax revenue is most serious problem because of its large share in prefectural tax revenue. Introduction of new tax base such as sales, capital ,value added has been suggested in various proposal in order to make enterprise tax revenue less sensitive to business condition.

The third criteria is distribution between local authorities. Local tax system should produce a relatively balanced distribution of revenue among local governments in relation to their expenditure needs. Large difference in tax base between localities may cause many undesirable effects which require intergovernmental fiscal equalization. Cigarette tax levied on number of cigarettes makes a good score for balanced distribution of tax revenue among localities. Also base of fixed assets tax is evenly distributed throughout the country. While regional disparity in financial capacity has been gradually reduced during post-war high economic growth era, a marked difference is still observed in per capita prefectural tax revenues among localities in FY 1994, the largest being Tokyo 183 thousand of Yen, the smallest Okinawa with 56 thousand of Yen. Japan has introduced the "local consumption tax" in April 1997. This tax is imposed as 25 percent of the national consumption tax (it constitutes 1 percent of the total 5 present tax). It is collected by the national tax office and the proceeds redistributed to the prefectures basically in proportion to

---

[24] Bennett,R. J.& Gunter K., op.cit., p. 250.

consumption. The local consumption tax could be expected to produce a relatively balanced distribution of revenues among localities.

The fourth criteria is local fiscal autonomy and 'fiscal equivalence'.[25] The power to determine tax rate and base allows sensitive local variations in fiscal burdens to local preferences which should encourage fiscal accountability. Despite strict uniformity, there are two options available to local government for setting tax rate and base in Japan. One is that central government sets fixed tax rate for a number of local taxes,but provides range for some other local taxes. But principle and practice differ. There are no localities whose tax rate is below the standard tax rate, because these localities are prohibited to issue local bond by Local Public Finance Law. It is hard to find any tax competition among local governments in Japan. On the other hand, all except one prefectures raised corporate tax over standard tax rate, but they did not increase personal tax for fear of electoral consequences. As a result almost all localities use uniform rate for the same tax base. For example, in FY1996, 2944 out of 3233 municipalities apply same standard tax rate on property tax base. The other option is concerned with the imposition of new taxes not listed in the law. Local government is given the authority to propose new taxes and must seek the approval of the MOHA and MOF. In FY 1996, only 14 prefectures and 21 municipalities are given permission to use a non-listed tax such as nuclear fuel tax on nuclear power plants. It is difficult to see how they can be accountable to their constituents at the margin, as both efficiency and local autonomy require.

C. THE RATIONALE FOR EQUALIZATION TRANSFER

Given Japan's history of strong collective preference for equal access to public goods, it is unrealistic to imagine that local autonomy would evolve toward a system in which substantial regional differences would reemerge.[26] Therefore, a role for the LAT is remain. However present LAT system is not complete one, but still evolving.

An effective intergovernmental transfer system, in general, should satisfy several criteria. The first criteria is revenue adequacy.[27] Local allocation tax is not a kind of general grant, but a kind of shared tax system. An automatic increase in major

---

[25] Ibid., pp. 250-252.
[26] Mochida, N. [1995], pp.10-11.
[27] Shah, A. [1994], pp.30.; Ma, J. [1996], p.2.

national taxes produced continuous increase in the financial pool of local allocation tax during rapid growth era. On the other hand, total fund of transfer is sensitive to business condition because major component of the fund consists of income-elastic national taxes. During the period of 1970-95, the rate of increase in financial pool for transfer has changed within the extent between -14.1 per cent and 43.5 per cent every year. An average rate of increase and standard deviation is 9 per cent and 11.8 per cent respectively. Indeed both short term borrowing from the Fiscal Investment and Loan Program of the MOF and deficit-covering local bond issue play a key role in filling the gap between total entitlement of local allocation tax and financial pool of the transfer in the post rapid growth era.

Future reform necessary for revenue adequacy is to make the financial pool less sensitive to business condition and more stable. One of these options may be to introduce an adjustment fund into LAT system. Adjustment fund which is often advocated by Ministry of Finance means that an extraordinary increase in financial pool of transfer could be carried over to the fund automatically and vice versa. Second option is calculating five national taxes by 5 years' moving-mean or changing the weight of each national taxes (ex. to increase the weight of consumption tax, to decrease the weight of corporate income tax). Third option is to return back to "the local finance equalization grant" recommended by Shoup mission in 1949. It may be difficult to chose the last politically, however, we need to consider the first or the second solution seriously in order to make the total fund less sensitive to busyness cycle.[28]

The second criteria is local tax effort.[29] Formula should not encourage fiscal deficit. In Japan basic financial revenue is measured by using figures of major tax base and standard tax rate. To retain incentive for local government to collect their own tax, basic financial revenue is calculated based on the prescribed percentage of the sum of local tax revenues. Regions with high tax effort are not penalized and regions with low tax effort are not encouraged. These arrangement does not follow what is known as the "gap-filling" approach.[30] As for tax effort, however, local tax system is a question. As mentioned above the base and rates of general tax cannot be determined by the independent initiatives of local government under the Local Tax

---

[28] On this subject, see, Fujita S. [1972],pp.143-147.

[29] Shah, A., op.cit., p.30.

[30] Shah, A., op.cit.,pp.33; Ma, J.,op.cit.,p.18; Ahmad E.,[1997],p.369.

Law. The tax base and the tax rates can be altered by the proposal of both the MOHA and MOF. This implies that a uniform rate is levied on the same tax base in all prefecture and municipalities. Present local tax system should be changed into more flexible system in which tax rate is determined at the discretion of local governments. In order to win national taxpayer's confidence, on the other hand, recipient local governments should express their efforts to reduce LAT by enlarging the relevant tax bases or using a non-listed local tax.

The third criteria is equity.[31] Probably strongest case for equalization transfer has been based on the premise of fiscal equity. Because local allocation tax is annually paid to local governments whose basic financial need exceed basic financial capacity, it varies directly with local fiscal needs and inversely with local fiscal capacity. The formula states that the national government transfer will fill the gap between each region's fiscal need and fiscal capacity to ensure that a region with reasonable tax effort will be able to provide a reasonable level of public services. Application of these formula can be found in Australia, Germany, Korea and United Kingdom as well as Japan.[32] Such approach actually corrected horizontal fiscal imbalance and ensured a minimun level of public service in Japan.

While, before 1970s, the transfer system contributed significantly to equality, after that as regional fiscal disparities have fallen over time, there has been less "inequality" to fix trough local allocation tax and the intensity of the equalization effect has fallen. Future reform, therefore, should be carried out based on not only equity criteria but also efficiency ground in order to eliminate or reduce "differencilal net fiscal benefits" which encourage fiscally induced migration.[33]

The fourth criteria is transparency and stability.[34] The formula should be announced and each locality should be able to forecast its own total revenue in order to prepare its budget. And formula should be stable for at least several years to allow long-term planning at the local level. Local allocation tax is distributed according to a uniform formula based on basic financial need and basic financial capacity. The application

---

[31] Boadway, W. R. & P.A.R. Hobson [1993],pp.88-90.

[32] Ma, J. op.cit., pp.31-32; Ahmad E.,op.cit.,Chap.5,6,10.

[33] As to the concept of "net fiscal benefit", see, Boadway, W.R.& P.A.R. Hobson, op.cit.,pp.76-90. Kanemoto,Y.[1997] also argues an efficiency case for equialization in detail.

[34] Shah, A.,op.cit., p.30.

of the formula contributed to remove intense negotiation and lobbying during the post war development. However the formula that consider not only the equalization of fiscal capacity, but also adjust for the expenditure needs are demanding in terms of data requirement, particularly those on expenditure needs. Calculation of the transfer became to be too complicated for local governments to forecast their own revenue(including the transfer) in order to prepare their budgets. A kind of special measure, such as borrowing from the Fiscal Investment and Loan Program of the MOF and deficit-covering bond issue, is not determined automatically as a matter of course, but based on arbitrary political negotiation between MOHA and MOF. Future reform is necessary to strengthen the transparency of present system.[35]

5. CONCLUDING REMARKS

The defining characteristic of Japan's system of intergovernmental fiscal relation has been the strong collective preference for equal access to public goods.[36] The Japanese people and government were willing to commit themselves after World War to the evolution of autonomy for their newly defined structure of local government. However, equal access to public goods and fair sharing of the burden to finance these goods were viewed as essential for economic and social development. Interregional redistribution is, therefore, the central issue for Japan's system of intergovernmental fiscal relations, as mentioned above. As Hayashi, T.[1992] points out,[37] fiscal equalization system has played a key role in maintaining the Welfare State in Japan. Japan's system of equitable tax allocations to the regions drastically reduces residents' Tieboutian voting with their feet between regions.

Japan's intergovernmental system has been well designed to enforce fiscal responsibility. The probability of a local government going bankrupt or getting itself in severe financial difficulties is less than in North American or Western Europe. As Reed, S. R. [1990] points out clearly,[38] Japan is like France in the sense that the

---

[35] Kaizuka, Keimei et al. [1987] proposes one feasible solution that use fewer variables (ex. population, area) to estimate directly a region`s aggregate fiscal needs.

[36] Mihaljek, D. op.cit., p.289.

[37] Hayashi, T. [1992], PP.119-132.

[38] Reed, S. R.[1990], pp.58-59

national government takes responsibility for enforcing proper financial practices on local government, while in other countries this responsibility lies more with the local electorate and the banking system.

However, current system faces considerable challenge in the medium term, given the changing preference of the public with respect to local autonomy. In 1990's, Japan has been faced second transitional phase after the Second World War. This means a shift away from a society which emphasizes equal access to public services and equitable sharing of the burden of paying for them , toward a society which gives priority to individual citizen's expressed preference. Where local governments are unable to set their own tax rates of taxation, the Layfield Committee's concept of local accountability does not function effectively. On this regards, current system need to evolve in the process of fiscal decentralization in order to redefine expenditure responsibilities, more flexibility in tax rate setting, and to enhance transparency in equalization transfer scheme.

REFERENCE

Ahmad Ehtisham (eds) [1997],*Financing Decentralized Expenditures- An International Comparison of Grants-,* Edward Elgar.

Bennett,Robert J.& Günter Krebs (eds) [1987], *Local Business Taxes in Britain and Germany*, Nomos Verlagsgessellschaft, Baden-Baden.

Boadway, W. Robin & Paul A.R. Hobson [1993], *Intergovernmental Fiscal Relations in Canada*, Canadian Tax Paper No.96, Canadian Tax Foundation.

Chihobunken Suisin Iinkai [1996], *Chukan Hokoku* (Interim Report - creation of decentralized Society -) ,29 March,1996.

———— [1997], *Dainiji Kankoku* (Second Recommendation), July, 1997.

Fujita, Sei [1972], *Nihon Zaisei Ron* (The Theory of Public Finance in Japan), Keiso-shobo.

Fujiwara, Toshihiro [1996] "The Role of the Ministry of Autonomy in Intergovernmental Fiscal Relations in Japan," discussion paper for the world Bank's EDI workshop on "Intergovernmental Fiscal Transfer," held in Hanoi.March 1996.

Hayashi, Takehisa [1992], *Fukushi Kokka no Zaiseigaku* (Public Finance of Welfare States), Yuhikaku.

Ishi, Hiromistu [1993], "Local Taxation and Intergovernmental Fiscal Relations," in *The Japanese Tax System*,2nd ed.,Oxford.

Ito, Hanya [1967], "Equalization of Local Finance in Japan,"*Finanzarchiv* N. F. 26, Heft, Boston:Little Brown.

Ito, Kobun [1996],"Zaisei bunken no gutaiteki sekkei (the design for fiscal decentralization)" in *Chihobunken no Senryaku* (The strategy for Decentralization), daiichi-syorin.

Jinno, Naohiko [1995],"Chihobunken to jichitaizaisei (Decentralization and Local Public Finance)", in *Jurist*, No.1074.

Kaizuka, Keimei et al. [1987], "Chihokofu-zei no Kino to Hyoka(Local Allocation Tax - Function and Evaluation-), "Ministry of Finance,*Financial Review*, No.4.

Kaneko, Masaru [1995],"Chihobunken to Zeizaigen Kaikaku (Decentralization and Reform of Local Finance)", in *Nenpo Jichitaigaku* (annual report of self-governing body), No.8.

Kanemoto, Yoshistugu [1997],*Toshi Keizaigaku* (Urban Economics), Chapter 9, Toyokeizai Shinposya.

Ma, Jun [1996], "Intergovernmental Fiscal Transfer: A Comparison of Nine Countries," paper presented for the workshop on " Intergovernmental Fiscal Transfer," held in Hanoi, March 1996.

Mihaljek, Dubravko [1997], "Japan," in Teresa Ter-Minassian ed. *Fiscal Federalism in Theory and Practice*. International Monetary Fund.

Ministry of Home Affairs [1996a], *Local Tax Administration in Japan*. not for sale.

————— [1996b], *Local Public Finance System*. not for sale.

————— [1996c], *Local Public Finance in Japan*. not for sale.

Miyajima Hiroshi [1996], *Bunken no Kosuto* (Cost of Decentralization),booklet No.44, Chihojichi Sogo Kenkyusyo.

Mochida, Nobuki [1990], "Chihokofu-zei Seido no Kozo to Kino (Structure and Function of the Local Allocation Tax),"*Keizai to Keizaigaku* (Economyand Economics, Tokyo Metropolitan University)no.65.

————— [1993], *Toshi Zaisei no Kenkyu* (Public Finance of Japanese Cities) ,University of Tokyo Press.

————— [1995] , "Balancing Equity and Decentralization", *Social Science Japan* No.5, Newsletter of the Institute of Social Science, University of Tokyo.

————— [1996], "Japan's Local Allocation Tax - An Equalization Transfer Scheme -", University of Tokyo, Faculty of Economics,*discussion paper series*, 95-F-32.

————— [1997]," Chiho zeizaigen kakuju no totatuten to kongono kadai (The prospects for Local Finance)", in *Zei* (The Tax), Volume52,No.9.

Reed, Steven R. [1990], *Nihon no Seifukankannkei* (Japanese Prefecture and Policymaking) , Bokutakusya.

Shah, Anwar [1994], *The Reform of Intergovernmental Fiscal Relations in Developing and Emerging Market Economies*, Policy and Research Series 23, The World Bank.

Ter-Minassian,Teresa (eds) [1997],*Fiscal Federalism in Theory and Practice*. International Monetary Fund.

Wolman Harold and Edward Page [1987], "The Impact of Intergovernmental Grants on Subnational Resources Disparities: A Cross-National Comparison, " *Public Budgeting & Finance*.

Yamauchi, Kenji [1996],"By whom, when and how is the Japanese Local Allocation Tax calculated ?," discussion paper for the World Bank's EDI, OECD and Council of Europe's workshop on "Intergovernmental Fiscal Transfers" held in Vienna,July 1996.

Yonehara, Junhichiro [1987],"Financial Relations Between National and Local Governments," in Shibata, T. (eds.),*Public Finance in Japan*, University of Tokyo Press.

CHAPTER15 FISCAL FEDERALISM IN AUSTRALIA

ROBERT J. SEARLE[*]

INTRODUCTION

The Australian Federation was formed in 1901 when the six British colonies on the Australian continent asked the British Government to pass legislation to form the Commonwealth of Australia. One of those colonies, South Australia, brought the Northern Territory into the Federation with it as a Commonwealth Territory. In 1913, the Australian Capital Territory (ACT) was formed when, as required by the Constitution, the Commonwealth Parliament annexed an area from New South Wales so that the national capital, Canberra, could be constructed.

The Commonwealth gave self government to the Northern Territory in 1978 and to the ACT in 1989. For most practical purposes, the powers and responsibilities of the Territories' Parliaments are now the same as those of the six States. The States[1] vary in population from over 6 200 000 in New South Wales to less than 200 000 in the Northern Territory. Their recurrent budgets vary from over $13 400 million[2] in New South Wales to less than $900 million in the ACT. In area, Western Australia is the largest at over 2.5 million km^2 and the ACT the smallest at 2 400 km^2. Further basic statistics on the States are held in Attachment A.

---

[*] Commonwealth Grants Commission, Australia

[1] Hereafter, the term State(s) includes the Northern Territory and the Australian Capital Territory unless the context requires otherwise.

[2] Australian dollars have been used as the unit of financial data throughout this paper. At the time of writing the paper, the market valued $1A at about $0.78US.

Each of the States and the Northern Territory also has a system of municipal government and there are about 775 local government authorities in Australia. The ACT, because it is largely a city-State, has not found it necessary to establish municipalities. Municipal government units vary in population from about 150 people to 800 000, in revenue from about $150 000 to $400 million, and in area from about 1 km^2 to 380 000 km^2.

The Australian Federation is therefore made up of the Commonwealth Government and six States and two Territories, with each State and the Northern Territory also having a municipal government level. The Commonwealth has a written constitution that has not changed greatly since it was agreed to by the colonies prior to Federation. The States have all powers that they did not hand over to the Commonwealth. Municipal government operates under State legislation.

Attachment B provides an extract of *The Constitution of the Commonwealth of Australia*, detailing the powers of the central government. The list of Commonwealth powers has been amended by referendum only twice — in 1946 when *Section 51 (xxiia)* was added to give social security powers to the central government, and in 1967 when the Commonwealth was given power to make laws in respect of the indigenous (Aboriginal) races. This does not mean, however, that the balance of power within the Australian Federation has been stable since it was formed.

When the colonies agreed to federate, they thought they had designed a constitution that would ensure their continued financial independence. Within ten years, however, the Commonwealth was found to have 'surplus' funds each year and a system of fixed per capita grants to each State was implemented. *Section 96* of the Constitution has been used ever since to transfer funds to the States. It states that:

> During a period of ten years after the establishment of the Commonwealth and thereafter until the Parliament otherwise provides, the Parliament may grant financial assistance to any State on such terms and conditions as the Parliament thinks fit.

Although not designed for the purpose, this section of the Constitution has been a major avenue through which the Commonwealth has expanded its influence in the public sector.

Table 1. Australian Public Sector 1994-95

Item	Per cent of Item at level			Item as per cent total
	C'wealth	State	Local	
REVENUE [a]				
Income Tax				
Individuals	100.0			39.4
Enterprises	100.0			12.6
Non-residents	100.0			0.8
Pay-roll Tax	29.5	70.5		6.7
Taxes on property				
Land tax		100.0		1.0
Municipal rates			100.0	3.6
Financial & cap trans.		100.0		4.3
Other property taxes		100.0		0.3
Taxes on provision of goods and services				
Sales Tax	100.0			8.4
Excise & Levies				
Commonwealth Excise Act	100.0			8.7
Agricultural Production	100.0			0.5
On Statutory Authorities		100.0		0.4
Taxes on International Trade	100.0			2.5
Taxes on Gambling		100.0		2.1
Taxes on Insurance		100.0		1.2
Taxes on activities and use of goods				
Motor Vehicle Taxes		100.0		2.4
Franchise Fees		100.0		3.0
Other Taxes	85.8	14.2		0.4
Mining Revenue [b]		100.0		0.7
Fees and Fines	69.9	3.5	26.6	1.0
Total Revenue	72.2	24.0	3.8	100.0
EXPENDITURE [c]				
General Public Services	55.6	36.7	7.7	8.0
Defence	100.0			5.8
Public Order and Safety	12.1	84.6	3.4	3.6
Education	10.9	88.9	0.2	13.2
Health	50.5	48.7	0.8	15.2
Social Security and Welfare	91.6	7.4	1.0	28.9
Housing and Community Amenities	1.3	60.9	37.8	1.3
Recreation and Culture	30.7	37.0	32.4	2.1
Fuel and Energy	78.8	21.1	0.1	0.7
Agriculture, Forestry, Fishing and Hunting	55.2	44.3	0.5	1.8
Mining, Manufacturing Construction, etc.	54.2	29.3	16.5	0.5
Transport and Communication	14.4	63.9	21.7	3.4
Other Economic Affairs	67.5	32.7	-0.2	3.1
Other Purposes	43.0	54.3	2.7	12.6
Total Expenditure	56.6	37.9	5.5	100.0

[a] Australian Bureau of Statistics, Taxation Revenue Australia, 1994-95 Catalogue No. 5506.0.

[b] Commonwealth Grants Commission, 1997 Update p 130.

[c] Australian Bureau of Statistics, Government Finance Statistics Australia, 1994-95 Catalogue No. 5512.0

Distribution of Responsibilities and Powers in the Australian Federation

Using a General Finance Statistics classification based on the United Nations' System of National Accounts, the practical distribution of responsibilities and powers between the three levels of Government in Australia in 1994-95 is shown in Table 1 which is based on actual expenditure and revenue patterns.

The most noticeable aspect of Table 1 is that while the sources of revenue are generally specific to one level of government, the expenditure pattern is much more complex. This has arisen largely because of:

- a belief (of at least the Commonwealth Government) that many revenues are more efficiently collected centrally;
- a conviction by the Commonwealth that it can manage the national economy more readily if it has greater revenue collection authority;
- an unwillingness of the States and the Commonwealth to share access to the major tax bases; and
- the Commonwealth's use of the tied grants power to influence the standard of most of the services provided by the States (although the Commonwealth has no power in education and health, for example, over 32 per cent of outlays in those areas are from its budget).

OVERCOMING THE FISCAL IMBALANCES

In 1942, the Commonwealth took over responsibility for the collection of income tax as a war time measure, and has held the power ever since. This added greatly to Commonwealth surpluses after the war and, as a result, the Australian Federation now has one of the largest vertical fiscal imbalances (VFI) measured by the international agencies. In its 1997-98 Budget Papers[3], the Commonwealth Government summarised the VFI in Australia diagrammatically as in Figure 1.

It can be seen very clearly from this that the Commonwealth raises much more revenue than it spends (even though a lot of its outlays are on State functions) and the States rely very heavily on grants from the Commonwealth to be able to provide the services they have responsibility for.[4] The municipal sector also relies on transfers of funds from higher levels of government, but to a much lesser extent than the States.

Figure 1. General Government Own-source Revenue and Adjusted Own-Purpose Outlays 1996-97 (estimated).

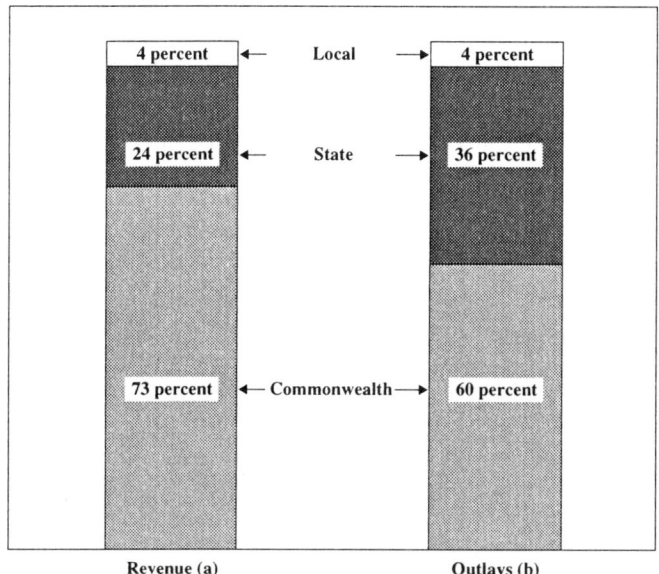

(a) Own-source revenue excludes the receipt of payments from other levels of government.

(b) The ABS measure of general government own-purpose outlays excludes payments to other levels of government and Public Trading Enterprises (PTEs), such as general revenue assistance, specific purpose payments (SPPs) and advances and subsidies, and interest payments on borrowings for other governments and PTEs. The adjusted measure adds back in to Commonwealth outlays SPPs 'through' the States (other than those for local government purposes). A corresponding adjustment is made to the State/local series. The adjusted measures for both Commonwealth and State levels of government abstract from all net advances, which is consistent with measures of the underlying deficit.

Some attempts have been made in the past to reduce the VFI. The States have given the Commonwealth full responsibility for funding what would otherwise be their functions (such as tertiary education) and the Commonwealth has given the States access to some tax bases (such as pay-roll tax). These actions have not satisfied the States, however, and there is growing pressure for an overhaul of the whole tax system.[5]

---

[3] *Federal Financial Relations 1997-98, Budget Paper No.3*, p 13. Australian Government Publishing Service, Canberra, 1997.

[4] Since the 1997-98 Commonwealth Budget, the High Court of Australia has found Business Franchise Fees levied by the States invalid. The Commonwealth now levies these fees, thus increasing the VFI further.

[5] In late 1997, the commonwealth and State Governments agreed that they would work towards a major reform of the tax system.

In addition to the vertical fiscal imbalance, there is also a considerable degree of horizontal fiscal imbalance (HFI) between the Australian States and Territories. Independent assessments by the Commonwealth Grants Commission[6] indicate that States' revenue capacities vary from about 77 per cent of the per capita Australian average to about 113 per cent of that average, largely due to variations in capacities arising from Land Revenue, Stamp Duty on Conveyances, Tobacco and Liquor Taxes, and Mining Revenue.

With the exception of the Northern Territory, the States' costs of providing the Australian average level of services are all assessed by the Commonwealth Grants Commission to be within 10 per cent of the Australian average. The Northern Territory, however, is measured as having a cost structure nearly 175 per cent higher than that average. The major influences on this aspect of HFI arise from differences in the socio-economic and demographic composition of States' populations, differences in the economies of scale in the provision of services and differences in the spatial distribution of population within the States' boundaries. In each of these areas, the Northern Territory is greatly different to the other States, giving it a very different cost and demand structure for State services.

It is probable that the HFI within the municipal sector in Australia is even larger than that experienced at the State level. However, because measurements of these differences are done within each State[7] and are not calculated on a fully uniform basis, it is not possible to give an accurate measure of the extent to which revenue capacities and costs of services differ between authorities.

The Fiscal Transfers

Transfers from the Commonwealth. By far the largest transfer of funds within the Australian Federation is from the Commonwealth to the State and municipal governments.

---

[6] The Commonwealth Grants Commission has responsibility for making recommendations to the Commonwealth Government on how untied financial assistance should be distributed between the States and is the subject of detailed discussion later in the paper.

[7] There is a Grants Commission established in each of the States and the Northern Territory, under State law but required as a condition of the SPP from the commonwealth, to advise on the distribution of untied funds provided to the States for transfer to municipal government authorities.

In 1995-96, the Commonwealth transferred over $33 500 million to the State and municipal governments, and spent another $890 million on the direct provision or subsidisation of services that would otherwise have been the responsibility of those governments. In summary, the transfers are presented in Table 2 below.

Tied grants **to** the States are for use within the States' budgets and fund normal activities of the States. Tied grants **through** the States are for activities for which the States have constitutional authority but which do not influence their budgets; such as the activities of their municipal authorities, the provision of tertiary education (for which the Commonwealth has accepted full financial responsibility) and primary and secondary schools run by religious and other non-government authorities.

One of the specific purpose payments (SPPs) through the States is for municipal government. In 1996-97, it was about $1165 million. This Commonwealth funding is only tied for the purpose of receipt by the States. It is passed on to municipal governments, on the recommendations of the State Grants Commissions, as untied funding.

The direct funding of State-type services by the Commonwealth is largely in the areas of Vocational Education and Training, and the provision of services for indigenous Australians, both of which are State functions but are now partly funded,

Table 2. Commonwealth Transfers to Other Levels of Government 1995-96 [a]

Transfer		$m
Untied Funds		
General Revenue Grants	Recurrent Purposes	15 700
	Capital Purposes	140
Tied Funds (to the States)		
Specific Purpose Payments	Recurrent Purposes	8 480
	Capital Purposes	2 555
Tied funds (through the States)		
Specific Purpose Payments	Recurrent Purposes	6 480
	Capital Purposes	155
Commonwealth direct expenditure or subsidisation of State-type Services		890
Total		34 400

[a] Based on data in *Commonwealth Financial Relations with Other Levels of Government 1996-97, Budget Document No. 3, AGPS, Canberra, 1995*, and Commonwealth Grants Commission sources.

with the agreement of the States, through statutory authorities of the Commonwealth. *Transfers from the States.* Until 1996-97, payments from the States to either the Commonwealth or their municipal sectors were of little importance in the overall fiscal transfer system in Australia. In June 1996, however, the Commonwealth 'asked' the States to assist it with its budgetary difficulties (it made acceptance of the request a condition of the total funds it would make available for transfer) and got their agreement to 'contribute' $1559 million over three years, on an equal per capita basis. Details of the States' contributions are shown in Table 3. That these contributions are on an equal per capita basis is of particular interest because of the efforts made to overcome horizontal fiscal imbalances (discussed later in the paper).

To give the States as much budget flexibility as possible in making these contributions, the Commonwealth agreed that they could individually decide how they went about meeting their commitment. In the event, some States opted to make payments back to the Commonwealth, some chose to have the Commonwealth reduce their untied funding, and others asked that their SPPs for welfare housing be reduced.

The last of these methods caused the Commonwealth some concern because it negated the 'national objectives' that had been taken into consideration when the SPPs for housing was being decided. For the 1997-98 contributions, the Commonwealth has continued to give the States as much flexibility as possible, but has indicated that it will need to consider more closely the acceptability of any proposals to fund them from SPPs, having regard to its policy objectives and the decisions underlying the

Table 3. Contributions by the States to the Commonwealth

	1996-97 $m	1997-98 $m	1998-99 $m
New South Wales	209.5	216.3	101.3
Victoria	153.4	158.1	73.8
Queensland	114.0	118.9	56.1
Western Australia	59.8	62.2	29.3
South Australia	49.9	51.2	23.8
Tasmania	15.9	16.3	7.6
Australian Capital Territory	10.4	10.8	5.1
Northern Territory	6.0	6.3	3.0
Total	619.0	640.0	300.0

[a] *Commonwealth Financial Relations with other levels of Government, 1996-97, Budget Paper No.3*, p 25. Australian Government Publishing Service, Canberra, 1996.

payments.

Traditionally, the States have not been generous in their assistance to the municipal sector, a situation that may be related to the States' financial capacity and to the revenue bases they have given their municipalities. In 1995-96, only the Northern Territory made untied grants to its local government authorities, and only the Northern Territory and South Australia made specific purpose payments to their municipalities. The different policy in the Northern Territory could be a result of the much younger municipal sector in the Territory, and the stage of development of many of the indigenous communities that have recently been granted municipal government.

Transfers from the Municipal sector. Except where they are paying for services undertaken on their behalf (under contract), the municipal governments transfer no funds to either the States or the Commonwealth.

Commonwealth to State Government Transfers
The transfers from the Commonwealth to the State sector are the major element of the fiscal transfer system in Australia and, as such, will be the focus of the balance of this paper. As indicated in Table 2 above, the payments are either specific purpose payments (SPPs) or general revenue grants (GRGs).

The total transfer is decided each year at the Premiers' Conference when the Prime Minister and Treasurer of the Commonwealth Government meet with the Premiers and Treasurers of the States to discuss the economic outlook and organise the fiscal transfer for the coming year. Because it controls the revenue, the Commonwealth has the upper hand in these discussions and the outcome does not often differ greatly from the 'offer' made to the States a few days before the Conference. For practical purposes, the value of the transfer is thus decided by the Commonwealth and set, each year, in the context of the budgetary position in which that Government finds itself. Because of the powerful position of the Commonwealth, the Premiers' Conference is often seen as a waste of time and simply an opportunity for the States to blame the Commonwealth for any reductions in services or increases in State taxes, and to campaign for tax reform.

This is not to say that the Premiers' Conference does not give the States some indication of the likely flow of funds in future years (at present, GRGs are guaranteed to increase annually in real per capita terms), but the Commonwealth always maintains the flexibility it feels it needs to manage the overall budget. While GRGs are guaranteed, for example, the total value of SPPs might be tied to the state of the economy and, at the Premiers' Conference, the States might be given only indicative SPP figures on an assumption that the economy remains unchanged.

The uncertainty in the total size of the transfer from the Commonwealth to the States is seen by the recipients (and many others) as a serious deficiency in the fiscal transfer system in Australia. Among their claims in this regard, the States say that:

- as the provider of important and wide-ranging services, they are entitled to greater security in financial planning than the present method allows;
- there is no pressure on the Commonwealth to minimise costs because it can force the States to take any pain associated with reductions in resource availability; and
- the Commonwealth could adequately manage the national economy without the degree of control it currently has.

Just as the value of the total transfer is decided very largely by the Commonwealth, so also is the split between SPPs and GRGs. That there is no overall policy on this aspect of fiscal transfers is another feature of the Australian system that some observers find surprising. While GRGs are decided at the Premiers' Conference in late March or early April for a Commonwealth budget in May, the negotiations on SPPs are held by relevant Ministers and senior bureaucrats over a period of months, both before and after the Premiers' Conference. Although the negotiating teams involved in the consideration of each SPP presumably have some instructions or guidelines from the Commonwealth Treasury and the Department of Finance and Administration, the total of the SPPs to be transferred seems to many to be no more than the accumulation of the individual outcomes of those negotiations.

In summary, there are no continuing policies on either how the total value of the transfer payments from the Commonwealth to the States should be determined, or how the transfer is divided between SPPs and GRGs. The Commonwealth, however, somehow takes into account its budgetary position, its desire to set minimum national standards in areas of State responsibility, and the States' desire for budgetary independence, to arrive at both the total size of the transfer and the share to be transferred as SPPs.

Specific Purpose Payments. Specific Purpose Payments to the States are used when the Commonwealth wishes to influence State expenditure priorities to satisfy national objectives. These funds must be spent on particular functions and their use is probably the easiest means by which the Commonwealth Government can achieve performance equalisation for any particular service provided by the States.

Over the period since 1990-91, the Commonwealth has used over 90 different SPPs to transfer funds to the States. This is not an accurate measure of the number of programs, however, because in some of them, government schools grants for example, there are a number of different sub-programs that are not detailed in the basic reference document — *Commonwealth Financial Relations with other Levels of Government, Commonwealth Budget Paper No. 3.*

The Specific Purpose Payments **through** the States are the funds transferred to the States for activities not provided through State budgets. The transfers are made in this way either as an administrative convenience or because the States and not the Commonwealth have the constitutional authority to perform the function. These large payments are where it could be argued that the involvement of the Commonwealth was initiated, at least in part, by the vertical fiscal imbalance in its favour.

Since the early 1970s, there has been a trend for SPPs to make up an increasingly

Figure 2. SPPs as a Proportion of Commonwealth Grants

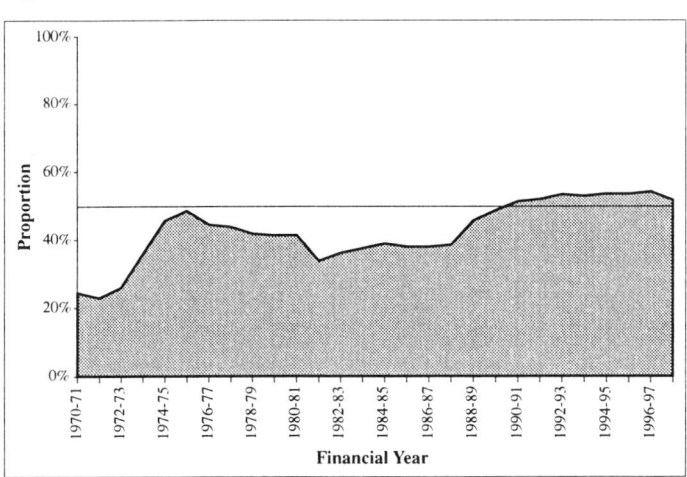

large proportion of total grants from the Commonwealth to the States.

The reasons for the two periods of increase in the proportion of SPPs over the last 25 years have been quite different. In 1972, Australia elected a new Commonwealth Labor Government after that party had been in opposition for 27 years, and it quickly expanded both the range and size of SPPs to initiate change and fulfil its social agenda. The increase in the late 1980s and early 1990s was because the escalation arrangements relating to SPPs at that time were more generous than those relating to GRGs. The current guarantee arrangements on GRGs (which will be in place until at least 1998-99) have resulted in a slight lowering of the SPP proportion in the most recent year.

Because there is no Government document that details the basis on which each SPP is distributed between the States, it is impossible to comment with any authority about the influence of equity on the distribution of these fiscal transfers from the Commonwealth. It is true, however, that the distribution of many of the major SPPs follows a pattern that is not dissimilar to that which the Commonwealth Grants Commission assesses as being appropriate if fiscal equalisation of the State Governments' capacities was the objective. It is also interesting to note that the distribution of some of the larger SPPs (such as those for health and education) has, over time, moved closer to the Commission's assessments.

The equitable provision of a service by State Governments can be more effectively achieved by the central Government through the use of SPPs rather than GRGs, because the decisions about the minimum level of service are being taken by one government. What is very difficult to achieve through SPPs, however, is an overall redistribution of fiscal capacity based on equity — it is difficult to use SPPs to adjust for differences in States' revenue raising capacities. This task is usually performed through the use of GRGs and systems designed to adjust funding for horizontal fiscal imbalance.

General Revenue Grants. As we have seen, untied funds or GRGs at present make up about 46 per cent of the total transfer of funds from the Commonwealth to State Governments in Australia and are the largest single avenue through which financial capacity is transferred. The decisions on the size of the transfer are taken by the Commonwealth Government and 'discussed' with the States at the Premiers' Conference.

306

The distribution between the States of the recurrent GRGs and nearly $4000 million of the SPPs (the majority of the Hospital Funding Grants) is based on per capita relativities recommended by the Commonwealth Grants Commission.

THE COMMONWEALTH GRANTS COMMISSION

Background and Method of Operation

The Commonwealth Grants Commission is a small, independent, advisory body that has been in existence for over 60 years. It has no Constitutional status but is widely seen as an integral element of Australia's federal structure.

Members of the Commission are appointed by the Commonwealth (on either a full-time or a part-time basis) after discussion of prospective candidates with the States who have an informal right of veto over nominees. They are appointed for their expertise and experience and do not represent any jurisdiction or organisation when working on Commission business. Appointees cannot be either Commonwealth or State employees and are usually drawn from academia, retired civil servants or business, although current salary structures in the Australian public sector make it very difficult to recruit from the last source. Appointments to the Commission can be for up to five years and Members can be reappointed.

The Commission is funded by the Commonwealth, has a professional staff of about 35 and, to stress its independence from the Commonwealth economic policy advising agencies, is given independent agency status within the bureaucracy and reports direct to the Minister for Finance and Administration.

The Commission cannot initiate its own inquiries and operates on terms of reference from its Minister, usually arrived at after negotiations between the Commonwealth and State Treasuries. In carrying out its inquiries, the Commission treats the States and the Commonwealth as equals in its deliberations. Although it presents its reports to a Commonwealth Minister, the Commission's usual procedure is to release it findings to the States immediately afterwards. Thus, although funded by the Commonwealth, the Commission could be seen to be working for the States — they are much more concerned about its findings than the Commonwealth which simply sets the amount to be transferred and leaves the decisions on distribution very largely to the Commission.

All proceedings of the Commission's inquiries are open to the public and it freely discloses the detailed calculations behind its results and findings. Every five years, the Commission reviews all aspects of its data and method of calculating the relative shares of general revenue funds to go to each State. In the intervening years, methods are unchanged and annual updates of the calculations incorporate the latest available data.

The principle the Commission follows in arriving at its conclusions (except to the extent that it is told otherwise in the terms of reference) is that of horizontal fiscal equalisation, a principle first enunciated by the Commission in 1936. It is:

that each State should be given the capacity to provide the average standard of State-type public services, if it:
- operates at an average level of efficiency; and
- makes the average effort to raise revenue from its own sources.

The Australian system is thus based on a principle of capacity equalisation within a federation. The States are given the capacity to achieve inter-personal equalisation of revenue imposts and receipt of services, but are left with the ultimate decisions of what levels of service are to be provided and what revenue efforts are to be made.

The first step in applying the principle is to decide what range of State-type services and areas of revenue raising should be considered in the equalisation assessments. The Commission looked at this in detail in 1990 and decided that all recurrent expenditures and revenues normally the responsibility of the States should be included. All capital transactions should be excluded, as should State spending on functions which are the financial responsibility of the Commonwealth, such as universities, even though they might remain the constitutional responsibility of the States. This has been the scope of Commission inquiries since 1993. As part of the 1999 Review, it is looking at this issue again and, in addition to all States' normal recurrent budgetary activities, it is considering bringing the recurrent cost of capital — that is depreciation — into its assessments. As a result, we may see an expansion of the scope of inquiries from 1999 onwards.

A number of conclusions follow from the implementation of the fiscal equalisation principle, and some aspects of its application are worth noting.

- The Commission deals with capacity and not performance equalisation. This is because Australia is a federation; the States have sovereign rights in functions they retained when the Constitution was written; and the grants the Commission is concerned with are untied grants. Capacity equalisation means that:
- a State many choose to levy low taxes, and have a reduced standard of public services compared with other States; or
- it may choose to have high-quality public services in some functions, but this will mean either a lower standard of other services, higher taxes overall, or an increase in debt for the State concerned; and
- a State that is less careful about the efficiency of its operations will not be able to provide services at average standards unless it has higher than average tax rates or increasing debt.
- The standard to which the Commission works is what has actually happened, what has actually been spent on a function, or raised in taxes — not what any group of experts thinks should have happened.
- The Commission's recommendations attempt to be policy neutral — as far as possible, the Commission makes sure that a State cannot get a larger share of the general revenue funding by changing its priorities or its policies.
- Central to the Commission's work is the need to measure or estimate 'disabilities'. These are influences beyond a State's control that require it to spend more (or less) to provide the same service as other States, or mean that it cannot raise as much revenue as (or can raise more than) other States from the same tax rates.

Thus, as stated earlier, the sources of fiscal imbalance between States are:

- different per capita costs in providing equivalent services; and
- different per capita capacities for raising own-source revenues.

The Commission's assessments of States' relative costs of providing services are shown in Figure 3. Apart from the obvious case of the Northern Territory, with its small population scattered over a large area (176 000 people in 1.35 million km^2), the Commission does not believe there to be great differences between the States. Victoria has the lowest cost at about 8 per cent below the national average. In Western Australia and Tasmania, costs are about 9 per cent above average.

Figure 4 shows the Commission's assessments of States' relative revenue raising

Figure 3. Relative Cost of Service Provision Ratios - 1995-96

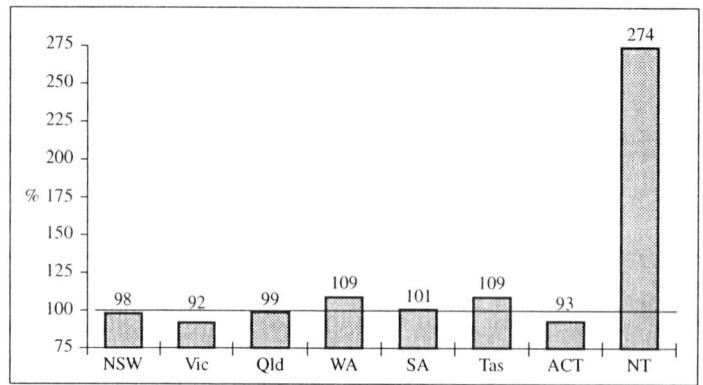

Figure 4. Relative Revenue Raising Capacity Ratios - 1995-96

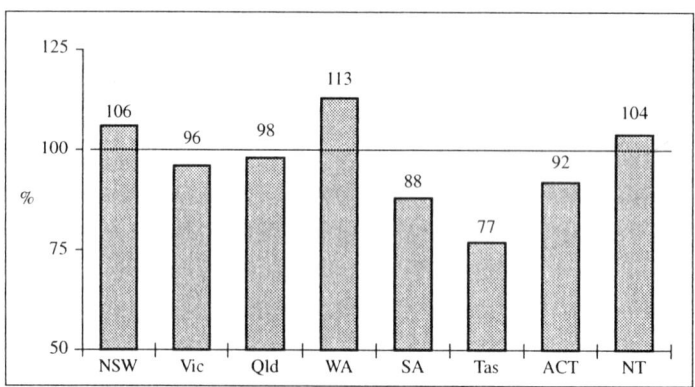

capacities. Tasmania, the poorest State, has a capacity 23 per cent below average. Western Australia, with its vast mineral resources, is assessed by the Commission as being 13 per cent above average in revenue raising ability.

The final outcome of the Commission's considerations is a set of per capita relativities which are its recommendations concerning the relative levels of per capita grant to which each State is entitled.

The per capita relativities recommended in the Commission's 1997 Update Report were:

310

State	Relativity
New South Wales	0.87819
Victoria	0.87835
Queensland	1.03737
Western Australia	0.99589
South Australia	1.19100
Tasmania	1.54974
Australian Capital Territory	0.88435
Northern Territory	4.89353
Australia	**1.00000**

But how does the Commission reach its conclusions of different revenue raising capacities and expenditure requirements?

Revenue Assessments

There are substantial differences between States in the per capita revenue they collect from their own taxes and charges (ranging, in 1995-96, from $1341 per capita in Tasmania to $2122 per capita in the Northern Territory). This is illustrated by Figure 5, which also shows the Australian average, or standard, revenue collected by the States in 1995-96 to be $1751.[8]

The differences in revenue collections are caused by:
* differences in the range of taxes levied;
* differences in the rates of tax charged; and

Figure 5. Total Own-source Revenue Per Capita - 1995-96

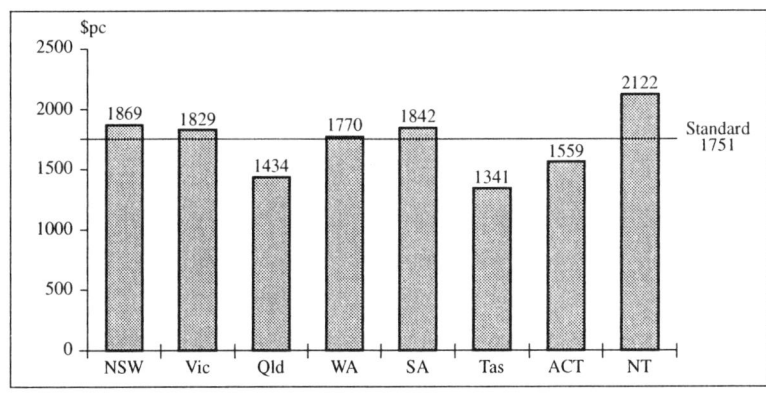

---

[8] Business Franchise Fees, which comprised 15.4 per cent of this revenue, have since been declared invalid by the High Court of Australia and are no longer collected by the States.

Figure 6. Total Own-source Revenue Per Capita - 1995-96

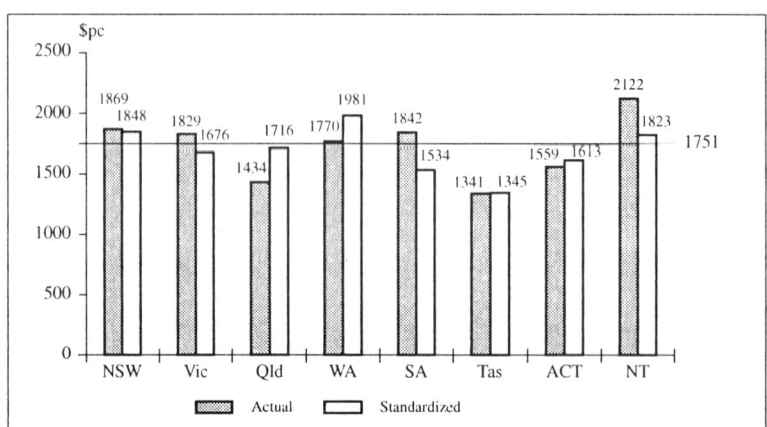

- differences in the capacity of States to raise revenue (ie revenue disabilities caused by differences in the economic and demographic positions of States which are beyond their control and affect the size of their revenue bases).

The first two groups of differences reflect policy choice by the State governments. Only the last one reflects non-policy influences that the Commission takes account of in its calculations. To accept the first two as reasons for variation in the per capita relativities would be to allow the States to influence their own levels of funding — which would destroy effort neutrality and be a serious inefficiency in the grant design system.

The aim of the Commission's revenue assessments is to measure the differences in the capacity of States to raise revenue. It does this by comparing the revenue each State would raise from its own sources if it made the same revenue effort as all the other States. That is, if they each imposed taxes at the average rates and collected their taxes with the average level of efficiency. The measured differences in capacity thus arise only because of differences in the size and structure of the States' revenue bases.

Figure 6 compares the revenue each State actually collected in 1995-96 with the Commission's assessments of what it would have collected under standard conditions. The Commission calls this the standardised revenue.

The task of estimating States' standardised revenues involves:

- deciding how to group revenue sources for assessment purposes;
- identifying and measuring the revenue base for each group of taxes; and
- measuring the standard revenue effort for each group of taxes.

Grouping Revenue Sources. After re-examining the scope and structure of its standard budget for the 1999 Review, the Commission has concluded that 19 categories are needed to best measure the differences between States in their ability to raise revenue. The classification, and the contribution of each category to total standard revenue, is shown in Attachment C.

It can readily be seen that many of the States' revenue sources, even in this grouped presentation, are only minor contributors to total own-source revenue. This is indicative of the problems of inefficiency and splintering the States see in their tax bases and, together with the level of VFI, forms the basis for their arguments for tax reform.

Measuring the Revenue Base. Once the assessment categories are decided by looking at the range of revenue sources used by the States, the Commission defines the revenue base for each one. Revenue bases are usually the legislative base for the tax and measured as the number or value of activities or assets subject to tax in the majority of States. For example, the revenue base for the tax on petroleum products is the number of litres of product sold; for stamp duty on conveyances, it is the value of land and other assets sold.

If no State, or virtually no State, taxes a part of the assumed revenue base, it is excluded from the measure of the revenue base. For example, most States exempt fuel used on farms from the petroleum tax so this is excluded from the revenue base in all States. Similarly, all States exempt small businesses from pay-roll tax and the Commission excludes the wages paid by such businesses from its assessments by adjusting data from which the revenue bases are measured.

In some instances, there are so many differences between States in how they impose a tax that it is impossible to get a common measure. In these cases, the Commission looks for a measure that is related to the particular tax but, if one is not available, it uses a broad measure of economic activity such as household income, State Gross

Product or industry profitability. Revenue from mining royalties, where one State has a much different policy to the others and where a measure of profitability is used, is an important example of where the Commission finds it necessary to apply this procedure.

When measuring revenue bases, it is also necessary to consider whether the level of activity in a State is influenced by the rate of tax imposed on it — that is, whether there are price elasticity effects. For example, some States use taxation policy as a deliberate means of influencing public health by discouraging tobacco consumption. The revenue bases, the volume of sales, should be measured as if al States operated at standard tax rates and, where necessary, the observed revenue all base of a State is adjusted for price elasticities.

Measuring the Standard Revenue Effort. Revenue effort is influenced by many things, including the rate of tax, the exemptions and concessions, and the enforcement effort. The Commission summarises the effects of all these things into the standard effective rate of tax or standard revenue effort. This is calculated as total revenue collected by all the States, divided by the total of their estimated revenue bases.

Where there is a common policy among the States to apply progressive rates of tax (for example, in Pay-roll Tax), the assessments take account of the differences between States in the value distribution of the taxable transactions. In effect, this is done by dividing the revenue base of each State into common value ranges, and performing separate assessments in each of those ranges.

Estimating Standardised Revenues. Estimating standardised revenue is achieved by multiplying each State's revenue base by the standard effective rate of tax. As the process can be described more easily by example, the following discussion of the Pay-roll tax assessment is used to illustrate the Commission's revenue assessment method.

Pay-roll taxes are collected from employers on the basis of the value of the wages and salaries they pay. The tax is in the range of 4 to 7 per cent of pay-rolls, depending on the jurisdiction and the value of the pay-roll. All States exempt small employers from the tax but there are differences between them in the definition of a small employer (in one State it is annual pay-rolls below $412 500, but in another it is pay-rolls below $700 000).

The revenue base is defined by the Commission as the estimated value of pay-rolls subject to tax; that is, the pay-rolls of public sector trading enterprises and private employers, except for small businesses where the pay-rolls are below the national average exemption level.

The starting point for the measurement of this revenue base is data from the Australian Bureau of Statistics on aggregate wages, salaries and supplements received by residents in each State. As such, the data include wages that are not taxed. The Commission therefore adjusts them for each State to exclude:

(i)   wages attributable to the general government sector; and

(ii) the estimated gross pay-rolls of private sector businesses with less than 20 employees in Australia (this corresponds to pay-rolls of about $500 000).

The adjustments are also based on data obtained from the Australian Bureau of Statistics.

Because the pay-roll tax rates applied by the States are progressive, it is necessary to take account of differences between States in the distribution of pay-rolls by size bands. This is done by dissecting the aggregate revenue base for each State into value groups, using details of pay-rolls and tax paid that are provided by the States from their tax collection records. The States' aggregate pay-roll tax assessments then become the accumulation of the separate assessments made for each value range. The assessments are done by applying the average rate of tax in each value range to the States' values of pay-rolls in each value range.

Figure 7 summarises the pay-roll taxation assessments for 1995-96. It shows that New South Wales and Victoria had above average revenue raising capacity and that the other States had below average capacity.

The above average capacities in New South Wales and Victoria arose because:

(i)   the wages, salaries and supplements per head of population in those States exceeded the Australian average;

(ii) the proportion of total wages, salaries and supplements attributable to private

Figure 7. Pay-roll Taxation Revenue Per Capita - 1995-96

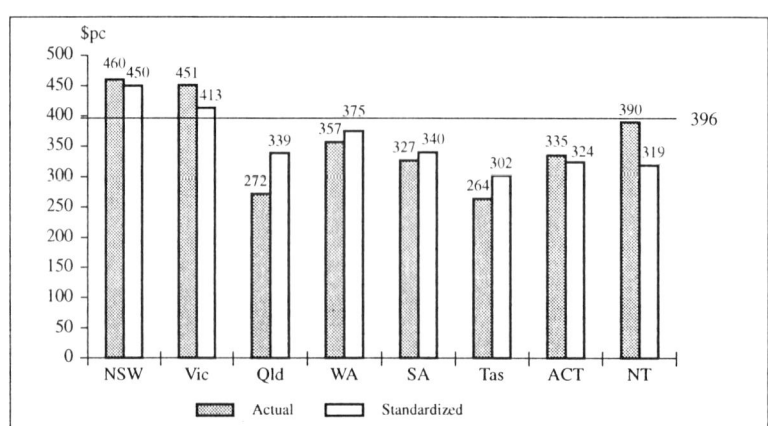

sector employers with more than 20 employees in those States exceeded the Australian average proportion; and

   (iii) New South Wales had an above average proportion of large pay-rolls.

Comparisons between the actual and standardised revenue for each State indicate how their revenue efforts differed from the average of $396. The actual revenues of New South Wales, Victoria, the Australian Capital Territory and the Northern Territory exceeded their standardised revenues because:

   (i)   these States applied the highest rates of tax;

   (ii)   the low tax effort in Queensland brought the standard down and therefore reduced all States' standardised capacities; and

   (iii) Victoria in particular has a very effective compliance program.

The actual revenue of Queensland was well below its standardised revenues because it applied the lowest rates of pay-roll tax and had the highest exemption level. The rates of tax in Western Australia, South Australia and Tasmania were also below average.

Expenditure Assessments

The Commission undertakes expenditure assessments in each of the 40 categories into which it classifies State recurrent expenditure. These are shown in Attachment D. As indicated earlier, the assessments are based on the calculation of disabilities (which can be either negative or positive), and are defined as:

316

influences beyond the States' control that result in them having to outlay different per capita levels of expenditure to achieve the same objective.

Disability Factors. For discussion purposes, we find it useful in considering expenditure disabilities, to distinguish between demand influences and cost influences. In practise, this distinction is not always clear but some examples might assist the explanation.

The most frequently used demand factor is **relevant population**. This defines the number of units able to demand the service. For some services it is the whole population of each State and States therefore have no per capita disability relative to one another. Hospital and police services are examples of where total population is applied as the relevant population. For other functions, schools for example, the relevant population is a subset of the total population and results in different per capita levels of demand for the service. It is not always measured in terms of human population and could be the number of properties or the number of mining establishments, depending on the service being considered.

A second demand influence, one that has several elements, is **population composition**. Different age and sex distributions often contribute to different levels of per capita demand, and the ethnic composition of the population may also affect demand. For example, the health status of the Aboriginal population in Australia is considerably worse than average and creates extra per capita demand for health services in States with higher proportions of Aboriginals. Differences in the proportion of the population in older aged groups, or without an ability to speak English, and differences in poverty levels, are also likely to be reflected in different demands for State services.

Another demand influence of interest is the **cross-border factor** which measures the net effects on a State's costs of:

- use by its inhabitants of services provided by other States; and
- use of its services by the inhabitants of other States.

The major instance of cross-border use of services in Australia is the flow of people into the Australian Capital territory (ACT) from the surrounding State of New South

Wales. The ACT services most used by the residents of New South Wales are hospitals, education, police, court facilities and social welfare provision. Without an adjustment to the assessment for this movement, the ACT would receive insufficient funds to provide the standard level of services, and New South Wales would receive too much.

Looking now at some cost influences, the **location of the population** is an obvious case in the vast areas of Australia. Other things equal, a more dispersed population costs more to service than a more concentrated one. Telephone and facsimile communication is more expensive over longer distances; travel in connection with the provision of services is more expensive; the average cost of freighting goods or transferring staff is greater; and the cost of compensating staff for working in remote and harsh locations may be greater. Population dispersion factors aim to measure and allow for differences in the influence of these types of costs.

Beyond a certain point of population concentration, however, urbanisation adds to costs. A large enough urban area will require the provision of a public transport service (nearly always at a net cost in Australia), and the larger the city the greater need for railways (nearly always more demanding on the budget than buses).

Other **demographic characteristics** may also affect costs. For example, providing services to migrants from different language groups imposes extra costs: the need for interpreter services; the more complex problems because they seek services later (health services in particular); and the extra time it takes to communicate. The effects of such demographic characteristics on costs are complex and the information available to measure them is often sparse.

Another cost differential arises from differences in economies of **scale**. The Commission measures these at two levels.

- **Administrative scale** relates to the additional expenditure of the States not able to take advantage of the economies of scale available to the more populous States. It concerns mainly policy development and administrative tasks carried out in central and regional offices, or specialised services (such as the legislature) provided centrally for the whole of a State's population.
- **Service delivery scale** refers to the differential costs of providing services at the point of service delivery (a school or a police station) arising from lower efficiency, because of population sparsity, in the use of staff and other resources at service outlets.

318

The last example to be discussed is **input costs**. The Commission has taken the view that the costs of some basic inputs into State government service provision are not within, or fully within, the States' control. A very important example is wages.

Salaries and related costs are a high proportion of total expenditure on State-government functions. The wage levels which a State pays its employees may be determined more by the general economic climate in the State, or by the centralised wage-setting system that operated in Australia until very recently, than by any action or inaction of the State Government.

The statistics clearly show, for example, that the level of private-sector wages in New South Wales is higher than elsewhere in Australia and it is accepted by the Commission that there are some flow-on effects into the State public sector. Obviously, however, States have some influence on the level of wages they pay, and the Commission has therefore approached the estimation of wage cost disability factors very cautiously.

Estimating Standardised Expenditure. To summarise an expenditure category assessment, Government Secondary Education can be used as a useful example to explain the process. In Table 4, it can be seen that the Commission assessed eight disability factors and combined their effects into an overall 'category disability'. It shows that Queensland has a disadvantage of nearly 10 per cent over the Australian average because of its high relevant population, but an advantage of 1.40 per cent through lower input costs. Its overall cost of providing the Australian average level of service is 8.15 per cent above average.

Table 4. Government Secondary Education Factors - 1995-96

Disability Factors	NSW	Vic	Qld	WA	SA	Tas	ACT	NT
Dispersion	0.9973	0.9921	1.0093	1.0106	0.9972	0.9952	0.9885	1.0710
Grade Cost	1.0014	1.0028	0.9966	0.9950	0.9992	0.9998	1.0016	0.9979
Input Costs	1.0120	0.9950	0.9860	1.0030	0.9910	0.9900	1.0080	1.0340
Relevant Population	0.9749	0.8874	1.0983	1.1639	0.9679	1.1422	0.9750	1.2226
Administrative Scale	0.9946	0.9946	0.9946	1.0065	1.0105	1.0304	1.0463	1.1139
Service Delivery Scale	0.9922	0.9906	1.0031	1.0153	1.0166	1.0380	0.9714	1.1141
Vandalism & Security	1.0023	1.0023	0.9973	0.9973	0.9973	0.9923	0.9923	0.9923
Cross-border	0.9965	1.0001	1.0001	1.0001	1.0001	1.0001	1.0660	1.0001
Category Disability	**0.9692**	**0.8658**	**1.0815**	**1.1941**	**0.9772**	**1.1917**	**1.0440**	**1.6605**

In simple terms, and again using Queensland as the example, the Commission calculates its standardised expenditure as the Australian average per capita standard, by 1.0815, by the Queensland population.

Equity and the Treatment of Specific Purpose Payments

The issue that now remains unanswered is how the distribution of the specific purpose payments (SPPs) between the States is taken into account by the Commission.

The necessity for the Commission to consider how to treat SPPs within its processes comes direct from the principle of fiscal equalisation. It is asked to work on the basis that each State should be given the capacity to provide the average level of services. The question then is:

> should the average level of services that is being considered include those funded by specific purpose payments?

The Commission believes that in many cases it cannot fulfil its objective of equalising States' capacities to provide services unless it includes those services funded by SPPs in its measurement of average levels of service, because the SPPs are contributing to States' capacities to fund services. It therefore includes the expenditure resulting from the SPPs in its expenditure standards and takes the variation in the receipt of SPPs paid to the States into account in arriving at its overall measure of States' needs for general revenue funding. It terms this procedure for treating SPPs the 'inclusion approach'.

The levels of standardised expenditure from which the SPPs are deducted is the Commission's assessment of each State's total expenditure requirement. Results based on the use of the inclusion approach thus adjust a State's level of GRGs to take account of its receipt of SPPs.

This treatment of SPPs fits into the model the Commission uses to determine the per capita relativities because each State's need for GRGs is measured, in per capita terms, as:

its Standardised Expenditure

plus	**the Standard Budget Result**
less	**its Standardised Revenue**
less	**its receipt of SPPs treated by the inclusion method.**

The standard budget result is simply the difference between total per capita expenditure and total per capita revenue included in the standard budget. There is no requirement for the Australian States to operate on a balanced budget and the Commission's standard budget therefore never balances. The assumption within the current assessment model is that the States have the same per capita capacity to operate at a surplus or deficit. However, this is being re-examined as part of the 1999 review because current State policies to fund non-income generating capital expenditure from recurrent surpluses have resulted in large standard budget surpluses.

The inclusion approach is one of four ways in which SPPs are treated by the Commission. The four approaches and the decision framework used to decide when each is used, are provided in Attachment E.

Some Small Difficulties

Not all States and Commonwealth Government Departments responsible for SPPs agree with the application of the inclusion approach and the issue is frequently raised for discussion. It is one of the most controversial aspects of the Commission's work. Few doubt that it is necessary to achieve fiscal equalisation, but is that the only objective of government, and how should other objectives be weighed against fiscal equalisation.

The most common criticism of the Commission's use of the inclusion approach is that it overrides the distribution of the specific purpose payment — a distribution arrived at after sometimes long and difficult negotiations before agreement is reached and signed by Commonwealth and State Ministers or senior officials on behalf of their governments.

In one sense, the Commission agrees with this criticism in that the financial distribution is over-ridden; but this occurs up to seven years after the event because the Commission (as instructed in its terms of reference) uses the previous five years on which to base its assessments. It is important to note, however, that the policy objectives are not influenced by the over-riding of the financial distribution. SPPs are usually distributed with a prospective view in mind, while GRGs are based on the analysis of retrospective data and (largely) on the assumption that nothing has changed. These points often appear to be overlooked by the critics.

The Commission also notes that relativities based on inclusion neither redistribute the actual levels of SPPs received in past years nor influence the distribution of such payments in future years; the process only adjusts the distribution of general revenue grants in a future year to reflect the requirements of fiscal equalisation based on the analysis of a past period.

There is some criticism of the Commission on the grounds that its processes are too resource intensive and its data requirements too demanding. Work done by the Commission, however, indicates that very few SPPs have as small a ratio of administrative cost to amount distributed as the GRG distribution.

On the issue of data requirements, it is true that the Commission has been the cause of a great expansion in management data relating to the public sector in Australia. This has not always been a bad thing, however, as the 'new' data are often used in making budgetary and other decisions and have greatly improved the basis of policy advice being given to the elected representatives.

The Involvement of the States
Because of the importance of the Commission's work to the States, they are directly involved in its procedures. This has been the case since the Commission's establishment in the 1930s and is seen as integral to the Australian system. The extent of this contact, and the openness of the Commission's work to examination by the States, contribute greatly to acceptance of the results.

For the five-yearly reviews of the data and methods used to make the assessments, the States:

- assist the Commonwealth in developing the terms of reference for the inquiry;
- assist the Commission in designing the events and timetable for the inquiry;
- assist in deciding the scope and structure of the standard budget, and the specification of other data collections;
- provide the data requested, both financial and non-financial;

322

- arrange for the Commission to visit State workplaces to get first-hand experience of disabilities and talk to service providers;
- make written submissions to the Commission on all aspects of the inquiry;
- attend conferences with the Commission and the other States to discuss the issues; and
- examine the Commission's preliminary findings and meet with the Commission and the other States to discuss them.

For its part, the Commission makes all submissions public, holds all its discussions in public and makes sure that any information given to one State is given to all others. It makes at least summaries of all its final decisions available to the States for examination as soon as the results of the inquiry are known, and makes further details, and even the minutes of its meetings, available on request once an inquiry has been completed.

The States have the results of an inquiry, and many of the calculations behind those results, for up to six weeks before the Report is discussed at a Premiers' Conference. During that period, they act as very efficient 'auditors' of the Commission's work and are supplied with any alternative calculations they require.

CONCLUSION

The Australian system of fiscal transfers has many good aspects to it but also has some problems. The work of the Commonwealth Grants Commission is one of the most developed approaches to fiscal equalisation, and is being studied with interest by a number of countries wanting to establish or reform their intergovernment fiscal transfer systems.

Some parts of the Australian system however — like the level of vertical fiscal imbalance, deciding the absolute level of the intergovernment transfer and the mix of tied and untied grants within that transfer — are not ideal.

The important thing to note is that it was designed for Australia and works fairly well in Australia. While it might be of interest to other nations, it is always necessary to design a system that suits the political and cultural environment of the nation to which it is to be applied.

For the observers that come to visit Australia and study the system, the things of most interest seem to be:

- the size of the VFI and the support for this by many in the Commonwealth Government;
- the lack of control over the size of the total Commonwealth/State transfer and its allocation between SPPs and GRGs;
- the independence of the Commonwealth Grants Commission and that its members are not political appointments and do not represent any other authority;
- the comprehensiveness of Australia's horizontal equalisation system;
- the Commission's approach to revenue and expenditure assessments;
- the interface between the distribution of SPPs and the distribution of general revenue grants; and
- the openness of the Commission's processes and the involvement of the States as both a source of debate and information, and as 'auditors' of the assessments of relative needs for funding.

ATTACHMENT A

Basic Data on States and Territories

	NSW	Vic	Qld	WA	SA	Tas	ACT	NT
Area and Population								
Area (km²)	801 600	227 600	1 727 200	2 525 500	984 000	67 800	2 400	1 346 200
Coastline (km)	1900	1 800	7 400	12 500	3 700	3 200	35	6 200
Population (1995-96)	6 152 256	4 521 457	3 317 541	1 747 235	1 476 007	473 216	305 544	176 260
Population per km²	0.30	1.19	0.93	0.96	0.49	0.79	2.11	0.80
Population Characteristics								
Net interstate migration (1994)	-13 541	-31 895	+49 066	+3 664	-3 466	-2 162	-151	-1 515
Capital city population (%, 1994)	61.9	71.4	45.6	72.9	73.2	41.0	99.6	46.0
Population under 15 (% 1994)	21.3	21.0	22.1	22.6	20.5	22.6	22.2	27.9
Population over 64 (% 1994)	12.4	12.1	11.2	10.2	13.6	12.4	6.9	3.1
Population born in non-English speaking countries (%, 1991)	15.2	16.9	6.9	12.0	10.8	4.0	14.1	9.3
Indigenous population (1991)	70 019	16 735	70 124	41 779	16 232	8 885	1 775	39 910
Crude death rate per '000 population (1993)	7.2	7.0	6.4	6.2	7.9	7.7	3.7	4.5
Perinatal death rate per '000 live births (1993)	8.5	7.5	8.1	7.3	7.6	9.5	7.2	19.3
Aged 15-69 with post-school qualifications (% of all aged 15-69)	43.7	38.1	36.9	42.1	38.2	36.7	48.9	37.1
Income characteristics								
Gross State Product per capita ($'000, 1992-93)	23.2	24.0	21.3	25.7	20.7	18.7	29.7	24.9
Household disposable income per capita ($'000, 1992-93)	15.6	15.8	14.0	14.8	14.3	13.1	19.8	15.2
Housing affordability								
Housing affordability index [a] (1993-94)	130.1	153.4	158.3	172.7	185.7	204.0	169.7	n.a.
Mean weekly rent (1994)	135	115	116	104	88	93	128	98

[a] The ratio of average household income to the average income needed to meet the repayments for an average established dwelling purchased by a first home buyer.

ATTACHMENT B

The Constitution of the Commonwealth of Australia - An Extract
Part V.- Powers of the Parliament

51. The Parliament shall, subject to this Constitution, have power to make laws for the peace, order, and good government of the Commonwealth with respect to:-

(i) trade and commerce with other countries, and among the States:

(ii) taxation; but so as not discriminate between States or parts of States:

(iii) bounties on the production or export of goods, but so that such bounties shall be uniform throughout the Commonwealth:

(iv) borrowing money on the public credit of the Commonwealth:

(v) postal, telegraphic, telephonic, and other like services:

(vi) the naval and military defence of the Commonwealth and of the several States, and the control of the forces to execute and maintain the laws of the Commonwealth:

(vii) lighthouses, lightships, beacons and buoys:

(viii) astronomical and meteorological observations:

(ix) quarantine:

(x) fisheries in Australian waters beyond territorial limits:

(xi) census and statistics:

(xii) currency, coinage, and legal tender:

(xiii) banking, other than State banking; also State banking extending beyond the limits of the State concerned, the incorporate of banks, and the issue of paper money:

(xiv) insurance, other than State insurance; also State insurance extending beyond the limits of the State concerned:

(xv) weights and measures:

(xvi) bills of exchange and promissory notes:

(xvii) bankruptcy and insolvency:

(xviii) copyrights, patents of inventions and designs, and trade marks:

(xix) naturalisation and aliens:

(xx) foreign corporations, and trading or financial corporations formed within the limits of the Commonwealth:

(xxi) Marriage:

(xxii) Divorce and matrimonial causes; and in relation thereto, parental rights, and the custody and guardianship of infants:

(xxiii) invalid and old-age pensions:

(xxiiiA) the provision of maternity allowances, widows' pensions, child endowment, unemployment, pharmaceutical, sickness and hospital benefits, medical and dental service (but not so as to authorise any form of civil conscription), benefits to students and family allowances: [inserted by No. 81, 1946, s. 2]

(xxiv) the service and execution throughout the Commonwealth of the civil and criminal process and the judgments of the courts of the States:

(xxv) the recognition throughout the Commonwealth of the laws, the public Acts and records, and the judicial proceedings of the States.

(xxvi)   the people of any race for whom it is deemed necessary to make special laws: [altered by No. 55, 1967, s. 2]

(xxvii)   immigration and emigration:

(xxviii) the influx of criminals:

(xxix)   external affairs:

(xxx)   the relations of the Commonwealth with the islands of the Pacific:

(xxxi)   the acquisition of property on just terms from any State or person for any purpose in respect of which the Parliament has power to make laws:

(xxxii)   the control of railways with respect to transport for the naval and military purposes of the Commonwealth:

(xxxiii) the acquisition, with the consent of a State, or any railways of the State on terms arranged between the Commonwealth and the State:

(xxxiv)   railway construction and extension in any State with the consent of that State:

(xxxv)   conciliation and arbitration for the prevention and settlement of industrial disputes extending beyond the limits of any one State:

(xxxvi)   matters in respect of which this Constitution makes provision until the Parliament otherwise provides:

(xxxvii) matters referred to the Parliament of the Commonwealth by the Parliament of Parliaments of any State or States, but so that the law shall extend only to States by whose Parliaments the matter is referred, or which afterwards adopt the law:

(xxxviii) the exercise within the Commonwealth, at the request or with the concurrence of the parliaments of all the States directly concerned, of any power which can at the establishment of this Constitution be exercised only the Parliament of the United Kingdom or by the Federal Council of Australasia:

(xxxix)   matters incidental to the execution of any power vested by this Constitution in the Parliament or either House thereof, or in the Government of the Commonwealth, or in the Federal Judicature, or in any department of officer of the Commonwealth.

ATTACHMENT C

Commonwealth Grants Commission Standard Budget 1995-96 - Revenue

Revenue Classification Category	$pc	Per cent
Pay-roll Taxation	396.06	21.59
Land Revenue	83.61	4.56
Stamp Duty on Conveyances	154.83	8.44
Financial Transaction Taxes	138.44	7.55
Stamp Duties on Shares and Securities	21.44	1.17
Gambling Taxation	187.91	10.24
Insurance Taxation	45.99	2.51
Vehicle Registration Fees and Taxes	124.78	6.80
Stamp Duty on Vehicle Registration/Transfers	57.71	3.15
Drivers' Licence Fees	14.97	0.82
Business Franchise Fees - Petroleum Products	83.96	4.58
Business Franchise Fees - Tobacco	144.25	7.86
Business Franchise Fees - Liquor	40.89	2.23
Other Revenue nec	11.01	0.60
Interest Earnings	43.80	2.39
Mining Revenue	57.14	3.11
Electricity and Gas	103.55	5.64
Metropolitan Water Supply and Sewerage	23.23	1.27
Other Enterprises	17.64	0.96
Hospital Patient Fees	38.08	2.08
Administration of Justice - Fees and Fines	29.60	1.61
Administration of Justice - Property Titles	15.86	0.86
Total Revenue [a]	**1834.75**	**100.00**

[a] Total State own-source revenue differs from the amount shown in the Commonwealth Grants Commission *Report on General Revenue Grant Relativities 1997 Update*, p 235. Total revenue includes Hospital Patient Fees, Administration of Justice - Fees and Fines, and Property Titles which have been offset to expenditure categories in the 1997 Update Report.

ATTACHMENT D

Commonwealth Grants Commission Standard Budget 1995-96 - Expenditure

Expenditure Classification Category	$pc	Per cent
Pre-school Education	18.57	0.62
Government Primary Education	303.01	10.18
Non-government Primary Education	22.88	0.77
Government Secondary Education	250.29	8.40
Non-government Secondary Education	27.09	0.91
Technical and Further Education	145.29	4.88
Transport of Rural School Children	25.54	0.86
Hospital Services	531.02	17.83
Nursing Home Services	48.19	1.62
Mental Health Services	46.24	1.55
Community Health Services	102.64	3.45
Police	154.75	5.20
Administration of Justice	68.83	2.31
Corrective Services	45.12	1.52
Public Safety and Emergency Services	24.73	0.83
Family and Child Welfare	46.89	1.57
Aged and Disabled Welfare	121.98	4.10
Other Welfare Services	21.44	0.72
Culture and Recreation	46.34	1.56
National Parks and Wildlife Services	14.98	0.50
Planning and Environment	18.22	0.61
Aboriginal Community Services	8.24	0.28
Superannuation	185.98	6.25
Other General Public Services	68.24	2.29
Agriculture and Fisheries	58.39	1.96
Brucellosis Eradication	0.88	0.03
Mining, Fuel and Energy	12.40	0.42
Tourism	11.99	0.40
Soil Conservation	6.20	0.21
Other Services to Industry	18.52	0.62
Road Maintenance	64.58	2.17
Other Transport	29.89	1.00
Debt Charges nec	176.62	5.93
Other Services	41.67	1.40
Urban Transit	142.53	4.79
Non-Urban Transport - Freight	14.63	0.49
Non-Urban Transport - Passengers	23.63	0.79
Country Water Supply and Sewerage	8.44	0.28
Housing	22.51	0.76
Other Trading Enterprises	-1.46	-0.05
Total Expenditure [a]	**2977.92**	**100.00**

[a] Total expenditure differs from the amount shown in the Commonwealth Grants Commission *Report on General Revenue Grant Relativities 1997 Update*, p 293. Total expenditure is exclusive of expenditure offsets such as Hospital Patient Fees, Administration of Justice - Fees and Fines, and Property Titles.

ATTACHMENT E

The Treatment of Specific Purpose Payments

The inclusion approach discussed in the paper is one of four ways in which SPPs are treated by the Commission. In summary, the four approaches can be explained as follows:

(i) The **inclusion method,** under which both the expenditure financed from the SPP and expenditure financed from State sources are included in calculating the standards used in the expenditure assessments. The SPP itself is treated as part of the Commonwealth revenue payments available to finance part of the total financial assistance requirement.

(ii) The **exclusion method,** where all revenue and expenditure related to the program which was the subject of the SPP is excluded from the revenue and expenditure standards used in the assessments.

(iii) The **deduction method,** under which the amount of the SPP is deducted from total expenditure on the program which was the subject of the payment.

(iv) The **absorption method,** under which expenditure financed from the SPP and expenditure financed from State sources are included in calculating the standards used in the expenditure assessments. The SPP is treated as though it were part of the general revenue pool distributed among the States.

The treatment given each SPP is arrived at separately after the Commission has asked itself the questions illustrated in Figure E-1.

Figure E-1. TREATMENT OF SPECIFIC PURPOSE PAYMENTS

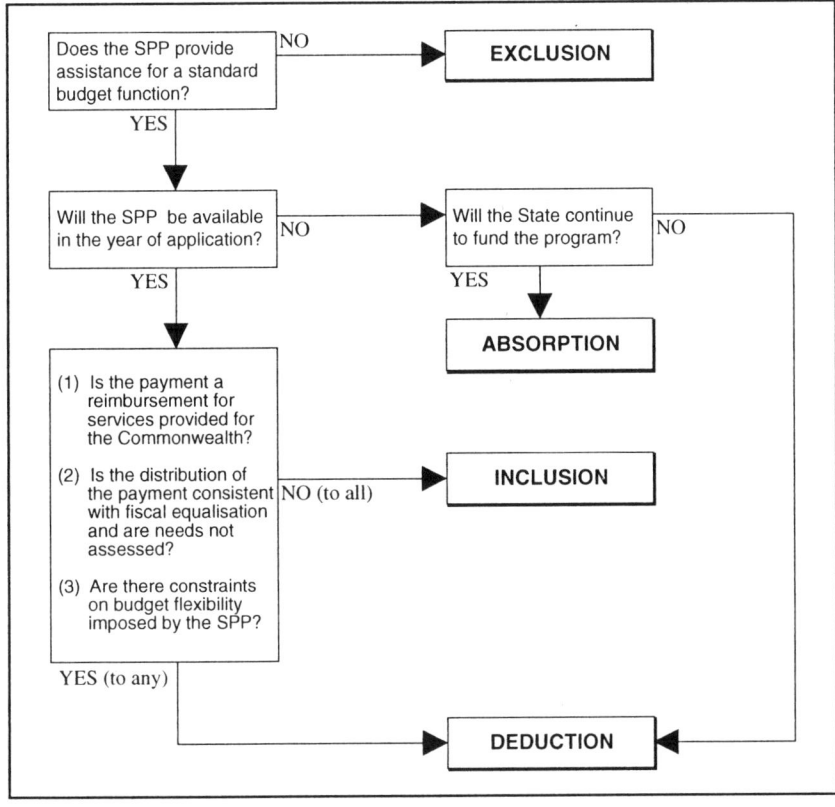

LIST OF CONTRIBUTORS

PETER BOHM, Professor, Department of Economics, Stockholm University, Stockholm, Sweden.

JAMES M. BUCHANAN, Advisory General Director, Center for Study of Public Choice, George Mason University, Fairfax, Virginia, U.S.A. (1986 Novel laureate in Economics)

SHINEMAY CHEN, Department of Public Finance, National Chengchi University, Taipei, Taiwan.

HAMID DAVOODI, Economist, Fiscal Affairs Department, International Monetary Fund, Washington, D.C., U.S.A.

FREDERICK ZU-LIU HU, Executive Director for Asia Economic Research, Goldman, Sachs & Co, 37th Floor, Asia Pacific Finance Tower, Citibank Plaza, Hong Kong, P.R. China.

JAKOB DE HAAN, Director of Research Institute SOM and Jean Monnet Professor of European Integration, Faculty of Economics, University of Groningen, P.O.Box 800, 9700 AV Groningen, The Netherlands.

TOSHIHIRO IHORI, Professor of Economics, Faculty of Economics, The University of Tokyo, Tokyo, Japan.

GERARD H. KUPER, Assistant Professor and SOM Research Fellow, Faculty of Economics, University of Groningen, P.O.Box 800, 9700 AV Groningen, The Netherlands.

JORGE MARTINEZ-VAZQUEZ, Professor of Economics, Economics Department, School of Policy Studies, Georgia State University, Atlanta, U.S.A.

NOBUKI MOCHIDA, Professor of Economics, Faculty of Economics, The University of Tokyo, Tokyo, Japan.

RICHARD A. MUSGRAVE, H.H.Burbank Professor of Political Economy Emeritus, Harvard University and Adjunct Professor of Economics, University of California, Santa Cruz, U.S.A.

THOMAS I. RENSTRÖM, Department of Economics, University of Birmingham, Edgbaston, Birmingham B15 2TT, U.K.

ROBERT J. SEARLE, Secretary, Commonwealth Grants Commission, Australia.

HIROFUMI SHIBATA, Professor Emeritus, Osaka University and Professor of Economics, College of Policy Science, Ritsumeikan University, Kyoto, Japan.

PAUL BERND SPAHN, Professor of Public Finance, Fachbereich Wirtschaftswissenschaften, Johann Wolfgang Goethe-Universität, Frankfurt am Main, Germany.

JAN-EGBERT STURM, Assistant Professor and SOM Research Fellow, Faculty of Economics, University of Groningen, P.O.Box 800, 9700 AV Groningen, The Netherlands.

DEBORAH L. SWENSON, Assistant Professor, Department of Economics, University of California, Davis, and NBER, U.S.A.

ALAN A. TAIT, Special Trade Representative and Director, Geneva Office of the International Monterey Fund, Geneva, Switzerland.

VITO TANZI, Director, Fiscal Affairs Department, International Monterey Fund, Washington, D.C., U.S.A.

VLADIMIR I. TIKHOMIROV, Deputy Director, Contemporary Europe Research Centre, The University of Melbourne, Melbourne, Australia.

SALLY WALLACE, Professor of Economics, Economics Department, School of Policy Studies, Georgia State University, Atlanta, U.S.A.

ZHANG XIAOQIANG, Director-General, Foreign Capital Utilization Department, State Planning Commission, P.R. China.

Board of Management of the International Institute of Public Finance (1997/98)